American Ambassadors at the UN

People, Politics, and Bureaucracy
in Making Foreign Policy

SEYMOUR MAXWELL FINGER

With a Foreword by Henry Cabot Lodge

HM

HOLMES & MEIER
New York   London

Published in the United States of America 1988 by
Holmes & Meier Publishers, Inc.
30 Irving Place
New York, NY 10003

Great Britain:
1–3 Winton Close
Letchworth, Hertfordshire SG61 1BA England

The first edition of this book was published under the title *Your Man at the UN* by New York University Press (1980).

This book has been printed on acid-free paper.

Library of Congress Cataloging-in-Publication Data

Finger, Seymour Maxwell, 1915–
  American ambassadors at the UN.

  Rev. ed. of: Your man at the UN. 1980.
  Includes index.
  1. United Nations—United States—History.
  2. United States—Foreign relations—1945–
  I. Finger, Seymour Maxwell, 1915– . Your man at
  the UN. II. Title.
  JX1977.2.U5F56 1988   341.23'73   86-19524
  ISBN 0-8419-1057-X (alk. paper)

Manufactured in the United States of America

For Alyce

Contents

Acknowledgments

I want to express my appreciation, for interviews and correspondence that provided valuable insights, to Ernest Gross, Henry Cabot Lodge, Philip M. Klutznick, Richard Pedersen, Charles Yost, George Bush, John Scali, William Scranton and Andrew Young, all former U.S. ambassadors at the UN; to Ambassadors Donald McHenry and Richard Petree; to Ambassadors William Barton (Canada), B. Akporode Clark (Nigeria), Nabil Elaraby (Egypt), Johan Kaufmann (Netherlands), Mahmoud Mestiri (Tunisia), Ivor Richard (United Kingdom), and Piero Vinci (Italy); and to Francis O. Wilcox, Samuel De Palma, Joseph J. Sisco, Charles D. Cook and Charles P. Noyes. These knowledgeable veterans of UN affairs shared their information, insights and wisdom generously.

Nancy T. Okada was most helpful throughout the book's preparation, providing invaluable advice and editorial assistance. She also either typed or supervised the typing of the various chapters of the manuscript cheerfully and efficiently.

I also wish to express my appreciation to Jacques Fomerand, Anne Gustave, Anne Risso, and Vi Manber for their help in researching files and data.

Professor Leon Gordenker, Princeton University, reviewed the original manuscript and provided extremely helpful suggestions and criticisms used in finalizing the text.

The College of Staten Island and the Graduate School, City University of New York, granted a fellowship leave that afforded me time for writing the book. The Rockefeller Foundation generously provided a fellowship grant that was of great assistance in researching for and preparing the manuscript.

I am deeply grateful to New York University Press, publishers of *Your Man at the UN,* who made it available for incorporation in the present volume and to Holmes & Meier Publishers for their generous cooperation in producing this book.

Foreword

Many meritorious changes could be made in the U.N.:

Member states should change it so that voting more nearly corresponds with the ability to carry out the things which are voted. Many detailed changes are proposed in the Report of the President's Commission on the Twenty-Fifth Anniversary of the U.N. published in 1971. I cite a few: small states should renounce their right to vote and should agree to become associate members; if any state pays less than one-tenth of one percent of the U.N. budget, it would become an associate member; the United States should commit itself in electing members of the Security Council to place primary emphasis on the contributions which the candidate can make; half of the ten elected seats in the Security Council would be rotated among the larger states. A nation of the size of Japan would always be a member of the Security Council.

The United States should be able to translate into political influence and power its status as a financial mainstay of the United Nations. We should not show undue respect for the General Assembly, the decisions of which, after all, are purely hortatory and do not have the force of law. Only the Security Council has the power to issue legally binding action orders and in the Security Council we are one of the "big five"—and each one of us has the veto. The Security Council is a good place for us.

Also, it would promote world peace if member states of the U.N. used the Assembly differently. At present there is a tendency to conduct roll call votes which tend to magnify and perpetrate the world's divisions. This is not the way to carry out one of the United Nation's main purposes: to be a center for harmonizing the actions of nations. The current tendency seems to be to act as though the General Assembly was a domestic legislative body. The General Assembly is not domestic, nor is it legislative. Its members do not represent districts carved out in proportion to population. Both the large and the small states each have one vote. The General Assembly more nearly resembles an international diplomatic conference. Its members, therefore, should be constantly trying to find ways to harmonize the actions of nations. They should be seeking consensus. They should be exchanging views in the lobbies and searching for forms of words which would have a harmonizing effect. They should not be agitating for roll call votes on contentious resolutions.

I also hope that members will rededicate themselves and strengthen their determination actually to suppress aggression—which, after all, is what the U.N. is all about, and which so many have forgotten. Remember Churchill's words that peace is not promoted by throwing small nations to the wolves.

I have no illusions about the difficulty of bringing about these changes, but I believe that an eloquent effort to do so is very much worth making. Since 1945, it is said, there have been fourteen international and twenty-four civil wars—all with substantial casualties. The world is still a dangerous place. We need the U.N.

Finally, we should always be mindful of the over-riding fact that the U.N. is the only purely international organization which is established on a world basis. This does not belittle regional organizations such as NATO or the useful work done by bi-lateral diplomacy. Modern war, however, is able, on a few moment's notice, to trigger off a world war. The presence in New York of a panel of men of ripe experience who can quickly devise measures to put out the fire can truly make the difference between life and death.

Max Finger has written a book of lasting value. He has carefully looked into all the things which make the U.N. a truly workable device and has shown how it all functions. He has worked for many years at the U.N. and has known virtually all the key personages. His book deserves the careful attention of all who are interested in what makes the U.N. tick.

Henry Cabot Lodge

Introduction

This is the story of people, politics, and bureaucracy in the making of American foreign policy at the United Nations.

The key actors are the American presidents since 1945 and the people they have chosen to represent the United States at the United Nations over the past four decades—the permanent representatives. We shall be tracing their influence on policy in a variety of situations.

This is not to deny the importance of objective factors that influence and at times determine the limits of a leader's action. The Soviet challenge after 1945, for example, demanded an American response, regardless of who led the United States. Yet it did make a difference whether Truman, Eisenhower, Kennedy, Johnson, Nixon, Ford, Carter, or Reagan was president. Any American permanent representative to the UN would have been involved in a cold war propaganda struggle with the Soviet Union; but the skill, forensic ability, stage presence, appetite for public debate, and political influence of Henry Cabot Lodge not only added to the intensity of the struggle but also spawned a number of important policy decisions that would not otherwise have occurred. Having been concerned with U.S. foreign policy for four decades—twenty-six years as a career diplomat, including fifteen at the UN, and fourteen years as a professor of international relations—I have been struck repeatedly by the extent to which a determined individual, enjoying the confidence of the president and backed by a competent staff, can exert policy leadership. People do make a difference.

Organization charts may depict an orderly process for arriving at policy decisions through the bureaucracy and ostensibly tell where the power lies. Yet anyone who is involved for any length of time in making or carrying out foreign policy soon learns which bureaucrats are alive and which are inert; which try to avoid responsibility and which assume it willingly; and which have real rather than ostensible influence on policy. When Henry Kissinger was presidential assistant for national security affairs, he—not the secretary of state—wielded the greatest influence on foreign policy. Dean Rusk, secretary of state under Kennedy and Johnson, observed: "The real organization of government at higher echelons is not what you find in textbooks or organizational charts. Confidence flows down from the President. That is never permanent and people don't like it. Besides, it fluctuates. People go up and people go down."[1]

Rusk also emphasizes the importance of entrepreneurship in a bureaucracy and points out that most bureaucrats do not struggle for power. "There is another struggle of far more consequence, the effort to diffuse or avoid responsibility. Power gravitates to those who are willing to make decisions and live with the results, simply because there are so many who readily yield to the intrepid few who take their duties seriously."[2]

Rusk's view is shared by Morton Halperin, an eminent scholar with Washington experience. "The bureaucratic system is basically inert; it moves only when pushed hard and persistently. The majority of bureaucrats prefer to maintain the status quo, and only a small group is, at any one time, advocating change."[3] As we shall see in the following chapters, the permanent representative and his staff at the United Nations have frequently been the advocates of a change in policy, with much greater assertiveness and influence than the usual Washington bureaucrat. They have had a sense of style in writing that is more likely to get the president's attention than dull bureaucratese.

A related point is made by George Ball, former undersecretary of state and, for three months, U.S. permanent representative to the United Nations. "If bureaucratic hypertrophy alienates people from their government they will yearn for a hero, the 'Master Player.' . . . Citizens now find their symbols of governmental authority in a few identifiable personalities primarily because the government itself is so huge and impersonal."[4] Ball refers to Dulles and Kissinger as "one-man foreign offices."

One "Master Player," Henry Kissinger, before he entered government service, set forth many of the reasons why presidents often go outside the bureaucratic structure in making policy or choosing emissaries. He pointed out that bureaucracies tend to become absorbed in routine.

"Serving the machine becomes a more absorbing occupation than defining its purpose . . . ": The quest for "objectivity"—while desirable theoretically—involves the danger that means and ends are confused, that an average standard of performance is exalted as the only valid one. Attention tends to be diverted from the act of choice— which is the ultimate test of statesmanship—to the accumulation of facts. Decisions can be avoided until a crisis brooks no further delay, until the events themselves have removed the element of ambiguity. But at that point the scope for constructive action is at a minimum. Certainty is purchased at the cost of creativity. . . .

All of this drives the executive in the direction of extra-bureaucratic means of decision. The practice of relying on special emissaries or personal envoys is an example; their status outside the bureaucracy frees them from some of its restraints. International agreements are sometimes possible only by ignoring safeguards against capricious action. It is a paradoxical aspect of modern bureaucracies that their quest for objectivity and calculability often leads to impasses which can be overcome only by essentially arbitrary decisions."[5]

Another factor that makes it increasingly difficult to use the bureaucratic machine in creative policymaking is the growing complexity of issues. An objective examination of all the relevant information and viewpoints leads to crushing bulk and mass. The president, or any other decision maker, may have a prodigious capacity to absorb material without getting mired down in it, but there are limits to what any one human being can absorb. Particularly in crises he must, in the end, rely on a few people whose judgment he trusts, sacrificing thoroughness to the need to make a decision.[6]

It is precisely this situation that has enabled certain American permanent representatives to exercise a direct and important influence on the making of foreign policy at the UN. A number of them were assertive, self-confident, and creative politicians; they had the special confidence of the president and could afford to take risks. Their staffs were large enough to analyze issues and prepare position papers but not so large as to get bogged down in bureaucratic slogging. While nominally subordinate to an assistant secretary of state, a strong permanent representative who is a member of the cabinet and has the president's confidence can go straight to the White House on important issues—and win. In numerous cases with which I am familiar and others that have been fully documented, important policy initiatives such as the proposal for the United Nations Development Program (UNDP) in 1957, the World Food Program in 1960, and the formulation of certain elements of U.S. policy in the Middle East in 1967 were initiated by the permanent representative and channeled directly to the president.

A great deal of attention will be directed to this relationship between the permanent representative and the White House because it is essentially the president who makes American foreign policy. The checks and balances spelled out in the Constitution are effective on domestic issues; for example, taxes, budget, housing, education, social security, unemployment insurance, offshore exploitation, and the regulation and encouragement of trade and industry. These are largely bread-and-butter issues where congressional control or deep involvement continues to be the norm. Moreover, many of these issues involve the jurisdiction of states and local communities, as well as the judiciary. By contrast, since 1945 foreign policy has been characterized by executive dominance, particularly in crises. Illustrative of this difference is the fact that between 1948 and 1964 the president prevailed on 70 percent of his proposals to Congress dealing with foreign policy and on only 40 percent of those dealing with domestic issues.[7] These figures actually understate the degree of presidential control of foreign policy; they take no account of the many executive policy decisions made without reference to Congress. On the other hand, the growing interrelationship between domestic and foreign issues may presage greater congressional involvement in the latter. Also, as a reaction to Vietnam and Watergate, Congress has become much more assertive on all issues, including foreign policy.

Executive dominance in foreign policy is not only an American phenomenon; worldwide, it is characteristic of every country that has an activist foreign policy, whether justified by efficiency, ideology, or the need for speedy action. Legislative bodies are, by their very nature, slow and cumbersome. In crises, such as the Korean War and the Cuban Missile Crisis, decisions are made by a small number of actors at the very top of the executive policymaking machine. Decisions on programs involve a wider group, including the Congress, and involve bureaucratic politics. In both cases the president is the central and key figure. On major programs, such as entry into the UN, the Marshall Plan, NATO, and national defense, the public and Congress have generally been supportive.[8]

Presidential preeminence in carrying out an activist foreign policy arises from a number of factors. First, he has the best apparatus in the country for gathering and evaluating information. Second, he is usually ready and willing to act and can do so more expeditiously than a Congress of 535 members. Third, because of the complexity of foreign policy issues, Congress will often make broad grants of power, as in the Tonkin Gulf resolution and in authorizing multilateral trade negotiations. Fourth, as commander in chief of the armed forces, he can commit them to action without a formal declaration of war, as in Korea and Vietnam. Fifth, he can communicate instantly with the people through television and radio. Finally, the president is nationally elected and, more than any other figure, represents the national interest and mood.

The American failure in Vietnam has had profound effects on relationships between the president and Congress. There is likely to be more restraint on future chief executives, at least for some years. Yet, for the reasons noted above, the president will remain the dominant actor as long as the United States has an activist foreign policy.[9] That is why in the pages to come great emphasis is placed on the relationship between the permanent representative and the president as crucial to his influence on foreign policy. Personal and political factors will also be stressed; they are important to the relationship.

Many of the U.S. permanent representatives have been influential politicians. The list begins with Senator Warren Austin and continues through Henry Cabot Lodge, an intimate of President Eisenhower; Adlai Stevenson, who twice won the Democratic party presidential nomination; Arthur Goldberg, who resigned from the Supreme Court to take the job; George Ball, a former undersecretary of state in the Johnson administration; William Scranton, a former governor of Pennsylvania and also a close friend of President Ford, and Andrew Young, friend and political ally of Jimmy Carter. Reagan's first appointee, Jeane J. Kirkpatrick, did not have an independent political base but drew great strength from her close ideological relationship with the President. (She had significant impact on policymaking, not only as permanent representative but also as a member of the cabinet and the National Security Council.) Although there have been many political appointees to such important embassies as those of London, Paris, and Rome, few if any of these have had the political clout of our more prominent permanent representatives to the UN.

Much attention will be paid to the personalities and political influence of these representatives. Years of experience with strong personalities like Lodge, Stevenson, Goldberg, and Ball have impressed on me how important the personality factors can be for the functioning and staffing of the U.S. mission to the UN and its role in making and carrying out policy. Even in a massive bureaucracy like the foreign policy establishment in Washington, individuals can make a crucial difference in what questions are raised, how policy is made, and how it is carried out—for reasons cited above by Rusk, Ball, Halperin, and Kissinger. Indeed, the very fact that the bureaucracy is so cumbersome provides at times a role for the "Lone Ranger" or the dedicated, tough, persistent advocate who is determined to get things done and will often bypass the bureaucracy. Although it is hard to document such personal impact precisely or consistently, interesting examples will be cited. From this analysis of the impact of personality, character, and style may emerge some useful conclusions about the *consequences* of having a certain type of person in charge of the mission—for example, politician, career diplomat, public figure, negotiator, fighter, activist-pacifier, and so on. The analysis might also shed some light on the question of how much (or how little) one person can accomplish.

We shall be looking not only at the role of the U.S. permanent representative in carrying out American policy at the UN but also at the influence the UN environment has on him and, through him, on American policy. Constant exposure to other delegations' viewpoints, daily contacts with officials of the Secretariat, and informal meetings in the Delegates' Lounge or the elevators of the Secretariat building with, say, representatives of nongovernmental organizations accredited at the United Nations or members of the local press all tend to focus attention on the United Nations itself and to stimulate analyses and perceptions of policy questions and issues from a United Nations perspective. In this sense, he tends to become the UN's ambassador to the United States as well as the U.S. representative to the UN. In the following chapters we shall consider numerous instances where the UN perspective gained by the U.S. permanent representative has had an impact on American policy on political and security issues in Korea, the Middle East, and Africa; on decolonization; and on economic development.

Furthermore, because the United Nations is a "standing conference machinery," the U.S. permanent representative is involved in an ongoing process of negotiations and multilateral diplomacy. His expertise in procedural matters, his access to intelligence not directly available to other officials of the American foreign policymaking bureaucracy, and his personal contributions to UN deliberations and the drafting and redrafting of resolutions all may be translated into effective power resources.

Finally, the U.S. mission to the United Nations differs from all diplomatic legations abroad in that its head does not necessarily report through an area assistant secretary. Although technically the mission reports to an assistant secretary for international organization affairs, the permanent representative has far greater prestige and leverage. He is a member of the cabinet and has often had such a close relationship with the president as to be able to bypass, on some issues, not only the assistant secretary but even the secretary of state.

All of this is not meant to indicate that the U.S. mission to the United Nations actually establishes U.S. foreign policy—sometimes in defiance of the government and the State Department. In fact, in an editorial commentary in the late 1970s, James Reston correctly pointed out that the job of U.S. ambassador to the United Nations could often evolve into an "elegant trap" and/or a "treadmill to oblivion."[10] Nevertheless, the U.S. mission to the United Nations is an extraordinary diplomatic entity, different in function and importance from any other embassy in the world.

Despite its significance, the role of the U.S. permanent representative has received scant attention from students of international organization and politics. Existing literature has, in general, focused (often from a purely legalistic and juridical perspective) either on the activities of national delegations at international conferences and international organization meetings[11] or on patterns of interactions among national organizational delegations in the General Assembly.[12] More to the point was Arnold Beichman's The "Other" State Department, published in the late 1960s; however, his book dealt with a United Nations that was very different from the one that exists today.[13] In the mid-1970s, E. Appathurai published two insightful accounts of the role of UN missions in the national policymaking processes. But the activities of the U.S. mission were only peripheral to the central argument, and the discussion remained broad in focus.[14] In brief, there is no single work that adequately describes and assesses the role of the U.S. permanent representative to the United Nations and his staff in the foreign policymaking process. Nor has there been any meaningful effort to articulate policy-oriented recommendations with a view of improving the performance of the U.S. mission in the decision-making apparatus of the United States. This is what we shall attempt to do in the pages that follow.

In Chapter I we shall consider the place of the United Nations in American foreign policy, examining available options in a UN and a world that have changed dramatically in the past four decades. In Chapter II, we shall describe the way USUN (the U.S. mission to the UN) works, the role of its chief, the functioning of its staff, and the ways it can influence the formulation and execution of policy. From this description and the seven narrative chapters that follow, tracing the history of USUN, we shall try in Chapter X to draw conclusions about the desired characteristics of the permanent representative, his staff (career or political), the composition of U.S. delegations to the UN General Assembly, and the current options the United States has in the UN and other international organizations.

Now a word about style and method. I have written this book on the premise that a serious work need not be dull. I have read all available books, articles, and documents; gained access to certain key telegrams and instructions; interviewed in person or by questionnaire virtually all living former permanent representatives, their associates at the mission, and officials and former officials at the State Department and the White House; consulted with certain foreign representatives; and drawn on my own experience of fifteen years working with Lodge, Wadsworth, Stevenson, Goldberg, Ball, Wiggins, Yost, and Bush. Notes at the end of each chapter, while very numerous, are used only to indicate sources. They contain no additional information; hence, the reader who does not wish to be distracted by notes may safely ignore them. Also, in the interest of readability, I have used "I" and "me" where called for rather than "the writer" or other third-person circumlocutions. For similar reasons I have used "he/his" when the reference is general but "she/her" for Jeane Kirkpatrick, the only woman representative to date (I hope the appointment has established a precedent).

NOTES

1. Dean Rusk, quoted in "Mr. Secretary on the Eve of Emeritus," *Life,* January 17, 1969, vol. 66, p. 62B.

2. Rusk, quoted in Roger Hilsman,

The Politics of Policy-Making in Defense and Foreign Affairs (New York: Harper & Row, 1971), p. 152.

3. Morton H. Halperin, *Bureau-*

cratic Politics and Foreign Policy (Washington, D.C.: Brookings Institution, 1974), p. 99.

4. George W. Ball, *Diplomacy for a Crowded World* (Boston: Atlantic–Little, Brown, 1976), p. 327.

5. Henry A. Kissinger, *American Foreign Policy* (New York: Norton, 1974), pp. 18, 23. See also John G. Stoessinger, *Crusaders and Pragmatists* (New York, Norton, 1979), and James D. Barber, *The Presidential Character,* 2nd ed. (Englewood Cliffs, N.J., Prentice-Hall, 1977), for analyses of the personal factor in the making of foreign policy.

6. See Halperin, op. cit., pp. 21–25.

7. John Spanier and Eric M. Uslaner, *How American Foreign Policy is Made,* (New York: Praeger, 1974), pp. 13–27.

8. Ibid., pp. 20–27.

9. Ibid., pp. 162–63.

10. James Reston, "Andy Young at the UN," *New York Times,* February 2, 1977. See also Clayton Fritchey, "Our Heroes at the UN," *Harper's,* February 1967, pp. 30–36.

11. See, for example, Johan Kaufmann, *Conference Diplomacy: An Introductory Analysis* (Dobbs Ferry, N.Y.: Oceana, 1968); John G. Hadwen and Johan Kaufmann, *How United Nations Decisions Are Made* (Leyden: A. W. Sijthoff, 1960); Dean Rusk, "Parliamentary Diplomacy—Debate vs. Negotiations," *World Affairs Interpreter* 26, 2 (Summer 1955): 121–38; Philip C. Jessup, *Parliamentary Diplomacy: An Examination of the Legal Quality of the Rules of Procedure of the United Nations* (Leyden: A. W. Sijthoff, 1956).

12. On this point see Richard F. Pedersen, "National Representation in the United Nations," *International Organization* 15, 2 (Spring 1961): 256–66; and Peter A. Baehr, *The Role of a National Delegation in the General Assembly,* Occasional Paper no. 9 (New York: Carnegie Endowment for International Peace, December 1970).

13. Arnold Beichman, *The "Other" State Department: The United States Mission to the United Nations—Its Role in the Making of Foreign Policy* (New York: Basic Books, 1967).

14. E. R. Appathurai, "Permanent Missions to the United Nations," *International Journal* 25, 2 (Spring 1970): 287–301, and *The Permanent Missions to International Organizations* (Brussels: Carnegie Endowment, 1975).

CHAPTER I

American Foreign Policy and the United Nations

Far-reaching changes in the international environment have posed new challenges to American policymakers. The relatively simple conceptual framework of the cold war, bipolarity, and containment has given way to a world where the Soviet challenge is more subtle, sophisticated, and complex; where the many facets of interdependence have become important to the United States, as dramatically demonstrated by the OPEC oil revolution; where the economies of the industrialized countries have become closely intertwined; and where the Third World, having found a new cohesion, dominates the agenda of the United Nations. Furthermore, to an increasing degree foreign policymaking involves a wide range of actors and interests—the world economy, monetary issues, resource availability, energy, technology, the seas and seabeds, the biosphere, and the food-population race—as well as the traditional political and security issues. Accordingly, foreign policy is no longer a monopoly of the State Department; it involves all branches of the government, and the issues often impinge on the domestic economy.

Almost all these issues are considered at the United Nations, usually not at the initiative of the United States. This does not mean that all of them can be best approached there, still less that the United Nations should be the chosen forum for negotiation on all or even most of the issues discussed there. It does mean that the United States must be concerned about how it deals with an issue raised in the United Nations, regardless of whether or not it intends to use that body as the place of tackling a problem substantively. Thus, the United States must decide which problems should be discussed at the UN but negotiated outside it. It must also determine which American policy objectives should be actively pursued in the United Nations and how to defend American interests in that body, whose agenda is now dominated by a Third World majority.

1

The questions we shall consider depend on this central issue: What is the place of the United Nations in American foreign policy in this new era?

When the UN was established, it had strong American support and participation. Even before its establishment, during World War II President Roosevelt made it clear that an international organization would be an important element of any postwar settlement. Much of the United Nations Charter was drafted in the State Department. Both during big power negotiations in Washington and at the 1945 founding conference at San Francisco, the United States was the strongest proponent among the major powers of a meaningful United Nations. The decision to establish the headquarters in the United States reflected a concern of other countries to assure full American participation. Less than five weeks after President Truman signed the Charter (June 24, 1945), the U.S. Senate ratified it by a vote of 89 to 2.[1] Speaking to the United Nations General Assembly on October 23, 1946, Truman declared that U.S. policy was "to support the United Nations with all the resources we possess . . . not as a temporary expedient but as a permanent partnership." Equally strong declarations of support were made by President Eisenhower and by three successive secretaries of state, Byrnes, Marshall, and Acheson.[2]

In the minds of the top American leadership in 1945, the overriding purpose of the UN was to contribute to the maintenance of international peace and security by providing a mechanism for great power leadership.[3] The veto on Security Council enforcement action by any of the five permanent members—China, France, Great Britain, the Soviet Union, and the United States—provided in Article 27 of the UN Charter was not based on any illusions about the benevolence of Joseph Stalin; rather, it was a realistic recognition of the fact that effective enforcement action could not be taken against the serious opposition of a great power without risking World War III.

By March 1947, Truman and other American leaders were frustrated and disillusioned by Soviet rearmament, Stalin's failure to implement the Yalta agreement regarding governments in Eastern Europe, his obstruction of a German peace treaty, and his anti-Western propaganda attacks. The response was the Truman doctrine, the Marshall Plan, and the rebuilding of American forces and military alliances as the main instruments of U.S. security. The UN, far from being an organization in which the great powers could concert their efforts to maintain peace, became an arena for battle between East and West. The Security Council was frequently stymied by Soviet vetoes. This led Gladwyn Jebb, the British permanent representative to the UN in the early 1950s, to remark in April 1953 that "it was chiefly the avoidance of hostilities on which the U.N. ought to concentrate, and not so much on how to resist aggression by military means."

In similar vein a former secretary general of the United Nations has observed:

> Some of the assumptions on which the UN was based have proved unfounded. . . . The Organization has, for example, proved to be of limited value as an instrument of collective security. . . . The idea of maintaining peace and security in the world through a concert of great powers . . . would seem to belong to the nineteenth rather than the twentieth century.[4]

In fact, since the Korean War (1950–53), such success as the UN has had in the maintenance of peace and security—and it has been significant— has been based on keeping Soviet and American troops *out* of a troubled area rather than using them as combined forces against an aggressor. UN peacekeeping forces were so used in the Middle East in 1956 and 1973 and in the Congo (now Zaire) 1960–64.

For the foreseeable future, it is not the UN but adequate American defense strength and the NATO alliance that must be relied on for deterrence or defense against any direct Soviet threat. But conflicts in various areas of the Third World—such as the Middle East, Africa, and Asia—have been very frequent since 1945 and are continuing. Here is where the UN peacekeeping role has been important. If such conflicts are not contained, they could draw in the USSR and the United States and touch off a major war. To deal with this threat, what Lincoln Bloomfield has called "spheres of abstention"[5] (areas where the United States and the USSR agree, tacitly or formally, to keep out) should be combined with strengthened UN and regional machinery for fact-finding, peacekeeping, and peaceful settlement. The role of the UN in preserving Zaire as a unified, nonaligned country and in helping to stop the fighting in the Middle East is a matter of record. The UN has also helped to deter or prevent at least a dozen other conflicts.

The record of these actions since the 1950s shows that UN peace-keeping, as distinct from enforcement action, has primarily been an auxiliary to political measures, an extension of political action intended to contain conflict and set the stage for peaceful settlement. The purpose has not been to apply military force in the classic sense of coercing the parties to submit to the UN's will but rather to install a political presence that carries out certain ancillary police duties. The late Adlai Stevenson aptly described this role in "No Mission But Peace; No Enemy But War," an article published by *McCall's* in October 1964.

The essential function of UN peacekeeping is far more political than military, from which fact follows a number of consequences. First, the mandate of a peacekeeping force must be compatible with the national security interests of the countries concerned, including those that contribute troops. In addition, the consent of the host government or governments on whose soil the force is to be stationed is necessary for entry of the force. The force itself should resort to violence only when necessary to defend itself and to carry out its primarily political mission. Finally, all principal parties in the conflict must be willing to cooperate with the force. If they are absolutely determined to fight, peacekeeping operations cannot stop them, but when they are willing to observe a cease-fire, UN forces or observers can reassure each side that the other is also under observation to insure honest performance.

Of all the major powers, the United States has most consistently supported UN peacekeeping. This support has usually been crucial, but it is equally true that only the willingness of middle powers—such as Canada, Brazil, Ethiopia, India, Yugoslavia, Ireland, and the Scandinavian states— to provide personnel and financing has made peacekeeping possible.

The withdrawal of UNEF on Egypt's demand in May 1967, followed a few weeks later by the Arab-Israeli war, cast a shadow on the future of UN peacekeeping. Yet six years later UN forces again became an important factor in keeping peace in the Arab-Israeli borders when UNEF II dramatically intervened at the conclusion of the 1973 Yom Kippur war. After calling for a cease-fire in resolutions 338 (October 21) and 339 (October 23), the Security Council, in resolution 340, paragraph 3 (October 25), decided "to set up immediately under its authority a United Nations Emergency Force to be composed of personnel drawn from states members of the United Nations except the Permanent Members of the Security Council." UNEF II was established on October 27 when the Security Council approved the report prepared at its request by the secretary general.[6] This followed a Soviet invitation to the United States jointly to intervene to stop the fighting (and thus save the Egyptian Third Army from annihilation), with a warning that the USSR might intervene unilaterally if the United States refused. This threat impelled President Nixon to order an alert of U.S. Armed Forces. Thus, the proposal of UNEF II by nonpermanent members of the Security Council was significant, not only because it helped to keep peace in the Sinai and to establish a basis for peacekeeping operations on which the USSR and the United States might agree, but because it might also have prevented a very dangerous Soviet-American confrontation in the Middle East. Moreover, UNEF II provides a workable precedent for future peacekeeping operations[7]—a precedent already followed on the Golan Heights and in Lebanon.

To diminish the prospects of a Soviet-American military confrontation, the UN and regional organizations should continue to be used to mitigate if not resolve conflicts among small- and medium-sized countries, particularly in Asia, Africa, and Latin America. To this end the United

States should give these organizations encouragement and appropriate support, while relying on its own strength and NATO to deter or counter any direct Soviet thrust.

This line of reasoning is evident in the conclusions of the Atlantic Council's Working Group on the United Nations:

> We believe there should be a new presumption in U.S. policy that the outcomes of most local conflicts will, in the long run, be more consistent with basic U.S. interests if recourse is made to the Security Council rather than if attempts are made to act unilaterally.
>
> The United States and its allies should sustain to the full the authority and capacity of the United Nations to interpose neutral peacekeeping forces between fighting parties whose actions menace international peace and security.
>
> We strongly urge new commitment by the U.S. government, in concert with a coalition of like-minded states of all persuasions and levels of development, to reactivate the machinery for peaceful settlement of disputes, which today languishes essentially unused.
>
> In our view the most effective U.S. posture would be that of international champion of the principle of nonintervention, except as intervention is used by the United Nations for legitimate peacekeeping of humanitarian reasons.[8]

Perhaps the UN as now constituted can deal with only a fraction of the security problems facing the United States. Yet experience has demonstrated that UN peacekeeping activities are in the United States' interest. One need only compare the costs and results of the UN Operation in the Congo (ONUC) with those in Vietnam.

The U.S. share of ONUC costs might have paid for four or five *days* of the war in Vietnam (see Chapter V). Yet the present government of Zaire, though not ideal, is certainly better in terms of U.S. interest than the one in Vietnam. Thus, while collective security as foreseen in the Charter has not worked, UN peacekeeping has become a significant element in American and world security. By October 1966 the postwar world had already witnessed some 379 instances of armed conflict, external and internal. In some 70 cases, the United Nations became involved either as a principal peacemaker or in a complementary role.[9] The record of conflict since 1966 has been at least as active. The UN role in preventing such conflicts from escalating into a world war has been a significant contribution to U.S. security.

The record on disarmament, another goal of the UN Charter, is as disappointing as on collective security, and for similar reasons. As we shall see in Chapter III, the mutual lack of faith between the Soviets and the United States has frustrated efforts to cut back on arms. On the contrary, arms expenditures around the world have continued to grow, currently amounting to over $900 billion. Again, as in collective security, it is not the UN that can take the action; it is the major powers, the protagonists— and their mutual distrust has prevented any real disarmament.

The nuclear arsenals and potentials of the USSR and the United States are so obviously superior to those of any other nation that the "balance of terror" clearly depends on these two countries alone. There- fore, any effort to slow down the nuclear arms race depends on agreements between the USSR and the United States, while the equally serious qualitative nuclear race also depends on Soviet-American negotiations. However, the UN is a valuable means of legitimizing Soviet-American arms agreements, and pressure from the General Assembly can serve a useful purpose by prodding the two superpowers.

GLOBAL ISSUES AND THE WORLD ECONOMY

American interest in the UN was initially centered on its potential role in collective security, and security concerns are still a key element for the United States. Now, however, concern with economic interdependence and global survival has assumed an ever growing importance. Indeed, viewed in the long term these issues are at least as important to the American people as the traditional political and security questions that dominated thinking about the UN in 1945. Harlan Cleveland has described our current situa- tion well:

> There is thus a long agenda of creative effort just ahead. Somehow the community of nations—or at least of those most concerned—will need to create a food reserve, assure energy supplies, depress fertility rates, stabilize commodity markets, protect the global environment, manage the ocean and its seabed, control the modification of weather at human command, rewrite the rules of trade and investment, reform the monetary system, mediate disputes, reduce the cost of military stalemate, control conflict in a world of proliferating weapons, keep the peace when it is threatened and restore the peace when it is broken.[10]

Although there may be some debate on the extent to which American economic policy should be influenced by UN debate, there are increasingly important global issues for which the UN, with its universal membership, is clearly the appropriate forum. These include safeguarding the environment; dealing with the race between population growth and food output; managing the ocean, its seabeds, and the resources under the seabed; assuring adequate supplies of energy and raw materials for a world economy that must grow to meet human demand; and dealing with the implications of human-controlled weather modifications. These are issues whose importance has been recognized primarily in the last decade and, with the possible exception of the law of the sea, were not even in the minds of those who framed the Charter.

We shall deal with the dimensions of these problems and efforts to cope with them in the last four chapters. In general they came to a head during the Nixon era (Chapter VII) and the Scranton-Young incumbencies (Chapter VIII)—as did the drive for a New International Economic Order. Here I shall merely sketch out the policymaking implications of this new agenda. Then, having analyzed the developments that are recorded in the next seven chapters, we shall take another look at policymaking for the future in the final chapter.

First, there will be more *multilateral* business. The trend is already apparent. Harlan Cleveland observes:

> In the late 60's when I had occasion to visit each U.S. Mission in NATO Europe, I made a point of asking what proportion of the business on each Ambassador's desk was strictly bilateral business and what proportion was essentially bilateral conversation about business done multilaterally. My estimate at the time was that the multilateral content of bilateral diplomacy ranged between 60 and 75 percent; now, nearly a decade later, the average is probably at the high end of the range.[11]

A similar estimate, 70 percent, was made by Ivor Richard, the British permanent representative to the UN in 1977. Of course, multilateral does not necessarily mean the UN—there are many other multilateral organizations of a functional and regional nature—but it is a fair assumption, buttressed by experience of the past decade, that the UN has shared in the increase in multilateral diplomacy.

Second, there is a growing tendency to build intergovernmental and transgovernmental networks associated with the work of the formal international organizations. Keohane and Nye have observed:

> Governments must be organized to cope with the flow of business in these organizations; and as governments deal with the organizations, networks develop that bring officials together on a regular, face-to-face basis. International organizations may therefore help to activate

"potential coalitions" in world politics, by facilitating communication between certain elites; secretariats of organizations may speed up this process through their own coalition-building activities. Leadership will not come from international organizations, nor will effective power; but such organizations will provide the basis for the day-to-day policy coordination on which effective multiple leadership depends.

From this perspective it is not surprising that—despite their weakness as "governments writ large"—the number of intergovernmental organizations more than tripled between 1945 and 1965.[12]

The United States participated in almost three times as many meetings in 1975 as in 1950, and fewer than half of the American delegates in 1964 came from the State Department.

Third, as Keohane and Nye also point out, international institutions help set the international agenda:

Governments must organize themselves to cope with the flow of business generated by international organizations. By defining the salient issues, and deciding which issues can be grouped together, organizations may help to determine governmental priorities and the nature of interdepartmental committees and other arrangements within governments. The 1972 Stockholm Environment Conference strengthened the position of environmental agencies in various governments. The 1974 World Food Conference focused the attention of important parts of the United States government on prevention of food shortages. The September 1975 United Nations special session on proposals for a New International Economic Order generated an intragovernmental debate about policies toward the Third World in general. The International Monetary Fund and the General Agreement on Tariffs and Trade have focused governmental activity on money and trade instead of on private direct investment, which has no comparable international organization.[13]

Fourth, the United States must decide how and where to deal substantively with the varied and growing items on this international agenda. When an issue is raised at the UN or a UN-sponsored conference, the United States must react by a given date. This does not necessarily mean that the United States should try to resolve the issue there and then. On economic matters, for example, I believe the United States would be better advised to use the World Bank group, the regional development banks, the International Monetary Fund, OECD, and GATT for negotiations and operations in the areas of aid, trade, and monetary policy. U.S.

interests would be best protected in those institutions, and they have a creditable operating record. In addition, there should be smaller "core" groups on specific problems and on the harmonization of economic policy among the major industrialized countries. On the other hand, there is a vital role for the United Nations General Assembly, UNCTAD, and the Economic and Social Council for the universal discussion of key issues. Experience has shown that over the years government attitudes and policies on major issues, although they cannot be imposed, can be educated and changed through this process.

Whereas other institutions may be preferable for *negotiations* on aid, trade, and monetary policy, the UN is an inevitable forum for *discussion* of these problems and has a virtually unique role on certain global issues. There is no other existing institution with universal membership to deal with the environment, the law of the sea, the race between population growth and food production, and political/security problems in the Third World. Even on economic issues, as presented in the New International Economic Order, the United States cannot afford to be indifferent or uninterested in the UN if it wants Third World cooperation on the global and political/security issues that are important to the United States.

Essentially it is in the long-run American interest to work with all willing partners around the world in meeting what Hedley Bull has called the principal sources of planetary danger; that is, "the war system, population pressure, the insufficiency of resources and the environment overload."[14] The United States would be well advised to avoid policies that are narrowly nationalistic, callous toward the developing countries, and shortsighted. As Lincoln Bloomfield has put it: "The truly hard-nosed advice may well be that which recommends interpreting the national interest far more broadly—that is, by taking bold moves to pool authority and giving a new lead to cooperative rather than unilateral direction."[15] The key question is: Should the main preoccupation of the United States be to gain some short-term political or economic advantage or should it be to contribute to the building of a civilized system of world order with effective means to manage mankind's common problems?

It is sometimes hard to keep this broad perspective in mind when the General Assembly adopts outrageous resolutions, as it has in recent years. The extremist rhetoric on economic issues, the campaign to delegitimize Israel by branding Zionism as racism and a veritable flood of other anti-Israel resolutions, the failure to deal with international terrorism, and the use of the General Assembly as a forum for vilifying the United States and other Western countries have produced widespread doubts about the value of the United Nations for the United States and have led to a congressional call for reassessment of our multilateral diplomacy.

One response has been confrontationist, as exemplified by Daniel

Patrick Moynihan, now a U.S. senator. Moynihan articulated his views some months before he was appointed U.S. permanent representative in 1975, in a *Commentary* article, "The United States in Opposition." Moynihan depicts a UN dominated by a hostile Third World majority, supported on anticolonial issues and economic complaints by the Soviet bloc. He argues that the Unites States and other liberal democracies, now in a minority position, should strike back in what he sees as ideological warfare with particular stress on civil and political liberty. He writes: "In Washington, three decades of habit and incentive have created patterns of appeasement so profound as to seem perfectly normal." "It is time," he contends, "that the American spokesman came to be feared in international forums for the truths he might tell."[16] Moynihan's performance as permanent representative in 1975–76 was true to his doctrine. We shall evaluate the results after looking at his record (Chapter VII).

Moynihan's successors, William Scranton and Andrew Young, adopted a more accommodating approach toward the Third World. In general, the difference was more in approach and tone than in substance. On southern Africa issues, however, even the substance of American policy moved closer to Third World goals of majority rule and racial equality (treated in Chapter VIII). But Jeane Kirkpatrick returned to the confrontationist style of Moynihan, and the U.S. policy toward South Africa became one of "constructive engagement" (Chapter IX).

We shall now look at the record of U.S. permanent representatives over the past forty years. Our focus will be mainly on their role in making and carrying out American foreign policy. Since many years of experience at the UN suggest that the personal characteristics of the permanent representative and his relationship with the president are crucial factors in his influence and performance, we shall be giving particular attention to those factors. We shall also be looking at the changing international scene and overall American policy, since these are the parameters within which the permanent representative must operate. At the end we should have a better insight into the role of our man at the UN—what it is, what it has been, and what it should be.

NOTES

1. *Congressional Record*, U.S. Senate, July 28, 1945, p. 8190.

2. Quoted in Arnold Beichman, *The "Other" State Department: The United States Mission to the United Nations - Its Role in the Making of Foreign Policy*, New York, Basic Books, 1967.

3. Lawrence Weiler and Anne Simons, *The United States and the United Nations: The Search for International Peace and Security*, (New York: Carnegie Endowment, 1967), pp. 39–40.

4. Hubert Myles Gladwyn Jebb, *The Memoirs of Lord Gladwyn*, New York, Weybright and Talley, 1972, p. 263. Speech by Kurt Waldheim on October 28, 1969, in *UN Monthly Chronicle* 6, 10 (November 1969): 85.

5. Lincoln P. Bloomfield and Amelia C. Leisse, *Controlling Small Wars: A*

Strategy for the 1970's (New York: Knopf, 1969), chap. 12.

6. UN Security Council, *Report of the Secretary-General on the Implementation of Security Council Resolution 340* (S/11052/Rev. 1), October 27, 1973.

7. S. M. Finger, "The Maintenance of Peace," in David Kay, ed., *The Changing United Nations: Options for the United States* (New York: Academy of Political Science, 1977), pp. 200–202. The literature on UN peacekeeping is extensive, but four books written since 1970 provide a good sampling: James M. Boyd, *United Nations Peacekeeping Operations: A Military and Political Appraisal* (New York: Praeger, 1971); Larry L. Fabian, *Soldiers Without Enemies* (Washington, D.C.: Brookings Institution, 1971); Indar Rikhye, *The Thin Blue Line* (New Haven: Yale University Press, 1974); and David W. Wainhouse et al., *International Peacekeeping at the Crossroads* (Baltimore: Johns Hopkins University Press, 1974).

8. The Atlantic Council of the United States, *The Future of the UN* (Boulder, Colo.: Westview, 1977). pp. xxii–xxiii.

9. Dean Rusk, cited in Beichman, op. cit., p. 31.

10. Harlan Cleveland, *The Third Try at World Order* (New York: Aspen Institute, 1976). See also Miriam Camps, *The Management of Interdependence* (New York: Council on Foreign Relations, 1974).

11. Cleveland, op. cit., p. 73. Ivor Richard, "Diplomacy in an Interdependent World," in Kay, op. cit., p. 4.

12. Robert O. Keohane and Joseph S. Nye, *Power and Interdependence*, (Boston: Little, Brown, 1977), p. 240.

13. Ibid., pp. 35–36.

14. Hedley Bull in Falk, R. A., *The Future of the International Legal Order* and *This Endangered Planet*," in *International Organization* 26, 3 (September 1972): 383–88.

15. Lincoln P. Bloomfield, *In Search of American Foreign Policy* (New York: Oxford University Press, 1974), p. 165.

16. Daniel P. Moynihan, "The United States in Opposition," *Commentary*, March 1975.

CHAPTER II

USUN: The U.S. Mission to the United Nations and the General Assembly

USUN is unique. Part of its uniqueness derives from the fact that it is at the United Nations. There is no other international organization with virtually universal membership and such an all-encompassing agenda. It deals with issues of war and peace, international disputes, the world economy, social development, human rights, international law, decolonization, refugees, the seas, and outer space. Because the UN has an agenda and a code (the Charter), the U.S. government is continually faced with decisions on a broad range of issues and a timetable determined by various UN bodies, USUN provides the eyes and ears in gathering information, the hand in executing policy, and part of the brain in formulating policy.

The extraordinary quality of the UN atmosphere is described by Arthur Schlesinger:

> It was not until I began making regular visits to the great glass tower glittering above the East River that I started to grasp the intensity of the UN life. It was a world of its own, separate, self-contained and in chronic crisis, where a dozen unrelated emergencies might explode at once, demanding immediate reactions across the Government and decisions (or at least speeches) in New York. It had its own ethos, its own rules, and its own language. . . . It had its own social life, an endless and obligatory round of evening receptions, where American non-attendance might be taken as an insult and lose a vote on an important resolution.[1]

Before coming to USUN I had served at four embassies and one consulate general abroad. In none of them—nor in eight years in private business—was there the frantic pace, the variety of issues, the wide range of personal contacts, and the incredibly long workday, repeated month after month, that a staff member finds at USUN. Nor was there a commanding political figure like Henry Cabot Lodge, Adlai Stevenson, or Arthur Goldberg as chief of mission.

True, there are American missions to many other international and regional organizations; such as the World Bank, the International Monetary Fund, other international specialized agencies, GATT, the Organization of American States, the OECD, and NATO. But each of these has a narrower range of membership or subject matter or both. None makes a similar pretension to being the "Parliament of Man." As the job at the UN is different and more complex, so must USUN be different and more complex. Also, as the web of interrelationships and the number of new nations has grown at an unprecedented rate, so has the task of the UN and USUN.

USUN is located in a twelve-story building at the corner of Forty-fifth Street and First Avenue, which is called United Nations Plaza in that six-block area. It faces the UN across the street and is thus ideally situated for contact with the Secretariat and other delegations. It can also be in instant communication with Washington, at any hour of day or night, and frequently is.

As of this writing, the staff at USUN numbers 117, of whom 36 are professionals dealing with substance. This is a large staff, comparable to those of the U.S. embassies in London and Paris; however, the latter do not have to deal with over 150 other countries and a Secretariat.[2]

USUN's staff grew in size until 1953, when it had 180 authorized positions, including 25 from the U.S. Atomic Energy Commission from 1948 to 1953. By 1954 Henry Cabot Lodge, as permanent representative, cut the staff to 115, eliminating all AEC positions and 40 others. There were then 59 members of the UN; in 1979 there were 152. Moreover, pressure from the new members has resulted in a greatly expanded number of committees and conferences dealing with issues of decolonization and economic development, adding substantially to the already heavy workload.

The statutory basis for USUN is laid down in the United Nations Participation Act of 1945 (Public Law 264-79), as amended in Public Law 341-81 (1949) and Public Law 208-89 (1965).[3] The permanent representative has the rank of ambassador extraordinary and plenipotentiary, as do heads of all embassies abroad. The 1949 act further provides for a deputy representative with ambassadorial rank. Starting with Stevenson in 1961, such rank was also accorded to the deputies for the Security Council, the Economic and Social Council, and the Trusteeship Council, all appointed with the advice and consent of the Senate.

Section 3 of the act stipulated: "The representatives provided for in section 2 hereof, when representing the United States in the respective organs and agencies of the United Nations, shall, at all times, act in accordance with the instructions of the President transmitted by the Secretary of State unless other means of transmission is directed by the President, and such representatives shall, in accordance with such instructions, cast any and all votes under the Charter of the United Nations." Since Section 2 provides, among other things, that members of Congress may be appointed as representatives to the General Assembly, Section 3 makes it clear that they are under the instructions of the president when serving in that capacity. Noteworthy also is the fact that the president may use channels other than the secretary of state to transmit instructions if he so directs.

Section 4 provides that the president must report to Congress at least once a year on U.S. participation in the United Nations, thus emphasizing congressional interest. Section 5 empowers the president to join with other countries in applying enforcement measures short of armed force under Article 41 of the United Nations Charter, an authority used only in the case of Rhodesia and South Africa.

The actual influence of USUN goes considerably beyond the provisions of the three acts of Congress. U.S. ratification of the UN Charter in 1945 carried with it certain obligations. For example, a vote by the U.S. representative in the Security Council on a binding decision taken under Chapter VII of the UN Charter can commit the United States to compliance with that decision. Even when policy is formulated in Washington, it cannot be sensibly designed without considerable information from USUN, which reports on the attitudes of other delegations. Often a conversation can be steered so that an authoritative foreign representative will say what the USUN officer wants him to say, and this can then be quoted in a telegram to Washington.

This practice and other maneuvers to affect the flow of information to policymakers is widespread in government, as shown in a study of Morton Halperin's. Among the maneuvers he describes are the following: selecting information and facts to support the position you favor; marshaling detailed facts on your side; structuring reports so that senior officials are most likely to see what you want them to see; circumventing formal channels; exposing participants informally to those who hold "correct views."[4] All of these devices are available to USUN, and an influential permanent representative with direct access to the president can do wonders in circumventing formal channels.

Between sessions of the General Assembly, USUN officers are in daily contact with representatives of other countries, providing the basis for reports and policy recommendations. During these informal contacts there is an opportunity to speak personally, without instructions, and to probe for areas of compromise and initiative without committing one's government. When there is a difference in viewpoint among various bureaus or departments in Washington, USUN can at times help to tip the balance on policy decisions.

Such influence is particularly important when there is a strong permanent representative with close ties to the president, as in the cases of Henry Cabot Lodge, Arthur Goldberg, Jeane Kirkpatrick, William Scranton, and Andrew Young. Since Lodge took the post in 1953, the permanent representative has had cabinet status and, on important issues, direct access to the president. Generally, he has not been career oriented in the Foreign Service sense and can take risks few other State Department officials would. Moreover, the performance of a leading political figure in public debates at the UN, with a large media contingent on hand, has often enhanced his public recognition and standing. This factor was important, for example, in Lodge's nomination as a vice-presidential candidate in 1960 and Moynihan's as a senator in 1976, and it enhanced the influence in Washington of Stevenson, Goldberg, and a number of other permanent representatives. Since the mission lives in a quasi-parliamentary environment, with an agenda and a Charter, it often becomes an action-forcing, action-inducing agency, notably in crises such as those of the Congo and the Middle East. Also, it often represents the UN to the United States as well as the United States to the United Nations. This latter function has been particularly evident on issues of colonization and economic development, where the existence of a Third World majority, an agenda, and an upcoming vote have forced the United States to make decisions on issues.

The Permanent Representatives and their staffs have also developed highly important relationships with the Secretary-General and his key subordinates, as we shall see in later chapters. Much of the planning and execution of operations at the UN depends substantially on the Secretariat, well-established relationships are extremely helpful to U.S. interests.

Another important USUN function is garnering quick reactions to world events. Casual conversations in the corridors and in UN Assembly halls can elicit a remarkably large and wide collection of well-informed opinions in short order.

Staff quality is also a factor. Writing in 1961, Chadwick Alger observed: "It is quite unlikely that the Government service has ever had officials in any posts who have demonstrated the devotion to their work, coupled with the necessary competence, of these men."[5] My own observation of the decade that followed indicates that this level of devotion and competence was maintained. Alger also wrote: "Only those with private incomes can presently afford to [live in Manhattan] without incurring personal hardships."[6] Again, my experience at USUN from 1956 to 1971 bears this observation out; I commuted twenty-seven miles each way. (In

1974, however, modest housing allowances were introduced, making it possible for officers without independent means to live comfortably in Manhattan.)

Given the heavy work load and the financial difficulties of living in New York without allowances, it is surprising that USUN has had such a high-quality staff. Part of the answer lies in the power and prestige its chief has usually had. Many competent long-term incumbents were recruited by Austin and Lodge, both important national figures, and Adlai Stevenson brought in his own strong followers to augment the existing staff. Lodge's power in the Eisenhower administration was such that he was able simply to wave off State Department inquiries about my transfer abroad, for example, though he probably would not hold on to an officer who felt a strong urge to leave. Then, too, the excitement and variety of the UN environment and the feeling that one's policy recommendations can make a difference are strong lures. For whatever reason, high-caliber people have not only come to USUN; they have stayed for much longer periods than is customary for Foreign Service personnel at American embassies around the world. As a result, many have acquired both rich experience and a UN-oriented viewpoint.

In sum, the quasi-parliamentary nature of the UN; the existence of an agenda and a Charter, with political forces pushing toward a deadline and a decision; the unusual importance of the UN as a place where information and persuasion on issues can be exchanged with unprecedented speed and informality; the quality and dedication of its staff; and the stature of the men who have served as its chief are factors that help to explain why USUN's policy influence has been such that it has at times been called "The 'Other' State Department."[7] Of these factors, the most important is the political strength, stature, and personality of the permanent representative and his relationship to the president.

Another element in the unusual status of USUN is the location of UN headquarters in New York since 1947. USUN must, in addition to the usual functions of a mission, assume host country responsibilities, acting as liaison to the city, state, and federal governments in connection with the privileges and immunities of all foreign mission and Secretariat personnel. It also means that USUN has a responsibility for relations with the American public that no other U.S. embassy has; nor does any foreign mission at the UN have it to a comparable degree. Further, the closeness to Washington produces a symbiotic relationship with the State Department. The constant communication by telephone, telegram, and air shuttle means that Washington can and frequently does get into details that no other government can. Department officials can tune in by direct line to any meeting of the Security Council, the General Assembly, or its committees. I can recall Arthur Goldberg's being called to the telephone from a negotiating session on the Middle East in 1967 to be told by President Johnson that his statement to the Security Council was excellent but he looked down at his paper too much! On the other hand, the symbiotic relationship affords USUN more opportunity for policy input.

USUN is also different from every other mission except the Soviet in that it represents a superpower with worldwide interests. In fact, because the USSR tends to concentrate on political and security issues at the UN and is less active on economic and social matters, the United States is actively involved in more issues at the UN than any other country.

I have deliberately omitted a detailed description of USUN's structure. It is not essential to the concerns of this book and has been adequately described by Arnold Beichman and James J. Wadsworth. Charts of the table of organization of USUN and the U.S. delegation to the General Assembly as of 1978 are included following page 38. They show no significant change from what Beichman has described.[8]

As the charts indicate, a U.S. delegation to the General Assembly is considerably larger than the staff of USUN. Later in this chapter we shall discuss its composition and functions. Hereafter, the terms "mission" or "USUN" will refer to the permanent representative and his staff and "delegation" to the larger group that participates in the General Assembly.

The significance of the U.S. delegation to the Military Staff Committee (MSC) of the Security Council warrants clarification here. The UN Charter foresaw this committee as a sort of allied command for forces to be provided under Article 43 of the Charter. However, negotiations on agreements in accordance with Article 43 failed; hence, there are no forces to command (see Chapter III). For the past three decades MSC meetings have been an empty ritual. Every second Thursday at 11:00 A.M. the MSC representatives of China, France, the United Kingdom, the USSR, and the United States meet for five minutes, during which the sole business is to decide on the date of the next meeting. Nevertheless, USUN has had a vice admiral, a navy captain, and colonels from the army and air force, with appropriate support staff, as its MSC delegation in residence. They are directly responsible to the Joint Chiefs of Staff of the United States. The other four delegations also have high-ranking military officers. No one doubts that all have intelligence functions along with their MSC duties. The vice admiral at USUN has served concurrently as commander of the Atlantic Fleet. The MSC unit at USUN has on occasion provided very valuable current information to the permanent representative, especially when there is Security Council concern with a combat area. Admiral McCain's services to Ambassador Goldberg during the Six Day War were especially helpful. The unit has also performed an important liaison function between the UN and the Pentagon in processing requests for logistical support and supplies for UN peacekeeping operations. In addition, the United States has used its MSC officers as advisers on peacekeeping negotiations. Nevertheless, most of these talented officers were underutilized. During the Carter administration the resident delegation was reduced to one officer, with the others on call in Washington.

MISSIONS TO THE UN AND THEIR ROLES

How have other countries managed their representation to the UN? Of 152 UN members, all but a few of the smallest have established missions in New York. There is evidence that the importance of such missions has been increasingly recognized. From 1945 to 1955 two thirds of the new members took up to three years to establish missions. Since 1955 two thirds of them have set up missions within three months of entering the UN.[9]

For a new nation, especially a smaller one, a mission at the UN offers significant advantages. First, it makes the nation's independence visible internationally. Second, it provides year-round access to an international crossroads. Its mission can transact bilateral business with the representatives of about 150 countries, including the observer missions of non-members such as Switzerland, the Holy See, and the two Koreas without the expense of establishing embassies all over the world. Third, much of the business carried on by the UN Secretariat in New York is of interest to governments. The secretary general and his staff are sources of reports, information, and advice unavailable elsewhere. Secretariat officials often offer help and advice in drafting resolutions. They frequently draft resolutions in their entirety, either in response to a delegation request, or by seeking out a delegation to present a resolution desired by a branch of the Secretariat. A Secretariat official may also advise delegations against submitting a draft resolution or propose substantial changes. Access to the secretary general for information, advice, or good offices can be very important to a country; indeed, the bulk of his time is devoted to such private consultations. Fourth, the UN Development Program and the Children's Fund can be important sources of assistance to new countries. Finally, meetings of blocs like the "Group of 77," which as of this writing has about 120 members from the less developed countries, are of great interest to their members, especially the new and less developed countries.

The proliferation and year-round activity of the missions to the UN is in marked contrast to the situation at the League of Nations. Then, only Japan and certain small and medium powers kept permanent delegations, whose legal status remained vague and whose contacts with the Secretariat were very little developed.

The late Dag Hammarskjold pointed to another important aspect of the "permanent conference" represented by the community of mission to the UN:

Over the years, the diplomatic representatives accredited to the United Nations have developed a cooperation and built mutual contacts in dealing with problems they have in common, which in reality make them members of a kind of continuous diplomatic conference, in which they are informally following and able to discuss, on a personal basis, all political questions which are important for the work of the Organization. . . . Public debate in the United Nations is dominated by the same differences among the parties as international political life as a whole. But behind closed doors these differences are diluted. The human factor carries more weight there, and confidential exchanges are possible even across frontiers which otherwise appear impassable.[10]

For the Republic of China, France, Great Britain, the Soviet Union, and the United States, the establishment of permanent missions became a necessity as soon as the Charter was ratified. Article 28, paragraph 1, stipulates: "The Security Council shall be so organized as to be able to function continuously. Each member of the Security Council shall for this purpose be represented at all times at the seat of the Organization." As soon as other members were elected to serve on the Council they, too, had to establish missions in order to "be represented at all times."

On December 3, 1948, the General Assembly recognized as "permanent missions" those national offices that member states had established in New York. It also recognized the permanent representatives and regularized procedures concerning their credentials.[11]

The UN diplomatic corps has now grown to the point where it involves some 158 missions employing more than 1,000 people. Let us now look at their functions.

First, there are the classic functions of representation at meetings, liaison with other delegations, information gathering, reporting, and the promotion of friendly relations with other states. The big difference is that these functions are carried out multilaterally with about 150 other countries instead of bilaterally with one. Smaller countries use their missions not only for multilateral functions at the UN but also to carry out bilateral negotiations with missions from countries where they are not represented.

Second, there are the functions of parliamentary diplomacy. These involve coping with an agenda determined by a majority; frequent public debates (daily during the General Assembly); rules of procedure that are subject to tactical manipulation; and a process of reaching formal conclusions, usually by voting. True, the General Assembly is not a legislative body. With rare exceptions its resolutions have no legal force; nevertheless, its procedures are similar to those of a legislative body. This is one reason why members of Congress find it relatively easy to adapt to service in a General Assembly delegation.

Richard Pedersen, who served more than fifteen years at USUN, makes the following observations about the unique characteristics of negotiating at the UN:

> The techniques of private negotiation are strongly influenced by the fact that a parliamentary test is intended before a final decision is taken. The provisions of the Charter, the rules of procedure in the General Assembly and the Security Council, and other institutional elements create a unique framework within which negotiations and parliamentary maneuvering take place. Notable among these elements are, of course, the veto in the Security Council and the two-thirds requirements in the General Assembly, elements which dominate the negotiation process as well as subsequent parliamentary activity. Closely connected with the aforementioned factors is the fact that in a public test of strength each state, no matter how large or small its actual power or its diplomatic influence, has only one vote in the General Assembly—the same as that of each other state. Thus the element of national power and influence is to some extent redressed in the UN in favor of small countries.
>
> Other characteristics of the UN that uniquely influence negotiations include the fact that all UN negotiation is in effect multilateral, as is also the "openness" of the activity, e.g., the fact that at any moment any of the negotiators may make a pure test of negotiating strengths by taking the issue out of private talks and into the public forum.[12]

Third, the proliferation of councils, boards, committees, and commissions, particularly in the economic and social fields, means that the range of action is much wider and often more technical than in traditional diplomacy. Consequently, technical specialists and lower-level personnel often have a more important role and greater discretion than they would have in a bilateral situation. Also, the wide range of questions promotes a greater degree of autonomy for the mission, as few governments can keep track of so many details and the government is more dependent on the mission for relevant information. In general, the smaller the country and the greater its distance from New York, the more autonomy a mission has.

Fourth, parliamentary diplomacy invokes greater informality than traditional diplomacy. So many decisions have to be made so fast that there is little time for protocol. Also, in the parliamentary atmosphere rank becomes less important. An adviser, even of junior rank, will often negotiate with an ambassador if they are both involved in fast-moving parliamentary negotiations. The use of first names after only brief acquaintance is prevalent.

Fifth, there is a propaganda function. Addresses to the General Assembly by presidents, prime ministers, and foreign ministers are frequently used as a propaganda vehicle, as are speeches, resolutions, and tactical maneuvers at other times. Pedersen refers to this propaganda function as "influencing opinion" and observes that a "considerable portion of the planning of every delegation must therefore be directed to the question of how it can most effectively use the United Nations to persuade the world of the validity of its government's policies." This raises considerations not only of a speech's content but also where, when, and by whom it should be delivered.[13]

The content must be considered carefully for its impact, not only on the immediate audience (e.g., the other delegates to the General Assembly), but also on wider audiences among the general public and abroad, if it is a major speech, as well as on the home government of the assembled delegates. Depending on the issue and the timing, a major speech may in reality be aimed at the wider world audience with little concern for the tactical situation in the General Assembly. Where the tactical aspects are more important, the statement may be assigned to a less prominent representative in a less prominent forum, such as one of the Assembly's committees. Where maximum impact on American public opinion is desired, a speech made by the president, the secretary of state, the permanent representative, or another prominent person will be made in the General Assembly or the Security Council shortly before noon, in order to meet media deadlines. The timing of rebuttal statements is also important. Henry Cabot Lodge, a permanent representative who was a skilled propagandist, made it a point always to reply promptly to Soviet attacks or charges so that the media could carry the rebuttal right along with the charge. Further, even though speeches are generally prepared by the professional staff, a leading political figure usually wants to put his own gloss on the statement; consequently, final wording is often a matter of negotiation. Speaking style and emphasis, however, cannot be negotiated and may be a significant factor, as is the prominence of a personality. Prominent senators like Knowland, Humphrey, Mansfield, and Javits have not only brought media attention but have also had a personal impact on other delegates, as have important industrialists, labor leaders, and artists. The choice of Dr. Charles Mayo of the Mayo Clinic to refute Soviet charges that the United States employed germ warfare in Korea was particularly effective.

Presidential addresses to the United Nations General Assembly are of particular impact when they launch a significant new program; for example, Eisenhower's "Atoms for Peace" proposal in 1953, which resulted in the establishment of the International Atomic Energy Agency, and Kennedy's proposal for a United Nations Development Decade. Similarly, Khrushchev launched proposals for "general and complete disarmament" in 1959 and the "immediate" elimination of colonialism in 1960. Also, the Soviets annually spice their foreign minister's address to the General Assembly by including a proposal for an "urgent and important" item to be added to the agenda. The urgency is rarely related to the issue itself but rather to getting media attention.

A sixth and most important function of the mission is its role in formulating and carrying out policy. As indicated above, the gathering and reporting of information may be used as a tool in influencing policy. On most issues the mission will make policy recommendations when reporting on issues anticipating an agenda item or looking for an initiative. If there is a competent staff and a chief who is respected in the capital, its recommendations carry considerable weight, since it is closest to the situation. If the chief (the permanent representative) is close to the head of government, his influence can at times be decisive and will consistently be an important factor in making policy.

Edward Appathurai lists the following factors that determine the degree of a mission's influence on policy:[14]

1. The nature of the issue. The more deeply it involves the country's basic interests, the more likely is the probability of opposition from other branches of the government.
2. The position of the permanent representative in the social and political hierarchy of his country, especially his relationship to the head of government.
3. Geographic position. The mission gets the relevant information first and most fully and it is in virtually constant contact with some 150 other missions. Appathurai writes: "In one sense every permanent mission can be considered as the Ministry of Foreign Affairs of a country with regard to multilateral decisions."
4. The attitude of the government toward the UN.

My own experience suggests that Appathurai's statement (quoted in item 3) must be modified, at least for USUN and other missions of major countries that are carefully instructed from their capitals.

The degree of a Mission's influence is bound to depend on the degree of its government's interest in the UN as well as the government's standing. In the 1950s and 1960s, South Africa and the United States stood at opposite extremes. South Africa saw the UN as a nuisance; its main interest was a defensive one, responding to attacks on its policy. The United States, by contrast, saw the UN as an important world forum and often as a valuable instrument in carrying out American policy. Even with countries of about the same size, the degree of interest varies greatly. The Netherlands mission to the UN has consistently exercised considerable influence, whereas Belgium's has been minimal. Naturally, there is a reciprocal relationship between a mission's influence at home and its influence at the UN, both reflecting the degree of the government's interest.

Other experienced observers point to the important role a delegation plays in modifying, interpreting, or even changing policy *after* it has received instructions on an issue. Pedersen observes:

> The influence of a delegation on policy may be exerted from the time when an issue first arises, but it is strongest after the consideration of an issue has begun. If a delegation reports, on the basis of its observations, that an objective cannot be achieved without modification, or if it recommends that the diplomatic cost of achieving the objective would be too high to justify pursuing it, its judgments necessarily carry considerable weight, as it is the only authority in a position at that moment to evaluate most of the available data. Missions and foreign offices naturally try to anticipate such a situation in preparing their policy positions, and missions to the United Nations customarily advise their foreign offices on the feasibility or viability of varying courses in advance. However, anticipation is not fact, and when anticipated difficulties actually arise, the influence of the negotiators is much greater than beforehand. As a source of information on the attitudes of other governments and delegations, as an agency of the government professionally concerned with effective use of the United Nations in foreign policy, and as a tactically minded unit which may be able to predict whether certain lines of policy may or may not be successfully carried out, a delegation is likely to exert substantial influence on policy formulation throughout the consideration of any individual issue.[15]

He also notes that there are occasional cases when issues must be decided immediately and UN delegations are compelled to vote without instructions from their governments; such votes may establish governmental policy.

James Hyde observes that an instruction or position paper may deal clearly and precisely with the issue at hand.

> However, it may contain vague language to hide rather than reveal differences of opinion. It may have intentional gaps because the critical decision cannot be made so far in advance or because the

Secretary prefers to keep it to himself. Also, it may purposely not indicate positions to which US representatives can retreat because some delegate may retreat too readily. In this case the paper may state that if a certain situation develops, the State Department should be consulted for further guidance.

Hyde reports cases in which it was easier for the State Department hierarchy to accept a suggestion from the mission after it received an instruction than it would have been to clear the same idea in the original State Department instruction. He concludes:

> In sum, the formulation of policy cannot be considered as at an end when the delegation is instructed and sent to the conference or meeting. There are inevitable changes and readjustments that occur during all the stages of implementation.[16]

In my own experience I can recall, when arguing about an instruction on the phone, being told to make the effort and report back. Only after the delegation was "bloodied" in making an effort we knew was doomed to failure would Washington be prepared to change the instruction. Such a tactic was usually used when the State Department had other critics at its back who had to be satisfied that an attempt had been made. More often, instructions could be changed before trial and failure if we could convince the Department that it was wrong.

Changes in instructions may also come about as a result of the negotiating process. Halperin observes:

> In a typical case the discussion starts with known governmental positions that are clearly inconsistent with each other and will, if maintained, create a stalemate. But the study of these positions, when they are all laid on the same conference (or luncheon) table, enables each representative to make a judgment about how much his own instructions would have to be bent in order to meet his colleagues—if they succeed in bending their instructions too. Each representative then reports to the government that a new proposition, not contained in anybody's instructions, might just make it possible to secure agreement. Each representative, in the elementary exercise of bureaucratic caution, attributes this composite formula to one or more other governments, and most of our allies are likely to attribute it to the United States. Without representatives who are willing to operate in that diplomatic no-man's-land beyond their formal instructions, the efficiency of collective diplomacy would be greatly reduced, and governments might just as well send messages directly from capital to capital even on issues that involve many nations.[17]

THE GENERAL ASSEMBLY: AN EIGHT-RING CIRCUS

To appreciate fully the pace, complexity, exhaustion, frustration, and excitement of a UN General Assembly, one must be an active participant in it.

The Assembly meets in Plenary and in seven main committees, each of which is a Committee of the Whole. Thus, at any given time the delegation of a major power must be involved in eight different arenas: preparing initiatives and positions; responding to the initiatives of other delegates; gathering information; drafting resolutions; preparing and delivering statements; consulting other delegations; negotiating with them; lobbying; and communicating and negotiating with one's own government. All of this takes place not only in the arenas, any six of which may be in session simultaneously, but also in the lounges, in caucuses, in interdelegation meetings, and at receptions and dinners. Moreover, items of identical, related, or similar substance will often be discussed in two or more committees simultaneously. The job of coordinating delegation positions into coherent policy requires constant attention.

On top of all this, one or more international crises may erupt during an Assembly session, bringing about concurrent sessions of the Security Council. In the fall of 1956 there were urgent sessions of the Security Council to consider the British-French-Israeli invasions of Egypt and the Soviet suppression of Hungarian freedom, then emergency special sessions of the General Assembly to deal with these issues after vetoes blocked Security Council action, all taking place while the regular eleventh session of the Assembly was approaching.

From the inception of the UN, American presidents from both parties have followed the practice of appointing prominent personalities from the worlds of politics, science, the academic community, and the arts to Assembly delegations. In even years there are always two senators; in odd years, two members of the House of Representatives, one Democrat and one Republican. Prominent and influential figures such as Senators Vandenberg, Connally, Mansfield, Knowland, Humphrey, Church, Sparkman, Javits, and Congressmen Bingham, Fascell, and Judd have served at one or more sessions.

Before he became secretary of state, John Foster Dulles, who had served on Assembly delegations as an appointee of President Truman, observed:

The influence of the Assembly depends largely upon the world attention it can attract, for only as it attracts attention can it have contact with world opinion, influence it, and be influenced by it. Thus, it is of utmost importance that the delegations should include both persons of international standing and prestige and those who have political authority in their own countries. . . .

If the delegations to the United Nations were made up of only subordinate officials, then, however capable they were, the influence of the General Assembly and indeed of the United Nations as a whole would be reduced almost to the vanishing point.[18]

Each delegation consists of five representatives and five alternate representatives, who have the same powers and functions in the Assembly. They are backstopped and guided by an unlimited number of advisers, principally from the permanent mission staffs.

The ten U.S. representatives usually include the permanent representative; the deputy permanent representative; the deputy to the Security Council; and at times the representative to the Economic and Social Council— all of whom now have the rank of ambassador. The other six or seven include two members of Congress, one Democrat and one Republican, and four or five others chosen for various reasons: prominence in politics, industry, labor, the arts, or the sciences; regional balance; payment of a political debt; ethnic balance; religious considerations; and the need to have at least one woman. Although this practice has occasionally resulted in a strange appointment, those chosen have generally been able and hardworking.

The main problem that arises is the tendency to appoint such representatives at the last minute. In the past, often the session was half finished before they got their bearings; in the meantime, they usually relied on their advisers. Repeated USUN recommendations that representatives be appointed well before the Assembly starts have been accepted in principle but not yet in practice. Even so, on balance, the impact of drawing on a pool of eminent persons has been quite positive. Many have brought inventive minds and fresh viewpoints or have been highly valuable in contacts with other delegations because of their personal prominence. Moreover, they return to their normal occupational worlds with an experience that can spread knowledge of the UN more widely.

It should also be noted that many representatives can serve only part-time at the Assembly. Members of Congress must return frequently to Washington for votes and other congressional business. Business executives like Henry Ford II and labor leaders like George Meany or I. W. Abel must continue to run their organizations. The delegation is organized so as to function with or without them; however, a special effort is made to accommodate assignments to their schedules so that their appearances may have maximum impact. The impact is worth the extra effort.

Representatives, especially those who come for only one Assembly session, lean heavily on their advisers, mostly USUN staff, with some from the State Department. This can be a difficult relationship; it often involves an eminent figure with an adviser half his age but who is an expert on the UN situation. It works surprisingly well. Congressmen and leaders of industry or labor have usually learned to use expert staff in their careers and take advice gratefully. Where the State Department's instruction or position paper runs contrary to his convictions, a representative can try to get it changed or ask to be given another assignment. For example, Senator Frank Church, as a member of the delegation in 1966, refused to take any position or make any statement in support of the war in Vietnam. It was no problem to use his very considerable talents on other items.

The assignment of agenda items, a very careful process, begins as soon as the names of the representatives are known. USUN staff officers, after looking into backgrounds and known positions, recommend the division of agenda items. An effort is made to assign a representative as much as possible to one committee so that he may develop relationships with his foreign counterparts. One of the two congressional members is normally assigned to the Fifth Committee, which deals with the UN budget, for obvious reasons. Naturally there is a tendency for most representatives to want the juicy, controversial political items that promise headlines and excitement, but there are not enough of these to go around. The permanent representative will usually go over the recommended list of items with each representative, stressing their importance and his particular abilities for dealing with them. Sometimes a representative assigned primarily to one of the other committees willl be given one or two newsworthy political items in the First Committee or Plenary to "sweeten the pot."

Usually these assignments are taken with understanding and good grace, although I can remember at least one notable exception. Barrett O'Hara, an aging Democratic congressman from Illinois, became so incensed by his belief that his colleague, Republican Peter Frelingheysen of New Jersey, was given more important items that he threatened to resign from the delegation a few weeks after the Assembly opened, in the fall of 1967. To a stunned audience of foreign representatives and advisers just outside the meeting room, he said he would take the floor in Congress to denounce USUN for treating congressmen with contempt. USUN's minister counselor, informed by telephone, made a hurried trip across the street to smooth O'Hara's ruffled feathers. Soon thereafter Ambassador Goldberg, the chief of delegation, sought out O'Hara, discussed the problem, made some adjustment in agenda items, and managed to keep O'Hara on the delegation, if not completely happy.

In the fall of 1960, when the General Assembly adopted a Declaration on the Granting of Independence to Colonial Territories and Peoples, Mrs. Zelma Watson George, a black representative on the U.S. delegation, stood up and joined in the applause. The United States had abstained on the declaration. Mrs. George was not reprimanded and continued to serve on the delegation on good terms with its other members, even though some questioned the appropriateness of her gesture.

In the opening weeks the secretary of state frequently heads the delegation, with the permanent representative serving as the chairman at all other times. The secretary uses his time in New York for intensive bilateral discussions with the presidents, prime ministers, and foreign ministers who come for the general debate. He may thus have valuable contacts with the spokesmen of several scores of countries in a few weeks, without the protocol hassle involved in official visits to Washington. Some secretaries, such as Marshall, Rogers, and Kissinger, have made the U.S. address in the Assembly's general debate. Others, such as Dulles and Rusk, have chosen not to do so, devoting their time at the Assembly to bilateral consultations and U.S. delegation meetings as well as running the State Department by long distance.

The chart on page 39A outlines the structure of the U.S. delegation in the fall of 1977 and is typical. In some years, however, there has been a senior USUN officer—the deputy representative, the alternate representative, or the minister counselor—who serves as coordinator and trouble-shooter. He must stay on top of the entire agenda, know what is going on in Plenary and each of the seven main committees, coordinate the delegation's activities, and see that remedies are brought promptly in each troubled situation. This may involve bringing in liaison officers to help with lobbying for votes, offering advice to the delegation executive officer for that committee, meeting with the representative, or occasionally making an off-the-cuff statement under pressure. If there is a misunderstanding, it may also involve arranging a private meeting between the representative and the chairman of the delegation.

The primary instrument for policy discussion is the delegation meeting, usually held at 9:30 A.M. two or three times a week. The secretary of state chairs meetings when he is present and usually gives at least one "inside" look at the state of the world. His presence is also valuable in discussing position papers; it sometimes enables changes to be made on the spot. When the secretary leaves, the permanent representative serves as chairman.

Usually the delegation will hear a brief report on the Plenary and each committee from the responsible executive officer, with comments invited. On important issues, time is set aside for discussion, starting with a presentation of the problem by the responsible staff officer. The representative to whom the item has been assigned is then asked to comment. Since the two have usually discussed the issue beforehand and come to an agreement, the representative rarely adds anything of substance. Then all present are invited to comment, starting with the representative and alternate representatives. Finally, the chairman summarizes the consensus. If there are agreed delegation recommendations for a change in position, the responsible item officer drafts a telegram to be cleared by the chairman and other delegation members directly concerned. Former Permanent

Representative James J. Wadsworth estimates that such strong disagreement happens only once or twice each session, but when the delegation "does feel that strongly, it has a good chance of success."[19] From my own experience of fifteen years, I would agree with Wadsworth's estimate of changes brought about by formal delegation telegrams; however, many more changes are brought about through less formal procedures. The responsible delegation officer, after consulting his representative, will often discuss the issue on the phone with a State Department counterpart; on larger issues, the permanent representative may call the secretary of state. After a meeting of minds, the agreed change will then be formalized by an exchange of telegrams. The full delegation discussion of issues is carried out at least as much to give the public representatives a sense of participation as to tap their wisdom.

The delegation meeting is usually preceded by a briefer, crisper staff meeting of the executive officers and liaison or "regional" officers; these meetings are held almost daily. Here protocol is at a minimum and the day's business is discussed tersely. Decisions are made about what issues should be taken up in the full delegation, which should be discussed privately with the chairman, and which warrant a phone call or telegram to the State Department. Also, liaison officers get the "party line" on the issues of the day and learn where the priorities are for lobbying. These staff meetings help to coordinate efforts, avoid contradictions from committee to committee, and promote effective teamwork.[20]

The "regional" officers referred to in the organization chart are also called "area" or "liaison" officers. Usually each has served in the area of his assignment, speaks the prevalent language, and knows some of the people representing the countries there.

The advisers are listed in three categories: senior advisers, advisers, and special advisers. There is no real difference between the first two, except for rank. The special adviser, however, is usually a senior person who comes in only for particular items on which he has expertise.[21]

TACTICS IN THE GENERAL ASSEMBLY

The Assembly's form of action is a resolution, just as a legislative body's form of action is a law. The comparison, however, is deceptive. A law passed by Congress that is not vetoed by the president or is passed over his veto has behind it the full and effective authority of the U.S. government; it will be enforced by the executive branch and the courts, unless it is declared unconstitutional by the courts. This is not so with a resolution of the General Assembly; with rare exceptions it is only a *recommendation* to governments and will have only as much effect as they choose to give it.

Some of the most important results of Assembly sessions do not come from resolutions at all but rather from changes in attitudes of key governments that result from both formal debates and informal talks during the session. Having represented the United States in the Second (Economic) Committee of the General Assembly from 1956 to 1963, and having watched closely since then, I have been impressed by the way prolonged discussion there can bring about major changes in attitudes on economic issues. When the notion of soft loans was first advanced by the less developed countries in the form of the Special United Nations Fund for Economic Development (SUNFED), the concept was rejected by the United States and most other industrialized Western countries. Yet in 1959 the United States led the way to the establishment of the International Development Association (IDA) as a soft-loan affiliate of the World Bank. Similarly, it took many years of discussion in the UN General Assembly and UNCTAD before industrial countries accepted the concept of nonreciprocal tariff concessions to the low-income countries; now this doctrine is generally accepted and has been put into practice. The notion of compensatory financing to help developing countries that produce raw materials weather the vicissitudes of erratic markets was put forth in the 1950s but made little headway. In 1974, however, compensatory financing was incorporated in the Lomé Convention, and in 1975 Kissinger proposed the establishment of a $10 billion facility in the International Monetary Fund (IMF) for this purpose.

These examples illustrate a point that I believe is valid for the future; that is, concepts can be taught and learned in the General Assembly, but successful operating mechanisms for major programs are more likely to be located outside the United Nations itself. Can anyone believe that the United States and other major Western countries would have provided SUNFED, or any other organization based on a one-nation, one-vote principle, with the major resources that were required for IDA? Would it have been possible to negotiate detailed trade rules in the Second Committee or the General Assembly? Would the developed countries even have dreamed of putting a $10 billion compensatory financing fund at the disposal of the General Assembly?

Another point is crucial with regard to the General Assembly and UNCTAD—that the voting majority of the Third World is most effective when used sparingly. Resolutions adopted over the strong objections of those whose cooperation is required for their implementation are meaningless. Their adoption in such circumstances does not change the minority position and may even tend to harden it and impede further negotiations. Far more effective has been the combination of pressure and patient negotiation, as in the establishment of the UN Special Fund in 1957 and in the agreement reached at the seventh special session of the UN General Assembly in September 1975 on the principles of a "new international economic order."[22]

Nevertheless, in a formal sense the Assembly still acts through resolutions as the only visible product of its deliberations, and activity revolves around them.

The first step is the decision by a delegation to take an initiative and draft a resolution. For the United States this might be done either in Washington and then checked with USUN or vice versa.

Next, for most resolutions, the delegation will choose and endeavor to secure cosponsors. It is usually desirable to cover a wide spectrum so that one will have advocates within as many geographic groups as possible. (Soviet bloc delegations will not normally cosponsor Western resolutions, except on certain disarmament issues where there has been prior Soviet–U.S. agreement.) At times a cosponsor may ask for a modification of the draft as a condition of cosponsorship. Such a request must be weighed carefully to be sure the change will not jeopardize other support or impair the American objective. Then clearance must be obtained from the State Department. At times the United States may find it expedient to have another delegation put forward the draft as its own; certain examples of this practice will be cited in subsequent chapters.

Once the draft has been presented, there is the task of winning support, meeting objections, and countering opposing moves, which may take the form of amendments, counterproposals, or a motion not to consider the proposal. Here is where behind-the-scenes cajoling, persuading, and appealing to friendships are used both by representatives to the committee and the area officers who work with their friends from each region. Johan Kaufmann, a thoughtful UN veteran who has been the Netherlands permanent representative to the UN headquarters in both Geneva and New York, lists the available instruments as follows: intellectual arguments; promises; overasking; underoffering; and threats, such as withdrawal of aid.[23] In my own experience at USUN I found that threats to other nations were rarely used; they can backfire, and other techniques were usually more effective. At times, when it was felt that a particular delegation was being uncooperative on an important issue and our bilateral relations with its government were good, approaches would be made to the capital. It was always politic, however, first to try to persuade the delegation, thus reducing both the number of capitals that had to be approached and the number of unhappy delegations.

Another notable fact is that representatives deal with each other over extended periods and on many issues. Anyone who acquires a reputation for being untrustworthy has little future at the UN, which is a glass house in more ways than one. Kaufmann and a Canadian veteran of the UN have noted that the negotiating process is carried out predominantly in private meetings.

> In such meetings personal relations are paramount. If a delegate is to be effective, it is necessary for him to know and approach the right person in the right delegation at the right time. If this approach is made under conditions of pressure and decisions are urgent, close personal understanding between the individuals concerned is of special importance.[24]

Kaufmann lists the qualities of conference diplomats as truthfulness and honesty; precision; calm and even-tempered; patience, modesty, and zeal; adaptability; loyalty; physical and mental endurance; speed; linguistic versatility; and courage in taking responsibility.[25] The linguistic versatility is important in fast-moving private negotiations, where interpreters are rarely present.

The need for precision might puzzle anyone who has read UN resolutions that are evidently ambiguous, but there may well be art even in ambiguity. When a decision must be made on a resolution and delegation positions do not quite mesh even after exhaustive negotiations, there are points where ambiguity may be introduced deliberately. Thus, delegations with varying positions can support the same text, interpreting it so as to fit their own positions. (An excellent example is Security Council resolution, 242, which is described in Chapter VI.) A negotiator is in trouble only when he does not recognize the difference between ambiguity and precision.

THE NEW MAJORITY IN THE GENERAL ASSEMBLY

In the first seventeen years of the United Nations' existence, the United States could manage to obtain a General Assembly majority on most of its initiatives. Thus, the United States took a number of steps to enhance the Assembly's authority. But, as the Third World majority has come to dominate the Assembly since the mid-1960s, the United States has been less frequently an initiator of resolutions and more often in a defensive or reactive posture. The United States has raised cries against the "tyranny of the majority", exercised its first Security Council veto in 1970, and has used it thirty-eight times since then. (The Soviet Union has used its veto 114 times, mostly before 1970.) In the Assembly the United States often stresses the need for negotiation, conciliation, and consensus rather than voting, in contrast to the emphasis it placed on votes in the early years. The delegation has had to place greater emphasis on defensive tactics, such as amendments, marshaling a blocking third in the Plenary on important questions, and appealing for patient negotiation rather than hasty voting.

At this point it might be well to look at the bloc politics that has come to dominate voting in the Assembly. (In the final chapter we shall make a more detailed analysis of possible American responses to the new situation.)

In the first decade the group politics situation was very favorable for the United States. The twenty Latin American states constituted more than a third of the memberships, which started at fifty-one and rose to fifty-nine by the end of the decade. On roll call votes involving "noncolonial" issues, sixteen of the twenty voted identically with the United States at least 89 percent of the time, and all twenty voted the same way as the United States on at least 70 percent of the votes. By contrast, the five Soviet bloc members voted identically with each other but voted with the United States only 7 percent of the time.[26] Clearly, the Latin American votes, combined with those of other friends and allies of the United States, provided a majority that could be rallied behind an American initiative with any reasonable amount of persuasion and adjustment of position or wording. In these circumstances it is understandable, if not entirely laudable, that the United States used the General Assembly as a cold war propaganda arena.

Now the voting situation in the various blocs has changed drastically, and so has the American position on the value of General Assembly resolutions and voting majorities.

The dominant bloc is the Afro-Asian group, which now constitutes a majority of the membership. (For various purposes, there are also separate Arab, African, and Asian groups.) As one would expect in such a large group, there is great diversity. There are large-, medium-, and small-sized members; oil rich and desperately poor; almost developed, less developed and developing; neighbors with border disputes that sometimes erupt into wars; coastal and landlocked states. Yet on issues of anticolonialism, antiapartheid, and economic development assistance they can usually unite. Moreover, on such issues they can generally count on the voting support of the Latin American-Caribbean group, now numbering thirty-three, regardless of how the United States votes, plus the eleven members of the Soviet bloc as well as China, Albania, and Yugoslavia. These issues now account for a substantial majority of the resolutions produced by the Assembly, with disarmament and the Middle East accounting for most of the others. Within the Afro-Asian groups the twenty-two Arab states exercise a powerful influence in pressing for drafts supporting Arab positions against the Israelis. Almost anything they present is assured of an overwhelming majority.

Appathurai observes that often the consensus or "unanimity" expressed by spokesmen for the Afro-Asian group on an issue is only a facade. Frequently states do not express their opposition in order not to offend other members of the group who attach particular importance to the issue. Thus, it is a privileged forum for a minority of extremists; they can present their position as if it were that of the group collectively. It is a serious inconvenience for states that have individual views and that, given the impassioned atmosphere of discussion on certain subjects, find themselves obliged to go along with a line of conduct at variance with their own views.[27]

Another negative aspect of group politics is a tendency toward inflexibility. In the 1950s and early 1960s a group of about a dozen representatives from states around the world could meet in a room and work out compromises that would carry overwhelmingly in the Second Committee. The negotiators would agree not to give in to extremists in their own geographic group, and the agreement would stick. A major change occurred at the first UNCTAD Conference in 1964; the Group of 77 developing countries was formed. Besides the Afro-Asian countries, it includes the Latin American nations and Yugoslavia and now has over 110 members. Kaufmann observes that, as group tactics have become more formalized, "the willingness to seek areas of acceptable compromise may be absent and, indeed, have been replaced by a sort of group inflexibility which makes the negotiation of compromise solutions more difficult."[28] The 77 have a three-fourths majority in UNCTAD and on its Trade and Development Board; obviously, they do not need to compromise to gain a majority. For practical reasons they have agreed to procedures that delay voting when there is serious objection from the developed countries in order to allow time for conciliation. They realize that a majority resolution has little meaning if it is not supported by the developed countries whose action is required.

The geographical groups also have their positive aspects. They are used for the selection of candidates for the presidency of the General Assembly, the Economic and Social Council, and UNCTAD; and for memberships on the Security Council, the Economic and Social Council, the UNCTAD Trade and Development Board, as well as various committees and commissions. They also serve as a center for the exchange and, to a degree, harmonization of views on issues before the UN. Especially for the new and smaller countries, they perform a tutorial and socialization function and provide information that individual missions might not have.[29] To a certain extent, too, the groups simplify communications and reduce the number of speeches. But the most important function these groups perform for the new and developing countries is undoubtedly their role in promoting the shared interest of their members. There is no question that the Group of 77 has managed to generate a collective pressure on economic issues that is much stronger than it would have been if left to individual members or smaller groupings. And the organized efforts of the African, Asian, and Afro-Asian groups has certainly increased the emphasis on decolonization. The question is whether the stress on cohesion may have brought inflexibilities in negotiation that hinder agreement with those whose cooperation is essential to progress. Moreover, the Afro-Asian group's support of Arab proposals has given the General Assembly an anti-Israel bias that prejudices the UN's standing as an impartial instrument for facilitating peace.

Caucus groups play a much less important role for the developed countries. The group known as Western European and Others (WEO) is used principally in connection with elections. The others include Australia, Canada, and New Zealand. For substantive discussions the tendency is to use smaller European caucus groups, such as the Nordic Group of five, the Benelux Group of three and the European Economic Community Caucus of nine.[30]

Little is known about the inner workings of the East European Group. Externally, it is the most cohesive group of all, with any deviation from the Soviet pattern being extremely rare, but Romania sometimes acts as a maverick.

The United States is not a member of any formal caucus group. This might be considered a handicap except that militarily the United States is one of the two superpowers and economically has twice the national income of the next largest nation, the Soviet Union. The UN Charter refers to the "sovereign equality" of members, and this is reflected in the fact that each member has one vote in the General Assembly. Yet, in truth, some members are "more equal" than others. Only China, France, Great Britain, the Soviet Union, and the United States are permanent members of the Security Council, with the power of veto; any one of them can frustrate the will of an overwhelming majority. The Soviet Union and the United States stand alone as superpowers, leading one member to remark in May 1970, "The majority of some hundred member states, it's two member states."[31] In 1964–65, for example, an entire General Assembly was conducted on a nonvoting basis rather than risk a showdown with the Soviet Union.

Superpower or not, the United States cannot do its job effectively at the UN unless it maintains wide contacts and is open to approaches from all sides. True, superpower strength can be effective in a negative sense. The United States can block action in the Security Council by a veto and can block most UN economic programs if it refuses to cooperate. It is thus in a good position to protect its own interests, in a narrow, nationalistic sense, even without the cooperation of other states.

But American national interests in the UN have always gone well beyond such a defensive, negative posture. There is no escaping the need for worldwide institutions to exchange views and to study and deal with critical problems affecting all humanity. Among them today are peace-keeping (to "freeze" local conflicts before they get out of control); limiting nuclear and conventional arms; coping with food shortages, unemployment, and mass poverty; limiting population growth; preventing environmental deterioration; controlling drug traffic and epidemic disease; setting safety standards for air and sea transport; and numerous other trans-national concerns.

None of these positive goals, essential to a livable world for the United States as well as other countries, can be approached effectively without widespread cooperation among member states. Consequently, the United States must reach out to states in all geographic regions, singly and in groups. Its mission and delegation must work constantly at persuading others to support American goals. Equally important, they must have sensitive antennas, to know in detail what other countries want and why. Changes in texts can be managed more easily before formal circulation. A true appreciation of others' goals can frequently result in agreement on common goals, by trade-offs, changes in texts, or persuasion. The mere act of listening closely, sometimes called the "persuasive ear," can win friends who will listen more sympathetically when an American position is being advanced.

For members of regional groups, contacts with other delegations or missions are built into their membership. The United States, on the other hand, must make a conscious effort to seek out other delegations. During the General Assembly this is the job of the regional officers; however, it cannot be done effectively unless *all* members of the delegation are involved. This means not only the usual receptions, lunches, and dinners but also carefully planned ad hoc caucus meetings, the casual cup of coffee or drink in the lounge, and frequenting the Delegates' Lounge. During the Assembly the Delegates' Lounge is full of valuable contacts, especially just before and just after lunch. There, individual brief contacts can frequently be made with four or five delegates in half an hour, faster and more effectively than by any other means. During my years as minister counselor, we made "lounge assignments" to make sure someone was there at all times, and many of us made frequent forays. The lounge is probably the best place to use antennas, but it offers only one of the many opportunities that must be used if the United States is to reach out effectively, as it must.

THE "CLASS STRUGGLE"—MISSIONS AND THEIR CAPITALS

"There is only one real class struggle nowadays—the struggle between the Missions and their governments." This facetious remark to the Second

Committee by the Japanese representative, Kakitsubo, in 1963 gave everyone there a good laugh, precisely because there was a grain of truth in it.

There is, first of all, an inherent conflict between field representatives and bureaucracies in the capital. In the U.S. case, operators in the field are prone to see Washington as a great bureaucratic sludge, slow to respond and comfortable with inertia.[32] The field operators are not alone in their thinking. Presidents, too, have despaired of the "built-in inertia" at the State Department.[33]

In substantial part, this tendency toward inertia results from the need to reconcile conflicting interests; for example, the Bureau of European Affairs versus the Bureau of African Affairs on colonial issues, Treasury versus AID and State on economic issues, East Coast versus West Coast fishermen on the breadth of the territorial sea. With each bureaucrat defending his own constituency, the easiest way to arrive at an agreement where nobody can be taxed by his constituents for losing ground is to leave things as they are. Thus, a major policy mutation usually must come from the president, who may on occasion be influenced by the thinking of a trusted emissary.

The negotiator in the field, by contrast, acquires a vested interest in moving toward a solution. American negotiators often become advocates for the maximum range of concessions in negotiations they are conducting. They want to claim success; the more they can offer, the more likely they are to achieve agreement.[34]

This inherent field-capital conflict is accentuated at the UN. First, the existence of a broad agenda requires a large number of negotiating decisions, which must often be made against a deadline. Robert Murphy observes:

> The UN may be required at any moment to consider almost any military, political, economic, or social problem anywhere on earth, under the seas, or in outer space. So the UN office of the State Department is supposed to examine, at least superficially, all the incredible deluge of documents, resolutions, surveys, complaints, reports which pour in from the member governments and all branches of the UN organization—the Secretary-General's Office, the General Assembly, the Security Council, the Trusteeship Council, the Economic and Social Council, and numerous special agencies.

A British observer depicts the General Assembly situation more graphically:

> the [resolutions] come flooding in, they are very long and complicated and, with the best will in the world, they really do present quite

a difficulty to the delegations in New York and Governments overseas. . . . Amendments are moved in New York of which we in the
capital cities have hardly seen the context—perhaps we get it on the
telephone—and in situations in which we are unable to appreciate the
full implications. Many of the member Governments, I can assure the
House, have given up the task in despair and give no instructions to
their representatives. Some have given permanent instructions to
abstain.[35]

For the United States the State Department's problems in controlling
policy have been accentuated further by the stature of its permanent
representatives. Men like Lodge, Goldberg, Scranton, and Young have had
direct access to the president and could, when necessary, bypass the State
Department. Thus, Arnold Beichman concludes:

With a Congress sympathetic to USUN as an institution [?], a
President who will probably always want at the UN his own rather
than the State Department's man, and the willingness of elite
Americans to serve as USUN Chief or in subordinate delegate posts,
USUN influence will continue to grow to such an extent that no State
Department policy either of rollback or containment of the USUN will
work. At best, the State Department can accept, as it has, a policy of
competitive coexistence with USUN.[36]

Technically, the permanent representative is responsible to an assistant
secretary of state for international organization affairs (IO). In practice, he
will often deal directly with the secretary of state or the president on
important issues. The following interview with George Ball is illustrative of
the relationship to the President:

"Mr. Ball, as U.N. Ambassador, will you regard yourself as the
lawyer for the Administration or a participant in policy-making?"
"Both. As a high official of the United States government I will
feel a very definite obligation to urge my views on the President, the
Secretary of State and the Administration. I'm sure this is one of the
reasons why the Presient asked me to serve, because he knows my
views, he's listened to them in the past; he has always given me my day
in court, and I'm sure he will now."[37]

By contrast, the assistant secretary is usually a career man with no
political power base. With a Lodge, a Goldberg, a Ball, a Scranton, or a
Young as permanent representative, he is far more likely to be the
permanent representative's lawyer than the other way around. The

presence of prominent American public delegates appointed by the president at the General Assembly, including two members of Congress, adds further to the delegation's power vis-à-vis the State Department. So, as noted above, does the fast-changing tactical interaction. When time is pressing, the permanent representative can state that he plans to pursue a certain course of action unless instructed to the contrary. Moreover, over most of the four decades the permanent representative has been buttressed by an experienced, able staff, many of whom were at USUN for long periods and were "UN-ized."

The late Robert Murphy, a distinguished career diplomat, considered that "the existence of a two-headed Foreign Office is potentially dangerous because it can seriously hamper coordination of foreign policy." As an example, he cited the Bay of Pigs invasion, where "Washington was persuaded to deny the use of the few American planes which with a great deal of luck might have enabled the weak Cuban invasion to succeed, and the absence of which guaranteed failure."[38] Elsewhere in his book Murphy wrote: "Personally, I have never regarded the U.N. as a divine machine from which happy solutions to our problems would miraculously flow. Nor have I feared the consequences even if the U.N. should collapse entirely."[39]

Murphy's lack of enthusiasm for the UN must have influenced his viewpoint. My own conviction that the United States has vital interests in the UN, on the other hand, makes me more favorable toward the idea of a strong permanent representative who will, in a sense, represent the UN to the United States as well as vice versa, even if this entails less neatness in making policy.

NOTES

1. Arthur M. Schlesinger, Jr., *A Thousand Days. John F. Kennedy in the White House* (Boston: Haughten Mifflin, 1965), p. 411.

2. USUN sources.

3. See "A Decade of American Foreign Policy, 1941–49," Senate Doc. 123, 81st Cong, pp. 156–62. See also, Arnold Beichman, *The "Other" State Department, The United States Mission to the United Nations. Its Role in the Making of Foreign Policy,* New York, Basic Books, 1967.

4. Morton H. Halperin, *Bureaucratic Politics and Foreign Policy,* (Washington, D.C.: Brookings Institution, 1974), pp. 158–68.

5. Chadwick F. Alger, *United States Representation in the United Nations* (New York: Carnegie Endowment, 1961), p. 27.

6. Ibid., p. 15. See also Richard Walton, *The Remnants of Power* (New York, Coward McCann 1968), pp. 212–13.

7. Beichman, op. cit.

8. Ibid., chap. 5. See also James J. Wadsworth, *The Glass House* (New York: Praeger, 1966).

9. E. Appathurai, "Permanent Missions to the United Nations," *International Journal* (Spring 1970): 288–89.

10. Dag Hammarskjöld's address to students' association, Copenhagen, Denmark, *United Nations Review* (June 1959): 22–23.

United States Mission to the United Nations

Organization of the
United States Delegation to the
32nd Regular Session of the
United Nations General Assembly

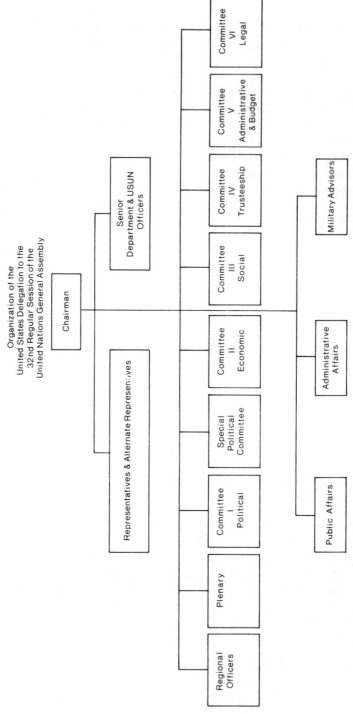

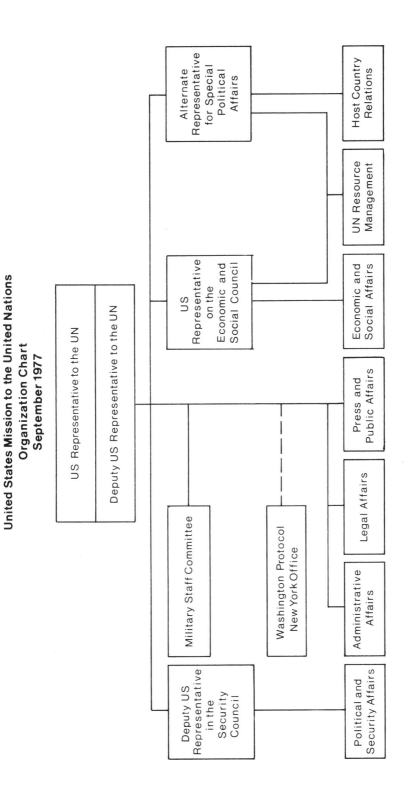

United States Mission to the United Nations
Organization Chart
September 1977

US Representative to the UN

Deputy US Representative to the UN

Deputy US Representative in the Security Council

Military Staff Committee

Washington Protocol New York Office

US Representative on the Economic and Social Council

Alternate Representative for Special Political Affairs

Political and Security Affairs

Administrative Affairs

Legal Affairs

Press and Public Affairs

Economic and Social Affairs

UN Resource Management

Host Country Relations

11. G.A. Res. 257 (III), December 3, 1948.

12. Richard F. Pedersen, "National Representation in the UN," *International Organization* 15, (Spring 1961): 258.

13. Ibid., p. 260.

14. E. Appathurai, *The Permanent Missions to International Organizations* (Brussels: Carnegie Endowment 1975), p. 71.

15. Pedersen, op. cit., 258–59.

16. James N. Hyde, "U.S. Participation in the U.N.," *International Organization* (February 1956): 25, 28.

17. Halperin, op. cit., p. 272.

18. John Foster Dulles, *War or Peace* (New York: Macmillan, 1957), p. 197.

19. James J. Wadsworth, *The Glass House* (New York: Praeger, 1966), p. 179.

20. Channing B. Richardson, "The U.S. Mission to the U.N.," *International Organization* (February 1953): 22–24.

21. Robert E. Riggs, *Politics in the United Nations* (Urbana, Ill. 1958), pp. 35–44, provides a good description of the delegation's structure and functions.

22. S. M. Finger, "United States Policy Toward International Institutions," International Organization (Spring 1976): 355–60. The same phenomenon is recorded by Harlan Cleveland, not only with respect to economic issues, but also anticolonial doctrine and some aspects of international law. Harlan Cleveland, "The Pace of Mutation," in *UN 30*, (New York: UNA/USA, 1975), p. 13.

23. Johan Kaufmann, *Conference Diplomacy, An Introductory Analysis* (Dobbs Ferry, N.Y.: Oceana, 1968), p.153.

24. John Hadwen and Johan Kaufmann, *How United Nations Decisions are Made* (Leyden: A.W. Sijthoff, 1960), p. 36.

25. Kaufmann, op. cit., pp. 130–36.

26. Riggs, op. cit., pp. 168–69.

27. Appathurai, *The Permanent Missions to International Organizations,* pp. 118–19.

28. Kaufmann, op. cit., p. 150.

29. David A. Kay, *The New Nations in the United Nations* (New York: Columbia U. Press, 1970), pp. 23–26.

30. Ibid., p. 25. The Western European Group, which then had five members, has grown to nine, now that Britain, Denmark, and Ireland have joined the European Economic Community and the Federal Republic of Germany has become a member of the U.N.

31. Appathurai, *The Permanent Missions to International Organizations,* p. 134.

32. Morton H. Halperin, *Bureaucratic Politics and Foreign Policy* (Washington, D.C.: Brookings Institution, 1974), p. 264.

33. Beichman, op. cit., pp. 201, 204.

34. Schlesinger, op. cit., p. 505.

35. United Kingdom, *Hansard's Parliamentary Debates,* 5th ser. (Commons), 653, February 5, 1962, pp. 53–54.

36. Beichman, op. cit., p. 196.

37. Ibid., p. 104, fn. 14.

38. Robert D. Murphy, *Diplomat Among Warriors,* (New York: Doubleday, 1964), p. 368.

CHAPTER III

The Early Years: Stettinius and Austin

Edward R. Stettinius, Jr., was not chosen as the first permanent representative to the United Nations because he had the special confidence of the president; he was offered the post when Truman decided to remove him as secretary of state.

Upon becoming president, Truman was concerned over the fact that, as the law then stood, his successor in the event of his death would be Stettinius, a man who had never run for elective office. On the day Roosevelt died (April 12, 1945) Truman told James F. Byrnes, former senator and erstwhile Supreme Court justice, that he was considering asking him to become secretary of state. Shortly thereafter, returning from Roosevelt's funeral at Hyde Park, Truman actually offered the job to Brynes, who accepted. Stettinius remained as secretary until June 25 in order not to disrupt the U.S. delegation to the San Francisco Conference negotiating the UN Charter. Byrnes succeeded him on June 30.[1]

Stettinius then accepted Truman's offer of the UN post. He tried to get cabinet status and to be able to report directly to the president but was thwarted on both counts.[2] He had no real knowledge of international relations nor any appreciable strength within the councils of government.[3] Truman felt confident that he, Byrnes, and Acheson could maintain full control of American policy at the United Nations. There is no evidence that Stettinius had any substantial impact in deciding policy issues. Owing to illness during the first session of the UN General Assembly, the job of leading the U.S. delegation fell to Adlai Stevenson. (See Chapter V.) Stettinius resigned abruptly after less than seven months as permanent representative, because he thought the position was not one of sufficient importance. He then became rector of the University of Virginia, his alma mater, serving for only a year until his death in 1949 at age forty-nine.

Although Stettinius had little impact on U.S. policy during his brief tenure as U.S. representative, as secretary of state he had played a major role in the establishment of the UN. Upon becoming secretary in November 1944, he included among his five major policy objectives the "establishment at the earliest possible moment of a United Nations organization capable of building and maintaining the peace—by force if necessary—for generations to come." In doing so, he reflected the convictions of his predecessor, Cordell Hull, and of President Roosevelt. He was the inspiration behind a large public information program that built up the American public's support of the UN in 1945. At the San Francisco Conference, Stettinius won the respect and affection of the U.S. delegates for the determination, enthusiasm, and dedication with which he approached the creation of the United Nations Charter.[4] Thus, although Truman did not intend to give Stettinius a policymaking role, the appointment was perceived by the public and by foreign governments as a recognition of the UN's importance to the United States.

Indeed, Truman did consider the UN important. In his *Memoirs* he records:

> I felt strongly about the idea on which the UN organization was based and had been supporting it in every way I could on the Hill. I wanted to scotch any rumors or fears in the U.S. and abroad that there would be any changes in the plans that had been made. It was with that in mind that I decided to issue a statement at once, reassuring our allies of my support of the coming [San Francisco] conference.[5]

Moreover, Truman kept in close touch with the U.S. delegation to the San Francisco Conference, starting with preparatory meetings in Washington and continuing through to the successful closing of the conference. He placed great stress on reaching agreement with the Soviet Union on points of difference to assure their participation. He signed the UN Charter in San Francisco on June 26, 1945, congratulated Stettinius on his "good work" as chairman of the delegation, and made a strongly supportive address at the Charter signing. And only six days after signing the Charter he submitted it to the Senate for ratification.[6] He also appointed strong and distinguished delegations to sessions of the General Assembly, including Eleanor Roosevelt, whose dedication, influence, and drive were major factors in the achievement of the UN's Universal Declaration of Human Rights in 1948. Other distinguished delegates were Senator Arthur Vandenberg, Thomas Connally, and Gen. George C. Marshall.

Truman also showed his interest in the UN by asking Warren R. Austin to succeed Stettinius. Austin, who had served over fifteen years as a senator from Vermont (1931–46), was highly respected by Democratic colleagues as well as by his fellow Republicans. Dean Acheson, then undersecretary of state, sensing that there would be a Republican victory in the congressional elections of November, urged the nomination of a Republican "internationalist" like Austin to head USUN in order to lift U.S. policy at the UN indisputably above domestic politics.[7] The move succeeded.

Austin had other important qualities. Truman considered him a very close friend, dating from their many years of service together in the Senate. Trygve Lie, then secretary general of the United Nations, described Austin as "one of the most thoroughly honest men I have ever met."[8] His able and distinguished deputy, Philip Jessup, said he was "devoted to Ambassador Austin—a fine Vermont gentleman and sincere public servant."[9] A former senior staff member of USUN wrote that Austin "exhibited the utmost patience and courtesy in allowing anyone to speak who wished to" at delegation meetings.[10] Another said Austin was superb in dealing with other delegations, who liked and respected him. He would consult other delegations fully before making moves in the Security Council, and they appreciated his courtesy, honesty, and openness to their viewpoints.[11]

Two respected scholars of international affairs, Lawrence Weiler and Anne Simons, have described Austin as "able, forceful and widely respected by both political parties." They note that his bipartisan acceptability was enhanced by the fact that, being sixty-nine at the time of his appointment, Austin clearly had no political career ahead. But they also noted that "his political standing within the Truman Administration was never such that he could be classified as a first-level negotiator. . . . Most of his instructions as well as his speeches on significant issues were delivered by teletype from Washington."[12] This was in sharp contrast with two of his strong successors, Lodge and Goldberg.

Austin was completely left out of Washington consultations on the Truman doctrine and the policy of containment. He saw President Truman's statement on the doctrine only one day before it was delivered on March 12, 1947. In the Security Council three weeks later, he supported the Truman doctrine fully as a necessary "short-term" measure meant "to strengthen the United Nations and to advance the building of collective security under the United Nations."[13] After NATO was established, Austin defended it in the same terms. He was thus able to reconcile his support of containment with his belief that a moral and righteous philosophy *eventually* would become established in international affairs.[14]

Unlike Lodge, Austin disliked both personal publicity and public controversy. In debates at the UN he rarely raised his voice or used a harsh word in response to Soviet propaganda against the United States. He felt strongly that the United States should not get "down in the mud" with the Russians. His replies to Soviet oratorical attacks were usually made only after careful preparation, thus enabling the Russians to gain the headlines unimpeded.[15]

Before the outbreak of the Korean War in June 1950, Austin's style was consonant with overall U.S. policy in the UN. In May 1948 Austin argued against any attempts to revise the Charter radically, which might drive the Soviet Union out of the UN. He warned: "Once this relative universality of membership is destroyed, such collaboration as now exists would cease, and a complete break between East and West would occur. The only possible bridge between the East and West would collapse; and yet the problem of bridging the gap between East and West is precisely the crucial problem of our time."[16] Although this statement was obviously cleared by the U.S. government, there was little progress in bridging that gap nor evidence that Washington sincerely believed it could be bridged. (The unsuccessful efforts on atomic weapons ban and military forces agreements will be discussed later in this chapter.)

With the advent of the Korean War in 1950, the cold war became increasingly embittered. The communist countries launched their "Hate America" campaign of 1951–53, culminating in their trumped-up germ warfare charges. This, in turn, resulted in strong American counter-propaganda efforts in the UN, with little thought to bridging gaps.[17] Austin, while he evolved over time into a "cold warrior" had neither the appetite nor the inclination for this propaganda warfare, which his successor, Lodge, enjoyed to the hilt and performed most effectively.

Austin, who had frequent bouts with ill health, received strong support from his two deputies, Philip Jessup and Ernest Gross. (It should also be noted that during the latter half of 1946 Herschel V. Johnson, a career Foreign Service officer, held an interim appointment as permanent representative so that Austin might finish his term in the Senate. Technically, Austin served as special advisor to Johnson, with the rank of ambassador.)

Philip Jessup, Austin's deputy until March 1949, was a highly respected professor of international law at Columbia University. He carried a major part of the burden at the UN on the Berlin Blockade, Palestine/Israel, and Indonesia. His incisive mind won him the confidence and respect not only of Austin but also of the president, the secretary of state, the secretary general, and other delegations as well. Jessup left USUN because Secretary Acheson wanted him for important special assignments. President Truman appointed him ambassador at large, and for the next four years he was a successful troubleshooter and adviser for Truman. Subsequently, he served on the International Court of Justice.

Jessup's successor as Austin's deputy, Ernest Gross, was also an international lawyer. He had served as assistant secretary of state for congressional relations and legal adviser of the State Department. Gross reports that when he asked for the UN job, Secretary Acheson could not believe he would want the post and thought he would be wasting his talents.[18] Acheson's doubts about the UN are also recorded by Jessup, who writes: "Acheson did not have much enthusiasm either for the UN or the Indonesian Republic."[19] Both Jessup and Gross indicate that much of the friction between Acheson and USUN resulted from USUN's greater concern with the struggle of colonial peoples for independence, while Acheson was NATO oriented and reluctant to take a position at the UN against our European allies. Gross sees this USUN-Washington friction as an inherent difference between multilateral and bilateral diplomacy. USUN is faced with an agenda and a Charter, which involves taking a position whenever another member raises an issue, in terms of written code. It also thinks in terms of Afro-Asian votes on other issues where there is competition for the votes of small nations. In bilateral relations, except for crises, Washington can usually choose whether or not to make a decision on a given issue at a given time and has been primarily concerned with military alliances and Soviet–U.S. relationships. As we shall see when considering specific cases, USUN has frequently attempted, with degrees of success varying from 0 to 100 percent, to move the American position toward greater support of self-determination for dependent peoples.

Because of Austin's protracted illness, Gross was frequently de facto chief of USUN and usually had to carry the ball in policy disputes in Washington on colonial issues. He kept Austin fully informed and cleared USUN positions with him on all important issues. Gross says that Austin's mental processes recovered completely from his 1950 stroke, even though it left him with certain speech difficulties. Austin kept himself fully informed at all times and decided USUN's position vis-à-vis Washington on all important issues.

Gross made frequent trips to Washington in order to work out policy differences, particularly on colonial issues. There he would negotiate with the assistant secretaries of state, particularly the heads of the various geographic bureaus—sometimes winning, sometimes losing, sometimes compromising. The full confidence of Austin, who had great prestige with the president and Congress, was a significant asset; however, Austin did not attempt to appeal directly to the president when Gross could not win State Department approval for a USUN position. Nevertheless, Gross states that USUN moved the American position at the UN significantly on items involving self-determination for Morocco, Tunisia, Indonesia, Eritrea, Libya,and Somalia.[20]

Even when the position could not be moved, USUN's attitude could make a difference. For example, on April 10, 1950, the Security Council was considering inscription of the question of Tunisian independence on its agenda. Gross, who favored inscription, had been instructed to abstain, his instructions being incorporated in a speech sent from Washington. But he added the following words at the beginning: "I express the following views of my government on this subject." UN newspaper correspondents had no difficulty in interpreting this sentence to mean that Gross disagreed with U.S. policy on this issue and so reported. Gross describes the scene that followed:

> After I read that opening sentence, from that point on it didn't matter what I said. The blunt tone of that sentence was enough. On the record nothing could be held against me by Washington because I had said what I was supposed to say. But when the Security Council recessed, I was surrounded in the Delegates' Lounge by a group of Asians and the small number of Africans then in the UN. They shook my hand and they were so pleased. What I had done was to make it possible to continue the dialogue.

As a result, Gross was called to Washington by John Hickerson, then assistant secretary for international organization affairs. He had already been lectured by Secretary Acheson about North Africa and had been told that relations with France were the "lodestar" of American foreign policy and therefore the United States could not play "U.N. politics." In Washington he was given anew the full background of U.S.-French problems on colonial issues and the extent to which these issues were a big domestic political problem for the French government. Gross said:

> What triggered this particular confrontation with the European desk [of the State Department] and with Acheson and [George] Kennan was that I had not given sufficient weight to the U.S.-France relationship nor taken account of the French domestic situation, that the battle in France was between the moderates on one side and the army and colonial administration on the other, that the latter were exercising more influence than the Qaui d'Orsay. However, the people in the African section of State were not unhappy at what I'd done.[21]

It would be a mistake, however, to view the USUN-Washington relationship as antagonistic across the board. On the contrary, as will become clear shortly, USUN was far more often a useful instrument of Washington's policy, which it carried out loyally and effectively.

Gross also emphasizes the far greater opportunity for informal discussion offered in the UN framework—that there can be a "casualness about an important issue." Thus, an informal, off-the-record conversation between Sir Benegal Rau of India and Gross resulted, after governmental consulations and approval, in the establishment of the UN Peace Observation Commission, whose function, rarely used, is to observe and report, upon request of the Security Council or the General Assembly, on any area of dangerous international tension.[22] Such informal exploratory conversations were used in verifying the Soviet position on ending the Berlin Blockade in 1949, in working toward a peaceful solution of the *Pueblo* incident in 1966, and in many other important but less known cases.

Another important function that took root under Austin, Jessup, and Gross was the development of thorough USUN staff work in preparing for sessions of the General Assembly. True, the final decisions on issues are made in Washington; however, good staff work at USUN on forthcoming items can make a very important difference in the way an item is presented for decision. John Ross, as senior adviser, played an important role in counseling Austin on policy and tactics.

Gross also attributes importance to the stationing of the representative to the Economic and Social Council (ECOSOC) at USUN. In the initial years the assistant secretary of state for economic affairs represented the United States at ECOSOC; this was just one, and not the most important, of his many official duties. The appointment of Isador Lubin as U.S. representative—a move initiated by Gross—set a precedent. From Lubin on, occupants of this post brought a USUN viewpoint into discussions of American economic policy. This has made a significant difference.[23]

Gross's legal mind was most helpful in working out the ground rules for the participation of American congressmen in delegations to the General Assembly. To bolster American support for the UN, Truman wanted bipartisan congressional participation each year, but the Constitution's separation-of-powers doctrine raised problems. As members of Congress, they were part of an independent, equal branch of the government. As delegates, they would be under instructions from the president, chief of the executive branch. Under the ground rules Gross prepared, subsequently accepted by both Congress and the president, congressional members of delegations to the General Assembly act under presidential or State Department instructions when serving in that capacity but otherwise retain the independence accorded them by the Constitution. Over the years, congressional participation has been most helpful in developing better understanding of the UN in Congress and maintaining the bipartisan nature of American participation in the UN. At times, as in the case of Walter Judd in the consideration of the UN Special Fund (see Chapter IV), a congressman's role has been crucial to success. Austin's stature with congressmen, based on the great respect he had earned during fifteen years as a senator, was an important factor in establishing the position of the permanent representative as chief of a delegation that included members of Congress at each session of the General Assembly.

IRAN, GREECE, SYRIA, AND THE INTERIM COMMITTEE

The first challenge to the Soviets came early. On January 19, 1946, Iran formally charged the Soviet Union before the UN Security Council with interference in Iranian affairs.

During World War II, Iran had been a vital connecting link for the Allies, with Soviet troops in the north and British in the south. In the Teheran Declaration of December 2, 1943, Roosevelt, Churchill, and Stalin had reaffirmed Iranian independence and integrity. At the London Conference of Foreign Ministers in September 1945, the British and Soviets had agreed that all their troops would be withdrawn by March 2, 1946. Instead, the Iranians charged, the Soviets were sending in more troops in November 1945.[24] Iran also charged that the rebel government in its province of Azerbaijan owed its existence to the Soviets and was supported by the Soviet military forces, which interfered with the shah's efforts to move in troops to put down the rebellion.

The Soviets argued that the dispute was not a matter which the Security Council was competent to handle and stated they would ignore any questions raised there in regard to this issue. The Security Council then agreed that the Soviets and Iranians should settle the matter by direct negotiation.[25]

The Soviets did not leave by the agreed date of March 2, 1946. On Truman's instructions, Secretary Byrnes then sent a blunt note to Stalin calling for compliance with the tripartite agreement and warning that the United States would take action if the matter were not satisfactorily settled. On March 24 Moscow announced that all Soviet troops would be withdrawn at once. Truman credited the withdrawal to his warning, "coupled with the moral force of the United Nations."[26]

On April 15, 1946, Iran informed the Security Council that it wished to withdraw its complaint against the Soviet Union. The next day Trygve Lie submitted a memorandum to the Security Council urging removal of the item, since the Soviets had already so requested and no other party had asked for inscription, nor had the Security Council ordered an investigation under Article 34 of the Charter. In a reversal of roles that subsequently became customary, the Soviets (Gromyko) held that, in view of Article 99, the secretary general "has all the more right and an even greater obligation to make statements on various aspects of questions submitted to the Security Council"; the U.S. representative said he was "not at all sure that the Charter can be construed as authorizing the Secretary-General to make comments on political and security matters." The Council's Committee of Experts rejected Lie's memorandum by a vote of 8 to 3 (USSR, Poland, France).[27] This example of practical consideration overriding principle was, of course, not unique.

In the fall of 1946 Iranian troops entered Azerbaijan, and the separatist regime of the leftist Tudeh party collapsed. Dean Acheson wrote of the incident: "Iran is no stronger than the United Nations and the United Nations, in the last analysis, is no stronger than the United States."[28]

The United Nations was also useful for American objectives in postwar Greece, faced by communist guerrillas. The main factor in the Greek government's eventual victory was its ability, strengthened by substantial U.S. aid under the Truman doctrine, to defeat the guerrillas in the field; however, the moral support of a majority at the UN was significant. A Security Council investigation, undertaken at Greece's request, substantiated Greek charges that Yugoslavia, Bulgaria, and Albania were supporting the uprising against the government. In the commission the vote on the report was 8 to 2 (USSR, Poland), with France abstaining.[29]

After Yugoslavia broke with Moscow in 1948 aid to the guerrillas subsided, and the Greek government was able to subdue them.

The experience in Greece and the intensification of the cold war led the United States to look to the General Assembly for support, since Security Council action could be stymied by a Soviet veto. At American initiative, launched by Secretary Marshall's statement to the General Assembly, the Assembly on November 13, 1947, adopted its resolution 3 (II) establishing an Interim Committee of the Whole that could act when the Assembly was not in session. This was the beginning of the American effort to build up the Assembly as an alternative to the Security Council and thus circumscribe the Soviet veto. The Assembly became an important forum for denouncing Soviet actions, mobilizing the pressures of world opinion, clarifying U.S. positions, and enlisting the support of the international community for policies the United States was undertaking or contemplating. The use of commissions and truce supervision in Greece, Korea, Palestine, Kashmir, and Indonesia gave the United States a role while keeping the Soviets out. Such devices were especially important to Washington during the 1946–49 period when the United States lacked disposable forces to intervene against Soviet actions in Eastern Europe, or in other trouble spots.

The Soviet bloc members refused to participate in the Interim Committee, but it served for a few years as a body where preparations could be made by the rest of the membership. It never met after 1955.

INDONESIA

The UN role in Indonesia was both more protracted and more significant than its role in Iran and Greece. After the Japanese were driven out by Allied troops in 1945, the Dutch reasserted their authority, which was resisted by Indonesian armed forces and guerrillas. The United States was convinced that Indonesia should have its independence, but as Jessup has pointed out, "it would have been inconceivable for the United States to have promoted the evolution of Indonesian independence through unilateral diplomacy. It was only with the aid of UN mechanisms that Indonesia was born in 1949."[30]

Despite Dutch objections, the British accorded de facto recognition to the Republic of Indonesia in March 1947, and the United States followed suit a few weeks later. Both countries voted for a Security Council resolution on August 1, 1947,[31] calling for a cease-fire and a peaceful settlement; they rejected Dutch claims that the fighting in Indonesia was an internal matter that, according to Article 2 (7) of the Charter, should be excluded from Security Council consideration.

Both in the Council and in the Good Offices Committee (GOC) the United States emerged as the key member. It consistently opposed proposals mandating the withdrawal of Dutch troops or compulsory arbitration. Dean Rusk, then director of UN affairs in the State Department, expressed it to Jessup as follows: "The United States cannot accept the role of world policeman either in a military or in a political sense if other permanent members refuse to join in action by the Security Council for maintaining peace. If the Security Council acted on the basis of the votes of seven members of which only the United States was really able to act, it would involve commitments we did not want and could not undertake."[32]

As for arbitration, Australia, Colombia, Poland, Syria, and the Soviet Union clearly favored it; Belgium, France, and Britain could be expected to oppose; and the United States and either Brazil or China could have provided the decisive votes in the Council. Instead, Jessup, who was in charge at USUN, successfully launched the idea of a Good Offices Committee, which the Council approved on August 25, 1947.[33] Constituted on September 18, the GOC's three members were Belgium, designated by the Netherlands; Australia, designated by the Indonesian Republic; and the United States, chosen jointly by Belgium and Australia.

In Washington Jessup consistently used an argument that USUN leaders repeatedly employed on colonial issues coming before the United Nations—that the United States must support nationalism in order to counter communism. In the cold war atmosphere this was the most effective tactic for gaining Washington's support of nationalism. Thus, the United States continued to put pressure on the Dutch for a peaceful approach toward Indonesian independence, using the GOC and the Security Council. At one point the United States warned the Dutch that if they did not move in good faith toward Indonesian independence, the United States would state in the Security Council that the Dutch were not carrying out the Renville Agreement, withdraw from the Good Office

Committee, recognize the Indonesian Republic, and establish trade relations with it.

On December 28, 1947, the Netherlands agreed to the GOC's proposals for a truce. A few weeks later, on January 17, 1948, it accepted the Renville Agreement setting out procedures for a peaceful settlement. When fighting broke out again, the Security Council called for a cease-fire on December 24, and on December 31 the Netherlands representative told the Council that the Dutch forces would cease hostilities within two or three days. This time the cease-fire held, and the two parties, assisted by the GOC with the United States playing the key role, came to a firm agreement. Sovereignty was formally transferred to Indonesia on December 27, 1949, and Indonesia was admitted to the United Nations nine months later—a notable success for U.S. policy exercised through the UN.[34] Unfortunately, for a variety of reasons, the United States did not pursue a similar policy toward the Vietnamese struggle against France.

STALEMATES—ATOMIC ENERGY AND FORCES AGREEMENTS

President Truman instructed the U.S. delegation to the first formal session of the General Assembly in London in January 1946 to work for the establishment of a United Nations Commission on Atomic Energy. This was in keeping with agreements reached in Moscow the preceding month, and a British proposal to establish the new commission was adopted on January 24.[35]

Meanwhile, a five-member committee chaired by Dean Acheson, then undersecretary of state, worked on a plan for international control of atomic energy. It was aided by a board of experts chaired by David E. Lilienthal. The result was a policy paper, usually referred to as the Acheson-Lilienthal Report.

In March, Truman appointed Bernard M. Baruch U.S. representative to the UN Atomic Energy Commission. Baruch transformed the Acheson-Lilienthal paper into a formal, systematic proposal and added a section calling for sanctions against violators. The result was the "Baruch Plan," which Baruch presented to the UN commission on June 14. Within hours the Soviets presented a proposal of their own plan, sharply in conflict with the American.

In essence, what the Soviets wanted was a plan that would provide for an agreement not to use atomic weapons, to cease bomb production, and to destroy existing atomic bombs (which only the United States had at that time). Only after these things had been done would the Soviets be ready to discuss arrangements for the exchange of scientific information and the establishment of controls. The American plan, by contrast, envisaged the prompt establishment of controls over raw materials out of which atomic weapons could be made. Only *after* such controls were established would the United States consider disposing of its stockpile of bombs. As Truman wrote to Baruch on July 10, "We should not under any circumstances throw away our gun until we are sure the rest of the world can't arm against us.[36]

The UN commission eventually adopted, over the objection of Poland and the Soviet Union, a plan essentially like the American one. In the Security Council, however, the Soviet negative vote constituted a veto, blocking further action.

In a situation of mutual trust the United States might have been satisfied with less far-reaching guarantees of compliance and the Soviets might have been ready to accept temporary inequality and even some inspection arrangements. As it was, disarmament debates at the UN became, for more than a decade, more of a battle for propaganda victories than a real effort at negotiation.

Because of this lack of mutual trust, a similar stalemate occurred when efforts were made to reach agreements on the provision of forces to the UN. Under Article 43, paragraph 1, of the UN Charter, "All Members of the United Nations, in order to contribute to the maintenance of international peace and security, undertake to make available to the Security Council, on its call and in accordance with a special agreement or agreements, armed forces, assistance, and facilities, including rights of passage, necessary for the purpose of maintaining international peace and security." The third paragraph of Article 43 states that such "agreement or agreements shall be negotiated as soon as possible on the initiative of the Security Council." These forces were to provide the UN with the military strength and facilities needed to act against an aggressor.

Early in 1946 the Security Council requested the Military Staff Committee to examine and report on the question of military agreements under Article 43. The committee's report, submitted on April 30, showed agreement on twenty-five articles but failure to reach accord on sixteen others.[37] Unfortunately, the sixteen concerned matters of a critical nature. They related to the size and composition of the armed forces to be contributed, the provision of bases, the location of forces when not in action, and the time of their withdrawal. The United States favored a large force with great striking power and so organized and located as to be readily available. The Soviets saw no need for a large force, insisted on the principle of equality with the United States not only in overall strength but in each category, and demanded clear definition of the conditions under which the force would be used. Since the Soviet Union had emerged from World War II with naval and air forces vastly inferior to those of the United States, it feared that acceptance of greater American strength in these two categories of the Article 43 agreements would prejudice its position. Its concerns were not alleviated by U.S. willingness to agree to larger ground forces from the USSR. Mutual distrust stalemated and prevented any progress. In fact, four decades have since elapsed without even a serious attempt at negotiations. The USSR has suggested Article 43 negotiations at various times during discussions of peacekeeping over the past decade, but the United States has shown little interest and the Soviets have not pressed the issue.

THE BERLIN BLOCKADE

Despite the mutual mistrust, the UN did serve a useful purpose in breaking an end to the Soviet blockade of Berlin.

On March 31, 1948, the deputy military governor of the Soviet zone, General Dratvin, notified the American military government in Berlin (OMGUS) that, beginning April 1, the Soviets would check all U.S. personnel passing through their zone for identification and would inspect all freight shipments as well as personal baggage. OMGUS rejected these conditions, pointing out that the three Western powers had been assured free access to Berlin at the time their troops withdrew from Saxony and Thuringia into their own zones. Thereupon the Soviets sealed off all highway, rail, and river traffic into Berlin, giving "technical difficulties" as the reason. By other means they made it apparent that the real difficulty was the currency reform to be introduced into West Germany, which would exclude the "East mark" then flooding Germany. The Soviets offered to reopen the approaches to Berlin if the Western powers would call off the currency changeover. Truman saw the maneuver as an attempt to force the Western powers out of Berlin.[38]

The Western response was a massive airlift to handle the food, fuel, and other requirements, not only of their own contingents, but also of the population of West Berlin. Then, Truman relates, the "Kremlin began to see that its effort to force us out was doomed. Russia's toughness and its truculence in the Berlin matter had led many Europeans to realize the need for closer military assistance ties among the Western nations, and this led to discussions which eventually resulted in the establishment of NATO. Berlin had been a lesson to us all."[39]

Formal efforts in the UN came to naught. On September 29, Ambassador Austin handed the secretary general a note charging that the Soviet action was a threat to the peace under Chapter VII of the Charter. The Soviets argued in the Security Council that there was no blockade in the sense of traditional international law and, therefore, no threat to the peace. They refused to take part in the Council's discussion of the item and stymied any action by the Council.

Nevertheless, the UN became a useful vehicle. Late in January 1949 the Kremlin released a series of answers by Stalin to questions submitted by American correspondents in Moscow. To a question regarding the Berlin Blockade, he replied that there would be no obstacle to lifting traffic restrictions if those imposed both by the three Western powers and by the Soviets were lifted at the same time. Truman and Acheson noted that for the first time since June 1948 the Berlin Blockade was not tied to the currency reform issue. Accordingly Acheson, with Truman's approval, instructed Philip Jessup to find out from the Soviet delegation at the UN if the omission had been intentional. On February 15 Jessup found an informal opportunity in the Delegates' Lounge to raise the question with the Soviet permanent representative, Jacob Malik. A month later Malik replied that the omission was "not accidental."[40]

Negotiations then began in earnest, and on May 4 a communiqué announced that the four governments concerned—Britain, France, the United States, and the USSR—had agreed that the blockade would end on May 12.

PALESTINE—THE BIRTH OF ISRAEL

In the Palestine case the UN was directly, formally, and actively involved. On April 2, 1947, Britain formally requested General Assembly consideration of the issue and suggested that a special session be convened at once to authorize a special committee to make a preliminary study.

The British had been given the Palestine mandate after World War I. London, in the Balfour Declaration of 1917, had promised a homeland for the Jewish people. The British had also made commitments to Arab leaders who were on their side during the war, notably the Hashemites. In 1922 they separated off about 80 percent of the territory, the part lying east of the Jordan River, which became Transjordan and is now the Hashemite Kingdom of Jordan. In the rest of the mandate the British were under Zionist pressure to allow increased Jewish immigration and Arab pressure to stop it. Following World War II, the Jewish survivors of the Holocaust in Europe were largely in displaced-persons camps in Germany, and it was clear that large numbers of them had nowhere to go but Israel. When apprised of this problem by Earl G. Harrison, his special representative sent to survey the situation, President Truman on August 31 sent a letter to Prime Minister Attlee urging the prompt issuance to Jewish displaced persons of 100,000 immigration certificates for Palestine. Attlee's reply stressed the difficulties that would be created in Palestine by a large-scale immigration of Jews and the need for prior consultation with the Arabs.[41]

The Jewish Agency for Palestine and other Jewish groups then proceeded to facilitate illegal Jewish immigration into Palestine, which it saw as the only way to get Jews there in the face of Britain's restrictive policy. Meanwhile, the struggle for a state of Israel intensified, both in Palestine, where violence was used, and abroad, through efforts to sway opinions of the governments and peoples of the United States and Europe.

As violence mounted in Palestine and pressures on the British for and against the Jewish homeland increased, they decided to bring the UN into the picture as a way of getting rid of the burden. The General Assembly, in the special session convened at Britain's request, on May 15, 1947, established the UN Special Committee on Palestine (UNSCOP), on which none of the great powers was represented. The committee agreed that the British mandate should be brought to an end and that, under UN auspices, a form of independence should eventually be worked out in Palestine. A majority of the committee further recommended that independence should take the form of two separate states, one Arab and one Jewish, with the city of Jerusalem under direct UN trusteeship.[42]

The Zionist leaders, although disappointed at the small area designated for the Jewish state, accepted UNSCOP's recommendations, as did the Soviet Union and the United States. The Arabs rejected them. Nevertheless, on November 29 the General Assembly adopted a resolution accepting the majority recommendations, including partition.[43]

On January 19, 1948, the Arab Higher Committee cabled the UN secretary-general, Trygve Lie, that it was determined to persist in rejecting partition and in refusing to recognize the UN resolution.[44] The Arabs' resistance, with clear indications that they were prepared to use military force against partition, caused tremors in London and Washington. On December 3, 1947, the British announced that they would end their mandate on May 15, 1948. Britain also declined to provide any forces to sustain the partition resolution, as recommended by the UN Commission on Palestine, which called upon all five permanent members to provide forces. In Washington the military talked about the inability of the United States to send troops to Palestine, and the State Department's Near East specialists were, according to President Truman, "almost without exception unfriendly to the idea of a Jewish state."[45] Accordingly, Austin told the General Assembly on March 19 that the United States would favor a temporary trusteeship for Palestine. He also stated that the UN lacked the power to enforce partition or any other type of political settlement.[46]

Lie was deeply discouraged by the apparent U.S. reversal of position. He felt that "Only the Soviet Union seemed to be seriously intent upon implementing partition, the United States clearly was not." Lie suggested to Austin that they both resign in protest. Austin would not resign and advised Lie not to do so either. According to Lie, Gromyko and Moscow urged even more forcefully that he stay—and he did.[47]

The General Assembly adjourned on May 14, the day before Britain's declaration that its mandate would terminate became effective. On that same day, May 14, Israel proclaimed its existence as a state. Within minutes Truman announced American recognition of the Provisional Government of Israel as the de facto authority of the new state. A half hour earlier he had instructed a staff member to communicate his decision to the State Department and Austin. Unfortunately, communications did not move swiftly enough. Austin got the news by telephone while the U.S. delegation was in the Assembly, only ten minutes before it came over the news ticker. He left the Assembly hall at once, apparently stunned and disheartened. Jessup, his deputy, got the news after it came over the ticker and had to ad lib a statement from the rostrum. Charles Noyes, who was with him in the delegation, thought Jessup did a brilliant job, particularly in the light of Jessup's own misgivings. Noyes also commented that, because it was so obvious that Austin and his delegation were taken completely by surprise, Austin's credibility remained intact. Nevertheless, the surprise was embarrassing to the U.S. delegation, which had been working all-out for a UN trusteeship, as instructed by the State Department.[48]

Arab armies poised on the frontier promptly attacked Israel and urged Arab residents of the new state to flee, with the expectation that they would return to their homes as soon as Israel had been eliminated. In fact, the Israelis beat back the attackers and took some land in Palestine that had not been given to the Jewish state under the UN partition plan. The Jordanian army occupied the West Bank (Judea and Samaria) and the old city of Jerusalem, and the Israelis took over the newer parts of the city.

In the UN Security Council, Austin appealed for a forceful reply to the international aggression (Arab) that had violated Palestine's borders. Such action was also supported by the Soviets; however, the British blocked any Council action until May 27, when a truce was finally agreed upon and Belgian, French, and American officers were assigned as observers.[49] The truce was accepted by Israel but rejected by the Arabs until Folke Bernadotte, the UN mediator, declared it effective June 11. A month later the truce ended and fighting resumed. On July 18 the Security Council again declared a truce, which held for three months. On October 16 the Israelis broke the cease-fire, advanced into the Negev, and occupied all of it except the Gaza Strip within six days. An Egyptian counterattack in December failed; the Egyptians then sent a message to the UN mediator, Ralph Bunche (successor to Folke Bernadotte, who had been assassinated on September 17), requesting a cease-fire from Israel, to be followed by troop withdrawals and armistice negotiations. Syria, Jordan, and Israel also agreed to negotiations.[50]

The successful negotiation of armistices on the island of Rhodes was in substantial measure due to the astuteness, extraordinary skill, sensitivity, patience, and dogged persistence of Ralph Bunche, who later received the

Nobel Peace Prize for his work. (He was also offered the job of assistant secretary of state in 1950 and U.S. deputy permanent representative in 1953 but refused both.) The General Assembly established a UN Conciliation Commission for Palestine (PCC), with three members (France, Turkey, United States), which was to carry the armistice foreward to peace.[51] Unfortunately, the positions of the parties were such that the PCC got nowhere with its task. Bunche said grimly after the 1956 and 1967 wars that he should have given back the Nobel Peace Prize.

KOREA

The North Korean invasion of South Korea on June 24, 1950, gave rise to the first use of combat troops under the UN flag and sharply intensified the cold war in the organization.

At the second session of the UN General Assembly in 1947, the United States had proposed that elections be held in the two zones of occupation, Soviet and American, by March 31, 1948, under UN supervision, as the first step toward the establishment of a national government. This government would establish security forces and then arrange with the occupying powers for the withdrawal of their troops. The Soviets countered with a resolution calling for the immediate withdrawal of all occupying forces and berated the United States for bringing the issue to the UN. (They had already helped to build a "People's Army" in the North.) The U.S. proposal, which established a UN Temporary Commission in Korea, was adopted with no negative votes and only the Soviet bloc abstaining.[52] The Soviets had rejected the U.S. proposal for all-Korean elections before the Americans brought the issue to the UN, and they found the idea no more palatable as a UN resolution, which they rejected. Elections were then held in South Korea in May 1948 under the supervision of the UN Temporary Commission. The resultant National Assembly met on May 31 and elected Syngman Rhee as president. In the North the Democratic People's Republic of Korea was proclaimed on September 9 and it announced that all Soviet troops would be withdrawn at the end of 1948.[53] Subsequently, American forces were withdrawn from South Korea.

The first news of the North Korean attack to reach UN headquarters came from the United States. At midnight of June 4, less than four hours after the United States learned of the attack, Assistant Secretary of State John Hickerson called Trygve Lie to convey the news and alert him to possible call for a Security Council meeting. Lie responded: "My God. . . . This is war against the United Nations!"[54] By the next day, when the Security Council met, the secretary general presented reports from the UN commission confirming that North Korea had initiated an all-out invasion.[54] On that same day, June 25, the Council adopted a resolution denouncing the action as a breach of the peace, calling for the cessation of hostilities and withdrawal of the North Koreans and calling on members to "render every assistance to the United Nations" in the execution of the resolution.[56] The Soviets, having walked out of the Security Council in January in protest over the continued presence of Chiang Kai-shek's representative rather than Mao's, were not there to exercise the veto.

President Truman was determined to help the South Koreans resist the North Korean invasion, both as an essential element in the policy of containment and to maintain the validity of the UN. He recalled how the failure of the League of Nations to act effectively against aggression in Manchuria and Ethiopia had contributed to its downfall. He wrote: "I was convinced . . . that to have ignored the appeal of Korea for aid, to have stood aside from the assault upon the Charter, would have meant the end of the United Nations as a shield against aggression."[57]

On June 27 the Security Council adopted a United States-sponsored resolution recommending that the members of the United Nations "furnish such assistance to the Republic of Korea as may be necessary to repel the armed attack and to restore international peace and security in the area."[58] (It made no mention of unifying North and South Korea.)

As North Korea's forces took Seoul and pushed rapidly southward, it became obvious that they would soon take the entire country unless ground forces as well as air and naval support were brought in by outside powers. India proposed that the People's Republic of China be seated in the Security Council on the understanding that they and the Soviets would support a cease-fire and withdrawal; Gromyko rejected the second part.[59] Then, on July 7, 1950, the Security Council, on U.S. initiative, adopted a resolution requesting that the United States establish a UN Unified Command, designate the commander, and report to the Security Council as appropriate.[60] The vote was 7 in favor, 0 against, with 3 abstentions (Yugoslavia, India, Egypt). Lie's suggestion of a committee to run the UN Command was rejected by Austin, who went all out in supporting Truman's position that the commander be an American.

Sixteen nations provided troop units for the UN Command, in response to the resolution, but the bulk of the forces were American and South Korean. The United States provided 50 percent of the ground forces, 86 percent of the naval and 94 percent of the air; South Korea accounted for 40 percent of the ground forces, 7.4 percent of the naval, and 5.6 percent of air support.[61]

In August 1950 the Soviets returned to the Security Council. Since it was obvious that they would veto any further Council resolution concerning the UN Command, the General Assembly became the organ through which the UN exercised its limited political guidance over the collective action.[62]

Meanwhile the UN Command, which had been pushed back to a small foothold around Pusan, executed a highly successful counterattack that soon drove the invaders out of South Korea. A brilliantly conceived landing at Inchon, behind enemy lines, was a key factor. The UN commander, Gen. Douglas MacArthur, urgently requested President Truman's authorization to continue his assault on the North Koreans into their own territory. On October 7 the UN General Assembly adopted, by a vote of 47 in favor, 5 opposed (Soviet bloc) and 7 abstentions, a resolution recommending "all appropriate steps to insure a condition of stability throughout Korea."[63] Two days later UN forces crossed the 38th parallel in strength, and by October 26 the R.O.K. Sixth Division reached the Manchurian border. MacArthur predicted complete victory in both North and South Korea by Thanksgiving.[64]

According to Charles Noyes, in our interview in January 1978, Britain, France, Turkey, and other countries with troops in the UN Command were most reluctant to give this much leeway to MacArthur in a vaguely worded resolution. USUN, almost to a man, shared that reluctance, fearing a Chinese reaction if MacArthur advanced beyond the narrow neck in North Korea. Secretary Acheson, however, took personal charge of this issue at the Assembly and would not accept language in the resolution that would have restricted MacArthur's movements. He wanted Washington to be in control.

Indian sources had warned that the Chinese would not tolerate UN Command forces on their frontier, but General MacArthur doubted that Peking would intervene militarily or that, if the Chinese did intervene, their action would cause serious military problems.[65] In this instance he was disastrously wrong. Chinese "volunteers" whose strength ultimately reached more than 300,000 began crossing the Yalu River in mid-October. MacArthur's proposal to bomb bridges and bases in Manchuria was rejected by Truman on the grounds that it could trigger a full-scale war with China. Instead, with his forces being battered by fresh, well-organized Chinese troops, MacArthur was instructed to consolidate them in the South.[66]

At the United Nations thirteen Asian and Arab nations sponsored a resolution looking toward a cease-fire, which the General Assembly adopted on December 14.[67] The resolution called for a three-man group to determine the basis on which a cease-fire might be reached in Korea. On January 2, 1951, the three men—Entezam of Iran, Pearson of Canada, and Rau of India—reported to the UN that their effort had failed; the North Koreans were unwilling to consider truce talks except on their own terms.

By late May a Chinese–North Korea offensive was thrown back. On June 1 Trygve Lie stated that a cease-fire approximately along the 38th parallel would fulfill the purpose of the United Nations; that is, to repulse the aggression against South Korea. Six days later Secretary Acheson made a similar statement. The United States distinguished between its political aim—a unified, independent, democratic Korea—and the military aim of repelling the aggression and terminating the hostilities under an armistice agreement.[68] At the monthly Security Council dinner in June, one of the first exploratory conversations over the possibility of a Korean armistice took place between Ernest Gross of the United States and Jacob Malik, the Soviet permanent representative.[69] Then on June 23 Malik indicated in a speech over UN radio that the Soviet government believed negotiations should be started between the belligerents in Korea. Two days later the Peking newspaper, *People's Daily,* stated that the Chinese people endorsed Malik's peace proposals.

On June 30, Gen. Matthew Ridgway, who had replaced MacArthur, broadcast to the commander in chief of the North Korean-Chinese forces in Korea that if, as reported, the communist commander was prepared to negotiate a cease-fire and armistice, Ridgway would send a representative to begin discussions. Two days later the communist side replied favorably, and on July 10 negotiations began at Kaesong, a town at that time between the lines.[70]

Unfortunately, negotiations for an armistice dragged on for two years. The most stubborn issue proved to be the question of whether there should be forcible repatriation of prisoners. President Truman, in a statement on May 7, 1952, declared: "We will not buy an armistice by turning over human beings for slaughter or slavery." The United States continued to hold firm on this principle.

Finally, on July 27, 1953, an armistice was signed. The Republic of Korea was restored in approximately the same territory as before the North Korean attack along the 38th parallel, with modifications to provide it with a better line of defense. Thus, the fundamental UN (and U.S.) objective was attained; aggression was stopped by the UN forces. The political goal of unification was not achieved; Korea is still divided.

In retrospect, it appears that the military aspect of the Korean War would not have been much different if the UN had not existed. More than 90 percent of the forces were American and South Korean, and the force commander was an American. The action to stop a communist aggression would have been taken as part of the containment policy of the United States even if the UN had not existed.

Yet the existence of the UN made a substantial difference politically. President Truman had a sincere commitment to the UN and instructed Austin to take the issue to the Security Council within hours of the North Korean attack. He said: "The foundations and the principles of the United Nations were at stake unless this unprovoked attack on Korea could be stopped." No alternative to acting through the UN was ever seriously discussed. Thus the mere existence of the UN was a sufficiently important feature of the world view of American policymakers that it foreclosed certain options, such as unilateral intervention. And the involvement of the UN meant that other countries could exercise influence on U.S. policy in Korea, even though General Assembly resolutions were often so ambiguous that MacArthur was able to conduct military operations according to his own lights.[71] In retrospect, it is most regrettable that the United States rejected its allies' proposals to phrase the October 7, 1950, resolution of the General Assembly so that clear limits would have been put on how far north MacArthur could advance. He was not, however, able to go forward with his proposal to bomb bridges over the Yalu. The decision against such action was made by President Truman, who feared it might trigger a wider war with China and the Soviet Union, but Truman's action was reinforced by consultations with other countries providing troops for the UN Command in Korea.

For the United States, working through the UN had other advantages. It buttressed the legal and moral authority of the United States and its allies in Korea. This, in turn, had an impact on public opinion and support in the United States and other democratic Western countries. It also associated fifteen other countries with the military operation, which, even though they accounted for only 10 percent of the troop strength, provided about $600 million per year in military support. They also provided support for economic sanctions against North Korea and Mainland China.[72]

That the United States was able to derive these advantages while carrying out the broad lines of its own policy through the UN is a tribute to the effectiveness of USUN and its well-cultivated relationships with other delegations and the secretary general, as well as to the shared view of other countries that the North Korean aggression had to be countered.

The Korean operation is the only one in which the UN Security Council has called upon members to provide military forces against an attacker since coming into existence in 1945. The Council was able to act in this unique case because the Soviets were boycotting it in June and early July; otherwise they would certainly have exercised a veto. Indeed, the veto is in the Charter because the framers envisaged that the use of force by the Security Council would not be ordered over the opposition of a permanent member. Clearly, members cannot be *ordered* to provide forces except by the Security Council with the concurring votes of all great powers.

Had the Soviets been there to exercise a veto, it would still have been possible to build an allied force to fight the North Koreans. Article 51 of the UN Charter states: "Nothing in the present Charter shall impair the inherent right of individual or *collective* self-defence if an armed attack occurs against a Member of the United Nations, until the Security Council has taken measures necessary to maintain international peace and security [italics mine]." Although South Korea was not a UN member, the communist attack against it, observed by a UN commission, could have been construed as an act requiring collective self-defense by the noncommunist nations. Although the Soviets could veto any Security Council action in support of such collective self-defense, they could not have prevented endorsement by a General Assembly majority that was then pro-Western.

Indeed, after the Soviet return to the Security Council in August 1950, the United States turned to the General Assembly for the support of the UN Operation in Korea and endeavored to build up the Assembly's role in the maintenance of peace and security. In September, Secretary Acheson proposed to the Assembly that it "organize itself to discharge its responsibility promptly and decisively if the Security Council is prevented from acting." He argued that, when the Council is obstructed by one member, the Charter did not leave the United Nations impotent. He noted that Articles 10, 11, and 14 vested in the Assembly "authority and responsibility for matters affecting international peace."[73]

The basis for so organizing the Assembly was laid out in the Uniting for Peace resolution, adopted on November 3, 1950, by a vote of 39 to 5 (the Soviet bloc).[74] The Soviets maintained then and still maintain that under the Charter only the Security Council—where they have to veto—can take action to maintain peace and security. Despite this position of principle, the Soviets did support General Assembly action in connection with the British-French-Israeli invasion of Suez in 1956, after the British and French stymied Security Council action by vetoes. Again, in June 1967, after a Soviet draft resolution on the Arab-Israeli war failed to get enough votes in the Security Council, the Soviets demanded and got an emergency special session of the General Assembly. Somewhat to their chagrin, the secretary general used procedures laid down in the Uniting for Peace resolution; these constituted the only basis he could find for calling an emergency session. (More details are provided in Chapter VI.)

While giving full recognition to the primary responsibility of the Security Council (Article 24 of the Charter) so long as it could act, the Uniting for Peace resolution sought to provide for Assembly supervision of military sanctions within the limits of its recommendatory authority. In case of a veto in the Security Council, an emergency special session of the Assembly could be convened within twenty-four hours by a procedural vote of any seven members of the Council or by a majority of the members of the UN. This has proved to be the only enduring institutional change introduced by the resolution, but its psychological impact was important in 1956–57 when the Assembly authorized establishment of the UN Emergency Force (UNEF) in the Sinai.

The resolution also provided that the General Assembly in such cases can make recommendations for collective measures including the use of armed forces when necessary, in cases of breaches of the peace or acts of aggression. A Collective Measures Committee was established to study and report on methods to strengthen peace and security, and members were invited to inform the committee of the measures taken to carry out this recommendation. The results of the committee's work were negligible. Only Thailand, Greece, Denmark, and Norway made relatively unconditional offers of national troop contingents, totalling about 6,000 men. The United States earmarked neither troops nor facilities, pointing to its current commitments in Korea. After three reports to the General Assembly, which were little noted and not long remembered, the committee was put on a standby basis by the Assembly in 1954.[75] It has not met since then.

The resolution also established a Peace Observation Commission to observe and report on situations in any area where the continuation of international tensions is likely to endanger the maintenance of international peace and security. The commission may function only when directed to do so either by the Security Council or the General Assembly, or by the Interim Committee if the Assembly is not in session. This commission of fourteen members, including all five great powers, has never been called upon to function; instead, ad hoc groups or committees, or representatives of the secretary general have been used, depending on the particular circumstance of each case.

Another by-product of the Korean War was the exacerbation of the Chinese representation issue. The problem was difficult enough for Washington in 1949 when the communists defeated Chiang Kai-shek's forces and gained control of the mainland. Right-wing politicians and commentators blamed the Truman administration for having "lost" China, impugning the loyalty and integrity even of such stalwarts as Dean Acheson and George Marshall.[76] The anticommunist hysteria, culminating in the bizarre, unscrupulous, and dangerously effective crusade by Senator Joseph McCarthy, made any move toward normal relations with the People's Republic of China difficult. The entry of hundreds of thousands of Chinese communist "volunteers" into the Korean War, inflicting huge casualties on American forces, made the difficult virtually impossible. The Indian delegation to the UN proposed in 1950 that Peking be seated in the Security Council so that it and Moscow would support a cease-fire fell flat when Gromyko emphatically rejected the second part. At a meeting in Washington in December 1950 British Prime Minister Attlee urged that the United States recognize Mao as a way of encouraging him to assert independence of the Soviets, a la Tito. Secretary Acheson expressed strongly the view that the United States should not reward Chinese communist aggression in Korea by according American recognition or allowing Mao's regime to represent China in the UN. President Truman backed Acheson's arguments and added that "we would face terrible divisions among our people at home if the Chinese Communists were admitted to the United Nations."[77] For the next two decades the United States used strong lobbying and a variety of devices to keep the People's Republic of China out of the United Nations until the dam broke in 1971.

Another fallout from the Korean War was the Soviet loss of confidence in Trygve Lie. His term was to expire at the end of 1950, and the Soviets made it clear they would veto his reappointment. Truman and Acheson were determined to veto any other candidate, and Austin, a good friend of Lie's, was fully in accord. They held to this position even though there were other good candidates friendly to the United States, including Carlos Romulo of the Philippines and Luis Padillo-Nervo of Mexico.[78] Finally, after strong American lobbying, in December 1950 the General Assembly voted to extend Lie's term. The Soviets noted that Article 97 of the UN Charter provides that the secretary general "shall be appointed by the General Assembly upon the recommendation of the Security Council." Since there had been no recommendation from the Council, they argued, the extension of Lie's term was invalid; consequently, they boycotted Lie for the rest of his stay at the UN. Finally, in 1953 Dag Hammerskjöld of Sweden was appointed secretary general by the Assembly on the recommendation of the Security Council, and Lie left.

THE AMERICAN ATTACK ON THE UN SECRETARIAT

It is ironic that Lie, who incurred Soviet wrath by supporting the U.S. position in Korea, had to endure an American attack on the Secretariat during 1952–53. Behind the attack were a fear of communist infiltration inspired by Senator McCarthy and disillusionment with the UN. Over-optimistic hopes for global peace through the United Nations had given way to the harsh realities of the cold war. The extensive use of the Soviet veto was resented by many Americans. Moreover, the United States was bearing the brunt of a costly and bloody war in Korea.

In October 1952 the Internal Security Subcommittee of the Senate Judiciary Committee opened public hearings in New York on the activities of U.S. citizens employed in the UN Secretariat. Of 24 suspect employees, seventeen invoked the Fifth Amendment on questions related to past or present associations with the Communist party. Of the seven who answered these questions, three acknowledged past membership and a fourth was implicated by the testimony of an outside witness.[79]

Lie moved promptly to stem American criticism. He took immediate action to discharge those temporary employees of U.S. nationality who had acknowledged communist affiliations on the grounds that an American communist was not a representative American citizen.[80] He also decided that those temporary employees who had invoked the Fifth Amendment should be dismissed, arguing as follows:

> United Nations immunity extended only to acts of Secretariat members in their official capacity. It did not extend to their outside activities or private lives. I felt strongly that a United Nations official should cooperate fully with investigations conducted by an official agency of his own government, at least in those countries where Western democratic traditions protected him from the exercise of arbitrary power. . . . Furthermore, by virtue of the very fact that a United Nations official was an international civil servant, special obligations were imposed upon him to conduct himself vis-à-vis the Member governments at all times in a manner above just reproach.[81]

The most difficult problem was the future of ten Americans with permanent contracts who had refused to answer certain questions. Lie constituted a three-man panel of eminent international lawyers, who recommended dismissal, and they were dismissed.

Subsequently the employees appealed to the UN Administrative Tribunal, which ordered reinstatement for four and compensation for the others. Lie refused to reinstate any of them. Thereupon the tribunal ordered compensation for all, totalling $170,730, plus pension rights in one case. The United States fought the award in the General Assembly, and as a result the International Court of Justice was asked for an opinion. The court, by 9 to 3, upheld the Administrative Tribunal. To avoid problems with Congress, the compensation was paid out of the tax equalization fund rather than the regular UN budget.[82]

It should be noted that the impetus for this attack on the Secretariat came neither from Austin nor from the executive branch. It came from extremists in the American public and reactionaries in Congress who, in fact, were aiming at Truman and Acheson as well as at the UN. Acheson, who was certainly not a blind idealist about the UN, made the following comment on the deplorable episode:

> From the outset we had urged that the United Nations should build a staff truly international in outlook, responsible and loyal to the organization and not nominated or directed by any national states. Secretary General Trygve Lie took the same view. Both he and we knew that citizens of Communist member states, some of whom would have to be included in the Secretariat, would be selected and directed by their respective governments, but neither of us wished United States citizens chosen by him to be in that category. I did not

want to claim a right to police his appointments and appointees, and, while he refused to appoint anyone suspected of subversive action against any government, he could hardly require appointments to turn upon a candidate's views in a field where the orthodoxy of one superpower became heterodoxy, or even criminality, as seen by another. Practical men could have solved the problem easily, but not so long as the two senators (McCarthy of Wisconsin and McCarran of Nevada) and the press saw it as a source of news and publicity. The day before the General Assembly opened, the Internal Security Committee (a subcommittee of Senator McCarran's Judiciary Committee), meeting in New York, opened a highly publicized hearing into the loyalty of Americans employed by the United Nations. Soon a federal grand jury opened a competing show on the same topic in the same city. Both called UN employees as witnesses, some of whom asserted their constitutional protection against self-incrimination. The result was highly unfavorable opinion of the United Nations in the United States and of the United States in the United Nations. If I needed confirmation of my opposition to having the UN headquarters in New York—which I did not—we had plenty of it during the autumn of 1952.[83]

Austin, like Acheson, could do little to stem the tide of the day. On the other hand, Robert Murphy notes: "While the Office of United Nations Affairs at the State Department was being half-smothered under a cloud of innuendo, the American delegation at U.N. headquarters was flourishing.[84] It is hard to pinpoint the reasons for this relative immunity, but Austin's prestige, the distance from Washington, and USUN's role in answering Soviet attacks may have been factors.

UNIVERSAL DECLARATION OF HUMAN RIGHTS

President Truman, in his address at the close of the San Francisco Conference on June 24, 1945, declared: "Under this document we have good reason to expect the framing of an international bill of rights acceptable to all the nations involved."[85] His seriousness was indicated by his appointment of Eleanor Roosevelt as the first U.S. representative to the UN Commission on Human Rights.

The eighteen-member commission began its work in January 1947 and elected Mrs. Roosevelt chairman. It also decided to draft a declaration and a convention, with Mrs. Roosevelt chairing the drafting committee. She plunged into the job with her usual energy, dynamism, and determination, driving herself and her colleagues hard and producing a declaration in a year and a half—a remarkable feat, considering its scope and the conflict of viewpoints. As one observer put it, she used "determined prodding combined with tactful persuasion and boundless graciousness."[86]

The major clash of viewpoints was with the Soviets, who emphasized the authority of the state, which defines the rights of individuals. The majority stressed the *inherent* rights of the individual, as in the American Bill of Rights. Mrs. Roosevelt exercised great patience in trying to reconcile viewpoints rather than simply to vote down the Soviets; however, they were important points of principle that could not be compromised, and in the end the Soviet bloc abstained on the declaration.

The Soviets also advocated that social and economic rights be included. Mrs. Roosevelt, a social humanitarian, was inclined to champion the view that these rights be included in the declaration; however, the State Department was lukewarm toward the inclusion of the newer rights in an international document. She persisted, and her stature on the American and the world scene was so imposing that Washington changed its instructions. Accordingly, six articles in the declaration are devoted to economic and social rights, such as a standard of living, education, rest and leisure, and participation in the cultural life of the community. This still left a difference with the Soviets, who insisted that the state must *guarantee* these rights, including full employment, while the majority saw the state's role as acting to *promote* the individual's opportunity to enjoy such rights.

On matters of wording Mrs. Roosevelt showed commendable flexibility. The original first article of the declaration read "All men are created equal," as in the U.S. Declaration of Independence. Mrs. Hansa Mehta of India objected that this phrase suggested the exclusion of women. It was changed to "All human beings." Mrs. Roosevelt agreed to change "created" into "born" after the communist representatives objected to a word that implied the existence of a divine creator.[87]

The commission's document then went to the Third Committee of the General Assembly, a Committee of the Whole, where eighty-one sessions were used to discuss it. It emerged from committee with no significant change in substance and was adopted by the General Assembly on December 10, 1948—now celebrated annually as Human Rights Day. The vote was unanimous, with 8 abstentions (6 from the Soviet bloc plus Saudi Arabia and South Africa).[88]

The declaration, a document not ratified by governments, is not legally binding on them. Nevertheless, it has had great impact. It is referred to in the constitutions of close to twenty new states. Referring to the legal status of a declaration, the UN Office of Legal Affairs stated:

> It may be considered to impart, on behalf of the organ adopting it, a strong expectation that members of the international community will abide by it. Consequently, in so far as the expectation is gradually

justified by state practice, a Declaration may by custom become recognized as laying down rules binding upon states.[89]

By that standard, the Declaration of Human Rights surely qualifies as an important document in international law.

Unfortunately, American leadership on human rights was later hobbled by congressional pressure against ratifying international conventions or covenants in this area.

THE EXPANDED PROGRAM OF TECHNICAL ASSISTANCE

Under the Truman administration the United States also took the lead at the UN on the issue of assistance to the less developed countries. In his inaugural address on January 20, 1949, Truman declared: "We must embark on a bold new program for making the benefits of our scientific advances and industrial progress available for the improvement and growth of underdeveloped areas"—a statement since known as Point Four.

The follow-through was not only a bilateral progam but also an American initiative at the UN that culminated in 1950 in the establishment of the Expanded Program of Technical Assistance (EPTA).[90] The UN and some of its specialized agencies had already been carrying out small programs of technical assistance. EPTA not only increased the scale of these efforts manyfold; it also brought the various specialized agencies together with the UN in a common effort, the first such common operational program. EPTA's program included the provision of experts and fellowships and the establishment of training centers.

As Truman left office in January 1953, the excessive optimism of the American public in 1945 had given way to the sober realization that power continued to reside in the strong states rather than in any organizational magic. The cold war had become the dominant fact of international life. The United Nations was seen much more as an arena for East-West confrontation than for cooperation. American security would be predicated on national armed forces and alliances rather than on the UN, which was not designed or equipped to deal with what was perceived as the main threat, the USSR. Truman's changed attitude is described by Dean Acheson: "He learned also, and learned quickly, the limits of international organization and agreements as a means of decision and security in a deeply divided world. Released from acceptance of a dogma that builders and wreckers of a new world order could and should work happily and successfully together, he was free to combine our power and coordinate our action with those who did have a common purpose."[91] Obviously, this statement reveals as much about Acheson as it does about Truman.

Austin, too, was converted over the years into a cold warrior, though more slowly because of his dedication to the UN and his strong moralism. His contact with the continued intransigence of the Soviets on all major issues at the UN, coupled with the administration's hard-line attitude, brought him to this view. Korea was the capstone; after early 1951, Austin appeared very pessimistic regarding any modus vivendi with the communists. Yet he remained committed to the ideals of the UN. He rationalized his position by arguing that the UN would attain those ideals through slow evolution; in the meantime, he shared Washington's view that the main immediate threat, the Soviet Union, must be dealt with outside the UN.[92]

Yet, because of Austin, USUN had established itself as an important entity, headed by a major political figure, and this tradition persisted. Cold war or no, the United States continued to consider the UN useful as a forum for cultivating other states and world opinion; as a place to deal with threats to peace and security in Asia, Africa, and the Middle East where a bilateral approach was inadequate; and as an institution where certain initiatives for international cooperation could be launched, such as the International Atomic Energy Agency and the Expanded Program of Technical Assistance. Recognition of this importance led President Eisenhower to designate Henry Cabot Lodge, a close and distinguished political ally, as his permanent representative to the UN.

NOTES

1. Harry S. Truman, *Memoirs,* vol. 1 (Garden City, N.Y.: Doubleday, 1955), pp. 22, 289, 326.

2. Dean Acheson, *Present at the Creation* (New York: Norton, 1969), p. 111.

3. Lawrence Weiler and Anne Simons, *The United States and the United Nations: The Search for International Peace and Security* (New York: Carnegie Endowment, 1967). A similar assessment of Stettinuis's abilities by Ralph Bunche will be found in Peggy Mann, *Ralph Bunche: UN Peacemaker* (New York: Coward, McCann & Geoghegan, 1975), pp. 108–36.

4. Richard L. Walker, "Edward R. Stettinius, Jr.," in *The American Secretaries of State and Their Diplomacy,* vol. 14. (New York: Cooper Square Publishers, 1965), pp. 60–86.

5. Truman, op. cit., vol. 1, pp. 108, 136.

6. Ibid., pp. 272–89.

7. Arnold Beichman, *The "Other" State Department: The United States Mission to the United Nations—Its Role in the Making of Foreign Policy* (New York: Basic Books, 1967), p. 138. See also Richard E. Neustadt, *Presidential Power* (New York: Wiley, 1960), pp. 46–57.

8. Trygve Lie, *In the Cause of Peace* (New York: Macmillan, 1954), p. 381.

9. Philip C. Jessup, *The Birth of Nations* (New York: Columbia University Press, 1974), p. 290.

10. James M. Hyde, "United States Policy in the United Nations," *Annual Review of United Nations Affairs* (1961): 254–67.

11. Interview with Charles P. Noyes, January 19, 1978.

12. Weiler and Simons, op. cit., pp. 568–69.

13. George T. Mazuzan, *Warren R. Austin at the U.N., 1946–1953* (Kent,

Ohio: Kent State University Press, 1977), pp. 9–10, 38–39.

14. Ibid., pp. 68–73.

15. Robert D. Murphy, *Diplomats Among Warriors,* p. 366.

16. Austin statement in U.S. Department of State, *Bulletin* 18, 463 (May 16, 1948): 625.

17. Weiler and Simons, op. cit., pp. 536–37.

18. Conversation with Ernest Gross, January 5, 1978.

19. Jessup, op. cit., p. 87.

20. Conversation with Ernest Gross, January 5, 1978.

21. Beichman, op. cit., pp. 178–79.

22. Ibid., pp. 181–83.

23. Conversation with Ernest Gross, January 5, 1978.

24. Truman, op. cit., vol. 1, pp. 522–23.

25. Truman, op. cit., vol. 2 (1956), p. 94.

26. Ibid., p. 95.

27. Andrew Cordier and Wilder Foote, *Public Papers of the Secretaries-General of the United Nations,* vol. 1 (New York: Columbia University Press, 1967), pp. 41, 87.

28. Acheson, op. cit., pp. 197–98.

29. Truman, op. cit., vol. 2, pp. 108–9. See also Robert Riggs, *Politics in the United Nations* (Urbana, Ill., U. of Illinois Press, 1958), pp. 96–98.

30. Jessup, op. cit., p. 92.

31. S.C. Res. 27 (1947), August 1, 1947.

32. Alastair M. Taylor, *Indonesian Independence and the United Nations* (Ithaca, N.Y.: Cornell University Press, 1960), pp. 390–91.

33. S.C. Res. 30 (1947), August 25, 1947.

34. Jessup, op. cit., p. 59.

35. Truman, op. cit., vol. 2, pp. 5–6.

36. Ibid., p. 11.

37. UN Security Council, *Official Records,* 2d year, 1947, Special Supplement 1.

38. Truman, op. cit., vol. 2, pp. 120–28.

39. Ibid., p. 130.

40. Ibid., pp. 30–31.

41. Ibid., pp. 132–42.

42. General Assembly Official Records, Nov. 26–29, 1947.

43. G.A. Res. 181 (II)A, November 29, 1947.

44. Lie, op. cit., p. 164.

45. Truman, op. cit., vol. , p. 162.

46. UN General Assembly *Official Records,* March 19, 1948.

47. Lie, op. cit., p. 171.

48. Conversation with Charles P. Noyes, January 19, 1978. See also Jessup, op. cit., pp. 290–91.

49. Mann, op. cit., pp. 222–42.

50. Ibid., pp. 248–58.

51. G.A. Res. 194 (III), Dec. 11, 1948.

52. G.A. Res. 112 (II), December 14, 1947.

53. Ruth B. Russell, *The United Nation and United States Security Policy* (Washington, D.C.: Brookings Institution, 1968), p. 364.

54. Albert Warner, "How the Korea Decision Was Made," *Harper's,* June 1951, pp. 99–106.

55. Leon Gordenker, *The UN Secretary General and the Maintenance of Peace* (New York: Columbia University Press, 1967), pp. 203–10.

56. Glenn D. Paige, *The Korean Decision* (New York: Free Press, 1968), p. 120.

57. Weiler and Simons, op. cit., p. 108.

58. John G. Stoessinger, *Why Nations Go to War* (New York: St. Martin's, 1974), p. 82.

59. Acheson, op. cit., pp. 419–20.

60. S.C. Res. 588, July 7, 1950.

61. Weiler and Simons, op. cit., p. 256.

62. Ibid., p. 269.

63. G.A. Res. 376 (V), October 7, 1950.

64. Truman, op. cit., vol. 2, pp. 365–66.

65. Ibid., p. 366.

66. Ibid., p. 373–93.

67. G.A. Res. 384 (V), December 14, 1950.

68. Acheson, op. cit., p. 531.
69. James Hyde, "U.S. Participation in the U.N.," *International Organization* 10 (February 1956): 31.
70. Acheson, op. cit., pp. 534–35.
71. Dennis Stairs, "The U.N. and the Politics of the Korean War," *International Journal* (Spring 1970): 308–20.
72. Weiler and Simons, op. cit., pp. 277–83.
73. U.S. Department of State, *Bulletin* 23 (1950): 524–45.
74. G.A. Res. 377 (V), November 3, 1950.
75. Russel, op. cit., pp. 131–33.
76. Acheson, op. cit., pp. 419–20.
77. Truman, op. cit., vol. 2, pp. 402–12.
78. Conversation with Charles P. Noyes, January 19, 1978.
79. *Report of the Secretary General on Personnel Policy* (Doc. A/236), January 30, 1953, p. 19.
80. Lie, op. cit., p. 388.
81. Ibid., pp. 395–96.
82. John G. Stoessing, *The United Nations and the superpowers* (New York: Random House, 1965), p. 46.
83. Acheson, op. cit., p. 698.
84. Truman, op. cit., vol. 1, p. 292.
85. William Korey, "Eleanor Roosevelt and the Universal Declaration of Human Rights," in A. David Gurewitach, *Eleanor Roosevelt—Her Day, Interchange Foundation* (New York, 1973), pp. 11–12.
86. Ibid., pp. 20–22.
87. Ibid., p. 22.
88. UN Gneral Assembly, *Official Records,* Dec. 10, 1948.
89. Korey, op. cit., pp. 27–28.
90. G.A. Res. 304 (IV), Nov. 16, 1949.
91. Acheson, op. cit., p. 732.
92. Mazuzan, op. cit., pp. 183–86.

CHAPTER IV

Henry Cabot Lodge

With the appointment of Henry Cabot Lodge, the role of the U.S. permanent representative assumed a new, higher level of prominence and importance. Lodge's enthusiastic, energetic, and effective support of the UN was in ironic contrast to the role of his namesake and grandfather who led the successful fight in the Senate to block U.S. participation in the League of Nations.

Lodge's principal source of influence was his close relationship with President Eisenhower. Eisenhower recalls that on September 4, 1951, Lodge, "an associate and friend of mine from wartime days," came to see him at NATO headquarters in Paris in order to persuade Eisenhower to run for the presidency. Lodge was active in the presidential campaign, managing the campaign for the Republican nomination and, after the election, represented Eisenhower during the transitional period in all parts of the executive branch except the Treasury.[1]

In November 1952 Eisenhower offered Lodge the post of permanent representative, saying, "I need you badly." He added that the job would "add a lot of experience to my life, for a year or a year and half or so [sic], fit me for even higher work and put me in the reserve for Secretary of State. The American case, he said, should be presented at the U.N. with life, cleverness and effectiveness. He stressed the importance which he attached to the U.N. and developing public support for it."[2] Based on written accounts, interviews, and four years of working with Mr. Lodge, it is clear that he did present the American case with unusual "life, cleverness and effectiveness" and that both he and the president worked earnestly and vigorously and effectively to build public support for the UN. Opinion polls showed American support rising from 55 percent in 1953 to 80 percent in 1960.[3] Of course this degree of support cannot be attributed entirely to the efforts of Eisenhower and Lodge; the period was one in which a UN majority could usually be found to support American policy and certain American objectives could best be advanced there; for example, bringing

72

about a French-British-Israeli withdrawal from Suez in 1956 and avoiding a dangerous Soviet–U.S. confrontation in the Congo (now Zaire).

Lodge's stature and influence were also enhanced by his continued close contact with the president. He was a member of the cabinet, and Eisenhower made it clear that he wanted Lodge's advice not just on UN matters but also on "politics generally." Eisenhower said he would ask for advice but urged that Lodge should not wait to be asked. In eight years the president wrote Lodge about 150 letters, who in turn wrote a much larger number to Eisenhower. And there was a great deal more oral and informal communication, by telephone and in many Lodge visits to Washington.[4] Moreoever, Eisenhower appointed Maxwell Rabb, as cabinet staff secretary; Rabb had been Senator Lodge's administrative assistant,[5] and this appointment gave Lodge an additional pipeline into the policymaking process.

Lodge's closeness to Eisenhower was further underlined by his appointment as special adviser to the president on November 15, 1973. In this capacity he counseled the president on many domestic political issues: he urged Eisenhower to lead public opinion, using television; to be the advocate of "modern Republicanism" and against reactionaries; not to attempt a purge of Republican mavericks in the 1954 congressional elections; to reject Senator McCarthy's smears against veteran Foreign Service professionals like John Service, John Carter Vincent, and Charles E. Bohlen; and to have presentations of policy made by an expert on Congress rather than someone expert only on the issue.[6] Although Eisenhower's degree of success on these issues varied, there is no doubt that this "extracurricular" role strengthened Lodge's relationship with the president and thus added to his influence in making policy for the U.S. role in the United Nations.

In answer to questions I asked him, Lodge, on October 21, 1977, wrote the following about his relationship with Eisenhower:

"I think in an average year I would breakfast with him twice a month and when Secretary Dulles was so seriously ill at the time of the Suez incident in '56, I was talking frequently with him on the telephone. . . .

I knew President Eisenhower so well that I could pretty well anticipate what he would think about a given subject. Of course, we always had instructions whenever there was time to draft them. But, as you know, a member will suddenly make a motion in the middle of the voting and the U.S. Representative has to meet the issue then and there. He must either vote "Yes" or "No" or abstain. Under those circumstances there is not even time to make a telephone call. But Washington never had to repudiate any decision that I took because I was so familiar with the thinking in Washington.

I was told by the President that whenever I thought I should have direct access to him, I should talk to him directly—man to man. I was to be the judge of whether to see him or not. As a practical matter, about 90% of the questions which we dealt with came to me through the regular policy-making machinery, who are a very competent group of people, and there was never any conflict or trouble.

Lodge's relations with the State Department are summarized in the following passage from his book:

The prime function of the U.S. Representative to the UN is to carry out foreign policy on the eighty-some issues which in those days confronted the U.S. in the course of the year. For this, I usually depended on the Secretary of State and his staff. But an event of great importance would almost invariably result in a message from the President himself—by telephone, by wire, or by letter. The U.S. Representative was also expected to make recommendations on policy to Washington and, where the matter was important enough, to the President personally. Membership in the Cabinet gave me unusual opportunities to learn what the President was thinking, as did breakfasts and other social events with the President. My memory is that my advice on UN matters was virtually always supported—except in cases where Washington had information unknown to me and which, had I known of it, would have led me to the same conclusion.[7]

In his letter to me on October 21, 1977, Lodge indicated that "scarcely any position was ever taken by the United States in the United Nations in which both Washington and the U.S. Mission did not play important parts." Still, on major crises such as Suez, in 1956, he consulted directly with the president. In at least one case he voted contrary to State Department instructions. Robert Murphy, then director of the State Department's Bureau of UN Affairs, gives the following account of a telephone conversation between them, after Lodge had voted contrary to instructions on a resolution concerning Korea:

I said, "Apparently our instructions failed to reach you." Lodge repeated, "Instructions? I am not bound by instructions from the State Department. I am a member of the President's Cabinet and accept instructions only from him." I knew that personal and official relations between Lodge and the President were exceptionally close. . . . But no one had warned me that Lodge regarded himself as independent of the State Department and I protested, "But you are also head of an Embassy, and our ambassadors accept instructions from the Secretary of State." After a moment's pause, Lodge replied, "I take note of the Department's opinion." I was flabbergasted. As an ambassador myself, I had acted under instructions for many years. . . . "This is a new situation to me," I said, "and I'll have to discuss it with the Secretary." Lodge replied coolly, "Yes, do that. He will set you straight." When I did report to Dulles, he listened carefully without comment until I finished, and then said, "This is one of those awkward situations which require special consideration. If it happens again, just tell me and I'll take care of it."

My personal relations with Lodge were always agreeable. Once I understood that the Secretary of State did not choose to challenge the virtual autonomy which Lodge claimed for his Embassy at the U.N., I realized it was not appropriate for me to do so. A word from President Eisenhower or a call from the Secretary of State personally were accepted by Lodge in good grace, but there were explosions from time to time if instructions, or even strong suggestions, were sent by the State Department to the American Mission at the U.N. headquarters. Lodge would tolerate no poaching on what he considered his own preserve. He was as anxious as anybody to promote a consistent American foreign policy, but he interpreted his functions as much broader than those of an ordinary ambassador. . . . Of course the State Department made every effort to have him participate in policy-making.

Murphy commented that, under Lodge, "our mission behaved less like an embassy than a second Foreign Office of the United States Government." Murphy had little enthusiasm for the UN. He wrote:

Personally I never regarded the UN as a divine machine from which happy solutions to our problems would miraculously flow. Nor have I feared the consequences if the UN should collapse utterly. . . .

Dulles respected the UN but he also regarded it at times as a receptacle where almost any stormy problem could be unloaded and stored away for a year or longer.[8]

Lodge did not challenge the great majority of instructions that came from the Department, accounting to literally hundreds each year. But on important political questions he would not accept an instruction written by some "faceless bureaucrat" (his term) as superior to his own judgment. He knew, as anyone does after a few months of working with the State Department, that the secretary of state actually sees only a tiny fraction of all telegraphic instructions that go out over his signature. Still, when a policy decision was made at the highest level, Lodge would carry it out faithfully, with no public display of disagreement, even though he might have opposed the policy vigorously in private. Since this happened with extreme rarity—Lodge was a strong advocate, respected by the president— he was generally at peace with himself in his role.

Another reason Lodge felt comfortable with his instructions was the close and loyal cooperation of Francis Wilcox, the assistant secretary of state for international organization affairs. Wilcox had been chief of staff for the Senate Committee on Foreign Relations when Lodge was a relatively junior member of the committee. On Wilcox's recommendation Lodge had been appointed as the Republican Senate member of the General Assembly delegation in 1950, even though he was fourth in seniority among members of the committee. Wilcox was most assiduous in consulting Lodge on policy issues, providing USUN with full opportunity for policy input while instructions were still in the formative stage. Wilcox likened his role to "the man on the flying trapeze," constantly bridging any differences between Washington and New York and loyal to both. In his experience, Lodge and Dulles did not battle for Eisenhower's favor on specific issues. Lodge recognized that Dulles was the president's principal adviser on foreign policy, and Dulles acknowledged that Lodge could confer directly with Eisenhower on policy issues when the latter two so chose. This did not weaken Dulles's overall authority.[9] Wilcox, incidentally, gave Lodge high marks for taking the trouble to call on other permanent representatives, as a matter of courtesy.

A British colleague, Gladwyn Jebb, made this assessment of Lodge:

> In no way an intellectual, Cabot was a first-class operator in the Security Council where he sometimes gave the impression of being, as it were, a power in his own right.

> Generally speaking, the State Department seemed to have a less tight hold on their representatives than under the Democratic administration when Dean Acheson with his brilliant team tended to dominate the show. Perhaps this was inevitable seeing that the Democrats during their long period in office had been able to create a corps of really admirable experts, which, under the American "spoils" system, could hardly, even with the greatest goodwill, be fully operated by the incoming Republicans.[10]

In addition to his closeness to Eisenhower and his role in the 1952 presidential elections, Lodge's experience, stature, and personality were also important in giving him an effective policy role. He had been a U.S. senator from 1936 to 1944 and again from 1946 to 1952, resigning in 1944 to serve in the U.S. Army during World War II and holding the rank of major general in the Reserve. (His defeat by John F. Kennedy in the 1952 Senate race in Massachusetts is, of course, what made Lodge available for the UN post.) Descended from distinguished forebears, tall, handsome, and articulate, he was fully self-confident, not plagued by any discernible self-doubts. He reached decisions quickly and slept well afterward. He did not hesitate to take responsibility or assume leadership nor to get criticisms off his chest when he thought someone on his staff or in Washington had erred or failed to do his job. Moreover, he picked his staff with great care and was keenly aware of how each one was performing. He liked people who would stand up to him and argue vigorously against his viewpoint.

For his deputy, Lodge picked an old friend, James J. ("Jerry") Wadsworth, who served with him for all of his eight-year tenure and succeeded to the job of permanent representative in the latter part of 1960 when Lodge resigned to run for the vice-presidency. (Eisenhower in 1953 had suggested Ralph Bunche, a highly regarded black assistant secretary general at the United Nations and a Democrat, as deputy, but Bunche declined.)[11] Lodge tended to entrust Wadsworth with responsibility in particular areas, notably disarmament, rather than use him as an overall operating executive. In fact, Lodge was his own operating executive, ably assisted by the minister counselor, James Barco, a highly capable, intelligent and tireless worker who ran the staff on a day-to-day basis. Barco, a relatively young man, was elevated to the minister counselor job because Lodge felt that men of his ability should be moved up fast in order to serve to their full capacities. For similar reasons Lodge promoted Charles Cook, a young man who had been appointed to USUN's staff by Austin upon graduation from Columbia Law School in 1950, as deputy counselor. He and Barco made the counselor's office the nerve center of the mission, serving as right-hand men to Lodge.

Except for Wadsworth and part-timers like Mason Sears, representative to the Trusteeship Council, and John C. Baker, representative to the Economic and Social Council, Lodge's staff was characterized by youth, ability, extraordinary diligence, virtual anonymity, and by no evident political party affiliation. (In the last two years of Lodge's tenure an active Republican from Massachusetts, Christopher Phillips, served full-time as representative to the Economic and Social Council.) Although I had an excellent working relationship with Lodge—in 1963, when he was ambassador to South Vietnam, he asked me to come out as his deputy—he did not know until I told him in 1974 that I generally voted for Democrats. The nonpartisan viewpoint at USUN was continued by Adlai Stevenson, who retained most of the same staff, except for the top five posts.

Only about 10 percent of the staff—three out of approximately thirty professionals—were career Foreign Service officers (FSOs) who had served elsewhere, as had also been the case under Austin. USUN was not an attractive post for FSOs. Living costs were very high; there were no rent allowances; entertainment funds were pitifully small; the twelve-hour day was normal; and an FSO was removed from the geographic bureaus that controlled future assignments. In recent years rent allowances have been provided, and the State Department has made it a matter of policy to fill most substantive posts with FSOs. Also, salaries have been raised substantially.

USUN, like virtually all embassies of any size, had a small sprinkling of CIA officers. Because the entire staff was stretched thin by the work load, the CIA people were heavily involved in regular mission functions; in fact, at least two were reprimanded by the CIA for doing so at the expense of their undercover work and eventually resigned. Of course other major missions to the UN also had intelligence agency personnel; in fact, the KGB types at the Soviet mission were frequently the most interesting to talk to, as they were not afraid of the KGB.

Lodge himself was a disciplined worker who also knew how to relax. He weekended or vacationed at his home in Beverly, Massachusetts, whenever he could and enjoyed sailing. He expected the staff work to be done for him and did not become involved in the details of arriving at positions, except on major political issues.

He worked on the principle that a large enterprise, such as USUN, is foredoomed to failure unless one can get truly able and responsible men to carry big parts of the load; he recruited, recognized, and rewarded talent. When a colleague first told me Lodge liked "punchy" prose, I thought of a prizefighter who had taken too many blows to the head, but this was quickly translated for me as brief, crisp, and clear memoranda and telegrams. He detested "bafflegab." His biographer, William J. Miller, refers to Lodge's attachment to "succinct, colorful language" and his "serene ruthlessness," which were both apparent at USUN. Miller also describes the helpful influence of his wife, Emily Lodge, with her "gentle manners, grace, inherent dignity and sensitivity."[13] When he lost his temper and started to upbraid someone—as he did often—she had an amazingly calming effect on him. Being the senior economic adviser gave me a sheltered position. Lodge was fully aware that he knew little about economics and gave me credit for knowing a lot more than I did.

Miller also observed a certain aloofness of manner, combined with brusqueness, in this self-confident patrician.[12] Yet Lodge was very popular with receptionists, guards, and other "little people." As a politician he always took time to greet them, often with a smile and a handshake, perhaps in the way the lord of the manor might mingle with the peasants, and they seemed to love it. He would also be at his charming best when entertaining foreign diplomats; he loved to sing at parties he gave for them, often in a duet with his old friend and deputy, Jerry Wadsworth.

For all his patrician manner, Lodge was earthy and practical. In talking to the staff about a visiting delegation of U.S. congressmen and their wives, he urged getting the wives seated comfortably as soon as possible because most had "weak feet and fat asses." Such visiting groups, as well as meetings of the General Assembly delegation, were planned in meticulous detail, with great attention to promptness, brevity, clarity, and showmanship—somewhat like the close-order drill of a well-trained infantry battalion.

As a staunch cold warrior, Lodge initially tended to share the Dulles view that nonalignment was somehow immoral, a kind of neutrality between good ("The Free World") and evil (Communism). Shortly after I came to USUN from Laos in September 1956, as economic adviser, I explained to Lodge at his request why some Asian countries were more concerned about avoiding starvation and bettering their lives than they were about the Soviet–U.S. struggle; consequently, they saw nothing wrong with taking aid from both sides. "Isn't that a kind of whorish attitude?" he asked. My reply: "Not if your needs are so great that all the help you can get from everywhere would still not be enough."

Subsequently, perhaps because of many contacts with Third World diplomats at the United Nations and his trips to their home countries, Lodge developed a better understanding of the nonaligned viewpoint. He even came to be extremely fond of Krishna Menon of India, long a thorn in the American side at the UN.[14] He was also a strong advocate of multilateral economic aid to the less developed countries, as a way of building political support at the UN.

On colonial issues Lodge urged that the United States go with the tide of self-determination in places like Algeria and Cyprus even at the cost of irritating France and Britain. In a letter to Eisenhower of June 26, 1956, he urged the president to recommend that Congress undertake a study of the progress toward self-government of the five remaining U.S. dependent territories—the Virgin Islands, Guam, Samoa, and the trusteeship islands in the Pacific—with a view toward setting target dates for self-government or independence. He also urged that the United States sponsor a resolution urging all countries with dependent territories to set target dates.[15] This proposal was rejected, apparently out of concern for our NATO allies, but it reflected a viewpoint that was to guide Lodge's recommendations for voting on a large number of colonial issues. His stand was undoubtedly influenced by constant exposure to Asian, African, and Latin American diplomats and his desire to win their support on issues important to the United States. These factors frequently made USUN an ally of the Bureau of African Affairs in the State Department in its policy struggles with the Bureau of European Affairs, not only in Lodge's day, but also Stevenson's Goldberg's, and Yost's. On the other hand, Lodge made no protest against the U.S. agreement on an Azores base with Portugal, a NATO ally, even though Portugal was then a colonial power in Africa, nor with South Africa on military space tracking stations there. These agreements appeared reasonable in the cold war optic that dominated Washington's policymaking in that era. For that matter, his successors, Stevenson and Goldberg, did not protest these agreements either. Nixon, of course, went much further in friendliness toward Portugal and South Africa.

PUBLIC RELATIONS AND PROPAGANDA

Eisenhower and Lodge both placed great emphasis on the UN as a forum for propaganda victories in the cold war. In his 1954 message to Congress on the State of the Union, Eisenhower described the United Nations as "a place where the guilt can be squarely assigned to those who fail to take the necessary steps to keep the peace" and "the only real world forum where we have the opportunity for international presentation and rebuttal."

Lodge's concern with timing, style, and effect and his ability as a speaker and debater suited him admirably for the role of propagandist. He told a Senate subcommittee on review of the UN Charter that "my guiding principle is never, never, never to let a Communist speech take place without having a speech from the U.S. on the same day, so that always the news story that is going out over the world has got something of the U.S. position in it." (Austin would sometimes wait days before replying.)[16] He also followed the practice of never allowing himself to be photographed shaking hands with a communist.

Particularly during his first three years, when there were few if any crises with which the UN could deal effectively (the Security Council met only forty-three times in 1953, thirty-two in 1954, and twenty-three in 1955), the emphasis was on cold war issues and winning votes over the Soviets. Given the overwhelming majority of members that would normally support the United States on political issues, Lodge's forensic skills, and an excellent staff, victories were predictable and frequent. Lodge used not only sharp rebuttal but also skillful tactics; for example, when the Soviets accused the United States of waging germ warfare in Korea, the United States succeeded in having the same issue referred to the Disarmament Commission, where it was buried. On that issue and on the American charge of communist atrocities against U.S. prisoners of war, the United States supported a UN investigation; the Soviets, by opposing investigation, lost propaganda points.[17]

At other times dramatic language or gestures scored heavily. In October 1957 when the Soviet foreign minister, Andrei Gromyko, charged in the UN General Assembly that the United States was inciting Turkey to attack Syria, Lodge not only refuted the charge; he declared, with memories of the Soviets' 1956 intervention in Hungary still fresh in the public mind: "Here is the arsonist, trying his best to start another fire and demanding his right to lead the fire brigade."[18] When an American U-2 plane was brought down over the Soviet Union and the Soviets brought the matter to the Security Council, Lodge countered by detailing Soviet intelligence activities directed at the United States. At an appropriate moment in the Council, with television cameras grinding, he whipped out from under the table a plaque of the great seal of the United States—a gift from the Soviet American Friendship Society to the U.S. embassy in Moscow—and showed where a microphone had been hidden. The Soviet resolution charging U.S. aggression was defeated, failing to win a majority.

Lodge was similarly effective when the Security Council considered the case of an American RB-47 plane shot down off the coast of Siberia while on an intelligence mission. He brought in large maps demonstrating that the plane was over international waters when it was shot down and proposed referring the matter to the International Court of Justice (ICJ). He also provided an expose of similar Soviet activities, as Eisenhower notes:

For example, he told of the appearance of the Soviet trawler *Vega* off the Atlantic coast of the United States in April of 1960. This vessel had gone so far as to attempt to retrieve one of the loaded test vehicles shot by our nuclear submarine *George Washington*. Cabot, tracing the path of this Soviet vessel to points thirteen miles off Cape Henry, Virginia, produced detailed photographs of this unusual "fishing" vessel with its numerous antennae capable of picking up long-range ultra-high-frequency radio and radar emissions. Twisting the knife, he pointed out that there had been no fishing gear at all on this so-called fishing boat; nevertheless we had photographed the *Vega, not sunk it.* He then continued with a series of other intelligence activities of the Soviets to include four aircraft flights in 1959 and two in 1960 that had come within twenty-five miles of United States territory, three of which had approached within five miles. Again he produced fairly close-range photographs, emphasizing again that we had photographed these planes but had not shot them down.[19]

The Soviet resolution condemning U.S. "aggression" failed, 2 votes for and 7 against. The U.S. resolution, calling for ICJ adjudication, was vetoed by the Soviets—not unexpectedly—giving the United States a propaganda victory.

In fact, the televising of these debates in 1960 made Lodge a nationally known and popular figure. When the Republicans were choosing a candidate for vice-president in 1960, and the choice apparently lay between

Lodge and Thurston B. Morton of Kentucky, Governor Thomas Dewey observed that Morton was better known to the delegates but Lodge was better known to the public—and Lodge was nominated.[20]

Lodge's comments at many staff meetings I attended made it clear that he had little faith in the success of disarmament negotiations—stymied since the rejection of the Baruch Plan—but he was determined not to give the Soviets a propaganda advantage in this area. This required not only opposing Soviet proposals that would redound to their advantage, such as banning the nuclear bomb, abolishing foreign military bases, or general and complete disarmament without international inspection, but also developing and advancing U.S. initiatives. For example, the U.S. proposal for establishing an International Atomic Energy Agency (IAEA) was presented at the UN by President Eisenhower on December 8, 1953, in a manner designed for maximum public impact. In 1955 Eisenhower presented his "Open Skies" proposal to the UN General Assembly, arguing that it could increase mutual confidence by providing better knowledge of capabilities and could be carried out without a disarmament agreement.[21] The Soviets, consistently opposed to inspection and reconnaissance, rejected the Open Skies proposal, but it still served U.S. propaganda objectives.

CONSTRUCTIVE PROPOSALS

A number of initiatives that were successful from a public relations standpoint were also constructive and substantive, such as the IAEA, the UN Special Fund (now the UN Development Program), and the World Food Program.

In *Mandate for Change,* Eisenhower describes his efforts "to promote development of mutual trust, a trust that was essential before we could hope for success in . . . specific disarmament proposals":

> I began to search around for any kind of an idea that could bring the world to look at the atomic problem in a broad and intelligent way and still escape the impasse to action created by Russian intransigence in the matter of mutual or neutral inspection of resources. I wanted, additionally, to give our people and the world some faint idea of the distance already travelled by this new science—but to do it in such a way as not to create new alarm.

> One day I hit upon the idea of actual physical donations of isotopes from our then unequaled nuclear stockpile, to a common fund for peaceful purposes. This would have to mean donations by both Russia and the United States—with Britain also in the picture in at least a minor way. I wanted to develop this thought in such a way as to

provide at the very least a calm and reasonable atmosphere in which the whole matter could be considered.[22]

Staffing by Adm. Lewis Strauss, Special Assistant for National Security Affairs Robert Cutler, and C. D. Jackson produced a plan for the IAEA and a speech at the UN General Assembly on December 8, 1953, in which Eisenhower made the following proposals:

> The governments principally involved, to the extent permitted by elementary prudence, to begin now and continue to make joint contributions from their stockpiles of normal uranium and fissionable materials to an International Atomic Energy Agency. We would expect that such an agency would be set up under the aegis of the United Nations. . . .
>
> Undoubtedly initial and early contributions to this plan would be small in quantity. However, the proposal has great virtue that it can be undertaken without the irritations and mutual suspicions incident to any attempt to set up a completely acceptable system of world-wide inspection and control.
>
> The Atomic Energy Agency could be made responsible for the impounding, storage, and protection of the contributed fissionable and other materials. The ingenuity of our scientists will provide special safe conditions under which such a bank of fissionable material can be made essentially immune to surprise seizure.
>
> The more important responsibility of this Atomic Energy Agency would be to devise methods whereby this fissionable material would be allocated to serve the peaceful pursuits of mankind. Experts would be mobilized to apply atomic energy to the needs of agriculture, medicine, and other peaceful activities. A special purpose would be to provide abundant electrical energy in the power-starved areas of the world. Thus the contributing powers would be dedicating some of their strength to serve the needs rather than the fears of mankind.[23]

Plans for the president's presentation and follow-up negotiations were worked out in consultation with Lodge. Fruitful negotiations for establishing the IAEA in 1956 were handled principally by Lodge's deputy and eventual successor, Jerry Wadsworth, and Georgi Zaroubin, Soviet ambassador to Washington. Wadsworth describes Zaroubin as forceful, gracious, and well intentioned, engaging in no vilification or propagandistic oratory and never going back on his word.[24]

This brings up another important point that most outsiders do not understand. It is not only possible but even usual for Russian and American negotiators to have good working and personal relations in private even when they are blasting each other in public debates. Lodge, for example, developed good personal relations with Nikita Khrushchev during the latter's 1960 visit to the United States and with Anatoly Dobrynin, then undersecretary general at the UN and later ambassador to Washington. In my last ten years at USUN, I had a number of friends at the Soviet mission and worked out agreements on a number UN matters of mutal interest, notably parallel positions on the level of UN budgets. Moreoever, many Soviet representatives seemed to respect an American who would present his country's case vigorously and effectively; some even said so—in private, of course. As long as a negotiator worked in good faith and kept his word, even toughness in private was not resented. A firm negotiator was more likely to carry weight with his own government if he became convinced that policy modification would be desirable.

In any event, the IAEA was established and it has contributed to the peaceful uses of atomic energy. Its potential contribution was reduced because the United States and other nuclear powers developed a preference for using other channels. Yet the IAEA is important as the agency for verifying compliance with the Nuclear Nonproliferation Treaty negotiated at the UN during Goldberg's tenure as permanent representative and in providing some fuel and technical assistance. Moreover, it is there to be used whenever the principal powers decide that its role should be enhanced.

ECONOMICS AND POLITICS

The UN Special Fund is another example of a project initiated for political and propaganda reasons but developing into a program of significant benefit to the less developed countries. In fact, evolved into the UN Development Program, it has become "the single most important United Nations cooperative effort."[25]

UN efforts on behalf of the less developed countries started in 1948, when the Economic and Social Council authorized the secretary general to provide experts and formalized a technical assistance program with a small budget. Then in 1949 President Truman's Point Four program for the United States inspired the Expanded Program of Technical Assistance, as a joint endeavor of the United Nations and the specialized agencies.[26]

While technical assistance was welcome, the less developed countries (LDCs) considered it inadequate by itself; they wanted a large program to provide capital for building infrastructure, such as bridges, harbors, roads, dams, and power stations. True, loans for such aid could be obtained from the International Bank for Reconstruction and Development (IBRD, or World Bank), but the interest rates were at money-market levels and the maturities were of the order of ten to twenty years. Leaders of the LDCs, notably Chile, India, and Yugoslavia in the late 1940s, argued that they needed grants or loans for a much longer term and at lower interest, given their difficulty in earning foreign exchange for repayment. Moreover, they wanted such a program under the control of the one-nation, one-vote General Assembly rather than the World Bank, where voting is weighted according to the level of capital subscription and three or four of the larger contributors can block a loan.

Under LDC pressure a Committee on a Special United Nations Fund for Economic Development (SUNFED) prepared in March 1953 a document providing a blueprint for such a fund.[27] It recommended a governing body with equal representation between the major contributors and other members—a concession designed to attract the former—and that operations should not begin until the equivalent of $250 million was available. While having majority voting support of more than three fourths of the General Assembly, SUNFED was resisted by those countries that could provide the major support, led by the United States.

On April 16, 1953, in an address to the American Society of Newspaper Editors, President Eisenhower, declared: "This Government is ready to ask its people to join with all nations in devoting a substantial percentage of the savings achieved by disarmament to a fund for world aid and reconstruction." (His statement revived a similar idea expressed by President Truman to the UN General Assembly a year and a half earlier.)[29] At U.S. initiative this concept was embodied in Economic and Social Council Resolution 482^A (XVI) of August 4, 1953.

Meanwhile, the president of the Economic Council, Raymond Scheyven of Belgium, was asked to sound out governments on SUNFED and submit his findings by 1954. Among the developed countries, Denmark, Italy, the Netherlands, and Norway indicated they would contribute to such a fund; and Belgium, France, and Japan said they would under certain conditions. However, negative replies came from Canada, the Federal Republic of Germany, Sweden, Switzerland, the United Kingdom, and the United States—the key countries, without which no such fund could succeed.

U.S. representatives reminded the majority in private negotiations over the year: "You can't run a dairy without a cow."

As years passed without the disarmament that would liberate the funds indicated by Truman and Eisenhower—in fact, military budgets have more than quadrupled since 1953—the initial glow generated by their statements dissipated. Lodge felt strongly that the United States would lose ground to the Soviets if we did not respond more sympathetically to the SUNFED drive. (The Soviets had declared in various UN forums that they would contribute to SUNFED if all other major contributors did.)

Accordingly, on May 11, 1956, Lodge wrote Eisenhower a letter proposing "UN Multilateral" under which the United States would earmark the $75 million per year then going into bilateral aid for a multilateral fund provided that other countries would match U.S. contributions so that this would constitute about one sixth of the total. Also built in would be a provision that no allocations would occur except with the approval of the World Bank.[29] Lodge's proposal was rejected in Washington, following strong opposition by George Humphrey, the powerful secretary of the treasury.

When I came to USUN as economic adviser in September 1956, one of the first things Lodge discussed with me was his desire "to get this monkey off our backs." He asked whether we could work out a "Baby SUNFED" of about $100 million, with the United States contributing up to one third, that would be welcomed by the LDCs and could gain acceptance in Washington. We then became involved in a hectic General Assembly, on which were overlaid emergency sessions to consider the Suez and Hungarian crises; hence, there was no opportunity to move ahead until 1957. Meanwhile, Paul G. Hoffman, a progressive Republican who had been administrator of the Marshall Plan and a strong advocate of economic aid, served as our delegate to the Second (Economic) Committee of the General Assembly. Because of Paul's interest and reputation, we had unusual opportunities to consult during the session with the most active leaders of delegations to the Second Committee as well as with knowledgeable Secretariat officials. A series of working lunches with the Canadian delegation was particularly useful. Although a majority of more than three quarters could have been mustered easily to establish SUNFED, its advocates wisely refrained from pressing the issue to a vote. Still, Hoffman and I advised Lodge in December 1956 that the LDCs were no longer interested in the 1953 Eisenhower promise; disarmament was elusive and their needs were pressing.

The first half of 1957 was devoted to a search for a new formula, in consultations involving USUN and the State and Treasury Departments. Early on I advised Lodge that a Baby SUNFED would not work. With some 100 countries and territories to be aided, $100 million would average out to $1 million each. Not many bridges or harbors could be built for that sum—putting a second level on the George Washington Bridge cost $185 million! Embarking on a Baby SUNFED would mean either that the contribution to development would be trivial or that the capital to be provided would have to be many times the amount envisaged.

Our answer was a program originally called the Special Projects Fund. This new fund, plus the existing Expanded Program of Technical Assistance, would have a joint target of $100 million, with the United States contributing up to 40 percent. It would not finance capital projects; rather, it would provide "preinvestment" assistance—resource surveys and the building of training institutions in LDCs, thus laying the groundwork for more and more effective capital investment, public and private, domestic and foreign.[30] Lodge put his full weight behind the proposal, and it was approved by Washington in time for the twelfth session of the General Assembly in September 1957.

The U.S. delegate to the Second Committee in 1957, Congressman Walter Judd, was a very different Republican from Paul Hoffman. An ardent supporter of Chiang Kai-shek, Judd told us shortly after he came to New York that, far from supporting the new Special Projects Fund, he believed that the existing Expanded Program of Technical Assistance should be abolished, with U.S. funds for multilateral technical assistance going directly to each specialized agency instead of being channeled through EPTA.

We did not argue with Judd but instead exposed him at small lunches and meetings to key representatives of LDCs and the more liberal developed countries (Canada, the Netherlands, and the Scandanavias). Gradually *they* changed his viewpoint. By December, Judd had not only fought hard for the Special Fund; he had become extremely popular with the LDCs, even with the Indians, Egyptians, and others who held views diametrically opposed to his on Chinese representation. His zeal, fervor, and honesty were appreciated, particularly after he changed his views on UN economic programs.

Judd helped greatly in achieving the compromise embodied in General Assembly resolution 1219 (XII), which provided for establishment of the Special Fund. It was largely worked out in backroom negotiations involving about a dozen delegations (not including the Soviet bloc), who then sold it to the rest. The United States promised it would stick to the agreement against any objections of recalcitrant developed countries, and the LDCs promised to do likewise with their recalcitrants; otherwise, no agreement would have been possible.

During the first days of negotiations we received instructions from Washington that we attempt to delete the word "Projects" from the title "Special Projects Fund," because the Treasury Department was afraid that it implied capital financing. Almost simultaneously representatives of the LDCs proposed its deletion because they were afraid it would imply that the new program could never go into such financing. The U.S. delegation was thus in the happy position of being able to acquiesce gracefully to the LDC request for deletion.

The agreement on the text of resolution 1219 was reached in a backroom negotiation at about 10:30 P.M. on December 10, subject to our obtaining clearance from Washington on a statement concerning the U.S. contribution. Walter Judd phoned Washington for approval and was told by John Hanes, Jr., then deputy assistant secretary of state, that "Congress wouldn't take that language." At that point, Judd exploded: "Hell, I'm a Congressman; I ought to know what they'll take!" That settled it.

During Second Committee consideration of resolution 1219, Judd pledged his best efforts with Congress to stabilize the U.S. contribution to the Special Fund and EPTA at 40 percent, then the level of our contributions to the EPTA program of $30 million. (Events proved he was a better judge of his congressional colleagues than Hanes.) This statement, an important factor in the successful negotiations, was remarkable for two reasons: (1) a few months earlier Congress had adopted a bill under which the U.S. contribution ceiling for EPTA would go down to 33⅓ percent; (2) Judd had arrived in New York three months earlier with serious doubts as to whether EPTA should be continued at all and with no commitment to the Special Fund. His contacts with Lodge, a fellow Republican, and with many other delegates from around the world changed Judd's mind, and he was all the more effective with Congress because of his record of staunch conservatism. From the UN standpoint, it was an excellent example of the potential value of exposing congressmen to the General Assembly and other delegates for three months.

The Soviets, for their own reasons, had denounced the proposal from the outset, arguing that it would spell the death of SUNFED. Some of the LDCs also feared such a result and, they told us, had asked whether the Soviets would agree to contribute $25 million to SUNFED regardless of what the United States did. When the Soviets refused, the LDCs felt they had no practical alternative to the U.S. proposal, especially since it did not actually close the door on SUNFED. Agreement was also helped greatly by Denmark and the Netherlands, both of which had supported SUNFED for years and were now urging the LDCs to accept the U.S. idea.[31]

In the General Assembly all delegations except the Soviet bloc, which abstained, supported resolution 1219. Subsequently, when the program was established in 1959 the Soviets joined in, but their annual contributions were meager and they had lost their credibility as friends of the LDCs on UN economic issues.

During negotiations, I had pointed out that the term "SUNFED" had negative connotations in the United States, where it was often described as a plan whereby we would put up most of the money and everybody else would decide how to spend it. As we groped for a term that would distinguish the Special Fund we had agreed on from the kind of fund still desired by the LDCs, I suggested, as a means of getting over a temporary negotiating roadblock, the term "UN Capital Development Fund," and it stuck. Indeed, in 1960 the General Assembly voted in principle to establish the UNCDF and in 1965 it was established; however, it has never received sufficient contributions to make it meaningful.[32] Significantly, countries like Saudi Arabia, Iran, Iraq, and Kuwait, which were strong SUNFED advocates, have not seen fit to make substantial contributions to UNCDF from the tens of billions of additional dollars they have earned through the twelve-fold increase of oil prices in recent years.

Yet the principle of multilateral soft loans did not die; it was incarnated in the International Development Association (IDA), established as an affiliate of the World Bank in 1959. IDA extends credits for up to fifty years at 1–2 percent interest, with an initial ten-year grace period during which there is no repayment. This is just the kind of capital assistance the LDCs had been demanding. The difference is that IDA comes under World Bank management and its weighted voting procedures. Where billions of dollars are involved, as they have been under IDA, it is almost inconceivable that the U.S. Congress and other parliamentary bodies would have voted the money for a fund under the ultimate control of the one-country, one-vote UN General Assembly. So, in my view, the establishment of IDA has been a great boon to the people in the LDCs.

In any case, the decision to establish the Special Fund, with the Soviets isolated, accomplished Lodge's political purpose; besides, it was economically sound and genuinely helpful to the LDCs. In his report to the president on December 19, 1957, he listed it among the four major accomplishments of the twelfth session of the General Assembly.[33]

When the Special Fund was established in January 1957, its eighteen-member Governing Council (half major contributors and half others) was to decide on a managing director on the recommendation of the secretary general. Because the United States would be contributing 40 percent, it was assumed that the job would go to an American. The official U.S. candidate was John Davies, who had earlier tried unsuccessfully to be elected director general of the Food and Agriculture Organization (FAO), but there was also a "Danish" candidate—Paul G. Hoffman. The Danish representative, Nonnie Wright, was lobbying hard for Hoffman, who was also very popular among the LDCs; he had headed the Marshall Plan, represented the United States in the Second Committee at the 1956 General Assembly, and had written in February 1957 a *New York Times Magazine* article advocating a massive increase in aid, including a new experimental fund of $100 million to conduct resource surveys.[34] As this broad support for Hoffman became evident, I urged Lodge to ask for new instructions. Since he was interested in political impact, I told him that we would in all likelihood win more political points with Paul Hoffman at the head of a $15 million Special Fund than with a relative unknown and $50 million. Lodge agreed and we next talked to Hoffman to find out whether a man who had administered a Marshall Plan running at $4 *billion* per year would accept the direction of a program that in its first year might amount to only $15 million (because of the provision that the United States contribution could not exceed 40 percent). Hoffman's reply: "I'd take it if it were 15 cents; it's the principle that counts." Our instructions were changed; Hoffman was approved and he remained for more than a decade. When the Special Fund and the EPTA were merged as the UN Development Program in 1965, Hoffman became administrator (chief executive) of the larger program. In no small measure it was due to Hoffman's superb advocacy (I never met a better salesman), his total dedication, and his standing with higher government leaders in Europe and the United States that annual contributions rose from $38 million in 1959 to $269 million in 1972. Hoffman was eighty when he retired in 1972.

THE "MALAYAN RESOLUTION"

Conscious of the political and propaganda success of the Special Fund, in early 1958 I sought another idea that would have intrinsic merit and also give the West a political and propaganda advantage. I drafted a resolution designed to encourage foreign private investment by asking the UN secretary general to (1) find out from the governments of less developed countries in what sectors of their economic development they would want foreign private investment and under what conditions; and (2) inquire of potential major investors in industrialized countries what sectors would most interest them and under what conditions.

Next I showed the draft to Henry Bloch, chief of the Finance Division in the UN Secretariat, who would be the principal action officer if the resolution were approved. Experience had demonstrated that Secretariat reaction to a draft resolution had a significant influence on delegation attitudes toward it as well as on its implementation. Bloch made a number of most helpful suggestions, which were incorporated in the draft. The revised draft was cleared by Lodge and the State Department without significant change.

Next there came the tactical question of sponsorship. Overt U.S. sponsorship would diminish chances of success. After a few weeks of getting acquainted with the new delegates, I found an ideal sponsor— Mohammed Sopiee, head of the Malayan delegation to the Second Committee. Sopiee saw considerable merit in the proposal and also thought that his identification with it would help him at home. He was a moderate socialist and wanted to make it clear in Malaya that he was not a doctrinaire opponent of private enterprise.

Sopiee assembled a group of cosponsors from around the world (Argentina, Australia, Canada, Denmark, Japan, Laos, Liberia, Nepal, New Zealand, Pakistan, Peru, Philippines, Sudan, and Thailand) for what came to be known as the "Malayan resolution"—General Assembly resolution 1318 (XIII). It was supported by all except the communist delegations, with the Yugoslavs exercising a benign neutrality while the Soviets thundered vainly against it.

The secretary general was highly pleased because he realized how important it was for the United Nations to have the confidence of important private interests in the United States and other industrialized countries. Moreover, since the needs of the less developed countries for capital and technology far exceeded what could be made available by governments, it was important to facilitate foreign private investment under mutually acceptable conditions. The process initiated by the Malayan resolution continued for more than a decade and resulted in many face-to-face meetings between government officials of the less developed countries and top industrialists and investment bankers from the developed countries. From the U.S. standpoint, it was also a political and propaganda plus, building links with Third World countries.

In fact, the key to better relations with the Third World representatives in the economic area was always a focus on their problems rather than an overt cold war approach, which turned them off. This was sometimes difficult for outsiders to understand. In 1958, when the late George Meany was U.S. delegate to the Second Committee, I drafted a general debate statement for him, emphasizing the problems of development and the American approach to them. I gave the draft to his political adviser, Jay Lovestone, who had at one time been a high official in the Communist Party of the U.S.A. and had, in disillusionment, become vehemently anticommunist. Lovestone returned the draft with the comment: "But you didn't attack the Russians." I replied, "The great majority in this committee don't care about our quarrel with the Russians. They're interested in development." He said Meany would not give the speech unless there was an attack on the Russians. I added a paragraph about the great gap between the Soviet protestations of concern for the less developed countries and the meagerness of their aid. Meany made the speech and our friends in the Second Committee simply ignored the anti-Soviet paragraph.

THE WORLD FOOD PROGRAM

In May 1960 Lodge called me to his office and said: "Max, the vice-president [Nixon] wants to do something about using food through the UN. Of course, he doesn't know anything about either one. Will you give me a short memo on it?"

Lodge's comment about Nixon, with whom he would run later in 1960, was typically candid. I had no desire to help Nixon, voting for his opponent every time he ran for president, but felt that the idea of channeling food aid through the UN and using it as an element of development was good. It would help to feed some people who would otherwise go hungry, assist economic development marginally, and help strengthen the role of the UN. I had doubts about the ability of the UN to manage efficiently a mammoth operational exercise comparable to the existing bilateral American program. Consequently, I worked out the skeleton of a program under which the UN would serve as a "clearinghouse" where food aid agreements could be arranged, with detailed negotiations and operations to be worked out by the countries concerned. Lodge handed the memo to Eisenhower, and it was then processed through channels to become a U.S. initiative at the 1960 General Assembly.

At the Assembly we prepared the ground carefully, recruiting an appropriate group of cosponsors. The aim in getting cosponsors was to assemble a group large enough to have influence in all the various geographical blocs except the Soviet, yet not so large as to be unwieldy in dealing with amendments. We also had to work out problems with food-exporting countries such as Thailand, which wanted to be sure that food aid would not interfere with their markets.

In order to maximize the political and propaganda impact, the United States used a favorite Soviet device—asking for priority consideration of the item. In this instance the Soviet delegate, Georgi Arkadiev, actually increased the impact by opposing the priority request vigorously and repeatedly. At one point he tactlessly commented: "What is the hurry? People have been hungry for a long time." As a result, the item got maximum attention at the UN and in the media. The *New York Times* gave it front-page coverage for three consecutive days. The resultant resolution, General Assembly resolution 1496 (XV), October 27, 1960, was adopted unanimously. It requested the secretary general and the director general of the FAO to prepare a report on the basis of which the next session of the General Assembly could take a decision on the establishment of a World Food Program.

In 1961 Orville Freeman became secretary of agriculture in the Kennedy administration. An able, energetic man, he succeeded in having the World Food Program established at FAO headquarters in Rome rather than at UN headquarters in New York. This defeated USUN's purpose of strengthening the UN politically by bringing the World Food Program under its aegis. It also placed policy responsibility in the Agriculture Department rather than in State, although the State Department would have input in the preparation of U.S. positions on the operation of the program.

The World Food Program has survived and grown, its essential soundness endorsed by a succession of American administrations. Between its inception in 1963 and the end of 1976, it provided almost $1.8 billion in food aid to the developing countries; of which the United States provided 35 percent. Like the Special Fund, it was thoroughly staffed out through all interested U.S. agencies before it became operational. The point is, however, that neither proposal is likely to have materialized if Lodge had not obtained a prior White House endorsement in principle. The problem for the bureaucracy then became not *whether* but *how*. Otherwise, they would in all probability have died in a morass of bureaucratic infighting and inertia.

SUEZ—1956

The eleventh session of the UN General Assembly was opened on November 12, 1956, instead of the usual September opening in substantial measure because Lodge had persuaded the secretary general and other UN members that it would be unwise to have the Assembly in session during the U.S. elections.* Lodge was concerned about a number of sensitive issues, particularly the Arab-Israeli dispute. It is doubtful, however, that Lodge or anyone else in the top levels of American government knew how explosive the situation would become.

Provoked by continued Fedayeen terrorist raids from bases in the Sinai Desert, Israel invaded Sinai on October 29, 1956, and advanced rapidly toward the Suez Canal. The next day Britain and France issued an ultimatum to Israel and Egypt calling for an end to fighting within twelve hours, the withdrawal of the forces of both sides to a distance of ten miles from each side of the Canal, and agreement by Egypt to allow Anglo-French forces to be stationed temporarily on the Canal for the purpose of separating the belligerents and insuring the safety of shipping. (Actually the Israeli, British, and French actions had been planned secretly in advance.)[35] The ultimatum was rejected by Egypt, thus opening the way for the Anglo-French invasion that was to start with the bombing of Egyptian airfields and other military installations by British aircraft based on Cyprus.

Eisenhower's reaction was one of dismay. The United States had not been consulted by the British or French, nor even informed in advance. "We could not permit the Soviet Union to seize the leadership in the struggle against the use of force in the Middle East and thus win the confidence of the new independent nations of the world. But on the other hand I by no means wanted the British and French to be branded as naked

---

*In 1948 this problem was handled by the decision of the members to convene the Assembly at the regular time (2nd Tuesday in September) but in Paris . . . presumably away from the pressures the media could have generated. In fact in 1956 there were proposals circulating to take the General Assembly to the United Kingdom. (Blackpool was the suggested locale.) The general breakdown in U.S.-U.K. communication alluded to later, kept this idea from taking hold. It is interesting to speculate on how much of what is hereafter described would have taken place if the UN General Assembly had been in session, in full regalia, in the United Kingdom at the time of the Suez and Hungarian affairs.

aggressors without provocation."[36] After all, Nasser had unilaterally nationalized the Suez Canal, commercially and strategically important to France and Great Britain, our NATO allies.

Following Eisenhower-Dulles-Lodge consultations on October 29, the United States called for an immediate emergency meeting of the Security Council and introduced a draft resolution calling upon Israel to withdraw its forces from Egypt without delay and asking all member states to "refrain from the use of force or threat of force."[37] Britain and France vetoed this draft resolution, as well as a Soviet draft the same night.

With Dulles ill—he entered the hospital a few days later for an ileitis operation—Lodge and his USUN staff, particularly Barco, Cook, and Pedersen, were largely responsible for initiating policy suggestions and drafting statements in the fast-moving situation at the UN. At the same time, they were involved in frequent consultations with the secretary general and his top deputies, Andrew Cordier and Ralph Bunche, along with other missions. As the Hungarian crisis broke out while Suez alone would have involved more than full-time operation, the key people at USUN, other active missions, and the Secretariat were involved almost around the clock for weeks. USUN feared that the British and French might organize a challenge to the Assembly's right to consider the question. It prepared a legal brief upholding that right and lobbied extensively for it; however, there was no formal challenge, perhaps as a result of the broad support for the move following the British and French vetoes.

On November 1 the Security Council, at the initiative of the Yugoslav delegation, invoked the Uniting for Peace procedure and called an emergency session of the General Assembly. The United States and the Soviet Union both supported this move; only Britain and France cast negative votes. In the Assembly, on November 2, Dulles condemned the resort to force by Britain, France, and Israel, which could "scarcely be reconciled with the principles and purposes of the United Nations to which we have all subscribed." In this attitude, the United States found support from a not particularly welcome source—the Soviet Union.

The two superpowers were able to agree on a compromise resolution sponsored by the United States, urging a cease-fire and a withdrawal of all forces behind the armistice lines. USUN lobbied extensively for the draft, securing solid Latin American support; it was adopted by a vote of 64 in favor, 5 opposed, and 6 abstentions. One of those abstaining was Lester Pearson of Canada, who claimed that the resolution had made "one great omission": it had not provided for a vital instrument to prevent another explosion in the Suez area—"a truly international peace and police force."[38] Even before Pearson spoke, there had been intensive consultations about such a force between USUN, Hammarskjöld, Andrew Cordier, Ralph Bunche, and the Swedish, Norwegian, Yugoslav, and Canadian delegations. Hammarskjöld was cautious and reserved at first, but then became convinced that this expansion of his authority was needed for the defense of Egypt and the principles of the UN Charter. Lodge also spent many hours with a skeptical Krishna Menon, who was finally persuaded to support the plan—an important factor, since India was then the leader of the nonaligned and had close relationships with Egypt and Yugoslavia. Subsequently, India and Yugoslavia provided a major part of the UN force in the Sinai. It was then decided that Pearson should be the official sponsor, and he introduced a draft resolution asking the secretary general to submit within forty-eight hours a plan for the creation, "with the consent of the nations concerned," of an emergency international force "to secure and supervise the cessation of hostilities." The United States gave the plan its strong support, declaring that it was interested in a solution that would "meet the immediate crisis as well as something that would go to the causes and into the more long-range subjects."[39] The Soviet Union felt that coercive action would be preferable, but did not object strongly to the Canadian plan. Thus, the General Assembly, on November 3, approved the Canadian draft resolution by a vote of 57 to 0, with 19 abstentions. The abstainers included the Soviet bloc, Britain, France, Israel, Egypt, Australia, New Zealand, the Union of South Africa, Portugal, Austria, and Laos.

U.S. policy in the Suez crisis of 1956 has been sharply criticized because it alienated, at least temporarily, two important NATO allies. In fact, former Secretary of State Dean Acheson believed that it came close to losing the United States its two closest allies, splitting the NATO alliance, and thus exposing Western Europe to a communist takeover.[40] Yet, for practical as well as moral reasons, Eisenhower, Dulles, and Lodge saw eye to eye on the policy adopted. There was, first, a sense of outrage because the British and French had not bothered to consult their NATO ally on so important a matter as military action in the Middle East. Second, from a purely military standpoint, the punitive expedition seemed to be foundering and thus could not be presented to the General Assembly as a fait accompli. The United States, by supporting the Anglo-French venture or even by taking a neutral view of it, would have risked the ill will of a large majority of the UN membership and, in addition, would have been in an embarrassing position if the military action failed or bogged down. Most important, the United States feared the intervention of the Soviet Union in the Middle East through "volunteers" and the risk of sparking a major war through direct superpower confrontation in the contested area.

According to Lodge, Eisenhower believed that the Soviets were prepared to use force to bring about foreign withdrawal and, where expedient, to use the Soviet presence in the Middle East to seize oil resources or deny them to the West.[41] Accordingly, the president used his full influence in persuading the British to back down. Once this decision was made, the UN "provided a convenient method whereby they [British and French] could extricate themselves with minimum embarrassment."[42]

While British and French disengagement was prompt, Israel was reluctant to withdraw in the absence of solid assurance of their security, including protection against terrorist raids from the Sinai. Eisenhower became impatient and asked: "Should a nation which attacks and occupies foreign territory in the face of United Nations disapproval be allowed to impose conditions on its own withdrawal?" But even Eisenhower noted that, contrary to his word, Nasser had sent Egyptian administrators back into the Gaza Strip after Israeli withdrawal. Finally, on March 1, 1957, Lodge affirmed at the UN that "a U.S.-Israel understanding that Israeli withdrawal was linked to free passage through Aqaba, and that any armed interference would entitle Israel to rights of self-defense under the U.N. Charter."[43] Nasser's proclaimed blockade of Aqaba in May 1967, in defiance of this understanding, triggered the Six Day War in June 1967.

HUNGARY

Unfortunately for the Hungarians, the climax of the crisis in Hungary coincided almost exactly with the Suez crisis. The two situations were dealt with at the UN in a series of round-the-clock meetings, as shown by the schedule of public meetings for the week of October 28–November 5.

Sunday, October 28, 4 P.M.–9:50 P.M. 746th Security Council meeting on Hungary.

Monday, October 29, 3 P.M.–3:25 P.M., 747th Security Council meeting on a French complaint of Egyptian assistance to Algerian rebels.

Tuesday, October 30, 11 A.M.–1:10 P.M., 748th Security Council meeting on Suez.

Tuesday, October 30, 4 P.M.–7:55 P.M., 749th Security Council meeting on Suez.

Tuesday, October 30, 9 P.M.–11:05 P.M., 750th Security Council meeting on Suez.

Wednesday, October 31, 3 P.M.–7:20 P.M., 751st Security Council meeting on Suez.

Thursday, November 1, 5 P.M.–7:40 P.M., 561st General Assembly meeting on Suez.

Thursday, November 1–2, 9:50 P.M.–4:20 A.M., 562nd General Assembly meeting on Suez.

Friday, November 2, 5 P.M.–8:50 P.M., 752nd Security Council meeting on Hungary.

Saturday, November 3, 3 P.M.–6:50 P.M., 753rd Security Council meeting on Hungary.

Saturday, November 3-4, 8 P.M.-3 A.M., 563rd General Assembly meeting on Suez.

Sunday, November 4, 3 A.M.-5:25 A.M., 754th Security Council meeting on Hungary.

Sunday, November 4, 4 P.M.-8:10 P.M., 564th General Assembly meeting on Hungary.

Sunday, November 4-5, 9:45 P.M.-12:25 A.M., 565th General Assembly meeting on Suez.

Monday, November 5, 8 P.M.-10:25 P.M. 755th Security Council meeting on Suez.

The public meetings were, of course, only the tip of the iceberg. Between them USUN was in ceaseless communication with Washington and other delegations.

The Hungarian crisis began with a revolution on October 23, 1956, against the government of Ernö Gerö, a lifetime Stalinist. It was apparently leaderless and unplanned, starting with demonstrations for more freedom and snowballing into a revolution because of widespread resentment at the use of disproportionate and deadly violence against the demonstrators. The revolt's success was assured, at least initially, when large Hungarian army units joined the revolution instead of following Gerö's orders to suppress it. Imre Nagy, a lifelong communist who had been imprisoned by the Stalinist regime of Mátyás Rákosi, was brought in to replace Gerö as prime minister and announced formation of a national government on October 30, but there is no indication that Nagy either led or encouraged the revolt.

By 2:00 A.M. on October 24 Soviet tanks entered Budapest. The Soviets claimed that they had come in response to a request from the Hungarian government on October 23, but a seasoned Hungarian observer has pointed out that the tanks were too far away to arrive when they did if they had waited for the request.[44] On October 25 Mikoyan and Suslov, the Soviet proconsuls in Budapest, forced Gerö to resign in the light of the widespread rage against him. On October 30 the Soviets pulled their troops out of Budapest, an action that confused some leaders in the West, but at midnight of November 3 Soviet troops reentered Buadapest and crushed the revolution.

The contrast between the UN's prompt and effective action in bringing about the withdrawal of the British, French, and Israelis from Suez and its failure to do anything effective about Hungary is a painful one. Criticisms were directed against the UN in general and the United States and Dag Hammarskjöld in particular. Anthony Eden, Britain's prime minister and one of the architects of the Suez invasion, observed bitterly:

Five days passed without any Council meeting on Hungary, despite repeated attempts by ourselves and others to bring one about. The U.S. representative was reluctant, and voiced his suspicion that we were urging the Hungarian situation to divert attention from Suez. The U.S. government appeared in no hurry to move. Their attitude provided a damaging contrast to the clarity they were showing in arraigning the French and ourselves.[45]

It is ironic that such doughty cold warriors as Dulles, Lodge, and Robert Murphy should be accused of a lack of zeal in condemning and trying to do something about the blatant Soviet aggression in Hungary. Why?

First, there was an information gap in Washington, as attested by Llewellyn Thompson, an experienced American Kremlinologist and in 1956 ambassador to Austria.[46] In part, this was because U.S. communications from Budapest to Washington and New York were slow. More important, the U.S. legation in Budapest had been without a chief of mission since August. It was difficult to keep up with fast-moving events in Hungary and evaluate the nature and strength of the Nagy regime.

Second, the revolution occurred two weeks before the U.S. presidential elections, hardly the best time for the president to focus on foreign policy issues. Moreover, Dulles was seriously ill with cancer and could not function with his usual vigor.

Third, the Anglo-French-Israeli invasion of Suez occurred right in the middle of the Hungarian crisis, distracting attention from Hungary and perhaps emboldening the Soviets. Endre Marton, AP correspondent in Budapest at the time, relates a conversation with a steelworker who asked him to translate the following to a British correspondent: "Is he English? Would he please convey our thanks to Mr. Eden for having stabbed our revolution in the back."[47]

Fourth, events moved very swiftly. Nagy's appeal to the UN asking that "the defense of this neutrality by the Four Great Powers" be put on the agenda of the Security Council at noon on November 1, was made just two and a half days before the Soviet troops reentered Budapest to crush the revolution. The Council met on November 2 and again on November 3, when the Yugoslav representative moved for adjournment of the session because, he said, the withdrawal of Soviet troops from Hungary had already started. Without information on Soviet intentions to strike (which they did at midnight), Lodge supported the Yugoslav motion. (It should be recalled that Yugoslavia, having broken with the Kremlin six years earlier, had every reason to sympathize with a Hungarian communist, Nagy, who wanted to take similar action.)

The real problem, however, was one of power and logistics. Eisenhower, Dulles, Lodge, and Murphy were convinced that any U.S.

intervention would have meant a military confrontation with the Soviet Union and possibly World War III. Eisenhower wrote: "Unless the major nations of Europe would, without delay, ally themselves spontaneously with us (an unimaginable prospect) we could do nothing. Sending U.S. troops alone into Hungary through hostile or neutral territory would have involved us in a general war, and, too, if the U.N., overriding a certain Soviet veto, decided [in the General Assembly] that all the military and other resources of member nations should be used to drive the Soviets from Hungary, we would inevitably have a major conflict."[48] Marton speculates that the West might have tried oblique threats, as the Soviets used in connection with Suez, or a tripartite demarche in Moscow recognizing Nagy's declaration of neutrality and urging Moscow to do the same, but Murphy, a realistic and astute veteran of many years of dealing with the Soviet Union, doubted that such tactics would have deterred them.[49] The experience with the Soviet suppression of the Dubček government in Czechoslovakia in 1968, when neither the president of the United States nor the United Nations faced an immediate crisis elsewhere, suggests that power and logistical factors were crucial in both cases. (Similar factors were apparently operative when the Soviets invaded Afghanistan in December 1979.)

Having decided against the use or threat of force against the Soviets, the United States moved to use the UN for exacting the maximum price in propaganda and world opinion from the Soviets. Lodge and his deputy, Wadsworth, with USUN staff, took charge of the tactics, getting appropriate clearances from State. Using the Uniting for Peace procedure once more, the United States and friendly delegations moved the discussion to an emergency session of the General Assembly immediately after the Soviet veto in the Security Council, November 3, of a U.S. resolution demanding that the Soviet Union desist from further military action and withdraw from Hungary. That same night the Assembly adopted, by 50 to 8 (Soviet bloc), with 15 abstentions, a U.S. resolution calling on the USSR in the strongest terms to cease its intervention. The resolution asked the secretary general to "investigate the situation caused by foreign intervention in Hungary, to observe the situation directly through representatives named by him, and to report thereon to the General Assembly at the earliest moment, and as soon as possible to suggest methods to bring an end to the foreign intervention in Hungary in accordance with the principles of the Charter of the United Nations." Although the resolutions went on to call on Hungary and the USSR to admit the secretary general's observers to Hungary and to urge all states to cooperate with him, the fact was that the responsibility had been transferred once again, this time to a single individual with no sovereign powers and no military or other resources, who was already fully engaged in carrying out the General Assembly's instructions of that same morning in another major crisis—Suez. The Assembly also asked Hammarskjöld to look into the humanitarian needs of the Hungarian people and to coordinate the sending of the necessary supplies.[50]

Hammarskjöld's proposal to go to Budapest was rejected by the Kádár regime, which also rejected the observers. The U.S. mission continued to prod Hammarskjold and the General Assembly, which passed a number of additional resolutions condemning the Soviet actions in Hungary, and the deportations, all of which were defied by the Hungarian regime and denounced by the Soviet Union. A five-member Special Committee composed of representatives of Australia, Ceylon, Denmark, Tunisia, and Uruguay, was appointed by General Assembly resolution 1132, and adopted by a vote of 59 to 8, with 10 abstentions.[51] They, too, were unable to gain access to Hungary, but submitted a report based on interviews with Hungarian refugees and available documents. Having examined the Special Committee's report, on September 14, 1957, the General Assembly adopted a resolution that found that the USSR had, among other things, deprived Hungary of its liberty and independence, imposed the Kádár government, and carried out mass deportation.[52] It also condemned those acts. Unfortunately, the Assembly had no power to take sanctions against the USSR, and the Soviets could veto any such action in the Security Council, which does have such power. By contrast, Assembly action in the Suez crisis was possible because all parties accepted the Assembly's resolutions and UNEF. (Israel's acceptance was reluctant, with the U.S. using a combination of pressures and assurances to bring it about.)

As a further means of making the Soviets and the Kádár regime pay a price before world opinion, the United States took the initiative to block acceptance in the General Assembly of the Hungarian delegation's credentials, a tactic that was used for several years. (A vote count by USUN indicated that it could not muster a majority for rejecting the credentials.)

Were the repeated efforts in the General Assembly worthwhile? János Radvanyi, a former official in the Hungarian Foreign Ministry, concludes that the Kádár regime, experiencing the verbal lashings of the General Assembly, decided to make some specific concessions.[53] Endre Marton observes that "in 1970 in Hungary there is more freedom, a fuller plate . . . and less evidence of police rule than in any other bloc country in Eastern Europe." He notes that Kádár is now popular and comments that "one of Nagy's greatest political mistakes was that he let himself be pushed into bypassing a phase of revolution" (by declaring neutrality so soon after his regime was established). He concludes that the Hungarian revolution did succeed after all, despite Nagy's mistakes, Washington's slowness in reacting, and the impotence of the West and the UN in the face of Soviet defiance.[54]

As for Lodge, there was little he could do in this situation except prod the General Assembly to condemn the Soviet actions, as he and USUN did. Radvanyi's assessment indicates that these efforts, however meager and unglamorous, were better than nothing.

LEBANON—1958

If the United States and Britain found themselves on opposite sides, at least initially, in the Suez crisis of 1956, they were clearly in tune in 1958. Both supported a Swedish resolution in the Security Council on June 11, 1958, to establish a UN Observation Group in Lebanon (UNOGIL) to observe and report any outside intervention in the struggle between Moslems and Christians there. Then, according to Robert Murphy, undersecretary of state, "we learned that Arab nationalists, under the direction of President Nasser of Egypt, were spending money to influence the swollen Moslem population of Lebanon and were sending clandestine arms to rebellious elements there." Appeals for help came to Eisenhower from the president and the prime minister of Lebanon, and when a violent leftist revolution occurred in Iraq on July 14, he decided to send U.S. Marines into Lebanon, "for the protection of U.S. citizens." and at the invitation of Lebanese President Chamoun. According to Murphy, UNOGIL could not confirm outside intervention but marine wiretapping did.[55] In any event, that crisis in Lebanon ended on July 31 when General Chehab was elected president, and the marines were out by October. Meanwhile, in a coordinate move, the British landed troops in Jordan, Iraq's neighbor, to stabilize the situation there.

There is no available evidence that Lodge either proposed or opposed the marine landing in Lebanon; however, USUN had been preparing contingency plans for three months before it occurred. As a result, USUN was able to act promptly in calling for a Security Council meeting and Lodge was able to put the best possible face on the operation. Lodge recalls that Hammarskjöld's anger, upon learning that the troops had landed, "was indeed memorable," a recollection confirmed by Brian Urquhart, a top aide of the secretary general's. Hammarskjöld believed that a solution was at hand at the time of the marine landing. He (and USUN) also feared that, once the pipeline that spewed U.S. marines on Lebanon's beaches had been turned on, it might be difficult to turn it off, even if clear evidence developed that the need had ended. Nevertheless, he decided to retain UNOGIL as a UN presence, and as noted above, the situation was resolved within a few weeks.[56]

The U.S. landing in Lebanon, seen in hindsight, may have been an overreaction, but Eisenhower and Prime Minister Macmillan felt that they could not afford to risk the overthrow of friendly governments in Lebanon and Jordan, as had occurred in Iraq. The fact that the U.S. image at the UN did not suffer any significant damage may be attributed to careful planning and skillful tactics by Lodge, as well as to his personal friendship with Hammarskjöld. There was also an element of luck; no marines killed or were killed.

Although the marine operation in landing involved no loss of lives, it did cost $200 million.[57] For comparison, the U.S. share of the cost of the UN Operation in the Congo (ONUC) was $168 million for a four-year operation dealing with an infinitely more complicated situation. This would suggest the wisdom of working through UN peacekeeping mechanisms rather than by means of unilateral intervention wherever possible.

LAOS

In 1959 Eisenhower was most anxious to avoid a further U.S. intervention in Laos, where the insurgents (the Pathet Lao), backed by the Vietminh, were making alarming advances against the royal government. On August 14 that government, with little knowledge of how the UN worked, asked for an urgent meeting of the Security Council—then requested a few weeks' delay so that delegation might arrive! On September 4 the Lao foreign minister requested that a UN Emergency Force, like the one in the Sinai Desert, be sent to Laos—an obvious impossibility in circumstances where the Pathet Lao was clearly unwilling to accept a UN peacekeeping operation. Nevertheless, the Italian president of the Security Council that month (Egidio Ortona) convened the Council to discuss the "Report by the Secretary General on the letter received from the Minister for Foreign Affairs of the Royal Government of Laos." The agenda was adopted, 10 to 1 (USSR).

At the Council meeting, France, Britain, and the United States presented a resolution to establish a subcommittee composed of Argentina, Italy, Japan, and Tunisia "to conduct such inquiries as it may determine necessary and to report to the Council as soon as possible." By a vote of 10 to 1 (USSR), the Council upheld the president's ruling that the resolution was procedural rather than substantive; consequently, under Article 27 of the UN Charter, the veto would not apply, and the resolution was adopted despite a negative vote of the USSR.[58]

The subcommittee was unable to find evidence of Vietnamese military intervention, which was hardly surprising, given the nature of the terrain, the difficulty in moving around, and the unwillingness of the Pathet Lao to permit observation in the area under its control. Nevertheless, its mere presence in Laos at the request of the royal government gave a temporary psychological lift to that government and made it easier for Eisenhower to avoid an escalation of American involvement.

The idea of the subcommittee and the tactics employed were

developed by USUN. Although then the senior economic adviser, I was co-opted as a sort of "nanny" to the Lao delegation to advise them against talking to the press or doing foolish things that their inexperience about the UN might prompt. They were all personal friends, dating back to my service in the American embassy in Laos in 1955–56; consequently, my assignment was pleasant and, according to subsequent commendations, helpful. Unfortunately, this brief respite for the government did nothing to stop the civil war and a succession of coups, and the Pathet Lao finally took over the country in 1975.

THE CONGO AND THE WADSWORTH INTERLUDE

Ironically, the UN's largest and most ambitious peacekeeping operation, ONUC, started in July 1960 when Lodge was about to leave his post and run for vice-president and Eisenhower was in his last months of office. Still, the crisis demanded an American reaction, and Eisenhower chose the multilateral route. Confidence in the secretary general and Lodge was a factor, along with a desire not to have a Soviet–U.S. struggle in the heart of Africa.

The Congo crisis and the U.S. and UN roles therein have already been thoroughly chronicled;[59] consequently, a brief sketch of the events in 1960 will suffice here. The Congo (now Zaire), became independent July 1, 1960, following many decades of Belgian rule that had given some attention to the physical well-being and economic needs of the indigenous people but had not trained them for self-government. Within hours an army mutiny and widespread lawlessness erupted, and thousands of Belgians fled. On July 11, Moise Tshombe, premier of Katanga Province, the wealthiest section of the Congo, declared that his province was seceding and requested Belgian troops to restore order. The next day the Belgian government announced that, since the government of Prime Minister Patrice Lumumba had been unable to protect the lives and interests of the remaining Belgians, Belgian troops would march into Leopoldville (now Kinshasa) as well.

On July 13 members of the Lumumba regime cabled Washington for help, but Lumumba immediately disavowed this appeal, stating that it had been meant as a request for a United Nations force composed of military personnel from neutral countries. (Lumumba did so on the advice of the U.S. ambassador designate to the Congo—Clare Timberlake—making his request orally to the secretary general's representative in Leopoldville, Ralph Bunche, who cabled it immediately to Hammarskjöld.) The secretary general called at once for an emergency meeting of the Security Council, which on July 14 adopted a resolution authorizing him to make arrangements for military assistance to the Congo. The vote was 8 in favor, including the Soviet Union and the United States, 0 against, with 3 abstentions—Nationalist China, France, and Britain. Thus was born the largest and most complex peacekeeping operation ever administered by an international organization. Lasting four years and costing about $402 million (of which the United States provided slightly less than 42 percent, or $168 million), ONUC at its height included almost 20,000 troops.[60] It also included a substantial program of technical and economic assistance.

Lodge and his staff at USUN were fully involved with Eisenhower, the State Department, and the UN Secretariat in planning and carrying out this complex operation. Within the State Department the Bureau of European Affairs worked to keep open the option of support for an independent Katanga but did not prevail.

On September 3, 1960, Lodge resigned in order to run for vice-president and was succeeded by James J. Wadsworth, his old friend and deputy. Wadsworth's three and a half months as permanent representative saw a serious aggravation of the Congo crisis and a hectic session of the General Assembly, at which Khrushchev, Castro, Tito, and many other world leaders appeared. In these waning months of the Eisenhower administration, U.S. policy was one of reaction rather than initiative.

In the Congo, Premier Lumumba was conniving with the Soviet bloc, accepting their military help, and refusing to accept a disinterested status for ONUC, as stipulated by its mandate. This set him at odds with the more conservative President Kasavubu, who, on September 5, 1960, exercising his constitutional prerogative, dismissed Lumumba for plunging the nation into fratricidal war. Lumumba, responded by dismissing Kasavubu. In the confusion, a young pro-Western colonel, Joseph Mobutu, took command of the armed forces. Allegedly the CIA was involved in Mobutu's coup.[61]

The superpowers now took opposing positions on the two rival factions in the Congo government. The United States pressed the United Nations to recognize the Kasavubu-Mobutu government, while the Soviet Union began to supply the deposed Lumumba with aircraft and trucks. The UN representative who was in charge of this critical phase of ONUC's operations in the summer and fall of 1960 was Andrew W. Cordier, executive assistant to Dag Hammarskjöld. Cordier's overriding concern was to uphold the Charter and to restore law and order in the war-torn Congo. In order to stop both Kasavubu and Lumumba from inflaming popular feelings even further and to prevent the outbreak of civil war, he decided to close all Congolese airports, to immobilize troops, and to shut down the national radio in Leopoldville. Three years later, Mr. N. T. Fedorenko, the Soviet delegate in the Fifth (Administrative and Budgetary) Committee of the General Assembly was to declare that, by this action, "Cordier had adopted a decision that broke Lumumba's back" and had thus started the United Nations on its pro-Western course in the Congo. Similarly, many highly placed U.S. officials later pointed to Cordier's decision as having "stopped the Russians." Cordier himself defended his action on the grounds that it had not been taken *against* one of the rival factions or *against* one of the superpowers, but *for* the law of the United Nations and the Charter.[62]

In the struggle for legitimacy, Kasavubu decided to press his case at the UN General Assembly. On November 8 he addressed the Assembly and demanded the seating of his representatives. The U.S. delegation lobbied intensively for him (I recall our private slogan: "No boo-boo on Kasavubu"), and he was backed solidly by the NATO countries, a majority of the French-speaking African states, and most Latin Americans. Finally, the Kasavubu delegation's credentials were accepted by a vote of 54 to 24, with 19 abstentions. Many conflicts and complications remained in the Congo Operation. (These will be discussed in Chapter V.)

In his brief but hectic few months as permanent representative, Wadsworth was a steady and cool-headed chief, running a well-organized staff that Lodge had built and left intact.

LODGE AND HAMMARSKJÖLD

At the outset of their relationship, Hammarskjöld was unknown to Lodge, and initially they regarded each other with reserve and occasional irritation. These were accentuated by the Guatemala issue in 1953, when Lodge successfully forestalled Security Council action on the complaint of the leftist Arbenz regime that the United States was aiding a coup against it, on the grounds that this was a regional issue to be dealt with in the Organization of American States. The Soviet motion for adoption of the agenda on June 25 was rejected by a vote of 4 in favor, 5 against, and 2 abstentions (Britain and France). By June 27 the Arbenz government had fallen and the issue was moot. Hammarskjöld felt that the Security Council should at least have considered the issue and was annoyed with Lodge.[63]

In August 1953 Hammarskjöld went to Lodge's home in Beverly, Massachusetts, for the weekend, accepting uneasily. He enjoyed himself so thoroughly in the Lodge family circle that he and Lodge developed a personal friendship that grew steadily, offsetting some official disagreements that arose later—for example, the U.S. intervention in Lebanon in 1958.[64]

Relations were further improved after Hammarskjöld's mission to China in 1955 resulted in the release of fifteen American fliers and by Hammarskjöld's masterful handling of the Suez crisis in 1956–57 and the Congo crisis in 1960.

On at least two occasions Lodge asked Hammarskjöld to talk to the secretary of state. While Hammarskjöld was negotiating for the release of the American fliers, Dulles was making condemnatory statements about the Chinese. In a phone call, Hammarskjöld persuaded the secretary to use more restraint. Again in the fall of 1956, with Lodge's full agreement, the secretary general phoned Dulles to explain why it was necessary to station a UN Emergency Force on Egyptian soil; Lodge himself had been unable to convince Dulles.[65] Washington's growing confidence in Hammarskjöld, as well as Lodge's good relations with him, was certainly a factor in Eisenhower's decision to encourage UN responsibility for the Congo crisis in 1960.

It is sometimes assumed today that the United Nations of the 1950s was a docile place where the United States could command a majority by snapping its fingers. In fact, Lodge and his staff had to work hard to sell American policies, cultivate other delegations assiduously, and make judicious compromises. Initiatives in the peaceful use of nuclear energy and in the economic field were used to build support among the less developed countries for things the United States wanted; even then the less developed countries commanded three fourths of the votes. As far back as March 1954 Gladwyn Jebb, the British permanent representative, observed: "The great days when we and the Americans largely ran the show were over. The era of the 'underdeveloped' countries was about to begin."[66] Of course, the task of the U.S. permanent representative is now far more difficult, as the Third World country membership in the UN has doubled since the early 1960s and has become better organized and more militant, but it would be an illusion to believe that American policies were automatically accepted in the 1950s. Even then, acceptance required hard work, sensitivity, judicious compromise, and occasional pressure.

At least one experienced observer, Ruth Russell, felt that the United States had worked too hard and expended too much influence in order to win votes on cold war issues.[67]

NOTES

1. Dwight D. Eisenhower, *Mandate for Change* (Garden City, N.Y.: Doubleday, 1963), pp. 84–85.

2. Henry Cabot Lodge, *As It Was: An Inside View of Politics in the 50's and 60's* (New York: Norton, 1976), pp. 46–47.

3. Alfred O. Hero, Jr., "The United States Public and the United Nations," in David A. Kay, *The Changing United Nations,* New York, The Academy of Political Science, 1977, p. 19.

4. Lodge, *As It Was,* p. 56.

5. Eisenhower, *Mandate for Change,* p. 118.

6. William J. Miller, *Henry Cabot Lodge* (New York: Heineman, 1967), pp. 120–24, 130–33, 154–55.

7. Lodge, *As It Was,* pp. 96–97.

8. Robert D. Murphy, *Diplomat Among Warriors* (New York: Doubleday, 1964), pp. 364–68. Henry Cabot Lodge wrote me on March 19, 1980 as follows: "I am sure that I never said that I was not bound by instructions from the State Department. Nor did I ever say, or think, that I did not accept instructions except from the President."

9. Interview with Francis Wilcox in Washington, February 23, 1978.

10. Gladwyn Jebb, *Memoirs*, p. 255.

11. Lodge, *As It Was*, pp. 61-62.

12. Miller, op. cit., pp. 351-53.

13. Ibid., pp. 326-27.

14. Henry Cabot Lodge, *The Storm Has Many Eyes* (New York: Norton, 1973), p. 132.

15. Lodge, *As It Was*, pp. 199-201.

16. Lodge, *The Storm Has Many Eyes*, p. 47.

17. Lawrence Weiler and Anne Simons, *The United States and the United Nations: The Search for International Peace and Security*, (New York: Carnegie Endowment, 1967), pp. 379-95.

18. Miller, op. cit., p. 281.

19. Dwight D. Eisenhower, *Waging Peace* (Garden City, N.Y.: Doubleday, 1965), p. 571.

20. Lodge, *As It Was*, pp. 211-12. In January 1960 Eisenhower had suggested to Nixon as possible vice-president not only Lodge and Morton but also Robert B. Anderson, Charles Halleck, Neil McElroy, John Mitchell, Nelson Rockefeller, and William P. Rogers (Eisenhower, *Waging Peace*), but by the summer the choice had narrowed to Lodge and Morton.

21. Weiler and Simons, op cit., p. 487. Weiler and Simons also describe the fruitless disarmament negotiations that gave rise to Lodge's cynicism, pp. 414-67.

22. Eisenhower, *Mandate for Change*, p. 252.

23. Ibid, p. 253

24. James J. Wadsworth, *The Glass House* (New York: Praeger, 1966), pp. 55-56.

25. Johan Kaufmann, "The Capacity of the U.N. Development Program," *International Organization* (1971): 938-39.

26. ECOSOC Res. 180 (VIII), March 4, 1949.

27. UN Doc. E/2381, March 18, 1953.

28. Robert Asher, *United Nations Economic and Social Cooperation* (Washington, D.C.: Brookings Institution, 1957), p. 487.

29. Lodge, *As It Was*, pp. 196-98, gives the text.

30. Many of these ideas had been incorporated in *A Forward Look*, a document prepared by the U.N. Secretariat looking toward the further development of the Expanded Program of Technical Assistance.

31. For an account of the negotiations from the Dutch and Canadian point of view, see John G. Hadwen and Johan Kaufmann, *How United Nations Decisions Are Made* (Leyden: A. W. Sijthoff, 1960).

32. Total contributions to the UN Capital Development Fund in 1979 were only $24.5 million, most of which was in non-convertible currencies.

33. Lodge, *As It Was*, p. 103. The other three accomplishments listed were: reduction of the U.S. share in the UN budget from $33\frac{1}{3}$ percent to $32\frac{1}{2}$ (it is now 25); defeating a Soviet move to condemn alleged U.S. "masterminding" a threat to the security of Syria; and dealing with the questions of Algeria and Cypress "to the satisfaction of the parties." Compared with the Special Fund, now metamorphosed as the UN Development Program with a budget of over $400 million annually, the latter two were distinctly transitory.

34. Paul G. Hoffman, "Blueprint for Foreign Aid," *New York Times Magazine*, February 17, 1957, p. 9. While advocating an increased UN role in resource surveys and technical assistance, Hoffman also stated: "As a practical matter the preponderant share of our aid program will have to be administered bilaterally, for the Congress of the United States cannot—and should not—give control over a huge sum of our money to any international agency."

35. John G. Stoessinger, *Crusaders and Pragmatists: Movers of Modern American Foreign Policy*, New York, Norton, 1979, pp. 114-24.

36. Eisenhower, *Waging Peace*, p. 83.

37. UN Doc. S/3712, October 29, 1956.

38. UN General Assembly, *Official Records*, first emergency special session, 562d meeting, November 1, 1956, p. 36.

39. UN General Assembly, *Official Records*, 563d meeting, November 3, 1956, pp. 55–71.

40. Dean Acheson, *Power and Diplomacy* (Cambridge, Mass.: Harvard University Press, 1958), pp. 109–16.

41. Lodge, *As It Was*, pp. 93–99.

42. Robert Rhodes James, "International Crises, the Great Powers and the United Nations," *International Journal* (Spring 1970).

43. Eisenhower, *Waging Peace*, p. 188.

44. Endre Marton, *The Forbidden Sky: Inside the Hungarian Revolution*, (Boston: Little, Brown, 1971), pp. 122–44.

45. Anthony Eden, *Full Circle* (London, Allen and Unwin, 1960, p. 286.

46. Marton, op. cit., pp. 291–92.

47. Ibid., p. 203.

48. Eisenhower, *Waging Peace*, pp. 256–57. See also Elmo Richardson, *The Presidency of Dwight D. Eisenhower*, (Lawrence, Kansas: Regents Press of Kansas, 1979), p. 99.

49. Marton, op. cit., p. 291.

50. Brian Urquhart, *Hammarskjöld*, New York, Knopf, 1972, p. 234.

51. G.A. Res. 1132 (XI), January 16, 1957.

52. G.A. Res. 1133 (XII), September 14, 1957.

53. Janos Radvanyi, *Hungary and the Superpowers: The 1956 Revolution* (Stanford, Calif.: Stanford University Press, 1972), concluding chapter.

54. Marton, op cit., pp. 264–67.

55. Murphy, op cit., pp. 396–402. In Lodge, *The Storm Has Many Eyes*, pp. 138–41, Lodge writes that the report that Egypt was involved in Lebanon later proved unfounded but that by that time the action had been taken.

56. Urquhart, op cit., pp. 278–81.

57. Murphy, op. cit., pp. 408–9.

58. Urquhart, op. cit., pp. 336–45. (For a Washington viewpoint see Roger Hilsman, *To Move a Nation* [New York: Doubleday, 1967], pp. 120–21.)

59. See, for example, Ernest W. Lefever, *Crisis in the Congo* (Washington, D.C.: Brookings Institution, 1965); and John G. Stoessinger, *The United Nations and the Superpowers* (New York: Random House, 1965), pp. 76–89.

60. Lefever, op cit., pp. 13–15.

61. Alexander DeConde, *A History of American Foreign Policy*, Vol. II, 3rd Ed., (New York: Scribners, 1978), p. 355.

62. Stoessinger, op. cit., p. 81. Hammarskjöld thought Lumumba had become "a dangerous, unstable man with dictatorial tendencies." Urquhart, op. cit., pp. 505–6.

63. Urquhart, op. cit., pp. 88–94.

64. Ibid., p. 131.

65. Beichman, op. cit., pp. 111–12, based on conversations with Andrew Cordier, former undersecretary general of the United Nations.

66. Gladwyn Jebb, op cit., p. 267.

67. Ruth B. Russell, *The United Nations and United States Security Policy* (Washington, D.C.: Brookings Institution, 1968), pp. 540–41.

CHAPTER V

Adlai Stevenson

In 1961 the United States was riding high at the United Nations. The election of the young, charismatic John F. Kennedy as president evoked waves of enthusiasm not only from American allies but also from the Third World. There were great hopes for a more liberal policy in the UN on southern Africa, economic policies toward the less developed countries, and disarmament. Kennedy's popularity was such that not even the Bay of Pigs debacle made any appreciable impact on the U.S. position at the UN.

Stevenson's appointment as permanent representative added greatly to the luster. Kennedy's choosing a man of such stature and international reputation was taken as a sign of the importance the new president ascribed to the UN. (His first appearance in the Security Council, on February 1, 1961, was greeted by a spontaneous outburst of applause.) In fact, Stevenson was to have less influence on American policy than his predecessor, Lodge, but few members of the UN perceived this in 1961.

The key factor is the relationship with the chief policymaker, the president, and the Kennedy-Stevenson relationship lacked the closeness, personal friendship, and mutual trust that characterized that of Eisenhower and Lodge. Whereas Lodge was important in Eisenhower's successful candidacy and never a rival for it, Stevenson had refused to remove himself firmly from consideration in the 1960 race and had rejected endorsement feelers from the Kennedy campaign staff.[1] Kennedy was also annoyed when Stevenson delayed for a week before accepting the UN post.[2] Stevenson wanted to be secretary of state, but Kennedy told him in late November that he had taken too many public positions on prickly political issues and would in consequence be too controversial for Congress. Given the margin of the election, Kennedy said that he needed most of all a secretary of state who could get along on Capitol Hill. Moreover, Kennedy privately questioned Stevenson's capacity for decision and no doubt also did not want a secretary of state with whom he feared he might not feel personally comfortable.

Finally, with whatever misgivings, Stevenson accepted the job as permanent representative because he found public life more exciting than private law practice, and he had a deep interest in the UN, dating back to its establishment.[3]

Arthur Schlesinger's view of the Kennedy-Stevenson relationship appears to me so perceptive and nuanced that it warrants quotation:

> Kennedy, who had an essential respect and liking for Stevenson, tried, when he thought of it, to make their relationship effective. He understood Stevenson's standing in the world and his influence on liberal opinion in the United States, admired his public presence and wit, valued his skills as diplomat and orator, and considered him, unlike most of the State Department, capable of original thought. . . . Kennedy fully expected, moreover, that people (including some of his own loyalists who still had not forgiven Stevenson for Los Angeles in 1960) would try to make trouble between Adlai and himself, and generally shrugged off the tales helpfully repeated to him of petulance or discontent in New York. On the other hand, certain of Stevenson's idiosyncrasies did try him; and his own effect on Stevenson in face-to-face encounter was unfortunately to heighten those which tried him most. The relationship was of course harder for Stevenson. He was the older man, and in one way or another Kennedy had denied him his highest hopes. Though Stevenson greatly respected the President's intelligence and judgment, he never seemed wholly at ease on visits to the White House. He tended to freeze a little, much as he used to do in the fifties on television shows like the *Meet the Press,* and, instead of the pungent, astute and beguiling man he characteristically was, he would seem stiff, even at times solemn and pedantic.[4]

Although Schlesinger's account shows that Stevenson had some influence in Washington, my own experience at USUN during the period 1956–65 indicates that he did not have the clout with Kennedy that Lodge had with Eisenhower. Schlesinger refers elsewhere to his uncomfortable position as a "middleman" between Kennedy and Stevenson, "two men whom I so much admired but whose own rapport was perhaps less than perfect."[5] Moreover, during Stevenson's tenure far more of the initiatives and initial speech drafts came from Washington.[6] Also, Stevenson hesitated to call the president unless it was absolutely essential;[7] Lodge and Goldberg had no such inhibitions.

Stevenson's relations with the secretary of state were courteous and showed a degree of mutual respect, but there was an underlying tension between them. Stevenson had agreed to take the UN post after Dean Rusk had been nominated as secretary of state; however, he had wanted the secretary's job and considered himself better qualified for it. He respected Rusk's intellect and industry but referred to him as "just a good technician" and too "wooden" at cabinet meetings. Rusk, on his side, had a high regard for Stevenson's performance at the UN, but more as an advocate than as a counsel, though he felt that Stevenson provided "a useful yeast and ferment." Rusk came to New York at the opening of each General Assembly for private talks with foreign ministers present there, as had become the custom, but he never spoke at the Assembly. Although both believed in containment, Stevenson was willing to go further in trying to end the cold war, and this caused some friction. Stevenson chafed at taking instructions from Rusk and in December 1961 tried to obtain a recognized channel to the White House; however, Rusk and Cleveland objected to this approach, and it was not very effective.[8]

THE STEVENSON TEAM—AND ITS LEADER

Stevenson brought in a top layer of aides of unusual competence and distinction. His main political adviser was Ambassador Charles W. Yost, deputy representative to the UN Security Council. Yost had worked with Stevenson in the preparatory and founding stages of the UN, and they had a high regard for each other. A career diplomat of the highest intelligence and integrity, Yost was the "professional's professional." He served as Stevenson's top adviser on political and security issues. Experienced, wise, and articulate, Yost drafted many of the key policy memoranda for Stevenson and was involved in all of them. Like most USUN personnel, he found the post a financial as well as a physical drain. In 1963, at Stevenson's suggestion, William Benton provided $3,000 to supplement Yost's salary. In the same year Kennedy asked Yost to become ambassador to Yugoslavia, a highly interesting and important post with much better pay and perquisites. But Stevenson asked Yost to stay with him, and he did, to Kennedy's surprise and irritation.[9]

As deputy permanent representative Stevenson chose Francis T. P. Plimpton, an old friend and former roommate at Harvard Law School and a liberal Republican. A highly successful lawyer and an intelligent gentleman, Plimpton was in general charge of the mission under Stevenson. He worked hard and effectively at his job and resented the use of the term "working level" to designate those below the rank of ambassador.

Plimpton also entertained foreign diplomats frequently and well, often using his country place on Long Island. Perhaps because of his wealth and distinguished family background, he could not seem to avoid a certain air of condescension toward Third World diplomats, even those he liked. On numerous occasions I heard him refer to the permanent representative of one foreign country or another as "that nice little fellow from ———."

Stevenson, though of similar background, showed no condescension in his manner; however, when he wanted to relax and enjoy life he habitually did so with people of wealth and position. Frequently, too, he asked Plimpton to represent him at the numerous UN social functions that he found boring, a function Plimpton fulfilled conscientiously and well. With his tendency for humorous hyperbole, Stevenson told John B. Martin, "Francis is my oldest friend but he has all the political sex appeal of a dead mouse."[10]

The post of representative to the Economic and Social Council was given new importance by according its new incumbent, Philip M. Klutznick, the rank of ambassador. Klutznick, a dynamic, hard-driving, and highly intelligent lawyer, had made a fortune in real estate development in the Chicago area and had been a supporter of Stevenson's campaigns. Because of his experience, skills, and energy, he was given responsibility not only for economic and social affairs but also for the U.S. interest in the UN's budget and finance activities. He was the principal negotiator of the UN bond issue of 1961, which kept the Congo operation financially afloat. It is indicative of the political affairs bias of most writers in the field that I could find no account of his activities at the UN in existing books except brief references in John B. Martin's two-volume biography of Stevenson.

Klutznick, a lifetime Zionist, had written a book about the Middle East called *No Easy Answers*, then still in galley form. At Stevenson's request, I read the manuscript and wrote him a memorandum about it. In my view, substantial sections of it were so pro-Israel and anti-Arab as to constitute an embarrassment to an American official at the UN. Stevenson, instead of speaking to his friend, Klutznick, on the basis of my memorandum, asked me to meet with him. Since Klutznick was slated to become my new boss, the situation was ticklish. In any case, I gave him my views with complete frankness, seeing no decent alternative. His first reaction was explosive; he said he would rather not take the job than alter the book. On reflection, however, he changed his mind and did revise the manuscript. Interestingly, it was the beginning of an excellent working relationship and friendship between us. (It is ironic that Klutznick, who became president of the World Jewish Congress in 1978, has been criticized by many Israeli hard-liners for his friendly relations with Egypt's President Sadat and his identification in 1976 with a Brookings Institution panel that recommended a comprehensive Middle East settlement. In January 1979 he became the Secretary of Commerce.)

The job of U.S. representative to the UN Trusteeship Council was also raised to the ambassadorial level, made full-time, and given to Jonathan Bingham, a liberal Democrat who is now in Congress. Two longtime personal friends, Marietta Tree, who frequently accompanied him on official and personal trips, and Jane Dick were named representatives to the Commissions on Human Rights and Social Development, respectively. The post of counselor of mission went to Charles Noyes, who had served at

USUN under Warren Austin; his job was mainly coordination, because the high-powered top layer left no room for a counselor with the power and policy impact that James Barco had had under Lodge.

At the staff level USUN was largely a carryover from Lodge. Richard Pedersen headed the political section; Albert Bender, the section dealing with the UN budget, personnel, and organization; and Max Finger, the economic and social section. Clayton Fritchey, a veteran of the newspaper and political worlds and a Stevenson friend since his service in the 1952 campaign, headed the public affairs section, but Frank Carpenter remained as press officer, as did most other personnel in the section.

It was a formidable array of talent but was not always as well managed and led as the staff had been under Lodge or was to be under Goldberg. The very existence of so many stars at the top, all with personal ties to Stevenson, made it more difficult to pull all parts of the staff together. Moreover, Stevenson was not a full-time mission chief. His prominence as a national and world political personality made enormous extracurricular demands on his time, such as correspondence, speaking engagements, meetings, and an important role in the Field and Eleanor Roosevelt Foundations. On top of all that, he led an extremely hectic social life even beyond the already exhausting official social activities involved in UN diplomacy. Perhaps out of frustration—he had a sense of having failed as a husband and a father and as a presidential candidate and of being bypassed on crucial national policy issues—he started eating and drinking far more than he should, bringing on an egg-shaped body that embarrassed him. As a highly sought after bachelor with a well-developed appetite for female company, he was also active as a ladies' man.[11] Unfortunately for his health, he would give up neither his conscience about working hard nor the pleasures of his social life and the comfort of lady friends. He was also plagued by a burdensome ex-wife; he often had to be concerned about her actions while also serving as the responsible parent for their sons. Furthermore, his deep and instinctive courtesy caused him to see far more people than was prudent, given the other priorities and demands on his time. He also kept up a prolific personal correspondence.

This indecisiveness plagued Stevenson in other ways. One biographer refers to him as "a bundle of unreconciled and unresolved contradictions."[12] Another, Martin, relates a sarcastic comment by Stevenson's wife in a letter replying to one of his: "I am very much impressed by your two bathrooms. How long does it take you to decide which one to use?"[13] Part of his difficulty in making up his mind on political issues arose from his excellent habit of looking at all sides of a problem rather than take a position prematurely. But the fact that he was beset by second thoughts and self-doubts was clear to his staff in his UN days, and this was a less laudable obstacle to decisiveness.

Another problem was cited by Lord Caradon, the former British permanent representative and a man of wide experience and objectivity, who thought that Stevenson was too fastidious for the ferocity and dirtiness of international negotiations. I can recall cringing for Stevenson when the Soviet representative, the sarcastic Nikolai Fedorenko, would attack him personally while Stevenson was too much of a gentleman to respond. I hated Fedorenko for it. Arthur Goldberg, accustomed to the rough and tumble of labor politics, had no trouble dealing with Fedorenko. (Stevenson was temperamentally disinclined toward personal animosities, but there was one public figure he loathed and despised—Richard Nixon, whom he considered sly, slippery, and thoroughly unprincipled.)[14]

Also, because of his self-doubts, Stevenson did not fight hard and aggressively in Washington on policy issues. With a president attuned to decisive action, surrounded by self-assured, assertive advisers such as McGeorge Bundy, Robert McNamara, and Walt Rostow, Stevenson might weigh in on policy, but his influence was rarely decisive. As has been noted, he simply did not have the clout that Lodge had with Eisenhower or Goldberg had in his first year and a half with Johnson.[15]

According to Arthur Schlesinger, 70 percent of the problem was a function of simply not being in the room when policy was being made in Washington. Thirty percent was that even when he was in the room Stevenson was not quite putting a legitimate point in a framework that would relate to the machine of government. "Stevenson had against him the whole apparatus of the Department of State except for Harlan Cleveland intermittently."[16]

John B. Martin quotes Stevenson's longtime, close friend George Ball, as follows:

After the Cuban missile crisis [1962] Adlai was only going through the motions. His role had become ritualistic. From then on he knew he was not going to have an impact on foreign policy—which was what was most important to him. Washington was a force of its own and he was not part of it. He was a member of the Cabinet but not really. He'd call me up and say, "I can't change anybody's view. The President is being misled and getting bad advice." But he didn't think for a minute that anything he said was going to change anything. It was an unhappy life, certainly not his finest hour. I loved Adlai but by the time he died I felt he was almost a caricature of himself—a hollow man. He was going through the motions, making speeches, yet with a feeling in his heart that it didn't make any difference to the world if he fell over and had a heart attack. I found it unattractive and terribly sad. Why should he spend his time with Marietta Tree and Ruth Field and Mary Lasker? They gave him adulation—they gave him the best food in New York—he went to every first night—it was an unhealthy business. So then he finally fell over and died. Ten days before he died, he had lunch with Rusk. I joined them for coffee. I said to him "Stevenson, you're so fat you're a slug." He patted his stomach. Rusk was paying no attention to him that day. Adlai was a terribly unhappy man. History had passed him by. His life had passed him by. He had no place to go. He talked about leaving the U.N. but had no place to go.

Martin then comments that Ball was "to some extent employing hyperbole. Stevenson probably realized much earlier, perhaps as early as the Bay of Pigs, that he would not exert decisive influence on much of policy. He continued to try, however. The defeatist mood that Ball was describing did not dominate until the last half year or so of his life."[17] Yet there was, for example, a notable difference between Ball's forthright opposition to American involvement in Vietnam and Stevenson's soul-searching, hesitating doubts about the intervention.

Stevenson was also deeply disappointed at being shut out of disarmament negotiations by both Kennedy and Johnson. He had proposed a nuclear test ban treaty in 1956, the first major American politician to do so, yet he had no significant role in negotiating the partial test ban treaty endorsed by the UN General Assembly in 1963.[18]

But there was also a strong positive side. Stevenson did have standing in the world, public presence, wit, an original mind, and great skills as a diplomat and orator, all of which Kennedy appreciated. He was also unusually decent and charming and had extraordinary energy. He genuinely believed in disarmament, the UN, relaxation of tension with the Soviets and assisting the development efforts of the poorer countries as a way of building peace and stability. In crises at the UN, notably in the Cuban Missile Crisis and the Congo crisis, he displayed an iron nerve and performed superbly. He was highly popular among other delegates, including those of the Third World. Achkar Marof of Guinea expressed a widespread feeling when he commented: "When I heard he died my feelings were exactly as if World War III had broken out. He was so identified with peace. I thought, who's going to succeed him? Who's going to exercise a moderating influence?"[19] And Arthur Goldberg told several of us at USUN that he would not have considered leaving the Supreme Court if a man of Stevenson's stature had not been the permanent representative before him.

Moreover, Martin notes, "his words at the U.N. moved millions, advanced the American interest, and strengthened the United Nations. Indeed, herein may have lain his greatest contribution. He did not enlarge the role of U.S. Ambassador to the UN, because he could not. But he did play another role, and in the long run perhaps a more important one; that of unofficial UN Ambassador to the United States."[20] And Robert Kennedy said:

President Kennedy always thought he did a good job of keeping people happy at the UN. He did not make mistakes. He represented in an articulate way the United States in foreign eyes as well as could be. He was the best Ambassador we could have had there.[21]

THE CONGO

Stevenson's first test came within weeks of his arrival at USUN, with a resurgence of the Congo crisis. Patrice Lumumba, the former prime minister, had been placed under house arrest by General Mobutu, who led the coup in September 1960. In November he escaped from Leopoldville, where he had been under UN protection, to join his leftist supporters in Stanleyville, but was recaptured by Mobutu's troops four days later. In January 1961 Mobutu turned Lumumba over to the Katanga regime, and on February 13 Katanga radio announced that Lumumba had been killed in an attempted escape the day before. (A UN commission investigating the matter reported on November 11, 1961, that Lumumba had in fact been executed.) In the meantime, Lumumba's lieutenant, Antoine Gizenga, had established a regime in Stanleyville that was recognized by the Soviet bloc and several of the more militant African states: The United Arab Republic, Ghana, Guinea, Mali, and Morocco.[22]

With civil war threatening, the Security Council met and on February 21 passed its strongest resolution to date, by a vote of 9 to 0, with France and the Soviet Union abstaining.[23] The prices paid to the various blocs among the UN membership were apparent in the provisions of the resolution—that Belgian and other military and paramilitary personnel be withdrawn, which was aimed directly at Tshombe's mercenaries; that the Congo parliament, in which Gizenga and the Lumumbist "radicals" could on most issues muster enough allies to command a majority, be convened; that the Congolese army be recognized; and finally that the UN should take "all appropriate measures" to prevent the occurrence of civil war and that these appropriate measures should include not only arranging for cease-fires, the halting of military operations, and the prevention of clashes, but also "the use of force if necessary in the last resort."

In any case, Stevenson did not have to fight Washington on this issue. Kennedy, like Eisenhower, was convinced that "if we didn't have the U.N. operation, the only way to block Soviet domination in the Congo would be to go in with our own forces."[24] Stevenson himself told the Security Council on February 15, 1961, that "the only way to keep the Cold War out of the Congo is to keep the U.N. in the Congo."[25] Strong support for this policy came not only from the president and Stevenson but also from the influential assistant secretary of state for African affairs, Mennen Williams and his deputy, Wayne Fredericks, as well as from Harlan Cleveland, the capable and supportive assistant secretary for international organization affairs, and Stevenson's old friend, Undersecretary of State George Ball.[26]

Efforts to terminate the civil war by negotiations with the Katanga regime proved fruitless; its secession was finally ended through military action in 1963, the UN Force acting in "self-defense," on the grounds that the Katanga troops were interfering with its communications lines. Negotiations between Leopoldville and the Stanleyville regime in 1961 were, however, successful. Under UN aegis, the Congolese parliamentarians, meeting in accordance with the Security Council resolution of February 21, 1961, reached agreement. On August 1 they selected as premier Cyrille Adoula, a moderate like President Kasavubu who had been a friend of Patrice Lumumba's, although he had a different political outlook. Antoine Gizenga, who had inherited Lumumba's mantle as leader of the leftist group in Stanleyville, was chosen as vice premier.[27] This parliamentary agreement was a brilliant success for UN "Good Offices."

After November 1961 there was little active consideration of the Congo in the Security Council, even though the operation continued for three more years.[28] As a result, the secretaries general, Hammarskjöld and U Thant, had to interpret existing instructions and work out procedures to deal with a situation that was always complex and often changed rapidly. That they remained true to the spirit of the resolutions and the UN Charter, despite tremendous political pressures (e.g., Khrushchev's attack on Hammarskjöld in 1960 and his call on the secretary general to resign), is a tribute to their integrity, impartiality, and political skills. Each kept abreast of the prevailing political currents at the UN, consulting the Congo Advisory Committee, composed of representatives of the countries contributing troops for the force, as well as a "Congo Club" of top Secretariat officials.[29]

The main axis of support for the secretary general consisted of the United States, India, and key African states. As Lefever notes, "India and the United States were the two countries the U.N. operation most depended upon, both for political support in New York and for military support in the Congo. Despite some differences in interpreting the mandate, the United States—India partnership remained solid throughout the Congo drama. The Congo operation would probably have collapsed if either New Delhi or Washington had withdrawn its support before the integration of Katanga in January 1963,"[30] This is particularly noteworthy, since India and the United States were so frequently at odds on other issues at the UN. India was the principal contributor of troops and military leadership during the crucial Katanga operation. The United States, like other major powers, did not contribute troops, but it was the mainstay for logistic, financial, and economic support. In New York, Stevenson met frequently with the secretary general and with other USUN personnel who were in almost daily contact with Undersecretary General Ralph Bunche and other UN officials concerned with the operation. The military officers at USUN performed a liaison function with the Defense Department in Washington in processing UN requests for logistical support and supplies, working closely with political officers at USUN and the State Department.

Thus, the United States was influential with both Hammarskjöld and Thant in carrying out the operation; however, its influence with them arose not so much from its logistical and financial support as from the fact that the American interest in stability in the Congo and a constitutional solution to the internal conflict there corresponded to a remarkable degree with the central objectives of the UN effort. Good personal relationships between USUN and Secretariat personnel, particularly Stevenson with Thant, made the cooperation smoother and more effective, but the decisive factor was the compatibility of interest.[31]

The UN Operation in the Congo ended in June 1964; however, the UN's civilian operation continued. Begun in 1960, this operation aimed to keep intact transport and communications; to sustain a decent level of public health; to further education and public administration; and to develop industry and agriculture. It was financed largely from the UN Congo Fund, made up of voluntary contributions from twenty governments. The United States at first contributed about three fourths and later about half of the total; the Soviet Union made no contribution.

Much more serious was the refusal of the Soviet Union, its satellites, and France to pay their share of the expenses of the UN Force in the Congo (discussed later in this chapter).

THE BAY OF PIGS

"The integrity and credibility of Adlai Stevenson," President Kennedy told Arthur Schlesinger on April 7, 1961, "constitute one of our great national assets. I don't want anything to be done which might jeopardize that."[31] Like the rest of the Bay of Pigs fiasco, this Kennedy aim went awry.

In New York, Adlai Stevenson was getting ready for a General Assembly debate of a Cuban charge that the United States had aggressive intentions against Cuba. Schlesinger briefed Stevenson on the invasion plans but left him with the impression that no action would take place during the UN discussion of the Cuban item. Stevenson wholly disapproved of the plan, regretted that he had been given no opportunity to comment on it, and believed that it would cause infinite trouble. But, if it was national policy, he was prepared to make out the best possible case.

After the Saturday (April 15) air strike, Paul Roa, the Cuban foreign minister, succeeded in advancing the Cuban item, scheduled for the following Monday, to an emergency session of the UN Political Committee that afternoon. In Washington, Harlan Cleveland tried to ascertain the facts about the strike. His office called the Bureau of Inter-American affairs, which in turn called the CIA. Word promptly and definitely came back that it was the work of genuine defectors, and Cleveland passed this information on to Stevenson. A few moments later Stevenson told the UN: "These two planes, to the best of our knowledge, were Castro's own air force planes and, according to the pilots, they took off from Castro's own air force fields."

Unfortunately, the CIA had not been truthful with the concerned bureaus of the State Department. Rusk, remorseful at the position into which State had thrust its UN ambassador, now resolved that the Cuban adventure should not be permitted further to jeopardize the larger interests of U.S. foreign policy.

The collapse of the cover story brought the question of the second air strike into new focus. The president and the secretary understood this strike as one that would take place simultaneously with the landings and have the appearance of coming from the airstrip on the beach. It had slid by in the briefings, everyone assuming that it would be masked by the cover story. But there could be no easy attribution to defectors now. Nor did the fact that planes were B-26s flown by Cuban pilots save the situation; despite the great to-do about "Cubanizing" the operation, they would still be U.S. planes in the eyes of the UN. Rusk, after his talks with Stevenson, concluded that a second Nicaraguan strike would put the United States in an untenable position internationally and that no further strikes should be launched until the planes could fly (or appear to fly) from the beachhead. Bundy agreed, and they called the president, who directed that the second air strike be canceled.[33]

The Bay of Pigs invasion was, of course, a disaster. Kennedy's decision against further air strikes was not based solely on a desire to avoid additional embarrassment for Stevenson at the UN; it was determined in the light of worldwide American interests and the intangible but important value of world opinion. It had also become clear that, with or without air cover, the invasion was doomed to failure. Yet the role of the UN as a mirror of world reaction and Stevenson's acute discomfiture were factors in Kennedy's decision to avoid further action that would compound the error.

Surprisingly, the standing of both Stevenson and the United States at the UN recovered quickly. It was generally perceived that Stevenson had not deliberately lied but had himself been duped, and there was much sympathy for him. As for the American standing, the United States was perceived to have stumbled but not to have embarked on a generally malign course in the world. It was not yet seriously involved in Vietnam and had a record of support for most majority objectives in the UN, such as economic development and the UN Operation in the Congo. Even on colonial issues the United States was considered to be a potential moderating influence on the European colonial powers. At the fall 1961 session of the UN General Assembly, Kennedy's address was received with great enthusiasm and Stevenson's prestige was high.[34] Indeed, in my fifteen sessions at the UN General Assembly, 1956–70, I cannot recall any other time that U.S. prestige was riding as high as in 1961—nor, as an observer, have I witnessed any since 1970.

THE CUBAN MISSILE CRISIS

The next crisis found Stevenson both fully informed and functioning as a key member of the Kennedy team, in sharp contrast with his role in the Bay of Pigs fiasco.

By September 1962 the United States was aware that Soviet aid to Cuba included surface-to-air missiles, but Washington thought they were essentially defensive and not threatening to American security. By October 15, however, air and sea surveillance revealed evidence of a secret buildup of sites for offensive nuclear missiles capable of reaching targets in the United States and most of the Western Hemisphere.

Since the missiles had not been fully emplaced, time was of the essence, and the exploration of alternative responses went on feverishly. The president worked with an ad hoc Executive Committee that included Stevenson.[35] The main alternatives that emerged were an air strike against the missile sites or a "quarantine" against Soviet shipments of military and related supplies. Attorney General Robert Kennedy, the president's brother, passionately opposed an air strike as a "Pearl Harbor in reverse."[36] Stevenson also opposed an air strike and agreed on the quarantine. By October 19 the president and the Executive Committee decided on it.

During the Executive Committee's discussion of alternatives, Stevenson emphasized the importance of diplomatic measures along with the quarantine. In this vein he suggested the possibility of a demilitarized, neutralized Cuba whose territorial integrity we would join in guaranteeing through the UN. This would have meant giving up the U.S. base at Guantánamo, but it would also have meant removal of the Soviet military presence from Cuba. He also suggested that the United States might agree to give up its Jupiter missile bases in Italy and Turkey. In 1961 the secretary of defense had urged removal of these bases on the grounds that they were obsolescent and vulnerable.[37]

The president, however, regarded any such political program as premature; he wanted to concentrate on a single issue—the removal of the Soviet missiles. Nevertheless, some of Stevenson's tactical advice was followed. For example, the president postponed his address announcing the quarantine to the nation from Sunday, October 21, to Monday evening in order to inform the members of the Organization of American States (OAS) of the action before it was under way. Kennedy also agreed to Stevenson's suggestion that the United States call for an emergency meeting of the UN Security Council.

When the Security Council met on October 23, Stevenson was able to announce that the OAS had just adopted, with 19 affirmative votes, a resolution calling for the immediate dismantling and withdrawal from Cuba of all missiles and other weapons with any offensive capability and recommending that member states take measures individually and collectively, including the use of armed forces that they might deem necessary, to insure that the government of Cuba could not continue to receive from the "Sino-Soviet power" military material and related supplies that could threaten the peace and security of the continent.[38] This endorsement of the U.S. quarantine was, of course, a substantial plus for the American political position.

Stevenson's suggestions for a possible trade-off of bases led some members of the Executive Committee to consider him too "soft." Accordingly, John McCloy, a Republican veteran of arms control negotiations, was added to the delegation, and he assisted Stevenson in the negotiations with the Soviets and U Thant into the spring of 1963.

As far as the presentation of the U.S. case was concerned, the hard-liners had no cause for concern. Stevenson was at his eloquent best in explaining the U.S. actions and in his indictment of Soviet aggression and duplicity.[39]

At the October 23 session, draft resolutions—by the United States on the one hand and by the Soviet Union and Cuba on the other—each condemned, and demanded the revocation of, the actions of the opposite party. Both drafts also, and significantly, urged the Council to call on the parties to enter into negotiations to "remove the existing threat" to peace or to "reestablish a normal situation." They were, in short, seeking a means of escape from an apparently closed situation. The Security Council members provided one by hearing the parties and then adjourning without voting on any resolution. This allowed the start of direct negotiations by the Soviet and American delegates under the Council's aegis and in consultation with U Thant.

On October 24 the secretary general appealed to both Kennedy and Khrushchev to refrain from aggravating the situation. To facilitate negotiations, he proposed the voluntary suspension of Soviet shipments, of American quarantine measures, and of Cuban construction of installations. The president declared, however, that only removal of the weapons causing the crisis could bring about a peaceful solution.

The secretary general then proposed, on October 25, that, to permit discussions, Soviet ships should stay away from the announced interception areas for the next few days and that U.S. vessels should avoid direct confrontation with Soviet ships. On October 26 the Soviet premier told U Thant that he had so ordered the Soviet ships; and the president, that American vessels would do everything possible to avoid confrontation if the ships stayed away. Work on the missile sites continued to aggravate the situation. Between October 26 and October 28, a number of messages crisscrossed between president and premier. The end result was an undertaking by Khrushchev to dismantle the offending weapons and return them to the Soviet Union, subject to UN verification; and by Kennedy that, if these commitments were implemented and no further weapons introduced (subject to verification), he would lift the quarantine and give assurances against any invasion.

It is important to put the role of the UN and Stevenson in perspective. The crucial factors in resolving the crisis were the American military superiority at that time, particularly in nuclear missiles and in the Caribbean area (by contrast, a U.S. military action against Soviet intervention in Hungary in 1956 would have been infinitely more complex and risky); the choice of a tactic, quarantine, that allowed time for the Kremlin to reflect on the situation and retreat with some face saving; and Khrushchev's willingness to back down rather than risk a nuclear holocaust.

The crucial negotiations were bilateral between Washington and Moscow, yet the UN made a significant ancillary contribution to U.S. policy objectives. Stevenson observed in a statement to the Senate Committee on Foreign Relations that the UN had been useful in the following ways: (1) it provided a world forum; (2) the secretary general's intervention on October 25 led to the diversion of Soviet ships that had been headed for Cuba and interception by the U.S. Navy—"an indispensable first step in the peaceful resolution of the Cuban crisis"; (3) the UN was the site of negotiations between the Soviets and Stevenson and McCloy; (4) the secretary general's offer to assure removal of the missiles by UN inspection was accepted by the Soviet Union and the United States; unfortunately, it was rejected by Castro, and the United States had to use its own means of verification.[40]

Ruth Russell points out that "the obvious role of the United Nations as a forum was useful in rallying the moral support of other governments in favor of peaceful settlement; and that its somewhat less obvious role, operating especially through the Secretary-General, was even more useful in allowing the nuclear dialogue to be reopened without either side appearing to concede its case.[41]

With the world poised on the brink of nuclear war, even these ancillary contributions must be considered of substantial value. As for Stevenson himself, the decision on what action to take in all likelihood would have been the same whether or not he had been involved in the Executive Committee. Where he did make an important contribution was in improving the American public posture, both by advising Kennedy on timing and procedures after the quarantine decision had been made and by his brilliant performance in the Security Council.

Ironically, Stevenson, who had performed admirably, was to suffer severe embarrassment about his alleged "softness." The incident is described as follows by a Stevenson biographer, Bert Cochran:

> In early December 1962 the *Saturday Evening Post* published an article by Stewart Alsop and Charles Bartlett purporting to disclose what went on inside the government during the crisis. The two authors, who obviously had received inside information, made the sensational charge that Stevenson was the lone dissenter from the crucial decision reached. They quoted an unnamed official as saying, "Adlai wanted another Munich. He wanted to trade Turkish, Italian and British missile bases for the Cuban bases." It also stated that "tough-minded" John McCloy had been assigned to work with Stevenson in the negotiations with the Russians at the UN because Stevenson was too weak to be entrusted with the responsibility.

> The article naturally made headlines and was the talk of the corridors for weeks thereafter. It was generally assumed that the White House had collaborated in supplying the information, and that the President was trying to force Stevenson's resignation. Newspapermen recalled that a previous Bartlett story had presaged the removal of Chester Bowles from the State Department. This interpretation was given further credence when Pierre Salinger, the White House press secretary, in response to inquiries, put out a statement that loftily acknowledged that Stevenson had "strongly supported the decision taken by the President," but left unanswered the accusation that Stevenson had opposed the otherwise unanimous decision and had advocated another Munich. Stevenson dealt with the article in a television interview. *He said it was "wrong in literally every detail" and that he had supported the idea of a blockade days before the decision was made* (Italics mine). "What the article doesn't say is that I opposed an invasion of Cuba at the risk of nuclear war until the peace-keeping machinery of the United Nations had been used." He was disturbed by the President's failure to back him up. He told Schlesinger, who was serving as the mediator between them, that Kennedy need not have been so "circuitous" if he wanted him to resign. When Schlesinger related this, Kennedy hotly denied that he had any such wish and said he would regard Stevenson's resignation "as a disaster." He explained that "from a realistic political viewpoint, it is better for me to have

Adlai in the government than out." It is possible that the press attack was meant to cut Stevenson down to size rather than to force him out.

By this time it had become clear that the intrigue to ruin him was backfiring, and was more damaging to the President's image than to the Ambassador's prestige. Kennedy had to make repeated statements expressing his confidence in Stevenson, culminating in the release of a laudatory personal letter. "The reaction was so intense and so strongly in Mr. Stevenson's favor," commented *The New York Times,* "that the President had to keep him on, even if he had wanted otherwise.[12]

Even so, the incident hardly indicates any real closeness between Kennedy and Stevenson.

As Cochran notes, Stevenson was not against the cold war or standing up to the Soviets when the situation demanded it. His differences with hard-liners in Washington were largely over tactics.[43] He did advocate greater flexibility in our relations with Moscow and Peking, raising questions over how long we should try to bar the latter from a seat at the UN. Kennedy shared Stevenson's desire for greater flexibility. In his first year in office Kennedy thought it would be useful for Australia and the United Kingdom to float a two-China resolution in the UN General Assembly, but domestic American politics made it difficult for the United States to move. Instead, a tactical device was adopted, obtaining a General Assembly decision that any substantive decision to change the representation of China was an important question requiring a two-thirds majority. This tactical maneuver, designed to gain a year until circumstances became more propitious, actually protected Taiwan's sole occupancy of the China seat for a decade.

STEVENSON, LYNDON JOHNSON, AND VIETNAM

After Kennedy's death, President Lyndon Johnson was effusive in welcoming Stevenson into the new administration. He said he knew that the late president had not been consulting him but said that was going to be changed. He also told Stevenson he wanted him to play a large role in the formation of policy.[44]

At first relations were better. Johnson was of the same generation and, Stevenson thought, understood him better. Stevenson applauded Johnson's choice of Humphrey as a running mate. But Johnson in fact turned out to be less interested in the UN than Kennedy had been. Stevenson soon found that he was having considerably less effective influence on policy than he had before, for all of Johnson's repeated expressions of admiration and need of him. Schlesinger observed: "It turned out that he was in worse shape with Johnson than he had been with Kennedy because Rusk quickly got more power," a judgment concurred in by Harlan Cleveland and supported by my own impressions at USUN. As Johnson became increasingly preoccupied with Vietnam, he relied more and more on Rusk, McNamara, and Bundy, his inner circle.[45] U Thant described Johnson's judgment of Stevenson as follows: "he had no sense of correct judgment of public opinion; his evaluation of events, both domestic and foreign, usually turned out to be incorrect. In the President's opinion, Mr. Stevenson was just an idealist with his head in the clouds." Stevenson himself noted that, though Johnson continued to urge him to stay on, he had little opportunity for close personal relationships or "low down" quiet talks with the President.[46]

The two men were quite different in background and style. Johnson considered Stevenson an effete aristocrat, and Stevenson thought Johnson's style was "cornpone." Also, Stevenson was disturbed over the American intervention in the Dominican Republic in 1965. But the most serious problem for their relationship was Vietnam.

Stevenson did not oppose U.S. intervention in Vietnam. He considered it part of the overall policy to contain communist expansion, which, in common with most postwar liberal Democrats, he supported. In the Security Council meetings of August 1964 he called the Tonkin Gulf incident "a planned, deliberate aggression against vessels in international waters" and assured the Council that the United States wanted "no wider war." The Council meetings were inconclusive, in part because Hanoi refused to participate despite the fact that the United States had raised no objection when the Soviets proposed that they be invited.

Stevenson agreed with Johnson and his Rusk-McNamara-Bundy triumvirate that Hanoi should be prevented from taking over South Vietnam by force. His chief and often agonizing difference with them was over the desirability and feasibility of a negotiated settlement. After the Tonkin Gulf incident Stevenson agreed that the United States should first increase its military efforts in South Vietnam to "give clear evidence of our firm purpose," then go to the UN Security Council and ask for a UN observer group to report on "infiltrations" and ways of enforcing the 1954 Geneva accords. Johnson had little faith in getting much from the Security Council, given the fact that the Soviets and the French were opposed to its taking action on Vietnam. The UN secretary general apparently felt the same way; on February 12, 1965, Stevenson reported that Thant urged reconvening the Geneva Conference parties to the 1954 agreements.[47] Replies from Washington made it clear that the United States was not then ready to go to such a conference.

Stevenson felt even more frustrated that, in his view, Washington had deliberately neglected chances for direct negotiations sought by the secretary general. U Thant first suggested to Secretary Rusk secret meetings between U.S. and Hanoi representatives, then sounded out Hanoi via the Soviets. According to Thant, Hanoi agreed within three weeks. Stevenson, after consulting Washington, told Thant nothing could be done until after the U.S. elections. Five months passed with no response from Washington. Then Stevenson, on his own initiative on January 18, 1965, saw Thant again. Stevenson then informed Washington that, according to Thant, all arrangements were completed for an ambassadorial-level meeting in Rangoon, pending U.S. concurrence and the naming of an emissary. On January 28 Washington declined on the grounds that holding such bilateral talks would cause the fall of the Saigon government and that the United States doubted Hanoi really wanted the talks. This angered Thant and bothered Stevenson.[48]

Washington's objections cannot be dismissed lightly. It is a tricky business to negotiate with the enemy of one's ally without the presence of the ally. And although U Thant was an honest man of goodwill (I knew him for ten years and some of his close associates even longer), it is far from certain that he had a clear commitment from Hanoi. Rusk was skeptical because Thant apparently did not know that Washington was providing secret large-scale aid to the government of Burma in its fight against communist rebels and could get corroborative information from that government about any proposed meetings in its capital if they were for real.[49] Moreover, Washington had seen the latest report of Blair Seborn, Canadian member of the International Control Commission in Vietnam, indicating that Hanoi was not prepared for serious talks to end its involvement in South Vietnam. Indeed Hanoi later denied that it had suggested any negotiations to Thant.[50] And on April 4, 1965, Thant told the United States he had received a message from Peking through the Algerians that the UN should not become involved in Southeast Asia and that Peking had no interest in a visit by Thant. Hanoi had also sent word that Thant would not be welcome there.[51]

In any case, in January 1965 Thant had disclosed that the source of his report that Hanoi would be prepared to carry out bilateral negotiations in Rangoon was a Russian agent. At the time neither the Soviet ambassador to the United States nor the Soviet representative to the UN knew about the maneuver, another factor in undermining the credibility of the report. Martin observes: "In addition Rusk—and probably Johnson as well— seems to have taken the general view that Thant was soft, wobbly and imprecise and to have lacked wholehearted confidence in him as an intermediary." Martin also provides a brief compendium of insiders' interpretations that indicate why Thant's initiative gained so little credence with the president and his top advisers. Moreover, there were many other efforts to arrange negotiations at the time, and Johnson did not like "negotiating from weakness."[52]

Unfortunately, Thant made numerous public statements about Vietnam that annoyed Washington, especially Rusk; as a result, Washington had little confidence in him. Thant might have been more successful in his efforts if he had emulated the public discrection combined with private negotiations that Hammarskjöld had used, for example, in securing the release of the American fliers from Peking. Undoubtedly the public utterance that jarred Johnson and Rusk the most was Thant's February 12, 1965, statement that the American people were not being given the "true facts" about Vietnam. It is now clear that Thant was right, but the statement was not the kind a secretary general should make in public when he wants the cooperation of the government concerned.

Along with his frustration over the failure of Thant's efforts to bring about negotiations, Stevenson was deeply disturbed about America's continued large-scale bombing of North Vietnam. Johnson ordered the sustained bombing in mid-February 1965, and it continued, with a week's pause in December 1965 and January 1966, throughout Johnson's term. (There had also been a strike against Hanoi in early February 1965, while Soviet Premier Kosygin was there, in retaliation for a Viet Cong attack on U.S. barracks in Pleiku—an action not likely to encourage Soviet help in bringing about a negotiated settlement.) Stevenson believed, as did Thant, that the bombings would harden Hanoi's resistance to negotiations.

Although Stevenson was deeply disturbed by the bombings and ardently sought negotiations for peace, there is no evidence that he disagreed with the basic American policy for preventing Hanoi from taking over South Vietnam by force. On June 21, 1965, a few weeks before his death, Stevenson met at USUN with a group of intellectuals who urged him to resign in protest against the U.S. policy in Vietnam. On this issue, as on many others, he saw both sides of the question, agonized over the consequences of each, and was profoundly disturbed when individuals whom he respected disagreed with him on an important issue, but he did not accept his critics' viewpoint. In a letter to one of the group, Paul Goodman drafted in Libertyville over the July 4 weekend but never mailed, he wrote: "Whatever criticisms can be made over the details and emphasis of American foreign policy, its purpose and direction are sound." He went on to urge that there should be no attempt to change the tacitly agreed East-West frontiers by force (containment) and that one should move from this position of precarious stability toward agreed international procedures for settling differences, building an international juridical and policing system, and working toward a genuine economic and social community. He stressed the need to check "Chinese expansionism." He believed in a negotiated peace based on the internationalization of the whole area's security and argued that a retreat in Asia or anywhere else would not help to move toward this ideal.[53]

Stevenson expressed the same viewpoint on BBC television on July 10,

1965, two days before his death. With respect to Vietnam, he said: "As we did in Europe, we shall have to draw a line between the Communist and non-Communist world areas so that neither power system can force a change by force."[54] Shortly before that he had written his son, Adlai III, about the many people who had urged him to resign in protest against the administration's Vietnam policy; he resented their assumption that he disagreed with the policy. Further, even if he did disagree, it was by no means certain that the most effective act was resignation; it might be better to stay and try to influence policy.

Stevenson, while accepting the doctrine that North Vietnam must be prevented from taking over South Vietnam by force, even at the cost of United States military intervention, differed with the President on the policy of military escalation. He argued that escalation carried more risk of worsening the situation than of persuading Hanoi to compromise. He thought that talks would be less risky than military escalation, even though Hanoi had given no indication that it would settle for anything less than control over all of Vietnam. He was proved right about the risks of military escalation; however, by June 11, 1965, he had concluded that "Peking and Hanoi are not interested in a peaceful solution as long as there is a prospect of winning by a military decision."[55]

With hindsight it is clear that the fundamental error was the tragic misperception by American policy makers of the true relationship between the Chinese and Vietnamese. A unified, Communist Vietnam has not become an instrument of Chinese aggression that would topple dominoes in Thailand, Malaysia, Singapore, Indonesia and the Philippines, as the U.S. feared in the 60's. On the contrary, China and Vietnam now pursue mutually hostile policies and even fought an undeclared war in 1979. It is evident that a Communist regime in all of Vietnam, or even all of Indochina, while bringing massive suffering and gross human rights violations to the people there, does not constitute a threat to American security—the only kind of threat that could have justified such a massive intervention.

Another tragic irony is the fact that Lyndon Johnson, who had opposed American military involvement in Vietnam when he was Senate Majority Leader, was the President who ordered the bombing and increased American troop strength in Vietnam from 16,000 to over 500,000. Johnson became convinced that, whether it was right or wrong to plant the American flag in Vietnam, the United States could not afford to lose face and credibility by leaving as a loser. As a result he took steps that cost tens of thousands of lives and spent over $150 billion that could have financed his War on Poverty and that fueled disastrous inflation. The costs of the American economy and social structure were enormous and are still being paid. The losses in international standing and moral position in the world are difficult to calculate but certainly substantial.

THE DOMINICAN CRISIS

Stevenson was disturbed by the U.S.-OAS intervention in the Dominican Republic in the spring of 1965, shortly before his death. He did not object to sending in a small detachment of marines to protect American citizens caught in the swirl of a civil war, but he was dismayed as the size of the force grew to 20,000 and President Johnson announced that the troops were there to prevent "another Cuba." Still, Stevenson himself, on instructions from Washington, stated in the Security Council: "The American nations will not permit the establishment of another Communist government in the Western Hemisphere,"[56] the essence of what has come to be known as the Johnson doctrine.

According to Eric Severeid, reporting on a conversation with Stevenson shortly before his death, Stevenson's objection may have been tactical. He reportedly asked Severeid: "Couldn't the President have waited, say three days so we could round up more Latin American support?" Stevenson also questioned the size of the force but apparently accepted Severeid's explanation of the need for it in view of the size of the barrier to be policed between the two fighting forces.[57]

Stevenson was also concerned about the precedent set for other regional organizations when the intervention became an OAS operation, a concern prompted by the UN secretary general's attitude. U Thant said: "If a particular regional organization under the terms of its own constitution, deems it fit to take certain enforcement action in its own region, it naturally follows that other regional organizations should be considered competent, because of the precedent, to take certain enforcement action within their own regions."[58] Thant specifically mentioned the Organization of African Unity and the League of Arab States; however, the next action came from another regional group, the Warsaw Pact, in 1968. An interesting parallel has been drawn between the Johnson doctrine, justifying the 1965 OAS action in the Dominican Republic, and the Brezhnev doctrine, which explained the August 1968 invasion of Czechoslovakia by the Soviet Union on the grounds that fellow socialist states had a right to protect another socialist state against counterrevolution.[59]

In the Dominican case the Soviet Union promptly brought the issue to the UN Security Council, condemning Washington's "armed intervention" as a violation of the Charter. It demanded immediate withdrawal of United States forces and denounced the Inter-American Force as illegal.

The crucial question was whether the action constituted enforcement action that, according to Article 53, would require prior authorization by the Security Council. Stevenson argued that the Inter-American Force was not aimed "at asserting any authority to govern any part of the Dominican Republic but were intended to preserve for the people . . . their right to choose their own government free of outside interference."[60] Thus, he contended, the OAS fell under Article 52, as appropriate regional action for the maintenance of international peace and security, and did not require prior Council approval.

The United States at first argued against any UN action, on the ground that it would complicate OAS activities. Uruguay, which had voted against the force in the OAS—where the United States had barely mustered the necessary two-thirds majority—worked in the Security Council for a compromise that would insert the Council into the situation without condemning the OAS action. Lacking strong Latin American support, the United States accepted a resolution that called for a strict cease-fire and invited the secretary general to report to the Council on the situation.[61]

Thant sent a small group to Santo Domingo, headed by Antonio Mayobre of Venezuela and including the secretary general's military adviser. This group was too small and its mandate too weak to interfere with the OAS activity; nevertheless, there was initially considerable mutual suspicion. Finally, a year after the intial intervention, during which there was considerable rightist opposition to the program of the Dominican Provisional Government, the promised national elections were held June 1, 1965, and a moderate constitutional government was elected, headed by Joaquin Balaguer. All three presidential candidates had called for the withdrawal of the Inter-American Force and the last troops left by September.

During the year there were sporadic, repeated meetings of the Security Council convened on the initiative of the Soviets every time the leader of the Dominican leftists asked for one. The meetings led nowhere, and there was little interest in them, either of the public or the UN delegations. Finally, in October 1966 the Dominican government expressed its appreciation for UN interest but declared that the Security Council's objectives had been accomplished and that, therefore, the UN mission be withdrawn—which it was forthwith.[62]

An interesting viewpoint was expressed by Walt Rostow. He writes that Antonio Mayobre (the UN representative in Santo Domingo) "had reacted initially with some passion against the intervention . . . but by the early months of 1966 he had come to the view that the process of democratization in the Dominican Republic had been set forward by fifteen years and with rare grace, he was prepared to tell this to me and others."[63]

Stevenson, however, had lingering doubts about the U.S.-OAS action right up to the time of his death. John B. Martin, one of his biographers, could find no comments on it in either his files or his public correspondence. (As noted, Stevenson was an effective advocate in the UN Security Council for U.S. policy.) Martin, who was ambassador to the Dominican Republic, 1962–64, and who served as President Johnson's personal representative to help in bringing peace in 1965, writes that Stevenson was perplexed but "not upset." Martin explained the U.S. operation, and "Stevenson seemed to accept the explanation."[64] Yet at a dinner in Paris shortly before his death, at which CBS correspondent David Schoenbrun was present, Stevenson called the operation "a massive blunder"—which Schoenbrun reported. Averell Harriman and Francis Plimpton thought Schoenbrun had misunderstood Stevenson, whom they had both known well for decades. Probably Stevenson had used hyperbole, not expecting to be quoted; even so, his remarks showed lingering, agonizing doubt.[65] The secretary general of the UN, U Thant, not only shared Stevenson's doubt; he considered the U.S. intervention a blunder that furnished a pretext for Soviet intervention in Czechoslovakia in 1968.[66]

AFRICA

Stevenson was more successful in moving American policy on Africa, particularly with respect to the Portuguese territories.

Portugal had friends in the Defense Department, which argued that the American base in the Azores was important to U.S. security and was concerned about NATO solidarity. For similar reasons, the Bureau of European Affairs wanted to support the Portuguese position at the UN, that Angola, Mozambique, and Portuguese Guinea (now Guinea-Bissau) were "provinces" of Portugal and therefore not within the competence of the UN (Article 2, paragraph 7 of the U.N. Charter precludes interference in the "internal affairs of states").

Both out of belief in self-determination and concern for African support on other issues, Stevenson courted the Africans, and effectively. Yost comments: "We had persistent differences with the Department on Africa. . . . The Africans were a nuisance to the Department but they meant votes to us. We kept the Department interested by saying it would affect Chirep [Chinese representation] and other things the Department was interested in.[67]

Stevenson's first success was gaining authorization to vote on March 17, 1961, in favor of a draft resolution sponsored in the Security Council by Ceylon, Liberia, and the United Arab Republic (Egypt) calling on Portugal to consider reforms to permit the Angolan people to exercise the right of self-determination. The resolution failed in the Security Council, 5 in favor and 6 abstentions; nevertheless, the U.S. vote represented a sharp break with the policy of the Eisenhower administration. Subsequently, a similar resolution was adopted by the General Assembly, 73 (United States) to 2 (South Africa and Spain), with 2 abstentions.

From that time on the United States continued to support self-determination for the people in all the Portuguese territories of Africa. (They are now independent.) But the United States refused to vote for resolutions calling for support of military activities against the Portuguese colonial governments. (It also came out strongly but unsuccessfully against India's use of force to take over the Portuguese enclave of Goa.) In any case, Stevenson was popular among the Africans, who considered him both sympathetic to their cause and a friend of the UN. In September 1962 he weighed in strongly by telegram, against the State Department's "increasing tendency to shy away from all mention of the Angolan self-determination, Portuguese territories in general, and from such revolutionary words as self-determination and independence."[68]

THE FINANCIAL CRISIS AND ARTICLE 19

The UN Operation of the Congo (ONUC) was kept going, as noted earlier, primarily by a confluence of African desires to get the Belgians out and the American desire to keep the Soviets out of the Congo. Thus, despite Soviet opposition after the fall of Patrice Lumumba in September 1960, the operation continued. But the Soviets, their satellites, and France manifested their opposition by refusing to pay their budget assessments for ONUC.

Since the Soviets had also refused to pay their assessments for the UN Emergency Force in the Middle East, the financial situation of the UN became critical. By the end of 1961 the UN had unpaid obligations of about $110 million and unpaid assessments of about $80 million. These figures might appear small when compared with the U.S. federal budget and national debt which were then over $600 billion each; however, in UN terms the deficit was huge and threatened to end ONUC. The UN's annual budget was $73 million, and ONUC was costing about $100 million per year. Unlike national governments, the UN cannot print money to cover deficits.   National contingents provided for ONUC were going unpaid, as were bills for material and other operating costs.

To keep ONUC going, USUN came up with a new idea for the UN—a bond issue. Phil Klutznick describes its origin as follows:

The idea of a Bond Issue was knocked around in our shop at the Mission with Al Bender [senior adviser on financial affairs] and his people having considerable to do with the origination of the idea. It took on a rather limited form at the beginning. I discussed it with Adlai who suggested I pursue it. As you know, Adlai *had little patience or time for the fiscal affairs of the U.N.* (Italics mine) The whole idea was given more character when we nearly folded the Congo Operation in the Spring, 1961. You will recall that all-night session where early in the morning we finally got a vote to finance the operation.[69] It became clear at that time that that was probably the last vote we could get if we did not come up with a better financing medium.

I spent some time with the Bureau of the Budget and with Harlan Cleveland and between us we finally got the green light from the Bureau. The question then arose whose initiative was it to be. I argued for the Secretary General to accept the idea and make it his own. Adlai and I had a date with the Secretary General [U Thant] for one late morning. He was coming in from Washington. At the last minute, he had to delay his arrival. He called me and asked me to go see the Secretary myself, which I did. The Secretary General was very sympathetic in the idea but wanted us to father it. I called his attention to the fact that it would be a difficult one at best and he was in a honeymoon period, which made it a certainty it could pass if he fathered it. He called in Eugene Black for a session in which we went over the whole matter and finally he reached the conclusion that he would propose it to the Fifth Committee, which he did. That was the beginning.[70] (U Thant "fathered" the bond idea so thoroughly he claimed credit for it in his memoirs, not even mentioning the U.S. role.) Thant, like Stevenson, had little interest in, or understanding of, UN finances, as his account of the Article 19 crisis reveals.[71]

It was far from the end. First there was a long struggle in the General Assembly, which on December 20, 1961, finally authorized the secretary general to issue United Nations bonds up to a limit of $200 million and "to utilize the proceeds from the sale of such bonds for purposes normally related to the Working Capital Fund"; that is, for paying ONUC expenses, inter alia. The bonds were to be repayable in twenty-five annual installments, bearing interest at 2 percent per annum on the principal amount outstanding; with the interest and amortization charges to be included in the UN's regular budget beginning in 1963.[72] The United States pledged to match bond purchases by all other countries combined and actually bought $85 million out of a total of $170 million.

The next step was to gain approval from a wary U.S. Congress. Just before the Senate hearings, Klutznick was asked to go to other countries to sell the bond issue and Francis Plimpton took over. He writes: "I have always suspected that the reason was that Senator Aiken had spread the word that I was the real father of the bond issue."[73] Congress finally approved but insisted on a commitment that delinquent members would have to pay their assessments or lose their right to vote under Article 19 of the UN Charter if their arrears exceeded more than two years' assessments.[74]

Thus, the bond issue assured continuation of ONUC and laid the groundwork for the Article 19 controversy that threatened to paralyze the UN in 1964 and 1965.

Those who supported the authority of the General Assembly were encouraged when the International Court of Justice, following a request for the Assembly for an advisory opinion, stated in a majority opinion of July 20, 1962, that the expenditures authorized by the Assembly for peacekeeping operations in the Congo and the Middle East "constitute expenses of the organization within the meaning of Article 17, paragraph 2, of the United Nations Charter."[75] Five months later, on December 19, 1962, the General Assembly accepted the opinion of the International Court of Justice by a vote of 76 to 17 (including France and 11 communist states), with 8 abstentions.[76]

By the time the nineteenth General Assembly would open in the fall of 1964, the Soviet Union and a number of other states would have arrears amounting to more than two years' assessments. By January 1, 1965, France would be in the same situation. Article 19 of the United Nations Charter provides:

> A Member of the United Nations which is in arrears in the payment of its financial contributions of the Organization shall have no vote in the General Assembly if the amount of its arrears equals or exceed the amount of the contributions due from it for the preceding two full years. The General Assembly may, nevertheless, permit such a Member to vote if it is satisfied that the failure to pay is due to conditions beyond the control of the Member.

So the battle was joined. The Soviets and the French, despite the International Court of Justice opinion and its acceptance by an overwhelming majority, were adamant on their refusal to pay. The real conflict was with the authority of the General Assembly under the Charter, which it was in the interest of the Third World majority to uphold. Yet, because of the commitment to the U.S. Congress when the bond issue was approved, the energy of USUN, and the tendency of the media to play up Soviet-American confrontations, the controversy appeared to be a cold war issue.

Having been involved with the issue from July 1964 to the denouement, I know that USUN did not perceive the action as an anti-Soviet maneuver, nor was that the attitude of those we dealt with in the State Department. Unless the arrears were paid, there was no way to reimburse the states that had provided contingents for ONUC and UNEF. These included poorer countries, such as Ethiopia, India, Tunisia, Indonesia, and Morocco, as well as Canada and the Nordic countries. How could one have future peacekeeping operations on a sound basis if the authority of the General Assembly to levy assessments were successfully challenged? If the General Assembly itself failed to enforce its authority under Article 19 in this instance, how could it do so in the future?[77] And there was also the commitment to Congress.

The Soviets and the French did not ask for exception under the second sentence of Article 19; that is, if the Assembly "is satisfied that the failure to pay is due to conditions beyond the control of the Member." They argued, despite the ICJ opinion and its acceptance by the General Assembly, that the assessments for ONUC and UNEF were not mandatory because the operations were, in their view, not conducted in accordance with Chapter VII of the UN Charter; hence, they had no obligation to pay. In their view only the Security Council could take action for the maintenance of peace and security, including financing.[78] (Curiously, France paid its assessments for UNEF, which had been authorized by the General Assembly, but not for ONUC, authorized by the Security Council. The Soviets paid for neither.)

As far back as March 6, 1964, Stevenson proposed to the Soviets that they pay enough to satisfy Article 19 on the assurance that they would not have to pay for future peacekeeping operations of which they did not approve. This offer was certainly not made in a cold war spirit. On March 21 the Soviets rejected it. Congress then passed a joint resolution calling upon Stevenson to insure that the defaulting countries paid up or Article 19 applied.[79]

At USUN during the summer and early fall of 1964 we spent hundreds of hours trying to devise formulas under which the Soviets and French could contribute amounts sufficient to obviate the application of Article 19, while still maintaining their positions of principle. We even devised schemes for American contributions that would not require new congressional appropriations, such as cancellation of a UN debt for certain U.S. services provided for ONUC and of "surplus accounts," representing assessments paid during a period when ONUC expenses were met from the proceeds of the bond issue. In fact, the United States has never collected a dime on these accounts anyway, because the deficit remained. Yet the amount nominally involved would have matched the sum in new funds that the Soviets would have to pay to avoid the applicability of Article 19. Nevertheless the Soviets, when approached by an intermediary group consisting of the Afghan, Nigerian, Norwegian, and Venezuelan ambassadors, would not promise any specific sum. Instead, they skillfully dropped hints of willingness to make a voluntary contribution, thus weakening the resolve of the smaller countries, but never mentioned how much, when, or how.

It became clear that most Third World countries, while agreeing with the Western position (minus France, Spain, and Portugal) on principle, were genuinely worried about the prospect that the Soviets, if deprived of their vote in the General Assembly, would leave the UN. For example, Ambassador El Kony of Egypt told Plimpton in my presence that Egypt needed the Soviet veto in the Security Council and would, therefore, oppose any action that would jeopardize the Soviet presence in the UN. Yet Egypt very much wanted UNEF to continue and had a stake, as a Third World country, in maintaining the authority of the General Assembly. At USUN we were convinced that the Soviets would find a way to pay if the Third World countries stood firm. Clearly, many African and Asian states did not see it that way, fearing a Soviet walkout, and their unwillingness to go to a showdown proved decisive.

Because of the widespread reluctance toward a showdown, U Thant suggested, after polling the membership, that the opening of the nineteenth session of the General Assembly be postponed from November 10 to December 1. There was general concurrence and no opposition from Washington. On November 13 Adlai Stevenson stated publicly that "voluntary payments could be made without prejudice to the Soviets or anyone else's legal views. Any arrangements for such payments consistent with the Charter and satisfactory to the Secretary General will be satisfactory to the United States."[80]

A crucial factor was the legal position of the man destined to become president of the nineteenth session, Ambassador Carlos Sosa Rodriguez of Venezuela, with whom Francis Plimpton and other USUN people had a number of meetings, Sosa, while believing that Article 19 should be applied against the delinquents, held that the General Assembly must take the decision. As an important question, this would require a two-thirds majority. Our head count indicated that we were close to that figure, but there was a real question whether we could get to a showdown vote at all. The U.S. view was that the loss of vote provision became automatic, since Article 19 states that a member "shall have no vote if the amount of its arrears exceeds the amount of its contributions due from it for the preceding two years." As a precedent, Mohammed Zafrula Khan, president of the fourth special session of the General Assembly in 1963, had ruled that Haiti's loss of vote was automatic unless and until it paid enough to remove the applicability of Article 19.[81] Should the president's ruling be challenged, the challengers would need a majority to set his ruling aside. Thus, only half the votes would be required to uphold Article 19's application instead of the two thirds required if the General Assembly had to take implementing action. Sosa, however, held firmly to his legal position.

Another factor that might have made a difference was the airdrop of Belgian paratroopers from American planes on Stanleyville on November 14, 1964, to rescue a group of white hostages from a leftist rebel group. Since the operation, whether intentionally or not, also helped Moise Tshombe, then prime minister of the Congo, to put down the rebellion, a number of African countries resented the action and the U.S. role in it. Francis Plimpton thought this caused support for the application of Article 19 to fall to less than two thirds.[82]

Feeling that the showdown would come December 1 when the Assembly opened, Dick Pedersen and I proposed that the United States delay its contribution to the UN Special Fund and the Expanded Program of Technical Assistance instead of making a pledge November 16 at the scheduled pledging conference. This maneuver, which was then approved in Washington, was intended to signal that financial irresponsibility on peacekeeping could undermine confidence in the UN. It was a carefully limited risk, since we knew the contribution would not be needed or made until 1965, and it became pointless when the expected December 1 showdown did not materialize. The United States did in fact make its contribution early in 1965, in ample time to avoid damage to the two programs.

Stevenson had paid little attention to the financial problem until it became a political crisis in 1964. He was disturbed about the potential damage to the UN. On November 20 he arranged a meeting with Fedorenko to discuss ways of avoiding an Article 19 confrontation and the idea of a no-vote Assembly was brought up. Stevenson reported this idea favorably to Washington, and according to Beichman, this came as "a total surprise and shock to Washington officials." Beichman reports that Rusk agreed at breakfast the next morning and asks: "Could he have done anything else?"[83]

In my opinion, Rusk could have disagreed if he had felt strongly about the issue. Apparently he did not, and it was difficult to tell from USUN what all the factors in his decision were. We did know that Ambassador Llewellyn ("Tommie") Thompson was concerned about the effect a UN confrontation would have on Soviet-American relations.

I doubt that the United States could have had a showdown December 1 even if it had insisted on it; the majority of Third World countries appeared determined to avoid a confrontation. Chief Adebo, the Nigerian permanent representative, probably spoke for many when he said: "Nobody is prepared to blow up the world Organization on the altar of a principle founded upon Charter provisions of an admittedly ambiguous character."[84] David Kay observes:

Regardless of its substantive content, the question of the application of Article 19 was transformed into a direct United States–U.S.S.R. confrontation, with the very existence of the Organization at stake. Primarily responsible for this transformation of the constitutional question of the applicability of the provisions of Article 19 into a highly charged political quesiton concerning the future of the Organization was the Soviet threat to leave the United Nations if Article 19 were invoked against it. In the face of this great power clash, the unity the new nations had demonstrated in 1963 dissolved, and these nations failed to take any decisive action designed to resolve the conflict. Faced with dissension within their ranks and a pervasive feeling of impotency over their own ability to affect the outcome of a direct great power collision, inaction and a willingness to agree to any subterfuge as long as it avoided this collision became the dominant themes of the political activity of the new nations at the abortive nineteenth session of the Assembly.[85]

Nevertheless, some of us at USUN would have preferred that the U.S. stand aside from any no-vote deal and wait to be persuaded not to press the issue on December 1. By hanging tough we might have induced Third World leaders to put greater pressure on the Soviet Union and France for contributions.

The General Assembly opened on December 1 and proceeded throughout the month without voting. This made little difference, since the first three or four weeks of any Assembly session are normally occupied by general debate while the real work of preparing resolutions and negotiating on them goes on privately. Where there were disagreements, the president of the Assembly, Alex Quaison-Sackey of Ghana, carried out a special "consultation" procedure in his office that amounted to an unofficial straw vote. He then stated to the General Assembly that a decision would be considered adopted if no objection were raised.

Meanwhile Quaison-Sackey and other representatives worked privately in efforts to resolve the crisis. The Afro-Asian states proposed a Rescue Fund to which all nations would make voluntary contributions. The Soviet Union, after protracted and laborious negotiations, told the secretary general it would make a contribution but refused to specify the amount and date of payment, demanding in return that the Assembly resume normal business and voting procedures. The United States refused to accept this proposal, describing it as a "pig in the poke."

Before the Assembly resumed in February, Ralph Bunche, on behalf of the secretary general, phoned Stevenson to suggest that the United States agree to let the nineteenth session proceed normally, including voting, with the understanding that the showdown would come in September. During USUN discussions I urged that we go along with this proposal, even though it was legally dubious. Having been in favor of a December 1, 1964, showdown, I had seen the erosion of Third World support for applying Article 19 during December and January and felt that it would continue. The only hope, as I saw it, was to say to the Third World countries: "Okay. You believe that this temporary suspension of the Charter provision (Article 19) will produce an adequate Soviet contribution. We'll go along, reluctantly, on the understanding that you and we together will insist that Article 19 be applied when the twentieth session opens in September if the delinquents [which by that time included France and ten other countries as well as the USSR] have not made adequate contributions by then." Politically, I felt, such a move would have aligned us with the majority and put the Soviet Union and France in a difficult position. Stevenson's other principal advisers disagreed, and Bunche's suggestion was rejected.

The General Assembly, having completed the bare essentials of its business—the budget and elections to fill vacancies—without voting, was getting ready to adjourn February 16. Then Halim Budo of Albania formally proposed that the Assembly proceed immediately on its normal work "in accordance with the Charter"—and asked for a decision by roll call vote. The president adjourned the meeting for two days for consultations. On February 18 he ruled there was a consensus against reconsidering the Assembly's previous decision not to vote. Budo challenged his ruling. Stevenson then stated to the Assembly that, so that the overwhelming majority might not be frustrated by one member, the United States would not object to one procedural vote, without prejudice to its position on the applicability of Article 19. Albania's motion lost, 2 (Albania, Mauritania) in favor, 97 against (including the USSR and the United States), and 13 abstentions.

Negotiations attempting to resolve the crisis continued during the spring. At USUN it became clear that a majority of countries would want to resume normal business when the twentieth session opened in September and that the pressure would now be on the United States rather than on the delinquents. There also appeared to be a weakening of ardor in Washington where some officials became concerned that enforcement of Article 19 against the USSR and France might create a precedent by which the Assembly could create a UN Capital Development Fund—which the United States opposed—and assess the United States for one third of its resources. There was also concern that an Assembly majority might someday launch a peacekeeping operation that the United States opposed. Nevertheless, at USUN the prevailing view, in which Stevenson concurred wholeheartedly, was that something should be done to resolve the financial crisis and thus strengthen the UN. We proposed that, at the San Francisco ceremony in June 1965 celebrating the UN's twentieth anniversary, President Johnson would announce American willingness to contribute $25 million to a Rescue Fund provided the Soviets contributed a similar amount. (The Soviet contribution would be in new funds and enough to take them out of the reach of Article 19, whereas the U.S. contribution would be largely in the cancellation of debts owed to us by the UN for logistical help in the Congo and certain "surplus accounts," none of which would be collectible unless the deficit was resolved.) Such an offer would have vastly improved the U.S. political position at the UN and put great pressure on the Soviets and French to contribute. State accepted the idea, and Stevenson, with staff help, prepared a draft for Johnson. Unfortunately, there was a leak to the press, which State Department insiders attribute to Harlan Cleveland. Two days before the San Francisco ceremony James Reston wrote a column in the *New York Times* predicting that Johnson would announce a compromise. Thereupon Johnson, who hated to be scooped, had the speech rewritten in Washington, completely eliminating any U.S. offer. As a result, the "celebration" in San Francisco seemed more like a dirge. (There is no evidence that Johnson had either accepted or rejected the idea of a $25 million contribution; what is certain is that the leak to Reston killed any chance the idea had ever had.)

After that it was clear that a majority could not be mustered to enforce Article 19 and that the USSR and France would make no contribution by September to make the question moot. Arthur Goldberg's statement on August 16 broke the voting deadlock (see Chapter VI); however, the authority of the General Assembly had been substantially weakened, along with the financial situation of the UN.

A number of writers have criticized the United States for its efforts to have Article 19 enforced. H. G. Nicholas, for example, writes:

> It was the U.S. that embarked in the mid-sixties upon the vain and harmful exercises connected with the invocation of Articles 17 and 19, which reduced the organization to the most degrading level of impotence. And this was an adventure which had its inception entirely in a belief that the Charter was some kind of timeless, self-enforcing prescription, whose wording could be construed without reference to the politics of the membership.[86]

Ruth Russell also criticizes the United States for becoming obsessed by legalistic arguments; she contrasts the American refusal to contribute to the Rescue Fund with the attitude of Great Britain, which contributed $10 million, Canada ($4 million), Japan, and the Nordic countries. These states had also paid their assessments, as had the United States; however, they chose to put belief in a stronger UN above arguments about legal responsibility.[87] A U.S. offer of $25 million, as advocated by USUN, would have helped substantially to put the UN on a sounder financial footing and put great pressure on the Soviets and French to match it. Unfortunately, Stevenson did not have enough influence on Johnson to maintain the offer after the press leak.

The real loss, however, was not to the United States so much as it was to the UN and the smaller- and medium-sized states that make up its majority. Their votes dominate the General Assembly, and their backdown on Article 19 meant that any major power, and other states as well, could defy the assessment power of the Assembly, one of its few real powers under the Charter. Indeed, given present moods of the Assembly majority, this "loss" may now seem comforting to Washington. As Stoessinger put it, the Article 19 controversy was really a conflict between those who wanted to maintain the United Nations as "static conference machinery" (the USSR and Gaullist France) and those who wished to endow it with increasing strength and executive authority.[88]

THE UN DEVELOPMENT DECADE

On the economic side, the United States continued to give strong support to the UN throughout Stevenson's tenure, although Stevenson himself took only a sporadic interest in anything nonpolitical. He was enthusiastically supportive of the work done by Klutznick, Bingham, and me on economic issues and enjoyed making the principal U.S. statement in Geneva when the Economic and Social Council met there each summer (which also gave him an opportunity to take a brief vacation in Europe); however, in New York it was impossible to get his sustained attention on economic or financial issues.

Early in the Kennedy administration (1961) Richard Gardner, then deputy assistant secretary of state for international organization affairs, phoned me from Washington and read a proposal for a UN Development Decade. He, Harlan Cleveland, and other Kennedy New Frontiersmen were strongly supportive of the UN and eager to demonstrate the new administration's interest. Their first idea was an International Development Year; however, the Treasury Department was concerned that designating a single year would bring pressure for more financial aid. It was then decided to propose a Development Decade, which emphasized aspects of development other than quantities of aid; for example, intensified international cooperation, better coordination, improved adaptation of science and technology, and better development planning.

I told Gardner that the ideas were all laudable but that they had already been put forward by the United States in 1958, in what was called at USUN the "Charting anew" resolution.[89] He replied that the principles might have been similar but the follow-through would be different, as the Kennedy administration was different from Eisenhower's. In fact, he and Harlan Cleveland labored mightily to make it so, and there were some constructive achievements even though the original proposal had little in the way of concrete commitments.[90]

Addressing the General Assembly on September 25, 1961, President Kennedy launched the proposal with the following brief reference:

Political sovereignty is but a mockery without the means of meeting poverty and illiteracy and disease. Self-determination is but a slogan if the future holds no hope.

That is why my nation—which has freely shared its capital and its technology to help others help themselves—now proposes officially designating this decade of the 1960's as the United Nations Decade of Development. Under the framework of that resolution the United Nations' existing efforts in promoting economic growth can be expanded and coordinated. Regional surveys and training institutes can now pool the talents of many. New research, technical assistance, and pilot projects can unlock the wealth of less developed lands and untapped waters. And development can become a cooperative and not a competitive enterprise—to enable all nations, however diverse in their systems and beliefs, to become in fact as well as in law both free and equal nations.[91]

The delegation then began consultations with a view to gathering a representative group of cosponsors in the Second (Economic) Committee, where the item would be considered. The objective was to have one or two cosponsors from each geographic area but to avoid having such a large group of cosponsors as to make the consideration of proposed amendments too complicated.

Because Phil Klutznick, our ECOSOC representative, was completely absorbed in getting the UN bond issue through the Fifth Committee, the responsibility for gaining Second Committee approval of the Decade of Development was almost entirely mine. Friends cultivated there during my previous four sessions, particularly among the Asian and African delegations, were most helpful in gaining support. Candor also seemed to help. In a private meeting, when the Indonesian and other Third World representatives asked what was new and concrete in the proposal, I answered frankly that there was nothing specific but that they would be unwise to reject the first offer from a new American president. The terms of the resolution were broad and positive; they had nothing to lose by accepting it and using it as a basis for concrete negotiations. In the end, that is what they did.

One problem of status was that the Indian prime minister had proposed to the General Assembly an International Cooperation Year. We accommodated the Indian delegation by entitling the resolution: "The United Nations Development Decade: A Programme for International Economic Cooperation."

We had another problem when one of the communist countries proposed an amendment by which the goal of the decade would have been to close the gap in income per capita between the developing and the less developed countries. Some of our cosponsors from less developed countries, in the sponsors' caucus, urged that we accept the amendment lest the resolution be lost. I argued that such a goal was clearly impossible and that we should not adopt language patently dishonest even to stave off a demagogic amendment. Instead, we stuck with a preambular clause reading as follows:

> *Noting,* however, that in spite of the efforts made in recent years the gap in *per capita* incomes between the economically developed and the less developed countries has increased and the rate of economic and social progress in the developing countries is still far from adequate.

We did, however, accept another very significant amendment in the key paragraph of the resolution, setting a quantitative target for growth in national income. This involved a struggle with Washington, where the Treasury Department was reluctant to see any quantitative goals specified, fearing that these would be translated into demands for more financial aid. As amended and adopted, the paragraph read:

> 1. *Designates* the current decade as the United Nations Development Decade, in which Member States and their peoples will intensify their efforts to mobilize and to sustain support for the measures required on the part of both developed and developing countries to accelerate progress towards self-sustaining growth of the economy of the individual nations and their social advancement so as to attain in each under-developed country a substantial increase in the rate of growth, with each country setting its own target, taking as the objective a minimum annual rate of growth of aggregate national income of 5 per cent at the end of the Decade.[92]

Ironically, the 5 percent goal was attained, and this was the feature of the decade—accepted reluctantly by Washington—to which the United States pointed with greatest pride in 1970.

The rest of the resolution was a list of general principles of conduct that would contribute to the goal set forth in paragraph 1; for example, stabilization of prices for primary commodities; a fair share of earnings from the extraction and marketing of natural resources; increased flow of private capital, help in working out economic development plans; accelerating the elimination of illiteracy, hunger, and disease; improved education and vocational training; intensified research; opening markets to the manufactured goods of the less developed countries. These principles had been largely accepted before 1961, and the full implementation of them remains a target in 1980. However, linking them together in one resolution, together with the 5 percent growth target, provided a rallying point for the less developed countries, and its unanimous adoption was a public relations triumph for the new Kennedy administration. It also provided the heads of specialized agencies such as the FAO, WHO, ILO, and UNESCO with reasons for projecting increased budgets. Also, in a companion resolution, the General Assembly raised the target of the Expanded Program of Technical Assistance and the Special Fund to a combined total of $150 million.[93] It had first been $100 million and by 1979 was over $600 million for the combined program, now known as the UN Development Program. There was also a substantial increase in financial aid during the first half of the decade, for which a good part of the credit should go to the Development Assistance Committee of the OECD; its member governments; and the World Bank and its new soft-loan affiliate, the International Development Association.[94]

Even so, the resolution would never have come through unanimously and so close to the original American design if the Soviet representative, Lavrichenko, had not been so disagreeable and inept. His vehement and often unfounded attacks against the United States and the resolution created a lot of sympathy for us. At a luncheon following one of Lavrichenko's tirades, Hector Bernardo of Argentina showed me two pages of troublesome amendments he had planned to propose, then ripped them up, telling all of us that this represented his response to Lavrichenko. During one of Lavrichenko's tirades, I slipped our United Kingdom neighbor a note saying, "I think this guy is being paid by the CIA." He wrote back, "This would be one of the few times they got their money's worth."

In 1970 the developing countries themselves took over the leadership in fashioning the blueprint of a second Development Decade. The resolution they presented was much more detailed and specific, including a target of 1.0 percent of the national income of the industrialized countries to flow to the developing countries, of which 0.7 percent should be public capital aid.[95]

THE UN CONFERENCE ON TRADE AND DEVELOPMENT (UNCTAD)

The year 1961 also marked the beginning of a new emphasis by the less developed countries on international trade as the primary instrument for economic development. In the 1950s the emphasis had been technical assistance and capital flows. The establishment of the Expanded Program of Technical Assistance in 1950, the Special Fund in 1958, and the International Development Association in 1959, had represented a significant response in those areas. Yet the fact remained that the most important source of foreign exchange earnings for the developing countries had been and would remain export proceeds; these amount to at least three times as much as foreign aid and private investments.

The trade picture as seen by the less developed countries appeared bleak. From 1950 to 1960 their share of world trade dropped from 30 to 20 percent; their exports lagged further and further behind their imports. Some of the reasons for these trends are evident. About 90 percent of the exports of the less developed countries still consists of foodstuffs and raw materials. World demand for these is growing rather slowly, owing to the switch to synthetics, their low "income elasticity of demand" (demand not very responsive to rising income), protectionist measures in many developed countries, and the developed countries' expanded output of the same products. At the same time, the production of many primary products by less developed countries has risen rapidly. As a result, prices of these products have tended to decline both in absolute terms and in relation to prices of the manufactured goods imported by less developed countries for their economic growth.[96] (The notable exception, of course, is oil in the 1970s).

These considerations prompted eighteen African, three Asian, and six Latin American states to put forward at the sixteenth session of the General Assembly in 1961 a draft resolution entitled "International Trade as the Primary Instrument for Economic Development." Most of its provisions were familiar and noncontroversial; they called upon governments to promote the expansion of world trade by avoiding "undue" protectionism, to make every effort to liberalize practices that unnecessarily limit the consumption and importation of commodities from the developing countries, and to pursue policies that would promote their industrial development.

The controversy arose over a paragraph calling for an international trade conference. The developed countries, particularly the United States, considered that GATT (the General Agreement on Tariffs and Trade) was the appropriate forum and opposed a separate conference. The developing countries felt that GATT's efforts were too much concentrated on trade in industrial goods and the concerns of the developed countries. The Soviet Union and its followers, which did not participate in GATT, supported the drive for a conference. The developing country leaders, with commendable patience and wisdom, amended the controversial paragraph so that the secretary general was asked to ascertain the views of governments "on the advisability of holding an international conference on international trade problems relating especially to primary commodity markets and, if they deemed such a conference advisable, the topics that might be considered for a provisional agenda." The resolution was adopted unanimously in the General Assembly.[97]

The developing countries could easily have pushed through their original text by a large majority, over the opposition of the major developed countries. Their choice of negotiation and compromise reflected their conclusion that such a "victory" would be meaningless; governments could not be forced to attend a conference, and it would be fruitless if the major developed countries did not come.

Of the 66 replies to the secretary general, 45 were favorable, 18 opposed (including most of the Western industrialized countries), and 3 were noncommital.[98] The Kennedy administration decided that the political cost of opposing the conference was greater than the risks involved, provided that satisfactory terms of reference could be obtained at the thirty-fourth session of the Economic and Social Council in Geneva. Once the United States, which had been the strongest opponent of the conference, changed its position, the other industrialized countries had no trouble in going along.

As usual with economic issues Stevenson did not become involved— nor, in general, did other U.S. permanent representatives. He did deliver the principal U.S. statement at ECOSOC in July 1962, stressing the importance of education, training, and technology in development. I drafted a statement that, because he was in Gstaad, Switzerland, for the weekend, Stevenson did not see until a few hours before he was to speak. Contrary to his usual custom of rewriting up to the last minute, Stevenson delivered the statement just as it was delivered to him. I am not sure whether this was a compliment to my drafting and knowledge of his style or an indication that he was preoccupied with other matters.

The draft resolution on convening the conference, to be known as the United Nations Conference on Trade and Development (UNCTAD), was sponsored by Brazil, Ethiopia, India, Senegal, and Yugoslavia. They were quite reasonable in private discussions of the text, which I carried on with L. K. Jha of India under instructions from Phil Klutznick. The resolution provided that the conference would concentrate on the problems of the developing countries (the United States did not want it to be a vehicle for promoting East-West trade), with a Preparatory Committee to meet in the spring of 1963 and report to the summer 1963 session of ECOSOC.[99]

At the General Assembly the pattern agreed to at ECOSOC became somewhat unstuck. A draft resolution introduced in the Second Committee by thirty-five states provided for enlarging the Preparatory Committee from twenty-four to thirty, convening the conference by June 1963, and appointing a secretary general.[100] In effect, the General Assembly was taking control of the conference away from ECOSOC; some of the developing countries left out of the Preparatory Committee by ECOSOC had revolted. I felt that those who had made an agreement with us at Geneva had welshed on the deal and told Janez Stanovnik of Yugoslavia as much. He explained that they were under great pressure in the caucus of developing countries and could do nothing else. Finally, as was usual in the Second Committee of those years, we reached a compromise that could be supported unanimously.

UNCTAD was to be held early in 1964, as originally planned at ECOSOC, but the Preparatory Committee was enlarged to thirty-four. Paradoxically, it was the United States that favored the final enlargement from thirty to thirty-four, in order to assure participation by the Federal Republic of Germany. In the thirty there were to be two participants from the European Economic Community, (EEC), or Common Market. For their own reasons the French double-crossed Germany, undoubtedly one of the world's major trading nations, and spread the word that the two EEC participants would be France and Belgium. France even opposed the increase to thirty-four but gave way when the overwhelming majority of the developed countries persisted, and the Federal Republic of Germany was named to the Preparatory Committee.

The Preparatory Committee devised a new formula for group representation, which had been and remains geographic in most UN bodies. Instead there was Group A (the Afro-Asian states), Group B (the industrialized market-economy states), Group C (the planned economy "socialist" states), and Group D (the Latin American states). Since the conference would have five committees, it was easy to decide that Group A, the largest, would have two chairmanships and each other group, one. Groups A and D wanted Janez Stanovnik of Yugoslavia to chair the committee on finance. The Western countries said: "Fine, that takes care of the Group C chairmanship." The Soviets, on the other hand, pointed out that Yugoslavia had sometimes been elected to UN bodies in the "Western Europe and other" category (Group B). Finally, the Afro-Asian representatives said that Stanovnik could be the candidate of Group A, thus making Yugoslavia, in effect, an Afro-Asian country.

UNCTAD I was held in Geneva from March 23 to June 16, 1964, and was, in retrospect, a historic event. Little was accomplished in terms of concrete negotiations on specific issues of substance; however, a major permanent UN institution was established that has articulated the demands of the developing countries.[101] The conference saw the birth of the Group of 77, representing the number of developing countries present; it still has that name, even though its members now number more than 110. It includes all Latin American, Asian and African countries, except Israel and South Africa, and one European country, Yugoslavia. This new cohesion of the developing countries, which has held together even after some of them became rich from oil exports, has been an important factor in pressing their demands.

Because it was feared, probably correctly, that the United States and other developed countries might not ratify an instrument setting up a new specialized agency, UNCTAD was established as a subordinate body of the General Assembly with membership open to all states that are members of the United Nations or of the specialized agencies. It now has more than 150 members. It has a large secretariat in Geneva, larger than that of many specialized agencies, with a 1979 budget of $55 million. Its activities are partisan in the sense that its main effort is to promote the interests of the developing countries on such matters as commodity prices, access to markets, transfer of technology, financing, monetary systems, shipping, and invisibles. Its activities have been carried out at four quadrennial conferences, and a fifth in Manila in 1979, as well as annual meetings of its sixty-eight-member Trade and Development Board, numerous special and technical committees, Secretariat documents and technical assistance as a participating agency of the UN Development Program. Incidentally, the name "Trade and Development *Board*" was chosen at the first UNCTAD in 1964 when, in informal discussions, I told representatives of the developing countries that the initially desired name, "Trade and Development Council," would unnecessarily offend Washington, which would regard it as an effort to undermine the authority of the Economic and Social Council.

This concern with securing cooperation from the developed countries rather than merely voting them down on economic issues—a concern that has, unfortunately, diminished in recent years—was also reflected in the conciliation procedures established by UNCTAD. Paragraph 5 of the founding resolution sets forth procedures "designed to provide a process of conciliation to take place before voting and to provide an adequate basis for the adoption of recommendations with regard to proposals of a specific nature for actions substantially affecting the economic or financial interests of particular countries."[102] The essence of the procedure is that in carefully outlined cases a certain minimum number of members (ten for proposals before a committee) may request postponement of the voting, if necessary to the next session, during which time a conciliation committee is to endeavor to reach agreement.

These conciliation procedures represented a compromise with what Richard Gardner and I had tried to achieve—a dual voting procedure under which there would have to be a majority not only overall but in each of the four groups. Although the procedures have rarely been used, the spirit behind them has engendered an emphasis on negotiation rather than on voting at UNCTAD. This is a realistic acknowledgment of the fact that governments, not UNCTAD resolutions, make policy. Changes in government attitudes are vitally important, whereas voting "victories" are hollow.

This reality must have been in the mind of Gamani Corea, secretary general of UNCTAD, when he observed:

It is true to say that UNCTAD's impact, UNCTAD's influence, extends beyond its own forum; its record goes beyond its specific achievements. UNCTAD had profoundly influenced attitudes, and decisions, and even actions, in virtually every forum that has concerned itself with the development questions. This in itself is an immense, a formidable, contribution.[103]

The United States, on its side, was not enthusiastic about the establishment of UNCTAD, nor has it developed much enthusiasm in the interim. It prefers trade negotiations in GATT, aid discussions at the World Bank, and monetary negotiations in the IMF, and acts accordingly. Yet it is impossible politically to ignore UNCTAD; hence, the United States has attempted—after George Ball showed how tough it could be at UNCTAD I—to be a constructive participant and has developed certain new policies at least partly as a result of discussions at UNCTAD; such as nonreciprocated, generalized special preferences for goods from the developing countries and advocacy of compensatory financing for developing countries in difficulty because of fluctuations in the prices of primary commodities.

THE UN DEVELOPMENT PROGRAM DEVELOPS

When the United States proposed the Special Fund in 1957, its main objectives were, in Henry Cabot Lodge's phrase, "to get the SUNFED monkey off our backs" and to expand the concept of technical assistance to larger preparatory and "pre-investment" projects. Another objective was to develop a stronger central management than existed in the Expanded Program of Technical Assistance (EPTA), where essentially the funds were apportioned among the specialized agencies in the Technical Assistance Board (TAB) rather than being distributed on the basis of country planning and project merit.

After two years of operation, the United States concluded that the Special Fund type of management should be extended to EPTA through a merger of the two programs. At its thirty-fourth session in the summer of 1961, ECOSOC, at U.S. initiative, established a Working Group to consider the advantages and disadvantages of a merger and report back to the council a year later. The specialized agencies and David Owen, chairman of TAB, were lobbying against the merger for the very reasons that the United States wanted it. The British delegation, perhaps out of sympathy for Owen, a Welshman who had been with the UN since its founding, were very wary of the merger. Phil Klutznick and I used the full weight of the U.S. contribution of 40 percent of the resources to lobby for support from the developing countries. Finally, a compromise was reached on the merger. Paul Hoffman, managing director of the Special Fund, would become administrator of the merged program, to be known as the UN Development Program, and Owen would be coadministrator. The Consultative Board of the Special Fund, which had consisted of the secretary general of the UN, the chairman of TAB and the president of the World Bank, was expanded to include all the specialized agencies. The merged program, UNDP, was established.

Also in 1961 came one of Paul Hoffman's greatest embarrassments. In May 1961, Hoffman, as managing director of the Special Fund, included in his program presented to the Governing Council a project calling for an allocation of $1 million for assistance to a five-year Cuban project at Santiago de las Vegas to study tropical animal husbandry, soil classification, conservation, and crop diversification. Coming a few weeks after the Bay of Pigs disaster, this was obviously a very senstitive domestic political issue in the United States. Yet Hoffman could not in good conscience avoid presenting the project, since the founding legislation of the Special Fund, resolution 1219, stipulated that the assistance furnished "shall not be accompanied by any conditions of a political nature," and the proposal, developed with the assistance of the FAO, appeared to be economically sound.

On a number of occasions, the Soviet delegate to the Special Fund Governing Council had objected to projects in Taiwan, South Korea, and South Vietnam but had never forced a separate vote on a particular project, and all were approved. Similarly, the United States had not attempted to block projects in communist countries such as Poland and Yugoslavia, and Egypt had not tried to frustrate projects in Israel. In each case a protest was made for the record, but no vote was taken. Yet in the case of the project for Cuba, the U.S. delegation was instructed to lobby intensively in order to round up enough votes to defeat the proposal. Since most members believed in the principle of shutting out political considerations and Hoffman had proposed the project, it soon became clear that the United States could not even come near getting the necessary votes to block it. Consequently, a decision was made not to press for a separate vote.

Instead, Phil Klutznick made a strong statement for the record, opposing the project on the following economic grounds: (1) Cuba had failed to take advantage of existing multilateral sources of technical assistance through the OAS; (2) the Cuban government had displaced or driven into exile qualified personnel at the same time that it had requested UN technicians to replace them; (3) the wholesale slaughter of livestock and misuse of other physical resources had raised doubts about the utility of any aid in livestock-raising techniques; (4) the existence of a bilateral technical assistance agreement with the Soviet bloc which would bring 300 agricultural experts to Cuba had mitigated the urgency of the need for the UN project. Adding that political and economic conditions were inter-related and that the manner in which a country was governed had economic consequences, Klutznick stated that the project had not received the approval of his government. He stated: "We have great respect for the judgment of the staff of the Special Fund. Under normal procedures, the Managing Director would examine any questions arising before entering into a plan of operations for any project. We are confident, therefore, that the project will not proceed until the staff has satisfied itself about the questions we have raised and is certain that the project can be completed successfully to the ultimate benefit to the Cuban people."

Hoffman's staff investigated the project for a year and a half and could find no valid economic reasons for canceling it. On February 13, 1963, the UNDP announced that it would proceed. There was a strongly negative reaction in the United States, including the Congress, but the project went ahead and the public clamor evaporated. Hoffman's standing as a dedicated UN civil servant was not damaged, since he stood up for principle, but he suffered personal discomfort.

Stevenson was not involved, leaving the problem to Klutznick in New York and Gardner in Washington.

THE UN INSTITUTE ON TRAINING AND RESEARCH (UNITAR)

In 1963 Harlan Cleveland received the impression that the Ford Foundation, with assets booming along with the stock market, could be prepared to give $2 million toward the establishment of a United Nations Institute to serve as a "think tank" for the secretary general. It turned out to be an illusion that gave rise to an institution.

Cleveland's deputy, Dick Gardner, sketched out plans for the institute and prepared a draft resolution for the General Assembly. Then Dick and I discussed broad outlines and tactics. The Ford Foundation would want Assembly approval, matching contributions from government and private sources, and assurances of a high-quality institute of the Rand Corporation type. The secretary general and his top associates are too much immersed in crises and day-to-day business to do long-range planning and research in depth on problems that confront the organization, both in keeping the peace and promoting economic development. Moreover, actual or potential Secretariat officials, particularly those from the new countries, could profit from specialized preservice or inservice training. These were the broad aims of the UN Training and Research Institute as we envisaged it. (The name was later changed to United Nations Institute for Training and Research, so as to provide a more felicitious acronym.)

For tactical reasons I suggested we ask that the question be discussed in the Second (Economic) Committee, where our network of friends was strong. Since the institute would have peace and security as well as economic and social aspects, it could have gone to the First Committee or the Special Political Committee if we had considered either of those forums as favorable. Also, I asked Nonnie Wright, the veteran and very popular Danish representative in the Second Committee, whether she would take the leadership of the proposal in the committee. She readily agreed and rounded up a representative group of sixteen cosponsors. The United States joined as the seventeenth cosponsor after the resolution was well along its way to approval in the committee. (This was the same Nonnie Wright who in 1958 had successfully initiated a campaign to name Paul Hoffman as managing director of the Special Fund, when the U.S. candidate was someone else.)

In committee the Soviets opposed the idea of an institute because it was a Western idea and designed to strengthen the role of the secretary general. The French were wary of it because they, too, did not want to see the role of the secretary general enhanced. Nevertheless, the resolution was approved by an overwhelming majority, including virtually all Third World countries.

Next came the problem of raising funds. Thant strongly favored the proposal. To help in getting contributions, he wanted a brochure describing briefly the aims and proposed structure of the new institute. Paul Hoffman, for whom I had done some drafting when he was U.S. delegate to the Second Committee in 1956, suggested to Thant that he enlist my services. Thant then asked Stevenson to lend me to the Secretariat to work on the brochure. Stevenson agreed to second me, as a result of which I worked on the project from Christmas through New Year's Day.

My draft was discussed with Thant's principal aides, who made suggestions. The most significant one came from Ralph Bunche who, as the official principally responsible for the UN's peacekeeping operations, did not want the term "peacekeeping" used as a topic of institute concern. We then substituted the phrase "U.N. operations in troubled areas." I also consulted at various stages with a key official at the Ford Foundation, in order to be sure we did nothing to offend an institution that was expected to contribute about half of the funds.

Thant then asked the UN High Commission for Refugees to second his fund raiser, Peter Casson, and the commissioner agreed. Casson, astute, persistent, and indefatigable, succeeded in raising $2.6 million in contributions and pledges from outside the United States. Then came the big surprise. The Ford Foundation rejected the secretary general's request for a founding contribution, though it expressed its willingness to consider requests for aid on individual projects on their merits.

The project had by that time gathered its own momentum; even though the assumption on which it was initiated proved to be unfounded. Thant and Casson persuaded John D. Rockefeller III to buy for $500,000 a five-story building on Forty-fifth Street and United Nations Plaza, facing the UN, and donate it as the headquarters for the institute. Moreover, the U.S. government, observing how many other governments had contributed, came up with $400,000 for the institute plus $100,000 for Adlai Stevenson Fellowships to be used for trainees from the new countries. Stevenson had died a year earlier, and the fellowship program was an appropriate memorial.

Unfortunately, UNITAR's problems were more than financial. To gain the confidence of leading foundations and universities, an executive director of outstanding reputation would have been required. Instead, the secretary general decided to make his choice on a political basis; this became clear when Dick Gardner and I went to see Thant's *chef de cabinet*, C. V. Narasimhan. Dick suggested John Holmes, head of the Canadian Institute of International Affairs. Narasimhan did not comment on Holmes's qualifications but stated flatly that the executive director could not come from a NATO country. Looking at his constellation of undersecretaries general, Thant decided that he should have another French-speaking African at that level in order to obtain a better geopolitical balance. He chose Gabriel d'Arboussier, a distinguished, charming and intelligent Senegalese. Unfortunately d'Arboussier had no standing with the Western foundations where most of the potential nongovernmental sources of support lay, nor with leading academic circles. It has been difficult to overcome the handicap of those early years, despite the appointment of subsequent Executive Directors of higher academic standing and reputation.

UNITAR has not become a Rand type of organization for the secretary general. It has, however, done commendable studies of economic and social issues and of the problems of negotiation, mediation, and the peaceful settlement of disputes. It has also performed an important training function. As of 1980, its research program on resources for the future has also carried out significant projects.

CONCLUDING THOUGHTS

Measured against his stature in the nation and the world and his own expectations, Stevenson's term as permanent representative could be considered a disappointment. He was not in the president's inner circle for policymaking. He was not on close terms with Secretary Rusk, with whom there was an underlying tension. His many other responsibilities and interests made him only a half-time representative. His reputation as an idealist gave him little clout on policy in the Kennedy and Johnson administrations, where the emphasis lay on being tough and practical. Moreoever, his own nagging self-doubts made him appear indecisive and handicapped him severely in policy disputes with the bright, self-assured men who counseled the two presidents—Bundy, McNamara, and Rostow; they also had the advantage of being there, in Washington, full-time. Finally, feeling deep frustration at his inability to move U.S. policy on major world issues, he exhausted himself by working and playing too hard and consequently lost some of his zest and effectiveness.

Yet Stevenson did a laudable job of representing the United States at the UN. His very presence was recognized as a sign that the United States attached importance to the organization. He assembled a distinguished and capable staff of top deputies. As we have noted, he had public presence, wit, an original mind, and great skills as a diplomat and orator. He was respected not only among Western delegates but also among those of the Third World as a distinguished, decent man who believed deeply in peace and justice. He was also superb in building support for the UN among the American people.

The tragedy was that Stevenson did not have more impact on the policies of Kennedy and Johnson. In retrospect, his doubts on escalating the war in Vietnam appear far wiser than the decisions of those bright, self-assured men whose counsels prevailed.

NOTES

1. Kenneth S. Davis, *The Politics of Honor: A Biography of Adlai E. Stevenson* (New York: Putnam, 1967), pp. 404–5.

2. Theodore Sorenson, *Kennedy* (New York: Harper and Row, 1965), p. 254.

3. Stevenson served most effectively and with great distinction as U.S. Delegation Press Relations chief, when the U.N. Charter was completed at San Francisco in 1945; as replacement for Edward Stettinius, U.S. Representative to the Preparatory Commission at London in 1946; and as Senior Adviser to the U.S. Delegation to the First Session of the U.N. General Assembly. He had hoped to become Permanent Representative in 1946, but the job went to Austin; he was, however, Alternate Delegate to the U.N. General Assembly in 1946 and 1947. See Bert Cochran, *Adlai Stevenson—Patrician Among Politicians.* (New York: Funk and Wagnalls, 1969), pp. 140–45. Also, John B. Martin, *Adlai Stevenson and the World* (New York: Doubleday), pp. 556–65, describes Stevenson's hesitation and dickering with Kennedy.

4. Arthur M. Schlesinger, Jr., *A Thousand Days: John F. Kennedy in the White House* (Boston: Houghton Mifflin, 1965), pp. 462–66. See also Martin II, op. cit., pp. 586–87.

5. Schlesinger, op. cit., p. 462.

6. Martin, op. cit., II, pp. 581–87. See also Arnold Beichman, *The "Other" State Department* (New York: Basic Books, 1967), pp. 145–46. See also Martin, op. cit., pp. 581–57.

7. Richard Walton, *The Remnants of Power* (New York: Coward McCann

1968), p. 26. Davis (op. cit., p. 459) reports that he was not consulted nor even adequately informed of important policy development with whose issue he disagreed personally but must defend before the U.N." Martin (op. cit., p. 650) quotes Stevenson as saying in a letter to Hubert Humphrey: "I feel that when he wants my point of view he will ask for it."

8. Walton, op. cit., p. 208-10. Also, Martin, op cit., pp. 588, 679-80, and Walter Johnson, *The Papers of Adlai Stevenson*, Vol. 8 (Boston: Little Brown, 1979), p. 21.

9. Martin, op. cit., p. 756 (II). For a fuller account of Stevenson's social and personal life, especially his personal letters, see Johnson, op. cit.

10. Martin, op. cit., p. 707 (II).

11. See John B. Martin, Adlai Stevenson of Illinois (Garden City, N.Y.: Doubleday, New York, 1976)(I), for a description of Stevenson's earlier love life, especially pp. 317-21 and 334-56. Martin writes:

Stevenson was unusually attractive to women all his life, and they attracted him. The ones who became close to him—and many more who tried— were nearly all bright, pretty, and rich, and several of them had newspaper connections. They were, most of them, also strong-willed, as his mother and sister had been. Unlike some political leaders, such as John F. Kennedy, Stevenson did not separate his political or official life from his private life. Kennedy had two sets of friends; those he worked with in politics or government, and those he saw socially, and to a considerable extent they were different people. Stevenson was inclined to mingle the two. The women in his life, except for his wife, gave him political advice. His most private letters to women are likely to contain his frankest views on public men and public issues—he confided more fully in women than in men. (p. 318)

His description of Stevenson's affair with Alicia Patterson is both fascinating and illumiating. His other love affairs, numerous and often lasting, are recounted elsewhere in this book as well as Martin's other book on Stevenson, *Adlai Stevenson and the World,* notably pp. 592-93, 637, 757-64. See also Lauren Bacall, *By Myself* (New York: Knopf, 1979), for additional comments on his lady friends and ravenous appetite, and Johnson, op. cit.

12. Cochran, op cit., p. 198.

13. Martin, *Adlai Stevenson of Illinois*, p. 258.

14. Ibid., p. 693; and Davis, op. cit., p. 421.

15. Walton, op. cit., pp. 212-17, describes the institutional problems that initiated Stevenson's influence on policy. Cochran, op. cit., p. 318, concludes that Stevenson's influence on shaping policy was negligible, that is he had "prestige without power."

16. Martin, *Adlai Stevenson and the World*, p. 761.

17. Ibid, pp. 747-48.

18. USUN telegram 851, September 21, 1962. A sanitized version is available in the Kennedy Library, Boston: NSF: Portugal 9/1/62-9/28/62, Box 154.

19. Cochran, op. cit., p. 336.

20. Martin, *Adlai Stevenson and the World*, p. 590.

21. Ibid., p. 591.

22. Ernest W. Lefever, *Crisis in the Congo* (Washington, D.C.: Brookings Institution, 1965), p. 51.

23. S.C. Res. S/4741, February 21, 1961. Text reproduced in Lefever, ibid., p. 193.

24. Schlesinger, op. cit., p. 575.

25. UN Security Council, *Official Records*, 943d meeting, February 15, 1961. See also Martin, *Adlai Stevenson and the World*, pp. 610-13.

26. Robert Hilsman, *The Politics of Policy Making in Defense and Foreign Affairs* (New York: Harper and Row, 1971), pp. 243-50.

27. Ibid., pp. 250-71. See also Lefever, op. cit., chap. 3 and 4. As Lefever

indicates, casulaties were high pp. 113–14).

28. The only notable action by the Council was its adoption on November 24, 1961, by a vote of 9 to 0 (France and Britain abstaining) of resolution S/5002, which in paragraph 4 authorized the secretary general "to take vigorous action, including the use of a requisite measure of force, if necessary, for the immediate apprehension, detention pending legal action and/or deportation of all foreign military and para-military personnel and political advisers not under the United Nations Command, and mercenaries." This provision was intended to strengthen the secretary general's hand in dealing with the Katanga secession, and it did.

29. Lefever op. cit., p. 120. Conor Cruise O'Brien, who was the UN representative in Katanga from June to November 1961, charges that Hammarskjöld bent to British pressure in September when UN troops used force in an operation aimed at ending Tshombe's secession. The UN's official report on the violence of September 13 described by UN troops as responding to attacks by the Katangese gendarmerie. O'Brien felt that this evasive and, in his view, distorted account encouraged the Tshombe regime to continue its secession, whereas a forthright UN campaign to end the secession by force would have succeeded quickly. It is difficult to judge the correctness of O'Brien's estimate of success. On the other hand, it is an established principle of UN peacekeeping operations that force is to be used only in self-defense, not for offensive operations. Even though the Security Council's resolution of February 21, 1961, authorized "the use of force, if necessary, in the last resort," this was to be done only "to prevent the occurrence of civil war in the Congo." Given the European, especially British, outcry against the operation and the principle that UN peacekeeping units use force only in self-defense, it is understandable that Hammarskjöld's

official version emphasized self-defense. See Conor Cruise O'Brien, *To Katanga and Back* (New York: Simon and Schuster, 1962), pp. 219–88.

30. Ibid., p. 62.

31. O'Brien, op. cit., pp. 40–67, alleges that three top Americans in the Secretariat—Cordier, Bunche, and Weischoff—actually formed the inner circle of Hammarskjöld's advisers. He does not challenge their loyalty to Hammarskjöld or the UN but argues that their cultural background necessarily influenced their viewpoints, a valid point. Weischoff died with Hammarskjöld in the plane crash of September 1961, and Cordier retired shortly thereafter. Bunche continued as U Thant's top adviser on peacekeeping until the end of ONUC in 1964, but he was a man of very independent mind. To my personal knowledge, he stubbornly and successfully resisted U.S. pressure to extend ONUC beyond June 1964 and never hesitated to disagree with Washington or Stevenson on other issues if his independent mind so indicated.

32. Schlesinger, op. cit., 271.

33. Ibid., pp. 271–73.

34. Ibid., pp. 484–86.

35. The members of the Executive Committee were:

Dean Rusk, Secretary of State
Robert McNamara, Secretary of Defense
Robert F. Kennedy, Attorney General
John McCone, Director of the C.I.A.
Douglas Dillon, Secretary of the Treasury
McGeorge Bundy, Adviser on National Security Affairs
Theodore Sorenson, Presidential Counsel
George Ball, Undersecretary of State
U. Alexis Johnson, Deputy Undersecretary of State
General Maxwell Taylor, Chairman of the Joint Chiefs of Staff
Edward Martin, Assitant Secretary of State for Latin American Affairs

Llewellyn Thompson, Adviser on Soviet Affairs

Roswell Gilpatric, Deputy Secretary of Defense

Paul Nitze, Assistant Secretary of Defense Intermittently

Lyndon B. Johnson, Vice President Ambassador Adlai Stevenson

Ken O'Donnell, Special Assistant to the President

Dan Wilson, Deputy Director, USIA For a full account of its deliberations, see Robert F. Kennedy, *Thirteen Days* (New York, Norton, 1969).

36. Walton, op. cit., p. 40.

37. Schlesinger, op. cit., pp. 810–11. In my interview (October 31, 1977) with Richard Pedersen, who had been senior political adviser in 1962, he told me that he and Charles Yost had worked with Stevenson in preparing this negotiating position.

38. Adlai E. Stevenson, *Looking Outward*, ed. Robert Schiffer and Selma Schiffer (New York: Harper and Row, 1963), pp. 97–98.

39. See ibid., pp. 79–112, for text of Stevenson speeches and his exchange with Zorin wherein he challenged the Soviet representatives to deny that there was offensive Soviet missiles in Cuba and said he was prepared to wait for the reply "until Hell freezes over." See also Davis, op. cit., pp. 482–85.

40. Stevenson, op. cit., pp. 125–28.

41. Ruth B. Russell, *The United Nations and United States Security Policy* (Washington, D.C.: Brookings Institution, 1968), p. 76.

42. Cochran, op. cit., pp. 324–25. It should be noted that Stevenson put forward his negotiating suggestions during a brainstorming session of the Executive Committee when all possibilities were being explored and he concurred fully with the Executive Committee's decision. Dean Rusk said: "The mix that turned out had a good Stevenson output in it. It was a place where his influence was significant. We were all doves and hawks trying to find an alternative to

force." Quoted in Walton, op. cit., p. 65. See also Beichman, op. cit., pp. 146–48; Martin, *Adlai Stevenson and the World,* pp. 722–23.

43. Cochran, op. cit., p. 318.

44. Martin, *Adlai Stevenson and the World,* p. 684.

45. Martin, *Adlai Stevenson and the World,* p. 782; and Davis, op. cit., pp. 488–90.

46. Johnson, op. cit., pp. 611–12, 667–69.

47. Martin, *Adlai Stevenson and the World,* pp. 827–28.

48. Walton, op. cit., pp. 141–2; and Davis, op. cit., pp. 494–98.

49. Walton, op. cit., pp. 144–45.

50. Martin, *Adlai Stevenson and the World,* p. 811.

51. Ibid., pp. 840–41.

52. Ibid., pp. 830–31.

53. Davis, op. cit., pp. 501–3; Cochran, op. cit., pp. 328–29; and Martin, *Adlai Stevenson and the World,* pp. 857–59.

54. Martin, *Adlai Stevenson and the World,* p. 861. See also Johnson, op. cit., pp. 781–82, 798–99 and 839 for evidence that Stevenson did not oppose "containment" in Vietnam.

55. Martin, *Adlai Stevenson and the World,* p. 856.

56. Quoted in Johnson, op. cit., p. 757.

57. Cochran, op. cit., pp. 326–28.

58. U Thant address, May 27, 1965, in *UN Monthly Chronicle* 2 (June 1965): 69.

59. Thomas Franck and Edward Weisband, *Word Politics: verbal strategy among the superpowers; New York, Oxford Univ. Press, 1971.* For a description and analysis of the Brezhnev doctrine and its implications, see Ivo Duchacek, *Nations and Men,* 3d ed. (Hinsdale, Ill.: Dryden, 1975), pp. 424–26.

60. UN Security Council, *Official Records,* May 3, 1965. See also Martin, *Adlai Stevenson and the World,* pp. 843–47. The United States also argued that the action was an exercise of self-

defense, invoking the January 1962 Declaration of Punta del Este, which had declared Marxism-Leninism incompatible with the Inter-American system and had urged OAS members:

> to take those steps that they may consider appropriate for their individual or collective self-defense, and to cooperate, as may be necessary or desirable, to strengthen their capacity to counteract threats or acts of aggression, subversion, or other dangers to peace and security resulting from the continued intervention in this hemisphere of Sino-Soviet powers, in accordance with the obligations established in treaties and agreements . . . such as the OAS Charter and the Rio Treaty.

Leonard C. Meeker, address before Foreign Law Association, U.S. Department of State, *Bulletin* 53 (1965): 62.

61. S.C. Res. 203, May 14, 1965.

62. UN press release M-1709, December 31, 1966, p. 7.

63. Walt W. Rostow, *The Diffusion of Power* (New York: Macmillan, 1972), p. 415.

64. Martin, *Adlai Stevenson and the World*, p. 844.

65. Ibid., pp. 860–61.

66. U Thant, op. cit., pp. 361–76.

67. Martin, op. cit., pp. 581, 589–90.

68. USUN telegram 851, September 21, 1962 (sanitized) in J. F. Kennedy Library, Boston: NSF: Portugal, 9/1/62–9/28/62, Box 154. See also M. A. Samuels and S. M. Haykin, "The Anderson Plan: An American Attempt to Seduce Portugal Out of Africa," *Orbis*, Fall 1979, pp. 649–69.

69. G.A. Res. 1619 (XV), April 21, 1961. The vote was 54 (including the United States, the United Kingdom, Canada, the Nordic countries, and 21 new nations) to 15 (including the Soviet bloc), with 23 abstentions.

70. Letter dated December 1, 1977, from Philip M. Klutznick to the author.

71. U Thant, op. cit., pp. 85–91.

72. G.A. Res. 1739 (XVI), December 20, 1961. The vote was 58 to 13 (France,

Belgium, and 11 communist states) with 24 abstentions.

73. Letter to the author from Klutznick, op. cit.

74. John G. Stoessinger, *The United Nations and the Superpowers*, (New York: Random House, 1965), pp. 98–102.

75. ICJ *Reports*, 1962, pp. 151, 179–80.

76. G.A. Res. 1854 (XVII), December 19, 1962.

77. For a detailed exposition of the U.S. viewpoint, see U.S. State Department, *Article 19 of the Charter of the United Nations, Memorandum of Law*, Washington, D.C.

78. Soviet memorandum.

79. Beichman, op. cit., pp. 149–53.

80. Walton, op. cit., p. 87.

81. See U.S. State Department, op. cit., pp. 2–8. Note also that on Jan. 2, 1980, Sudan was informed by the UN Secretariat that it had lost its right to vote under Article 19, this without General Assembly action. *The New York Times*, Jan. 17, 1980, p. A-9, col. 1.

82. Walton, op. cit., pp. 87–91.

83. Beichman, op. cit., pp. 155, 163.

84. UN General Assembly, *Official Records,* A/C.121, April 29, 1965, p. 5.

85. David Kay, *The New Nations in the United Nations*, (New York: Columbia U. Press, 1970), p. 129.

86. H. G. Nicholas, *The United Nations as a Political Institution*, 4th ed. (England: London, Oxford University Press, 1971), p. 264.

87. Russell, op. cit., pp. 440–43.

88. Stoessinger, op. cit., p. 110.

89. G.A. Res. 1316 (XIII), December 12, 1958.

90. The achievements are described in Richard N. Gardner, *In Pursuit of World Order* (New York: Praeger, 1974), pp. 124–40.

91. Statement by President John F. Kennedy to the UN General Assembly, September 25, 1961.

92. G.A. Res. 1710 (XVI), December 19, 1961.

93. G.A. Res. 1715 (XVI), December 19, 1961.

94. Gardner, op. cit., pp. 126-31.

95. G.A. Doc. A/8124/Add. 1, October 20, 1970.

96. Gardner, op. cit., pp. 161–63.

97. G.A. Res. 1707 (XVI), December 19, 1961.

98. UN Doc. E/3631/Add. 1–4, May 10, 1962.

99. ECOSOC Res. 917 (XXXIV), August 3, 1962.

100. G.A. Doc. A/C/L. 648/Rev. 2/Corr. 1, November 14, 1962.

101. G.A. Res. 1995 (XIX).

102. Ibid.

103. Statement by Gamani Corea at a meeting of the UNCTAD Trade and Development Board marking UNCTAD's tenth anniversary, August 1974.

CHAPTER VI

Arthur J. Goldberg

Arthur Goldberg arrived at USUN with a strong mandate. He came as "the representative of Lyndon Johnson,"[1] who had persuaded him to leave a lifetime job in the Supreme Court. Johnson referred to him as "an old and trusted friend of mine" and "a counselor of many years," who would sit in the cabinet and would "always have direct and ready access to, and the full and respectful confidence of, the President of the United States and the Secretary of State." He added: "In his new office, he will speak not only for an administration, but will speak for the entire nation."[2]

The fact that Johnson sought Goldberg strengthened the new permanent representative's position, at least initially. The president called Goldberg on July 16, 1965, shortly after Adlai Stevenson's death, and said that he needed "an outstanding American to deal with the crisis at the U.N." and to guide him to an early settlement of the Vietnam War. After another phone call from the president, Goldberg went to see him at the White House. While waiting in the anteroom, Goldberg was approached by a presidential assistant, Jack Valenti, who inquired whether he might not also be interested in the post of secretary of the department of health, education, and welfare. Goldberg, with typical sensitivity, resented being treated like a job applicant, having come because the president had invited him to discuss the UN post. He told Valenti: "I'm not an applicant for any post—including the U.N. one." The president, who must have had some indication from Valenti of Goldberg's reaction to the HEW post, never mentioned it; instead, Johnson reemphasized how much the nation needed a man of Goldberg's stature at the UN. Goldberg again deferred his decision.

Shortly thereafter Johnson asked Goldberg to accompany him to Bloomington, Illinois, for Adlai Stevenson's funeral, and on the plane coming back to Washington they had a long conversation. Goldberg told Johnson that leaving the Court would be a grave step and that he would need assurance before finally deciding on acceptance, not only that the UN ambassadorship would be elevated in general foreign policymaking, but that he would be a principal adviser and participant in all decision making leading to a negotiated peace in Vietnam. He asked Johnson whether he was committed to such a peace. The president replied that he was and that one of his basic reasons for asking Goldberg to assume the UN post was to get the benefit of "America's greatest negotiator in reaching a peaceful solution; and soon."[3] (Another strong reason that became evident later was Johnson's desire to create a Supreme Court vacancy for his old friend, Abe Fortas. Goldberg was aware that Fortas might be chosen but thought at the time that Fortas would be a good appointment.)

The weekend before Goldberg resigned from the Court he and his wife were guests at Camp David. That same weekend Secretary of Defense McNamara presented a proposal for calling up the Reserves for service in Vietnam. Goldberg told Johnson that if this were done he would withdraw his acceptance of the UN post because, to him, calling up the Reserves meant the equivalent of a formal declaration of war. Johnson did not give the order.[4] Still, Goldberg was aware of Johnson's plans for a massive increase in U.S. forces in Vietnam. Upon arriving at USUN in July 1965, he told some of us in private that the publicly announced increment that month, from 75,000 to 125,000, was only a beginning; by the end of 1966 there would be over 400,000 American troops in Vietnam. And there were.

Goldberg had valid reasons for insisting on a clear mandate before accepting the UN post. His seat on the Supreme Court was the most revered position in the law and a lifetime appointment on the olympian heights that included generous pensions for himself and his wife. He would be trading these for a hectic, backbreaking job in the hurly-burly of UN politics where he would serve at the president's pleasure. Yet he was intrigued by the new post. He had great, perhaps exaggerated respect for the potential of the UN in "the effort to bring the rule of law to govern the relations between sovereign states. It is that or doom—and we all know it."[5] He observed that "in one generation the U.N. has created more international law than in all previous generations in man's history."[6] Shortly thereafter he said, "I consider the role of the U.S. Representative to the United Nations to be a dual one. He, of course, first represents the President of our government at the United Nations, but second, he also represents the United Nations to the American people."[7]

Another factor, as noted above, was Goldberg's sincere conviction that his efforts at the UN and in cabinet meetings could help to end the war in Vietnam. Having been at USUN for nine years when Goldberg arrived and having witnessed Stevenson's frustration, I was privately skeptical from the beginning about the extent to which the chief of our mission could have an impact. Hanoi, the Soviets, and the French did not want a UN role.

When, in January 1966, the United States did attempt to get UN Security Council action on the issue, we managed with great effort to get the bare 9 votes (out of 15) required for inscription of the item. The ninth vote (Japan) was conditioned on the understanding that the Council would not actually meet on this item until private consultations indicated that a meeting would be constructive—which never happened. The one point of agreement among the Council members was that the 1954 Geneva accords should be the basis of any new settlement.

Goldberg's efforts were not helped by the fact that the United States resumed the bombing of North Vietnam shortly after it requested Security Council consideration. According to Norman Cousins, the resumption of bombing on January 30, 1966, also derailed a meeting Cousins was to have with a Hanoi representative in Warsaw in February. Another meeting of Washington and Hanoi representatives in Warsaw envisaged for late 1966 was also aborted because of escalated U.S. bombings on the eve of scheduled meetings.[8] Small wonder that Goldberg's efforts at the UN were doomed to frustration.

Another clue to Goldberg's frustration on Vietnam is provided in Walt Rostow's book, *The Diffusion of Power*. Rostow described Johnson's national security policy as one built initially around Rusk, McNamara, and Bundy. Goldberg is mentioned as one who came "occasionally" to the Tuesday luncheons where crucial policy discussions took place. He suffered from an inherent handicap in having to be in New York most of the time, even though he did attend the formal National Security Council sessions regularly and worked superhuman hours to be in Washington for a policy role there while doing a superb job of running USUN. As Rostow was so close to the president, it is a significant indication of Rostow's attitude toward the UN that his lengthy book covering more than a decade of foreign policy starting in 1958 makes only this one reference to Goldberg in his capacity of permanent representative in the UN. There is no reference whatsoever to other occupants of the post during the period covered— Lodge, Ball, Wiggins, Yost, and Scali. Lodge is mentioned only as ambassador to Vietnam, Ball as undersecretary of state, and Goldberg a number of times as secretary of labor.[9]

I witnessed another indication that Johnson had used some hyperbole in describing his belief in the importance of the UN. Goldberg had suggested to the president that he invite the secretary general and the UN diplomatic corps to a White House reception. On Thursday, June 9, 1966, the president called and said he could receive them the following Tuesday! Goldberg told us that, however short the notice and hectic the preparations, we had better make the best of it; the president was not likely to reschedule the reception for any other time. With yeoman efforts on all sides the UN group arrived at the White House Tuesday evening and were treated to the full splendor of a White House reception. Unfortunately, halfway through the agonizingly long receiving line—consisting of more than 100 ambassadors and their wives plus a larger number of other dignitaries—the president became bored with the whole exercise and retreated to his private quarters upstairs, until he was persuaded to come back down and finish the job. The secretary general, who had expected to have a private substantive session with the president, had to settle for a casual chat. By then, of course, Thant's public criticisms of U.S. actions in Vietnam had not endeared him to either the president or the secretary of state. Thus, while a visit by the secretary general and the UN diplomatic corps to the White House was an unprecedented event, it did little to convince the visitors of Johnson's belief in the UN, which, in any case, was not profound.

Still another element in Goldberg's acceptance was the fact that he, the Chicago-born son of a poor Jewish immigrant, would be succeeding the illustrious Adlai Stevenson. In fact, he told some of us at USUN that he would not have considered the job if Stevenson had not been his predecessor.

I suspect, too, that Goldberg, a man of prodigious energy and drive and still in his fifties, did feel a little restless on the Court, though I do not doubt his statement that he did not seek the UN job or any other post. Lyndon Johnson wrote in *The Vantage Point* that Goldberg had been "bored" on the Court and wanted to leave.[10] Goldberg became so incensed upon reading this statement that he telephoned the former president and told him in no uncertain terms that Johnson's statement that he had solicited the appointment was completely unfounded, as Johnson had reason to know. He also demanded the return of one of Mrs. Goldberg's paintings that the president had been given after strong hints, stating: "It's mine and you don't deserve it."[11]

In any case, the record shows that Johnson went to great lengths to persuade Goldberg to accept the post, agreed to Goldberg's conditions, and gave him a strong mandate. Moreover, Goldberg had frequent access to the president, long talks with him, and some impact on national policy, at least for the first two years of his tenure. This was particularly true with regard to the Indo-Pakistan War of 1965, the Middle East crisis in 1967, Rhodesia, Southwest Africa, and the *Pueblo* incident (issues discussed later in this chapter). Unfortunately, he had little influence on the main issue that led him to take the UN job—Vietnam.

Goldberg also insisted on having *all* available information on issues confronting the U.S. government. He was keenly aware of Stevenson's acute embarrassment at having to provide false information to the Security Council in the Bay of Pigs incident because he was not privy to the truth and he was determined not to be placed in that position. Also, he had been in the OSS during World War II and was thus fully aware of the many sources of intelligence, overt and covert, available to the president. At his insistence, he and his top associates saw not only State Department traffic but also the relevant output of the CIA, the FBI, the Department of Defense, and the National Security Agency. Having the full picture was of enormous importance in developing policy input and in negotiating with other delegations, notably in the Middle East crisis.

Overall, I consider Goldberg to have been one of the most effective of all the distinguished and capable men who have served as permanent representatives over three decades, during half of which I was at the USUN. As one astute UN correspondent put it, he restored the mission "to a new level of efficiency."[12] He had a creative and retentive mind, prodigious energy, a well-developed sense of organization, and a strong interest in his staff, which had to work extremely hard to keep up with him. His influence with the president—he phoned him often—and Johnson's personal confidence in him meant that Goldberg's well-developed positions on UN issues would often become U.S. policy. Probably about 80 percent of the action proposals and instructions on which USUN operated during his tenure originated with Goldberg or under his guidance. Also, in contrast with the Stevenson era, USUN normally prepared the first draft of speeches, giving it a tactical advantage in bargaining with the State Department in negotiating over the final text.

Goldberg was certainly the best negotiator I have ever seen, at the UN or anywhere else. He was always thoroughly prepared; knowledgeable on all aspects of the issue; aware of what arguments the other side was likely to make; judicious in weighing the strengths and weaknesses of the respective positions; clear in exposition; and calm, patient, and scrupulously honest. This last quality was particularly important at the UN, which is a "glass house" in more ways than one, where bad faith is quickly detected and a reputation for it spreads fast. His long experience with labor negotiations had sharpened his natural talents.

His main weakness was in public speaking, where he compared poorly with Lodge or Stevenson. He had a nasal monotone that sounded dreary in any lengthy public statement, and certain mannerisms made him look pompous. In private discussions and negotiations, however, his keen mind and sensitivity made him a superb interlocutor. Nor should one exaggerate the importance of public speeches at the UN; they rarely change a mind or a vote. The real action is in the private negotiations, especially one-on-one conversations; that is where minds are changed—and that is where Goldberg was at his best.

Goldberg prided himself on good faith negotiations and not "pulling a fast one." For example, on December 19, 1965, a group of African delegations, supported by other anticolonial states and the Soviet bloc, were advancing a resolution calling for the dismantling of all foreign military bases. Their speeches were anticolonial in nature, and privately they told us that the resolution was not aimed at American bases but colonial bases; however, the text made no such distinction. Consequently, the United States urged that it be amended or withdrawn. We also argued that, if the resolution were put to a vote, a two-thirds majority should be required, since Article 18 of the UN Charter specifies that "recommendations with respect to the maintenance of peace and security" are important questions. The sponsors of the resolution replied, curiously, that the issue was indeed important but not an "important question" for voting purposes. As a result, a procedural vote was called for, to decide whether or not the issue was an "important question." Looking around the General Assembly hall I observed that half the African delegations were absent on that Friday afternoon and that we could win the procedural vote. Apparently the Africans present realized the same thing; they asked for a postponement until Monday, December 22. I urged Goldberg to insist on proceeding to a vote, calculating that we could also defeat a motion to adjourn. Also, I had seen the same delegations press relentlessly for a vote when the United States wanted a postponement. But Goldberg, acting as a gentleman, agreed to the postponement. Over the weekend the sponsors lobbied feverishly, using group pressure to enforce anticolonial solidarity and insure the presence of all possible supporters Monday. As I expected, this made the difference; they won the procedural vote and the resolution was adopted. After its adoption Goldberg made a statement to the Assembly declaring the resolution "ultra vires," since the voting procedures had violated Article 18 of the Charter.

In retrospect I am convinced that Goldberg was right. As a resolution of the General Assembly, the recommendation was not binding on its members, and in fact no state with foreign military bases paid any attention to it. Moreover, even if that resolution had been defeated, a future Assembly would have adopted something similar. By agreeing to the postponement, Goldberg gained a reputation for good sportsmanship and fairness that helped him during the rest of his term at the UN.

Another Goldberg gesture made him popular with Americans in the UN Secretariat. All U.S. premanent representatives had cultivated good relations with the secretary general, Andrew Cordier, and Ralph Bunche. Also, some of us at USUN developed good working relations with Secretariat officials dealing with our areas of concern. Yet the vast majority of Americans in the Secretariat had little contact with USUN; few had ever been invited there, and many felt neglected or snubbed. Secretariat personnel from most other countries had far more frequent contact with their national missions. I suggested to Goldberg that we do something to improve our relations with Secretariat Americans, and he agreed. In early

June 1966 he invited all 1,528 U.S. citizens employed at the UN to an "American Day" reception at the mission and to meet Vice-President Humphrey. It was a great success. Few had ever been inside the mission before, and the gesture was appreciated. Moreover, Goldberg was able to announce that day the settlement of a grievance by the U.S. employees of the Secretariat, which had previously been brought to his attention by the secretary general. They had been obliged since 1960 to pay the U.S. social security tax at the high "self-employed" rate, since the UN could not be taxed as an employer. Goldberg, with Humphrey's help, obtained a U.S. government ruling that henceforth they would pay the lower rate charged for employees.[13]

Unfortunately, he was not able to remove one of the handicaps of USUN itself—the sparsity of funds for necessary entertainment. Except for the Russians, there was no other large country on as tight an entertainment budget as the United States. With the fiscal year ending June 30, we had no money for the American Day reception and had to go to private sources.

On other occasions we had to resort to various stratagems. My wife and I would pay off accumulated social obligations by having inexpensive buffets on the top floor of the mission. For two successive years we entertained delegates to the Fourth (Decolonization) Committee by having a wine-tasting party, with free wine and cheese provided by the California Wine Growers Association.

Goldberg wanted to break out of the stodgy pattern of formal dinners and receptions and still live within our tight representation budget. In the fall of 1966, during the General Assembly, he decided to invite foreign delegates to two dinners aboard American passenger ships in port. He asked me to negotiate with the ship company president for "very wholesale" prices. The company was most accommodating, offering a price of $800 for about 200 guests at each party, which would cover the raw cost of the food and beverages used. Unfortunately, at the second dinner a freeloading reporter for a Chicago newspaper started inquiring about the terms offered by a shipping company that received U.S. government subsidies. This disturbed Goldberg, who then instructed me to renegotiate the contract so that we would pay every cent of the full cost. With heavy heart, knowing what a dent it would make in our available funds for the year, I renegotiated for triple the original price!

Goldberg was always sensitive about the press. He read at least four newspapers every day and would react sharply to any adverse story. The veteran newspaperman, Frank Carpenter, who served as press officer for Lodge, Stevenson, and Goldberg, advised him not to get excited "just because some guy writes a story in the newspaper," but his advice had little impact on our chief.

THE GOLDBERG TEAM

Initially Goldberg followed the practice of his predecessors, appointing prominent noncareer people at the ambassadorial level, backstopped by experienced professionals. The exception was Career Ambassador Charles Yost, who had been Stevenson's deputy representative to the Security Council and remained in that position under Goldberg. Yost, a superb professional, was Goldberg's principal adviser on political issues, providing a rare incisiveness and sound judgment.

Francis Plimpton, Stevenson's deputy permanent representative and former law school roommate, was as much surprised as any of us when the news of Goldberg's designation came over the news ticker. He apparently expected to stay on and was disappointed when Goldberg accepted his offer to resign. Perhaps in a Freudian slip, he referred to Goldberg a number of times as "Goldwater"; Plimpton was a liberal Republican by conviction and probably had little affection for the leader of the party's right wing.

To replace Plimpton, Goldberg picked Dr. James M. Nabrit, the president of Howard University. Nabrit had been one of the NAACP's top lawyers in the civil rights struggle but was now something of an elder statesman in the black community. While at USUN Nabrit continued as president of Howard and maintained his residence in Washington, commuting back and forth. He did not concern himself much with day-to-day operations, but we all profited from his wisdom.

One factor in Nabrit's appointment was Goldberg's desire to have a distinguished black man in the number two position. Goldberg's appointment came on the heels of outstanding achievements by President Johnson on civil rights, and he was fully in tune with Johnson on this issue. I can recall being at Goldberg's official residence for a Passover seder with diplomats, labor leaders, rabbis, and black leaders where we sang labor songs and "We Shall Overcome." Goldberg also decided we should have a black female on the mission's eleventh (executive) floor and, since my secretary was due to leave, that her replacement should be black. I said the color did not matter as long as she was competent. In due course came Brenda Lee, a beautiful and extremely bright girl, fresh from Saigon. By that time Goldberg had been succeeded by George Ball, who had no interest in Brenda's color, but I did get a bright and good-humored secretary out of the process.

James Roosevelt, eldest son of the late president, became U.S. representative to the UN Economic and Social Council, with the rank of ambassador. A big, outgoing, genial backslapper, a former congressman, Jimmy was very popular with other delegations and a good team man. His one-year tenure corresponded to a period when U.S. economic policy in the

UN had become largely defensive and reactive, and this did not fit his activist temperament.

The other ambassadorial slot, representative at the Trusteeship Council, went to Eugenie Anderson, a power in Minnesota politics and an ally of the vice-president, Hubert Humphrey. She had previously been ambassador to Bulgaria and Denmark and was skilled in diplomacy as well as politics. During her last year, however, she became heavily involved in Humphrey's 1968 presidential campaign and had little time for her work at the UN. I filled in for her on all colonial issues, although she did return to New York for three weeks in June to serve as president of the Trusteeship Council.

Rounding out the top layer was Richard Pedersen, who had been at USUN since 1953 and had served as chief of the political section. Dick had the rank of minister counselor and continued to concentrate on political issues and the Security Council. I served as deputy counselor, with responsibility for coordinating the mission's activities in the economic, social development, financial, personnel, legal, and decolonization areas. Thus, our office became the nerve center of the mission, as James Barco's office had been under Lodge. Pedersen and I also served as troubleshooters at various UN meetings, either as advisers or as representatives, whenever a situation was important, sensitive, or difficult. (Subsequently Dick became the senior adviser with ambassadorial rank, and I took over as minister counselor.)

A year and a half later came a major shift. Nabrit had returned to Howard after a year at USUN, and Yost succeeded him as deputy, only to leave shortly thereafter in retirement from the Foreign Service. About the same time, Jimmy Roosevelt resigned to take a job with the Overseas Investor Service in Geneva. Thus the number two, three, and four slots in the mission were open; the expectation of most people, including me, was that they would, as usual, be filled by political appointees. On the contrary, Goldberg decided that he wanted experienced, competent career professionals. As deputy he choose William Buffum, a career Foreign Service officer with many years of experience in the State Department's Bureau of International Organization Affairs. Buffum had been deputy to Joseph Sisco, then assistant secretary for International Organization Affairs, who recommended him. Dick Pedersen became deputy representative to the UN Security Council.

Goldberg offered me the post of representative to the UN Economic and Social Council (ECOSOC) vacated by Roosevelt. The offer was tempting, since I had found dealing with economic issues at the UN highly gratifying; however, family considerations would have made it difficult to spend long periods abroad at meetings of ECOSOC and its various subsidiary and affiliate bodies. I therefore, suggested to Goldberg that he offer the ECOSOC slot to Eugenie Anderson. If she wanted it, I would take her place as representative to the Trusteeship Council, while continuing as executive coordinator of the mission and of the General Assembly delegations, as well as general troubleshooter. He agreed to ask her, and she took several weeks to think about it. In the meantime, President Johnson decided to offer the ECOSOC job to an old friend, Arthur ("Tex") Goldschmidt, who had spent many years in the UN Secretariat dealing with economic and technical assistance matters. Thus, Eugenie was foreclosed from shifting and remained for a time as representative to the Trusteeship Council. Goldberg decided that he would nevertheless nominate me for ambassadorial rank as senior adviser, in which capacity I did in fact deal with many issues of decolonization and trusteeship, as well as political, economic, peacekeeping, legal, budget, and personnel questions.

The new team of predominantly career ambassadors was sworn in on January 27, 1967, marking a new departure for U.S. representation initiated by Goldberg. As a team it was the hardest-working and most competent group of top assistants I saw during fifteen years at the mission—a judgment I could make leaving myself out of the calculation. Our standard working day was about twelve hours; Goldberg worked longer. This strength was to prove particularly important during the Middle East crisis, including the Six Day War in June 1967, which we shall discuss later in this chapter.

Another feature of the Goldberg era at USUN was the mobilization of the wives. President Johnson depended significantly on his wife and set a style in Washington for wives of the cabinet officers to help their husbands in their jobs—a style that Goldberg characterized as "two for the price of one." Dorothy Goldberg plunged energetically and wholeheartedly into her part of the job, not only at social functions hosted jointly by her husband, but also at coffees and teas for the wives of foreign diplomats at the Goldbergs' official residence in the Waldorf Tower and in visits to foreign wives who had suffered family calamities or tragedies. She also enlisted the services of our wives, some of whom had other responsibilities that made the added social duties a hardship. In her book Mrs. Goldberg writes that she "related better to foreign wives than to our own."[14] One reason was that some of "our own" had to live in the suburbs because we had neither rent allowances nor government-paid quarters. Arriving at midtown at 10:00 A.M., well groomed and well coiffed for a morning coffee session with foreign wives, after a late official dinner the night before, was not a joyous event, particularly since the wife usually had no servants and had to keep her own household running. Yet, like her husband, Dorothy Goldberg worked hardest of any of the wives, and I can remember fondly her bringing us sandwiches and coffee during a midnight break at the Security Council.

Another Goldberg innovation was a monthly report to the two living former presidents, Truman and Eisenhower. These reports, known by the staff as the "Harry and Ike letters," kept the two men regularly informed of all significant developments and invited their comments. Truman, by then very advanced in years, sent polite acknowledgments but no substantive comments. Eisenhower, on the other hand, frequently gave views and opinions in his letters of reply. In any case, it was a wise stroke on Goldberg's part, helping to build bipartisan sympathies for American policies at the UN.

ARTICLE 19

It was left for Goldberg finally to break the Article 19 deadlock discussed in the previous chapter. By the time he came on the scene in July 1965, it was obvious that there was no way the General Assembly would apply the loss-of-vote sanction in Article 19 of the Charter to those countries that were two years in arrears in paying their assessments because they would not pay their share of the Middle East and Congo peacekeeping operations.

Goldberg shuttled back and forth between New York and Washington to take soundings with key congressmen, the State Department, the secretary general, other delegations, and his own staff. All were agreed that the General Assembly must assume its normal activity in September, including voting. Goldberg's preference, which eventually prevailed, was to make a statement in August to the Special Committee on Peacekeeping Operations outlining the legal correctness of the U.S. position but indicating that, in view of the apparent consensus of the General Assembly not to bring the Article 19 question to a decision, the United States would not seek to frustrate the consensus. There was a general agreement with this position at USUN, although some of us also felt that there would be no great tragedy in raising the issue as a matter of principle and losing, if this would sit better with Congress. Goldberg, however, was concerned that there might be a strong reaction in Congress and among the American people against the UN if the United States were defeated on such an issue. He succeeded in persuading the key congressmen to go along. He also journeyed to Gettysburg and persuaded Eisenhower, who was preparing to attack the proposed course of action, not to do so and to help in meeting congressional reaction.[15]

Accordingly, Goldberg made his statement ending the impasse on August 16, 1965, to the Special Committee on Peacekeeping Operations. After reviewing the history of the General Assembly's actions in assessing the costs, the advisory opinion of the International Court of Justice supporting the Assembly's actions, the Assembly's vote by an overwhelming majority to accept the ICJ's opinion, and its evident unwillingness to apply Article 19, Goldberg declared:

> The United States regretfully concludes, on ample evidence, that at this stage in the history of the United Nations the General Assembly is not prepared to carry out the relevant provisions of the Charter in the context of the present situation. From private consultations, from statements by the principal officers of the Organization, from the statements and exhaustive negotiations within and outside this Committee, from an informal polling of the delegations—indeed from the entire history of this affair—the inevitable conclusion is that the Assembly is not disposed to apply the loss-of-vote sanction of Article 19 to the present situation.
>
> We regret exceedingly that the intransigence of a few of the Member States, and their unwillingness to abide by the rule of law, has led the Organization into this state of affairs.
>
> The United States adheres to the position that Article 19 is applicable in the present circumstances. It is clear, however, that we are faced with a simple and inescapable fact of life which I have just cited. Moreoever, every parliamentary body must decide, in one way or another, the issues that come before it; otherwise it will have no useful existence, and soon no life.
>
> Therefore, without prejudice to the position that Article 19 is applicable, the United States recognizes, as it simply must, that the General Assembly is not prepared to apply Article 19 in the present situation and that the consensus of the membership is that the Assembly should proceed normally. We will not seek to frustrate that consensus, since it is not in the world interest to have the work of the General Assembly immobilized in these troubled days. At the same time, we must make it crystal clear that if any member can insist on making an exception to the principle of collective financial responsibility with respect to certain activities of the Organization, the United States reserves the same option to make exceptions if, in our view, strong and compelling reasons exist for doing so. There can be no double standard among the members of the Organization.[16]

For 15 years the United States did not exercise the option "to make exceptions if, in our view, strong and compelling reasons exist for doing so". But starting in 1980 it withheld its portion of expenses for the UN's P.L.O.–related activities and in 1985–86 Congress unilaterally legislated deep reductions in US paid assessments; these will be discussed in

Chapter IX. Thus the authority of the General Assembly on financial matters was seriously weakened, especially with regard to the major powers.

THE INDO-PAKISTAN WAR—1965

The outbreak in August 1965 of large-scale hostilities between India and Pakistan quickly demonstrated the need for a fully functioning UN. Because the presidency rotates monthly in alphabetical order, Goldberg happened to be president of the Security Council when the question came there in September. Drawing on his experience in settling labor disputes, he emphasized the importance of private negotiations among the members to reach agreement rather than making speeches at each other in the Council chamber. The result was a cease-fire agreement that a new group of UN observers had some difficulty in persuading the parties to carry out.[17]

Ruth Russell gives the following succinct summary of ensuing events:

At that time, both the Soviet Union and the United States wanted to keep the violence from spreading; but Communist China supported Pakistan's truculence and accused Moscow of conspiring with Washington to dominate the world through the United Nations. The withholding of foreign economic and military aid from both parties succeeded in forcing an end to the fighting before a military decision. (Although India appears to have been leading at the time, both sides later claimed to be winning.) Perhaps to avoid the Chinese charges, the Soviet Union offered its good offices to the two governments in direct negotiations. President Ayub and Premier Shastri accepted, meeting in Tashkent in November 1965 with Premier Kosygin. This effort resulted in a formal accord, most importantly to withdraw to military positions held prior to the outbreak of hostilities; but politically little was accomplished except to open a door through which further negotiations might be undertaken. Unfortunately, the sudden death of the Indian Prime Minister, immediately after signature of the agreement, made further progress more difficult. Certain measures to restore economic relations were about all the advance made.[18]

RHODESIA

Goldberg had an important impact on American policy toward Rhodesia. He helped in moving Washington to strong support of majority rule and against the Ian Smith white minority regime.

In October 1965, perceiving signs of an early unilateral declaration of independence by Smith, a group of new nations rushed through the General Assembly a resolution condemning any attempt by the Rhodesians to seize independence and calling upon the United Kingdom to use all possible means to prevent such a declaration.[19] The United States voted in favor, along with the overwhelming majority; only Portugal and South Africa voted against the resolution; France abstained and the United Kingdom did not participate in the voting. When the white Rhodesians went ahead anyway, the Assembly adopted a resolution that condemned "the unilateral declaration of independence made by the racialist minority in Southern Rhodesia" and recommended that the Security Council consider the situation as a matter of urgency.[20] At the request of the United Kingdom the Security Council met on November 12, 1965, to consider the Rhodesian situation. Thus, the British were finally abandoning their position that neither the United Kingdom nor the United Nations had the right to interfere in the territory's internal affairs. During November 1965 the Security Council passed resolutions that condemned the unilateral declaration of independence, called upon all states to refrain from recognizing or assisting the regime, requested all states to break economic relations with Southern Rhodesia, and requested the establishment of an embargo on oil and petroleum products to Southern Rhodesia.[21]

The resolution on the oil embargo was a compromise between a British draft and one submitted by thirty-six African states. The African draft called for the *mandatory* employment of "all enforcement measures" and a finding that the situation in Rhodesia constituted a threat to international peace. This was the language of UN Charter Chapter VII and implied that the use of force could be among the measures contemplated—much further than the British were willing to go. Goldberg suggested rephrasing the statement to read that "the situation . . . is of extreme seriousness . . . its continuance in time constitutes a threat to peace and security." This was the language of Chapter VI, which envisages seeking solutions by negotiations and other means of peaceful settlement. Also, members were *requested* to apply the embargo, not ordered to do so at that stage. (Later, mandatory sanctions were ordered by the Council.) The Africans agreed to accept Goldberg's language both because it avoided a British veto and because it could be interpreted to mean that, if the situation persisted, the Security Council could reopen discussion of the question of mandatory and more pervasive sanctions or even force. This was a typical example of Goldberg's skill as a negotiator, using careful ambiguity, his acceptability on both sides, and his policy clout in Washington.

During the following year the United Kingdom negotiated with Smith on the principle of No Independence Before Majority Rule (NIBMAR), but the negotiations failed. Under strong African pressure the United Kingdom in December 1966 asked the Security Council to approve for the first time since its founding selective, mandatory sanctions against a regime. During a week of discussion the African states made a concerted attempt to alter the British draft drastically to include more commodities and to provide enforcement provisions to insure that the Council's edict was carried out. The African states also sought to have the Security Council deplore the British refusal to use force against Rhodesia and to call upon the United Kingdom to withdraw all previous offers to the Rhodesian regime and to declare flatly that it would grant independence to Rhodesia only under majority rule.

Although the British successfully resisted the African attempt to have the Security Council order the use of force and dictate the terms of settlement, the Africans did succeed through amendments in strengthening economic sanctions in the resolution. On December 16, by a vote of 11 to 0, with Bulgaria, France, Mali, and the Soviet Union abstaining, the Security Council approved a ban on the purchase of twelve of Rhodesia's chief exports and the supply to Rhodesia of oil and oil products. Not only did this mark the first use of mandatory sanctions by the Security Council, but the Council itself emerged as a new instrument in the politics of decolonization.

Goldberg sincerely believed in the sanctions approach. In our strategy meetings at USUN and his policy discussions with Washington, he drew a parallel with the American South, where economic pressures had helped significantly in the civil rights struggle. He also argued that U.S. trade and investment in black Africa and Rhodesia would become increasingly important; consequently, on both moral and practical grounds, the United States should support the economic sanctions. Goldberg knew, too, that Britain would not use force against the Smith regime, as demanded by the Africans, and he considered it important, therefore, to support the economic sanctions that the British offered as an alternative means toward majority rule. The British, who were not likely to have used armed forces anyway, were warned by Undersecretary of State George Ball that the United States would not bail them out if a "quick-kill" action hurt their balance of payments.

Goldberg had to wage a strong policy battle in Washington on the sanctions issues. Aligned against him were Defense; NASA (concerned about its tracking stations in South Africa); and Commerce and Treasury, the latter two because of economic considerations. This time, however, the State Department had a solid front in supporting sanctions, despite the misgivings of Undersecretary George Ball. The assistant secretary of state for African affairs, Mennen Williams, and his deputy, Wayne Fredericks, were strong and determined, and they found strong allies in IO (International Organization Affairs) and L (Legal), as well as the staff of the National Security Council. This time EUR (European Affairs) went along willingly, since the British wanted the sanctions. In this battle within the Washington bureaucracy, Goldberg's interventions were highly important, especially after Williams and Ball left in 1966. Then it was Goldberg who provided leadership to the prosanctions groups, ably backstopped in Washington by Joseph Sisco, the IO assistant secretary, who was both vigorously assertive and completely responsive to Goldberg's lead.[22]

Goldberg had to answer many American critics, notably Dean Acheson, who considered the sanctions a dangerous precedent for similar action whenever violations of human rights were involved. Goldberg argued that there were a number of unique elements in the Rhodesian situation.

> Here we have witnessed an illegal seizure of power by a small minority bent on perpetuating the subjugation of the vast majority. Moreover, in this situation the sovereign authority with international responsibility for the territory has asked the United Nations to take measures which will permit the restoration of the full rights of the people of this territory under the Charter. . . .

> Law in the United Nations, as in our own society, is often developed on a case-by-case basis. We should analyze each action of the U.N. political organs with due regard for the facts of each case and be careful of hasty generalizations. Because the Security Council considers the situation in Rhodesia, with its unique legal and factual elements, as constituting a threat to the peace requiring the application of mandatory sanctions, does not absolve it from an independent exercise of judgment in different situations.

> Moreover, each of the Permanent Members of the Security Council has the power to prevent the use of enforcement measures in other situations where it may deem them to be inappropriate.[23]

The Security Council subsequently established a committee of all fifteen members to monitor compliance with the sanctions, report violations, and make recommendations to the Council.[24] It also added to the economic sanctions until they became virtually total. In the initial years the United States, along with the United Kingdom, supported the committee's activities wholeheartedly, not only with implementing action of its own, but also with reports, including information from intelligence sources, about violations by others. This caused some irritation to Japan and certain European countries, mostly Western and some Eastern, where forbidden Rhodesian goods were entering in substantial quantities. Nevertheless, throughout Goldberg's term the United States continued its energetic support for the sanctions. I was U.S. member of the committee until August 1971 and served as its chairman for a time.

The sanctions did not budge the Smith regime in Rhodesia. Portugal denounced them as contrary to the UN Charter, since the resolution mandating the sanctions did not have "the concurrence of the permanent members," as called for in Article 27, paragraph 3. France and the Soviet Union had abstained. If the language of that article is read literally, the Portuguese interpretations would be correct; however, the practice at the UN for twenty years had been to consider a Security Council resolution validly adopted if it had the required majority and no permanent member voted against it. (It will be recalled that the Soviets were boycotting the Security Council in June 1950 when the Council approved a resolution calling on member states to provide troops, supplies, or services to help repulse the North Korean invasion.) Consequently, the Portuguese argument was rejected by the secretary general, obviously supported by practice and by the membership in general. Indeed, the practice of not considering abstention or nonvoting by a permanent member as a veto has continued to this day; changing it would seriously hobble the effectiveness of the Security Council.

Nevertheless, Portugal refused to comply with the sanctions, and the ports of its "province" of Mozambique were used fully by neighboring Rhodesia. South Africa also provided Rhodesia with transit and port facilities, as it helped generally to sustain the illegal Smith regime. Rhodesian products, especially chrome, the principal export, were transshipped from South Africa under fraudulent certificates of origin describing them as South African products. Importers did not examine the documents too closely, as the terms were generally advantageous to them, nor did the officials of most importing countries. Moreover, vehicles and other goods needed by Rhodesia were obtained through South Africa and Mozambique, often at higher prices because of the need for transshipment and fraudulent documents. Many products formerly imported began to be manufactured in Rhodesia, usually at a higher price than had been paid for imports before sanctions were imposed. Thus, Rhodesia suffered some economic inconvenience from the sanctions, but the pressure did not bring the Smith regime to submit or to change its racist policy.[25] The Africans in the committee and on the Security Council, therefore, demanded the extension of sanctions to Portugal and South Africa and British use of force to bring Smith down. The British, backed by the United States and other Western allies, refused these demands. Their zeal for the existing sanctions against Smith was at least in part an effort to placate the Africans without taking the steps demanded.

Throughout Johnson's term the United States supported the British policy of sanctions and stayed one step behind them. This policy and Goldberg's relations with the Africans were remarkably successful. Occasionally the Africans were irritated by U.S. reluctance to go further but never so seriously as to lead them to jeopardize relations with the United States.

SOUTHWEST AFRICA

Goldberg's stamp of influence on American policy was unmistakable in the issue of Southwest Africa in the fall of 1966.

South Africa had received a League of Nations mandate over Southwest Africa following World War I. Alone among such mandate recipients it refused to place Southwest Africa under a UN trusteeship, and this was a great source of frustration to the Africans. Between 1946 and 1960 they mustered majorities for more than sixty General Assembly resolutions on Southwest Africa, but these were ignored by South Africa.

In 1960 Liberia and Ethiopia (former League of Nations members) brought the problem to the International Court of Justice as a contentious case. After six long years the ICJ in July 1966 declined to give judgment on the grounds that Liberia and Ethiopia did not have standing.[26] South Africa interpreted this 8 to 7 decision on technical legal grounds as a vindication of its position, but virtually all other governments were as shocked as they were surprised. Inevitably, Southwest Africa received priority attention from the Assembly in the fall, with the anticolonial powers demanding an immediate confrontation with South Africa. The United States and Great Britain led an opposition strong and flexible enough to get a compromise resolution adopted almost unanimously. Resolution 2145 (XXI), October 27, 1966, adopted by 114 to 2 (Portugal and South Africa), with 3 abstentions (France, Britain, and Malawi), represented a milestone and a personal triumph for Goldberg. It declared South Africa's forty-six-year-old mandate terminated on the grounds that it had failed to live up to its obligations and responsibilities toward Southwest Africa, which it placed "under the direct responsibility of the United Nations." Goldberg had to wage a strong policy campaign in Washington, aided by the State Department's Bureau of African Affairs and Assistant Secretary for International Organization Affairs Joseph Sisco; after all, he was advocating U.S. support of an unprecedented action by the General Assembly, with our British and French allies abstaining. He won.

At the UN Goldberg was helped by the credibility he had gained with African representatives on the Rhodesian issue and other colonial questions and by his gentlemanly behavior on the military bases resolution. Another factor was his successful fight in Washington to ban the sale of American military planes to South Africa.[27] Also, the Western caucus functioned well, endeavoring to reconcile positions insofar as possible and cooperating even where, in the case of Britain and France, they voted differently. Goldberg took the lead in negotiating with the African delegations and working out the compromise resolution 2145.

Resolution 2145 also set up an Ad Hoc Committee on Southwest Africa to recommend practical means for administering the territory so that the people might "exercise the right of self-determination and achieve independence." The Ad Hoc Committee was unable to agree on a single set of recommendations; instead, it submitted three draft resolutions to the General Assembly, one representing the African viewpoint, another the Latin American, and the third the Canadian, Italian, and U.S.[28]

The stalemate in the Ad Hoc Committee was repeated in the fourth special General Assembly during April–May, forcing a number of compromises in the draft resolution finally adopted. This was essentially a merging of the Afro-Asian and Latin American positions and was sponsored by seventy-nine states. It established an eleven-member council for Southwest Africa responsible to the Assembly, to administer it until independence, if possible, to be attained by June 1968. The council, to be based in Southwest Africa, was to "enter immediately into contact with the authorities of South Africa" to arrange for the transfer of administration and the withdrawal of South African police and military forces and other personnel. The resolution also provided for a UN commissioner for Southwest Africa and requested the Security Council "to take all appropriate measures to enable . . . the Council of Southwest Africa to discharge [its] functions and responsibilities."[29]

The resolution was adopted 85 to 2 (Portugal and South Africa), with 30 abstentions, including all permanent members of the Security Council except China. The U.S. abstention, as explained by Goldberg during the debate, was based on its view that an initial attempt must be made to reach a peaceful solution through dialogue. He stated:

> I do not know—nobody can know—whether such a dialogue [with South Africa] would be fruitful. But I do know that public opinion in my country, and indeed in many parts of the world, would not understand a policy which seems ready to resort to immediate coercion rather than explore the possibilities of peaceful progress.[30]

Thus, with Goldberg in the leading role, the United States had gone as far as it felt it could go in support of the African delegations. Even when it could not go all the way, the United States abstained rather than vote against the resolution and did so in the most conciliatory manner possible. This sympathetic attitude, even in disagreement, was to pay dividends for the United States in the Middle East crisis that followed.

THE SIX DAY WAR

Goldberg's role in negotiating with Soviet Foreign Minister Gromyko and Ambassador Dobrynin during the 1967 Middle East crisis has been called "the apogee of his career at the U.N."[31] In fact, his role throughout the crisis could be described as his finest hour at the UN.

In May 1967 the Soviet Union warned Egyptian authorities that Israel was preparing to attack Syria. Reports by UN truce observers (UNTSO) failed to find any evidence of such preparations, and the Soviet ambassador to Israel refused an Israeli invitation to visit the Syrian border to see for himself. Meanwhile, President Nasser was being taunted by other Arab leaders for hiding behind the protection of the UN Emergency Force (UNEF) in the Sinai. Nasser used the unconfirmed (and probably untrue) Soviet report as a reason for placing Egyptian forces in a state of readiness and, on May 18, demanding the withdrawal of UNEF; both actions were contrary to the 1956–57 armistice agreements.[32] It is noteworthy that neither Syria nor the Soviet Union saw fit to bring the alleged Israeli threat to the attention of the Security Council. Israel, under threat of strangulation, saw one outside guarantee after another vanish. She had withdrawn her forces from the Sinai in 1957 on two understandings: (1) that a UN force would keep her border with Egypt tranquil and the Gulf of Aqaba open; (2) that the major maritime powers would guarantee access to Aqaba.

On the first, Secretary General U Thant acceded promptly to Nasser's request for withdrawal of the force, an action subsequently attacked sharply by critics and defended staunchly by U Thant.

There is no doubt whatsoever that U Thant had to withdraw the force if Nasser was sufficiently determined to oust it. A lightly armed force of 5,000 men, sent to keep peace, not to fight, and dependent for logistics on the Egyptians—such a force could not have resisted a determined Egyptian army. If the two sides were determined to fight, leaving UNEF would only have exposed its troops to fruitless casualties and might have done permanent damage to the willingness of states to provide contingents for any future UN peacekeeping operations.

Moreover, the contingents of India and Yugoslavia—countries tightly aligned with Egypt as leaders of the nonaligned—had already pulled out of the line without waiting for the secretary general to act, leaving only about half the force there.

The only real question, therefore, is whether Thant had to respond so promptly. I felt at the time—and still do—that he should have played for more time. President Nasser, three years after the Six Day War, told a correspondent that he did not want the whole force withdrawn, only part of it.[33] Whether or not this statement is taken at face value, Thant might have volunteered to go to Cairo to discuss the matter, perhaps giving Nasser a face-saving way of backing down. This is speculation, of course, but it is hard to see why even this slight possibility was left unexplored.[34]

So the force was withdrawn, and the first outside guarantee dating back to 1956–57 vanished.

On the second, the United States consulted the other Western maritime powers about action to fulfill the pledge that Aqaba would be kept open to all shipping. I saw the replies. One government after another found reasons not to act. It was said around the U.S. mission to the UN, not entirely in jest, that the fleet of maritime powers that could be assembled would consist of a Dutch admiral commanding an American destroyer (our navy was heavily committed to Vietnam and elsewhere). London and Washington did issue statements on behalf of the maritime powers protesting the announced blockade of Aqaba, but these were peremptorily rejected by Egypt.[35]

U Thant learned of the blockade while en route to Cairo on May 22, *following* his decision to terminate UNEF. Upon his return to New York he alerted the Council to the fact that Israel considered the blockade a casus belli. He then stated:

> In my view, a peaceful outcome to the present crisis will depend upon a breathing spell which will allow tension to subside from its present explosive level. I therefore urge all the parties concerned to exercise special restraint, to forego belligerence and to avoid all other actions which could increase tension, to allow the Council to deal with the underlying causes of the present crisis and to seek solutions.[36]

The United States, along with Argentina, Brazil, Canada, Denmark, and the United Kingdom, consulted other Council members on a draft resolution calling on all parties "to forego belligerence" (i.e., not blockade Aqaba) in order to provide a "breathing spell" that would "allow the Council to deal with the underlying causes of the present crisis and to seek solutions." This proposal had the support of at least nine of the fifteen members—the required majority unless a permanent member cast a veto. In the Council when Ambassador Goldberg pleaded for such action without delay, the Soviet representative (Fedorenko), echoed by Bulgaria, accused him of creating "hysteria" and argued that there was no cause for excitement. India, apparently reflecting Nasser's views, also denied any urgency. Thus, the Council was stymied right up to the very eve of the outbreak of fighting—another fact that Israel remembered.

Though the Council was stymied, this was a time of feverish activity at USUN. In fact, from May 15, when Nasser requested UNEF's withdrawal, to August 15, I had one Saturday and one Sunday off, on different weekends, and we had numerous Council sessions that went into the next morning. Goldberg was a stickler for advance planning, complete information, meticulous preparation, and full consultation with other delegations.

One vivid recollection stands out. On Sunday, June 4, we had just been to an afternoon meeting of cooperative delegations at the Danish mission on Third Avenue and Forty-second Street and had managed to arrive at a "breathing spell" draft resolution that could command the necessary nine-vote majority. As we walked up Second Avenue on our way back to USUN, someone had a pocket radio with the news turned on. It was reported that the Israeli troops were relaxing at the beaches. Goldberg commented: "I don't like that. With the Israeli mobilization system they could be ready in two hours." How prophetic!

Meanwhile, President Johnson had been very active in trying to prevent the war. To the end of his term, he made it clear to Israeli officials that he regretted their decision to go to war on June 5. On May 22, 1967, when Nasser announced the blockade, he sent Prime Minister Kosygin a strong message urging a maximum effort in the cause of moderation and underlining the danger that American and Soviet ties to nations in the Middle East could bring about difficulties neither wanted, not only in the Middle East but elsewhere. During the war itself American forces in the Mediterranean were strengthened and directed to within fifty miles of the Syrian coast when a June 10 message from Moscow raised the possibility of Soviet military intervention. But the major business between Moscow and Washington over the hot line was, in effect, a high-level review of what was going on in New York; that is, an attempt to achieve a cease-fire.[37]

In a further effort to prevent war, Johnson sent former Ambassador Charles Yost to Cairo in late May. Yost reported that the Egyptian leaders were dismayed by what they had themselves wrought. They were aware that the Aqaba blockade might be treated as casus belli by Israel. They were by no means ready for war, yet hesitated to lose face in the Arab world. Consequently, they welcomed the suggestion of an exchange of vice-presidential visits with the United States, and the Egyptian vice-president was preparing to go to Washington as the first step in the exchange. Yost believes they were looking for a face-saving way out of the crisis they had precipitated, with Soviet encouragement. But war broke out before the visit could take place.

When fighting broke out on June 5, the U.S. delegation moved promptly that morning to get Council agreement on a resolution calling, as a first step, for an immediate cease-fire. Once again there was opposition from the USSR, Bulgaria, and India, which insisted that the resolution also call for withdrawal to the June 4 positions. The entire day and evening were spent in wrangling and negotiations, while both the Israelis and the Egyptians told Council members around the fringes of the chamber that their armies were having great success. The most intensive negotiations took place between the United States and the USSR, the latter apparently carrying the proxy of the UAR; these were adjourned overnight, at Fedorenko's request.

Because we were getting full and accurate information about the fighting, we had no difficulty in agreeing to Fedorenko's request for delay. Just before going in to the room for negotiations with the Soviets that evening, I had asked Ambassador Joel Barromi of the Israeli delegation how things were going. He had just phoned Jerusalem and said: "We are picking up more shoes than we did in 1956." (The retreating Egyptian soldiers discarded their shoes so they could run faster.) This corresponded to the reports from the U.S. sources. I advised Goldberg to stand firm on our draft resolution text, and this was his own inclination as well.

By the next morning, June 6, the rout of the Egyptian forces was evident. We had also received an intercept of a Moscow instruction to Fedorenko to accept the U.S. draft. When Fedorenko phoned Goldberg to signify his acceptance, Goldberg—the shrewd and careful negotiator— said, "Fine, Nikolai: Now we must agree on the interpretation." Thus, the initial U.S. draft, calling for a cease-fire in place, was accepted by the Soviets and adopted by the Council on June 6.

It is interesting to conjecture what might have happened if this resolution had been adopted on the morning of June 5 when it was originally proposed and Israel had not advanced very far into the Sinai. Later that week similar cease-fire resolutions called for a halt to fighting between Israel and Jordan and Syria, respectively. Much credit was due to Hans Tabor, of Denmark, who presided with great skill over the Council's deliberations in the month of June. It was he who presented the laboriously negotiated cease-fire resolutions as presidential proposals, thus facilitating unanimous adoption.

The Soviet delegation, while accepting the cease-fire resolutions adopted by the Council for the three fighting fronts, continually pressed for the condemnation of Israel as the "aggressor" and for the immediate withdrawal of all forces to the lines existing on June 4. Goldberg and others on the Council resisted such a one-sided condemnation, noting that the blockade of Aqaba and other Egyptian actions could hardly make that country an innocent party. Withdrawal to the June 4 lines would only restore the dangerous situation of that date. He also argued that the Council must go beyond the immediate crisis and seek a stable peace. This position was supported not only by Canada, Denmark, and Britain but also by Argentina, Brazil, China, Ethiopia, and Nigeria, in part as a result of intensive consultations and Goldberg's skill and persuasiveness.

Goldberg again showed his metal on June 10. The Council met at 4:30 A.M. on a Syrian complaint that Israel was violating the June 10 cease-fire, advancing farther into Syria, and bombing Damascus. Fedorenko, the

Soviet representative, demanded immediate condemnation of Israel and introduced a draft resolution to that effect. Goldberg argued that the Council needed authentic information and urged that General Bull, the UNTSO commander, be asked to report. Even after Bull reported that an air attack against Damascus was going on, Goldberg remained calm. He raised questions as to whether the report was based on firsthand information and whether reported Syrian artillery fire on Israeli villages had been verified (U.S. intelligence had indicated the latter). What was needed, he said, was a comprehensive report as to what was going on in the entire area. Further reports from Bull indicated that there had been some bombing seven to ten kilometers south of Damascus, about fifteen minutes after the agreed cease-fire time and that an hour and a half after the agreed cease-fire time there was continued artillery fire from Syria on positions in Israel. Bull also reported that the Israeli defense minister, Dayan, told him that Israel would implement any cease-fire proposals made by Bull. The Soviets introduced a resolution condemning Israel. Goldberg, pointing to the violations by both sides, won support for revising the Soviet text. As a result, resolution 236 (1967), as adopted unanimously June 12, condemned "any and all violations of the cease-fire" (Goldberg's language). It also reaffirmed the cease-fire and called for the prompt return of troops to their positions of June 10 and full cooperation with the UN Troop Supervision Organization in implementing the cease-fire. This time the truce held.

On June 14 the Soviets introduced a draft resolution, which "vigorously" condemned Israel's "aggression" and demanded that Israel "should immediately and unconditionally remove all its troops . . . and withdraw them behind the armistice lines."[38] Goldberg argued that it would be unrealistic to expect Israel to act as if there were peace, by withdrawing its troops, while the Arab states continued to insist that there was a state of belligerency—Nasser's justification for blockading Aqaba. This line of reasoning had majority support. When the Soviet draft was put to the vote on June 14, it was supported by only 4 states—Bulgaria, India, Mali, and the Soviet Union itself—with 9 votes required for adoption.[39]

Fedorenko thereupon announced that, the Council having failed, the Soviets would request an emergency special session of the General Assembly. He insisted on this course even though other draft resolutions were still before the Council, including a U.S. draft that, Goldberg stated, was open for discussion, modification, and revision. Ironically, the only relevant rule of procedure for convening an emergency session had been inserted under the Uniting for Peace resolution of 1950, a resolution the Soviet Union had so often denounced because it was related to the UN action in Korea and because Moscow maintains, as a matter of principle, that only the Security Council may take action to deal with the maintenance of peace or threats to international peace and security.

One hour before the Assembly began its first substantive session on June 19, 1967, President Johnson made a speech over all media laying down the fundamental policy of the United States. He declared that peace in the Middle East must be made by the parties themselves and that it must be based on five principles:

—first, the recognized right of national life;
—second, justice for the refugees;
—third, innocent maritime passage;
—fourth, limits on the wasteful and destructive arms race,
—and fifth, political independence and territorial integrity for all.

American policy since that date has been based on those principles as well as on the concept that peace must be made by the parties themselves. Variations have occurred mainly on the question of how much outside assistance, mediation, or prodding might be helpful.

Debate at the 1967 emergency session centered largely on two draft resolutions—one, sponsored by Yugoslavia, India, and a group of "nonaligned" countries, was close to the UAR's desiderata, that is, immediate, unconditional withdrawal of all Israeli forces to June 4 positions; the second, sponsored by a group of Latin American countries, linked withdrawal by Israel of "all its forces from the territories occupied by it as a result of the recent conflict" to ending "the state of belligerency."[40] The vote on the first was 53 in favor, 46 against, and 20 abstentions; on the second, 57 in favor, 43 against, and 20 abstentions. Since this was an important question requiring a two-thirds majority, neither was adopted. The superficial observer might conclude that the session was thus a failure. In my view, it was a highly significant exercise, more so than at other sessions when resolutions were adopted that obviously could have no effect. The result was a general recognition that if Israel were to act as if there were a state of peace by withdrawing from good defensive positions, the Arab states concerned could not persist in a state of belligerency vis-à-vis Israel. Thus, the groundwork was laid for Security Council resolution 242 of November 22, 1967—the only basis for solution accepted unanimously by the Council and by the nations directly concerned.

Another significant result of the emergency session was the decisive rejection of Soviet and Albanian resolutions that sought to brand Israel as an aggressor.

In the latter stages of the emergency session the Soviets initiated bilateral negotiations with the United States in an endeavor to find a generally acceptable formula. The Soviets chose their ambassador to Washington, Anatoly Dobrynin, to lead their side, apparently because they had more confidence in him than in Nikolai Fedorenko, their ambassador to the UN. But when Dobrynin suggested negotiations with Secretary of State Dean Rusk, he was advised that Ambassador Goldberg had the responsibility for the United States. The Dobrynin-Goldberg negotiations proceeded very well in New York; a draft resolution was worked out that was acceptable to the UAR, Jordan, the Soviet Union, and the United States—but not to Israel. The United States was nevertheless ready to go forward with it; however, violent opposition from Algeria and Iraq caused the UAR to draw back. The Soviets—with evident reluctance and discomfort—abandoned the endeavor, much to the relief of Israel.

Yet these negotiations were not in vain. Along with the Latin American resolution, referred to above, they helped to pave the way for the Security Council action in November.

During the general debate of the twenty-second general session of the General Assembly, progress was made toward understanding among the prime ministers and foreign ministers of the interested countries. Consequently, when the Security Council met in November to consider the Middle East question, it was able to build upon the Latin American resolution of the emergency session; the Soviet, American, UAR, and Jordan discussions of July; and the discreet private sessions that took place during the general debate.

The resolution finally agreed upon unanimously in the Security Council was put forward by Lord Caradon, the British representative, but the draft was largely Goldberg's[41] Virtually all fifteen members of the Council engaged in the consultations that resulted in the agreed text, with critical negotiations taking place between Goldberg, Lord Caradon and Vasily Kuznetzov, the Soviet first deputy foreign minister.

Since the various parties have given different interpretations of the text it might be well at this point to refer to the Security Council records of the discussion that took place there. Most of the controversy about resolution 242 has revolved around paragraph 1, concerning "withdrawal of Israeli armed forces from territories occupied in the recent conflict." The Arabs and Soviets have claimed that this means *all* territories. I know from my own experience with the negotiations that the resolution would not have been accepted by a substantial number of members of the Security Council and certainly not by Israel if the word "all" had appeared. This is what Lord Caradon alluded to when he introduced the draft resolution to the Security Council on November 20 and said, "Since then I have been strongly pressed by both sides—I emphasize, by both sides—to make changes particularly in the provisions regarding withdrawal. But I came to the conclusion that to make variations under pressure from one side or the other at this stage would destroy the equal balance which we had endeavored to achieve and would also destroy the confidence which we hope to build on our effort to be just and impartial."[42]

It is ironic that the Latin American resolution, which failed to get the required two-thirds majority at the fifth emergency special session of the General Assembly in July because it was strongly opposed by the Arabs and their friends, was actually more favorable to the Arab position than resolution 242. The former called for the withdrawal of forces from *all* occupied territories. Even the text agreed to by Goldberg and Dobrynin on July 19 called upon "all parties to the conflict to withdraw without delay their forces from *the* territories occupied by them after June 4, 1967 [italics mine].[43]

There is also some irony in the fact that Goldberg, a Zionist sympathizer, had the principal role in negotiating the cease-fire resolutions and the basis for a settlement, resolution 242. Many American Jews regretted that he was placed in that role, fearing that Goldberg would lean over backward to prove that he was objective. In fact, his fairness was recognized by the Arabs; only Ambassador Tomeh of Syria attacked him personally in the Security Council debates, and Syria was so virulently anti-American at that time that its representative would have attacked any U.S. representative. By contrast, the Egyptian representative, Ambassador El Kony, was personally very friendly with Goldberg. The two would usually embrace when they met in the corridor after bitter Security Council debates on the Middle East in 1967.

It is also significant that President Johnson and Secretary of State Rusk consciously gave Goldberg the main responsibility for the Middle East negotiations.[44] As noted above, the Soviets, who had more confidence in the negotiating ability of their ambassador to Washington (Dobrynin) then their UN representative (Fedorenko), were directed to Goldberg when they sought bilateral talks, and Dobrynin came to New York for talks with Goldberg. One factor may have been that Johnson and Rusk were deeply involved with the war in Vietnam, then at its peak, while Goldberg could concentrate on the Middle East. Even so, Johnson's delegation of authority to Goldberg was a mark of great confidence, which, from my own observation, was well placed.

THE PUEBLO INCIDENT, NUCLEAR NONPROLIFERATION, AND OUTER SPACE

Goldberg and the United Nations again proved useful to American policy in January 1968, when North Korea seized the U.S.S. *Pueblo.* According to U.S. evidence, the *Pueblo* was seized on January 23 at least thirteen miles offshore, which would have put it in international waters even by North Korean standards. Secretary Rusk denounced the seizure as an act of war, and feelings in the United States were running high. The Joint Chiefs of Staff recommended a military strike to liberate the *Pueblo* and its crew, but Goldberg, with Rusk's support, persuaded President Johnson to use the United Nations as an escape valve to allow emotions to be vented against North Korea's action.[45] Johnson, who had his hands full in Vietnam, was not eager to undertake another military action, yet the seizure could not be ignored.

At the Security Council Goldberg presented a strong case, using detailed maps to show that the *Pueblo* had definitely been in international waters. The debates were carried live on television, so that the American public did not have a sense of inaction. And while the debates were going on, Hungary's permanent representative to the UN, who unofficially represented North Korea as well, received word from North Korea to communicate to Goldberg that they were prepared to negotiate the release of the crew.[46]

Parallel with the diplomatic effort at the UN, Johnson had ordered a strong naval buildup in the Sea of Japan, called up 14,000 navy and air force reservists and alerted and reinforced land-based tactical air units in South Korea. The Soviets countered with a naval buildup of their own and a strongly worded warning to the United States not to use military force. As a result of the channel of communication opened through the Hungarian ambassador at the UN, the United States by early February requested closed meetings with North Korea at Panmunjom, and on February 6 the carrier *Enterprise* was sent south and away from Korea, signaling the abandonment of any military options. The Soviet military buildup was also halted.

The negotiations at Panmunjom did, in fact, lead to the release of the crew of eighty-three, after eleven months. Thus, although the conditions were onerous, the main American objective was achieved—and peacefully.

Despite this success, by February 1968 Goldberg's relations with the president began to sour. The Viet Cong–North Vietnamese Tet offensive that month was a shattering defeat for the United States and South Vietnam, with huge losses of lives, and it brought home to Goldberg the futility of his efforts to help end the war either through the UN Security Council or the secretary general. Johnson, on his side, was dismayed by the U.S. failure in Vietnam under his presidency, and this did not help his disposition. When arrangements were finally concluded for four-party negotiations (the United States, South Vietnam, North Vietnam, and the Viet Cong) in Paris, Johnson chose Averell Harriman and Cyrus Vance as his representatives. This must have been a bitter blow to Goldberg, who had made his reputation as a negotiator and had accepted the UN post in large part because he hoped thereby to help bring about a peaceful settlement in Vietnam.

Goldberg would have resigned in early 1968; however, President Johnson asked him to postpone his resignation long enough to guide the

Nuclear Non-Proliferation Treaty to endorsement by the UN General Assembly.[47] The treaty had been under consideration for several years. On November 23, 1965, the General Assembly adopted, by a vote of 93 to 0, with 5 abstentions, a resolution setting forth the principles on which the treaty should be based.[48] In 1966 both superpowers began to work in earnest on a formula for a treaty. But they were deterred from assuming a joint initiative by one stubborn problem, that of inspection. The Soviet Union favored the International Atomic Energy Agency (IAEA) as the main inspection organ for the treaty; whereas the United States, under pressure from the Western European countries, preferred the European Atomic Energy Community (EURATOM) as the inspection organ for its European allies.

Since both countries felt that a nonproliferation treaty was urgently needed, they set to work to overcome their differences. The Soviets' concern was heightened after China became the fifth nuclear power, and the specter of a potential German nuclear power was particularly disturbing to them. On August 24, 1967, after intensive secret negotiations, the USSR and the United States submitted separate but identical drafts in the Eighteen Nation Disarmament Committee, (ENDC), leaving blank the article that was to embody the inspection provision.

In the ENDC a number of nonnuclear powers objected to the draft on the grounds that it did not provide adequately for their security. After lengthy negotiations the two superpowers, presenting a common front, managed to get an agreed report to the General Assembly on March 14, 1968. In the meantime, they also overcame their one remaining difference on inspection. It was agreed that the IAEA verification procedures would ultimately apply to all nonnuclear states but that EURATOM would have an inspection role for its members during a transitional period.

Goldberg had participated briefly but effectively in the ENDC negotiations with the nonnuclear states, supplementing the efforts of William H. Foster, who represented the United States at the ENDC. He so impressed Vasily Kuznetzov, the Soviet first deputy foreign minister, that the latter asked Goldberg to take the lead in negotiating General Assembly approval in New York.[49]

In the Assembly many specific reservations were proposed by nonnuclear states of Asia, Africa, and Latin American, seeking stronger guarantees and expressing displeasure at what they perceived as a double standard. Their objections were met in part when the superpowers agreed to provide security assurances to the nonnuclear powers through a formal Security Council resolution.

Finally, on June 12, 1968, the General Assembly endorsed the treaty to halt the spread of nuclear weapons. The vote was 95 in favor, 4 against, 21 abstentions, and 4 not voting.[50] On June 19, 1968, the three nuclear powers on the Security Council gave their formal pledge to assist any nonnuclear country that was threatened by nuclear aggression. A resolution in the Council welcoming these pledges of assistance was passed by a vote of 10 in favor and 0 against, with 5 abstentions (Algeria, Brazil, France, India, and Pakistan).[51]

Goldberg could well be proud of his role in securing this endorsement. The Soviet and American delegations worked closely together and lobbied hard for the endorsement, but Goldberg was the leader in persuasion and negotiation of the compromises that made the endorsement possible. He resigned shortly after the successful conclusion of the NPT exercise.

He had accomplished a great deal—resolving the Article 19 crisis, helping to bring about a cease-fire in the India-Pakistan fighting, negotiating cease-fires and resolution 242 in the Middle East crisis of 1967, bringing U.S. positions closer to African objectives in Southwest Africa and Rhodesia, helping to settle the *Pueblo* crisis, and playing a key role in the negotiation of the Nuclear Nonproliferation Treaty and the treaty banning the stationing of weapons of mass destruction in outer space.[52] But he had not been able to get the UN to help bring peace in Vietnam, for reasons completely beyond his control, nor to bring about a resolution of the dispute over Chinese representation. On the principle of universality, he favored having all divided states in the UN—North and South Vietnam, North and South Korea, East and West Germany, and the two Chinas— but the key nations involved were not ready for such a solution.

BALL AND WIGGINS

Goldberg's resignation came with seven months left in the Johnson administration. To fill the gap the president persuaded George W. Ball, former undersecretary of state in the Kennedy and the early Johnson administration, to take over.

Ball had never shown much interest in the UN, even while his old friend, Adlai Stevenson, had been the permanent representative. He had headed the U.S. delegation to the UN Conference on Trade and Development in 1964, where he decided to show the less developed countries that the United States could be firm. In his own words,

I felt compelled to tell (UNCTAD) that what they were seeking was not politically feasible. Labor-intensive industries in the United States were then pressing hard for restrictions on imports from the less developed countries, using the old argument about the unfair advantages of cheap labor. Refutable as it was by the rational answers we persistently gave, the "cheap labor" contention always found strong resonance in the Congress. Since we were, thus, hard-pressed to resist discriminatory restrictions against imports from the poor countries, it was quite impracticable to propose that we encourage those imports by preferential treatment. Although I disappointed the UNCTAD Conference and no doubt created the impression that I was indifferent to the predicament of the poor countries—which was far from the truth—it would have been a great disservice had we raised expectations we could not fulfill.[53]

While I believe candor is admirable on most occasions and generally admire George Ball greatly, I think he was wrong at UNCTAD. The United States, by staking out negative positions on this and other objectives of the less developed countries, became the lightning rod for all their frustrations.

On the other hand, Ball alone among President Johnson's high-level advisers openly took the negative on Vietnam. In October 1964, after the Tonkin Gulf incident but before massive American intervention, he wrote a hundred-page memorandum advocating a withdrawal from the "gluepot" of Indochina or, if that could not be done, at least a concentration upon the ground war in South Vietnam itself rather than "going North" with air power.[54] In the fall of 1961 Ball had warned President Kennedy against a commitment in Vietnam.[55]

Ball had many other admirable qualities. He was a man of broad knowledge and experience, with a keen analytical mind, a good sense of humor, and a likable, outgoing personality. He was also the most articulate man I have ever met. I have seen him dictate into a recorder the complete text of a lengthy statement, which would come out not only logical, coherent, and well organized but also well styled and with good syntax. Naturally, he was superb with ad lib statements in the Security Council.

In the one test that came during his brief tenure, the Soviet invasion of Czechoslovakia, Ball did an outstanding job. When the issue came before the Security Council in August 1968, he was brilliant in his presentation of the case against the aggression by the Soviet Union and its Warsaw Pact partners. The Soviet representative, Fedorenko, opposed even inscription of the item, arguing that this was an internal matter for the "socialist" (communist) countries that should not be discussed in the Council (as the United States had argued that its intervention in the Dominican Republic crisis of 1965 was a matter for the OAS, not the UN Security Council). After inscription, Fedorenko contended that the Soviet forces had been "invited" into Czechoslovakia, but he had difficulty in specifying who issued the invitation. He also used what came to be known as the Brezhnev doctrine— that fraternal socialist countries should intervene whenever one of their number was threatened by a counterrevolution.[56] Beyond that, Fedorenko repeatedly filibustered into the wee hours of the morning, hoping to stretch out the Council's consideration of the item until Czech Prime Minister

Dubček, then in Moscow, could either be pressured into requesting that the item be removed from the agenda or replaced by someone who would. Ball was just as determined to keep the proceedings going until a resolution could be brought to a vote.

Tactically, at least, the West won. On Saturday, August 22, Foreign Minister Jiri Hayek appeared at the Council. He looked straight across the room at Fedorenko and declared: "No one in the government of Czechoslovakia invited your troops; no one wanted your troops." That same afternoon the Council voted on a draft resolution presented by Brazil, Canada, Denmark, France, Paraguay, the United Kingdom, and the United States condemning the invasion and calling upon the USSR and its allies to withdraw forthwith. The vote was 10 in favor, 2 against (Hungary and the Soviet Union), and 3 abstentions (Algeria, India, and Pakistan).[57] Because the Soviet Union is a permanent member of the Security Council, its negative vote constituted a veto.

I have often heard people argue that the UN could become much more effective if Article 27 of the Charter were amended to remove the veto. I disagree. In this instance, even if the resolution had been declared adopted, would the Soviets have obeyed? If they refused, how could they be forced out without starting World War III? And how many in the West would have wanted another great war? What was required here was a Soviet willingness to go along with the majority view, not a procedural change.

Of course, we knew in advance that the Soviets would veto the resolution. Why work for days and nights to arrive at a veto? The United States was not prepared to use force in Czechoslovakia, yet the Soviet aggression could not be ignored. The matter had to be fully aired in the Security Council and the Soviets forced to pay a price at least in world public opinion for their brutal suppression in Czechoslovakia. And pay they did. A number of Western communist leaders opposed the aggression, and Peking denounced the Brezhnev doctrine as a manifesto of "socialist imperialism."[58] Clearly, China feared that Moscow might wish to assure the purity of the communist faith in China by a similar military intervention. Yugoslavia and Romania opposed the Brezhnev doctrine for similar reasons.

Referring to these fears, George Ball later wrote:

I was acutely aware of their apprehensions, since as ambassador to the U.N. at the time, I spent long hours with the Yugoslavs and with the Romanian Foreign Minister. It gave them little comfort to reflect that Soviet intervention would be undertaken in the same spirit of "fraternal solicitude" Moscow had shown other socialist republics. They knew only too well the meaning of that term; it was the same kind of fraternal solicitude Cain had shown his brother Abel.[59]

Following the Soviet veto, the United States consulted with friendly delegations from around the world as to next steps. We gave serious consideration to inscribing the Czech item on the agenda of the twenty-third session of the UN General Assembly that opened the next month. We did not do so because virtually all of the Western European countries thought such a move would be counterproductive, especially since the Soviets had installed a puppet regime that would represent Czechoslovakia in the Assembly. Denunciations of the Soviet action were made, of course, in the Assembly's general debate.

In September, Ball resigned to campaign for Hubert Humphrey in the 1968 presidential election. He detested Richard Nixon, as had his friend, Adlai Stevenson, and he could not rest with the thought that he would stand aside while there was still a chance of defeating Nixon.

Ball's successor was James Russell Wiggins, editor of the *Washington Post*. Russ Wiggins knew he would have the job for only a few months, but he was retiring from the *Post* anyway and accepted the UN assignment to help Lyndon Johnson, his friend. There were no crises during his tenure; the most startling development was the announcement that Jacqueline Kennedy would marry Aristotle Onassis. Out of deep conviction and concern, Wiggins strongly supported the Swedish initiative to hold a UN conference on environment. He was an altogether delightful man, well informed, experienced, wise, and extraordinarily good-natured.

NOTES

1. *New York Times Sunday Magazine*, February 6, 1966, p. 16.

2. Arnold Beichman, *The "Other" State Department*, The United States Mission to the United Nations: Its Role in the Making of Foreign Policy, New York Basic Books, 1967, p. 114.

3. Dorothy K. Goldberg, *A Private View of a Public Life* (New York, Charterhouse 1975), pp. 193–94.

4. Ibid., p. 195.

5. Goldberg acceptance statement at the White House, July 20, 1965, in *The Defenses of Freedom—The Public Papers of Arthur J. Goldberg,* ed. Daniel Patrick Moynihan (New York: Harper and Row, 1966), p. xv.

6. Ibid., p. 5. Address to the Conference on World Peace Through Law, Washington, D.C., September 17, 1965.

7. Ibid., p. 65.

8. Norman Cousins, "Journeys with Humphrey," *Saturday Review,* March 4, 1978, pp. 11–14.

9. Walter W. Rostow, *The Diffusion of Power* (New York: Macmillan, 1972), pp. 358–60.

10. Lyndon B. Johnson, *The Vantage Point: Perspectives of the Presidency 1963–69*, New York, Holt, Rinehart Winston, 1971, pp. 543–45.

11. Dorothy Goldberg, op. cit., p. 223.

12. Louis B. Fleming, *Los Angeles Times-Mirror*, July 17, 1966.

13. Beichman, op. cit., pp. 145–46.

14. Dorothy Goldberg, op. cit., p. 224.

15. Beichman, op. cit., p. 174.

16. USUN press release 4615, August 16, 1965, pp. 3–4.

17. S.C. Res. S/211, September 20,

1965, and S.C. Res. S/215, November 5, 1965.

18. Ruth B. Russell, *The United Nations and United States Security Policy* (Washington, D.C.: Brookings Institution, 1968), p. 187.

19. G.A. Res. 2012 (XX), October 12, 1965.

20. G.A. Res. 2024 (XX), November 11, 1965.

21. S.C. Res. S/216, November 12, 1965 and S.C. Res. S/217, November 20, 1965. Res. S/217 called for an embargo on the shipment of oil to Rhodesia.

22. See Anthony Lake, *The "Tar Baby" Option* (New York: Columbia University Press, 1976), pp. 62–122, for a full account of the U.S. policy toward Rhodesia, Goldberg's role in it, and the impact of the sanctions.

23. U.S. State Department press release 304, December 29, 1966, pp. 6–7.

24. S.C. Res. S/253 (1968).

25. Lake, op. cit., see also Chapter VIII of this volume.

26. See ICJ *Reports*, 1966, Southwest Africa, Second Phase, Judgment.

27. Beichman, op. cit., pp. 97–98.

28. UN Doc. A/AC.129/L.6, March 15, 1967.

29. G.A. Res. S/2248 (S-IV), May 18, 1967.

30. USUN press release 49, April 20, 1967.

31. Drew Middleton, *New York Times*, July 26, 1977.

32. Arthur S. Lall, *The United Nations and the Middle East Crisis, 1967* (New York: Columbia University Press, 1968), pp. 8–19.

33. Nasser interview with Eric Rouleau in *Le Monde,* Paris, February 19, 1970.

34. For U Thant's rationale, see S.C. Doc. S/7906, May 26, 1967, paragraphs 1–8.

35. S.C. Doc. S/7925, June 2, 1967.

36. S.C. Doc. S/7906, May 26, 1967, paragraph 14.

37. Rostow, op. cit., pp. 417–19.

38. UN Security Council document S/7951/Rev. 2.

39. Lall, op. cit., pp. 46–115, provides a lucid, carefully documented and detailed account of the Security Council's proceedings in June, to which I am indebted. Lall's appendix includes the texts of all relevant resolutions and draft resolutions. For an account of the Soviet and U.S. roles during private negotiations, see my statement in *The Big Powers and the Present Crisis in the Middle East,* ed. Samuel Merlin, (Cranbury, N.J.: Associated University Presses, 1970), pp. 92–140.

40. See G.A. Doc. A/L.572/Rev. 3 and G.A. Doc. A/L523/Rev.1, fifth emergency session of the General Assembly.

41. Dorothy Goldberg, op. cit., p. 250. writes that the "concept and language were Arthur's work"; this corresponds to my own recollections.

42. Subsequently Lord Caradon confirmed that omission of "all" and "the" in the phrase "from occupied territories" was deliberate and expressed his own interpretation of resolution 242 to mean that Israel should withdraw to *"secure and recognized boundaries.* [italics mine]." Lord Caradon, "Is Peace Possible?" in S.M. Finger, ed., *The New World Balance and Peace in the Middle East,* (Cranbury, N.J.: Associated University Presses, 1975), p. 221. See also Lall, op. cit., p. 254, for confirmation that Caradon rejected an Arab effort to use the term "all the territories" in resolution 242.

43. Lall, op. cit., pp. 208-10, states that the text agreed to by the United States and the USSR was based on a new Latin American draft. See also Security Council records of debate on November 17 (S/PV/1373).

44. Rostow, op. cit., p. 419

45. Dorothy Goldberg, op. cit., p. 250.

46. Ibid., pp. 250-51.

47. Ibid., p. 250. Mrs. Goldberg writes that the Nonproliferation Treaty was

the achievement in her husband's UN career "in which our family takes the most pride."

48. G.A. Res. 2078, November 23, 1965.

49. Dorothy Goldberg, op. cit., pp. 247–52.

50. G.A. Res. 2373, June 12, 1968.

51. S.C. Res. 255, June 19, 1968.

52. Officially known as "The Treaty on Principles Governing the Activities of States in the Exploration and Use of Outer Space, including the Moon and Other Celestial Bodies," which entered into force on October 10, 1967.

53. George W. Ball, *Diplomacy for a Crowded World* (Boston: Atlantic–Little, Brown, 1976), p. 282.

54. Tom Wicker, *J. F. K. and L. B. J.: The Influence of Personality Upon Politics* (New York, Morrow, 1968), p. 249.

55. Ibid., p. 269.

56. In Brezhnev's words, "The sovereignty of each socialist country cannot be opposed to the world of socialism of the world revolutionary movement." From "Sovereignty and International Duties of Socialist Countries," *Pravda,* September 25, 1968, as translated into Ivo Duchacek, *Nations and Men,* 3d ed. (Hinsdale, Ill.: Dryden, 1975), p. 424.

57. UN Security Council, *Official Records,* S/PV/1445, August 22, 1968.

58. Duchacek, op. cit., pp. 425–26.

59. Ball, op. cit., p. 107.

CHAPTER VII

The Nixon-Kissinger Years:
Yost, Bush, Scali, and Moynihan

CHARLES YOST

Charles Yost, who became the U.S. permanent representative in January 1969, was the first and thus far the only career diplomat to serve in the post.

Yost was, in fact, the "professional's professional." Entering the Foreign Service as a young man, he rose through the ranks to the top grade, career ambassador. This is a rank held at any given time by only ten to twelve outstanding diplomats. He served with distinction in Eastern Europe, the Middle East, and the Far East, and the State Department before becoming ambassador, successively, to Laos, Syria, and Morocco. Soft-spoken, slight in build, and given to understatement, Yost had a professional diplomat's caution about emotionally charged language and belief in quiet diplomacy rather than spectacular public confrontation. Yet he was as firm as a rock on principle and relentlessly logical, incisive, and realistic in analyzing situations. Goldberg's deputy, James Nabrit, referred to Yost as "the most stubborn quiet man I ever met."

Yost brought other unusual qualifications to the job. He had worked closely with Edward Stettinius and Adlai Stevenson at the founding conference of the UN in San Francisco in 1945. Stevenson was so much impressed with him that he asked Yost to become his deputy for the UN Security Council in 1961. Yost was then ambassador to Morocco, with all the perquisites of a chief of mission overseas—residence, servants, car, chauffeur, and generous allowances—none of which he would have at USUN. Nevertheless, he accepted, because of his deep and sustained belief in the importance of the UN and his high regard for Adlai Stevenson.

I recall lunching with Yost while he was still weighing Stevenson's offer. We had known each other in Laos, where he was the ambassador and

I was chief of the political section in 1955–56. When he raised the question, I told him that his coming to the USUN would be a personal sacrifice, given the grueling schedule and the loss of perquisites, but it would be a great thing for the United States. Knowing Yost, I am sure that our lunch conversation was mainly a matter of renewing friendship and that his mind had already been made up. In any case, he came to USUN and remained there from early 1961 to his retirement from the Foreign Service in 1966, earning the highest praise from both Stevenson and Goldberg.

Yost devoted the next two years, 1966–68, to research and writing at Columbia University, the UN Association of the USA, and the Council on Foreign Relations. However, as noted in Chapter VI, there was a brief interlude in May 1967 when he went to Egypt at President Johnson's request in an effort to avert war in the Middle East. Yost is the author of innumerable classified think-pieces for the State Department as well as many published articles and three thoughtful books on foreign policy and the human condition: *The Age of Triumph and Frustration* (1964), *The Insecurity of Nations* (1968), and *The Conduct and Misconduct of Foreign Affairs* (1972).

Yet President Nixon did not pick Yost because he shared a deep belief in the UN or desired to strengthen the organization. On the contrary, Nixon had a generally negative attitude toward the UN. For political reasons he wanted a Democrat in his cabinet. Although the UN post carried cabinet status, he considered it of little real importance. Initially he offered the post to Hubert Humphrey, whom he had just defeated in the presidential race. Humphrey declined, as Nixon must have expected he would. He then approached Sargent Shriver, former President Kennedy's brother-in-law. Shriver expressed great interest but stated certain conditions for acceptance. Among other things, he required a pledge that federal poverty programs would not be cut. Nixon then told Secretary designate Rogers to inform Shriver he had decided against him because he found it "intolerable to have a prospective ambassadorial appointee making demands relating to domestic policy."[1] Then the job was offered to Yost, who had supported Humphrey's campaign but was essentially a career diplomat rather than a political figure.

Some insight was provided by Arthur Goldberg, at a lunch we had in early 1971, after George Bush had succeeded Yost. Goldberg told me Nixon had phoned him to get his views about a Yost appointment. Goldberg replied: "You won't have as much trouble with him as Lyndon Johnson had with me." Goldberg said he knew that was what was on Nixon's mind.

It is significant that in his Memoirs of 1,090 pages, *R N,* Nixon does not mention Yost even once. George Bush is not mentioned in his UN capacity either. John Scali, the third and last Nixon appointee, is mentioned only in connection with the Yom Kippur war in October 1973, as reporting developments in the UN Security Council. Significantly, the UN is not mentioned even once during the long section of Nixon's memoirs covering his vice-presidency.

Yost himself was under no illusions. When I saw him in 1978 he said he knew from the outset that Nixon had a negative attitude toward the UN. Nevertheless, he accepted the post, believing that Nixon might otherwise have chosen someone hostile toward the UN.

Moreover, Nixon's principal adviser on foreign policy was Henry Kissinger, presidential assistant for national security affairs. Kissinger, an outstanding advocate of realpolitik and balance-of-power politics,[2] had no more respect for the UN than Nixon did. Samuel De Palma, assistant secretary of state for international organization affairs during 1969–73, recalls being told by Kissinger: "Don't bother me with that UN crap."[3] De Palma says that, on occasions when Kissinger did not want to be bothered, his deputy, General Haig, was conscientious about seeing that critical issues at the UN were at least brought to the president's notice. Kissinger and Nixon concentrated on great power relationships.

By contrast, Yost considered balance-of-power politics a failure. In *The Insecurity of Nations* he writes: "The system of national egotism, armaments, alliances, balance of power, deterrence, challenge and response has brought no security to its strongest proponents, to Germany, to Russia, to France, to Britain, to Italy, to Japan, to China. It has brought temporary security to the United States only because this country has hitherto been protected by distance and allies, but even the United States is now subject to the loss of half its population in a few hours." He notes that the military power of the United States has increased vastly since 1949 while its national security has been rapidly diminishing. He believes that "great power may be fully as hazardous as great weakness. . . . National power, even relatively disinterested power, inevitably provokes fear and eventually more-or-less matching counterforce. Uncontrolled national power, moreover, creates in those who possess it an almost irresistible temptation to use it; but its use, even for seemingly legitimate ends, provokes still more fear and still more counterforce. The law of disproportionate response, triggered by such fears, quickly takes over." He concludes: "The inherent insecurity of nations in the modern environment is such that there may be no safety for mankind except in a fundamental reform, as early suppression of the nation-state system."[4]

Yet Yost had few illusions about the UN. He noted that it has no standing armed force, no decisive power to control national armaments, limit national conflict, or enforce peaceful settlements.[5] The Security Council is often immobilized by great power antagonisms and the veto. The General Assembly can only recommend to governments, not order; the "sovereign equality" of its members and the influx of mini-states progressively dims its reflection of real power and hence the impact of its recommendations; and "the preoccupation of its more numerous and least powerful members with the vestigial problems of colonialism distracts it wastefully from the major problems of today and tomorrow."[6]

Nixon and Kissinger would certainly agree with this catalogue of weaknesses. The difference is that they considered the weaknesses a reason for ignoring the UN on most major political and security issues, at least for four years and nine months, that is, until the Yom Kippur war, when the UN became an important element in separating Arab and Israeli forces. Yost, on the other hand, considered the weaknesses an agenda for reforming and strengthening the UN. This should be effected by the restoration of great power cooperation, primarily in the gradual reinforcement of multilateral peacekeeping through the United Nations. In *The Insecurity of Nations* he concludes: "The revival and reinforcement of the United Nations no doubt seems, and at the moment may be, Utopian. The point to be made again and again, to be hammered unmercifully into our proud, hard, silly heads, is that the attempt to achieve the security of nations by national means under modern circumstances is still more Utopian."[7]

Yost's inability to convince Nixon and Kissinger on measures to strengthen the UN was a foregone conclusion. His influence on policy was reduced even further by the weakness of the secretary of state's position in Nixon's foreign policy councils. Nixon had appointed William P. Rogers as an old and trusted friend whose open, low-key manner might help in dealing with Congress, not as a man whose judgment on foreign policy was to be valued. It soon became apparent that the President's principal adviser on foreign affairs was Kissinger, not the secretary of state. Yost, having no clout with either the president or Kissinger, had to work through the State Department and its chief, who himself had little impact.

Even when Rogers signed a memorandum to the president at the behest of Yost or Assistant Secretary De Palma, he would not fight for it if the president disagreed. De Palma recalls drafting a memorandum for the secretary's signature recommending against a cut in the U.S. contribution to the UN Educational, Scientific, and Cultural Organization (UNESCO). There was no formal reply; the president simply wrote on a corner of the memorandum: "To hell with this outfit. Let's gut it. RMN."[8]

When asked what issues he had been able to exert an influence on, Yost replied: "One percent and the high commissioner for human rights."[9] This was a shorthand way of indicating that the U.S. delegation had been authorized to vote for a 1970 resolution on the second United Nations Development Decade and to support a Costa Rican proposal to establish a high commissioner for human rights, which remains unfinished business. These were, as Yost would be the first to acknowledge, marginal achievements. In fact, as we shall see in discussing specific issues, Yost was able to exercise a constructive influence on a number of issues, but none was of decisive importance. The further an issue from the vital concerns of Nixon and Kissinger, the more likely Yost was to have an impact.

The obverse of this observation is illustrated by Yost's role on the Middle East, which was of prime concern to Nixon and Kissinger. Throughout 1969 and the early part of 1970, Yost was engaged in four-power talks at the UN with the representatives of Britain, France, and the Soviet Union. When these talks became more serious than Kissinger wanted them to be and the Soviets endeavored to get into terms of settlement, Yost was instructed to slow up the process.[10] In fairness to Nixon it should be noted that the Soviet proposals would have had the major powers make judgments on boundaries (total Israeli withdrawal) and impose them on the parties. The United States, while taking the position that any changes in the prewar borders should be "insubstantial," held that a durable peace agreement must be negotiated by the parties themselves.[11]

Conversely, Yost was able to gain State Department and White House support for a more flexible position on guidelines for future UN peacekeeping operations, which did not cut across any vital current Nixon/Kissinger concern. Negotiations had started in the aftermath of the Article 19 crisis over the refusal of the Soviets to pay their share of the costs of UN peacekeeping operations in the Congo and the Middle East. At first the United States had encouraged the middle-sized and smaller powers to come forward with guidelines to assure better preparation and more reliable financing of future operations. This effort foundered on the rock of unyielding Soviet and French opposition. Then, encouraged by the other members of the Special Committee on Peacekeeping Operations, the United States undertook intensive negotiations with the Soviet representatives in an effort to agree on guidelines.[12]

The exercise was a USUN initiative from the outset, but there was constant consultation with Assistant Secretary De Palma and his special assistant, Nathan Pelcovits. To accommodate the Soviets, we started discussions on a model that would fit even their restrictive interpretation of the Charter; that is, "U.N. Military observers established or authorized by the Security Council for observation purposes pursuant to Council resolutions." Discussion began in a Working Group of eight countries, consisting of the four officers of the committee (Mexico, Canada, Czechoslovakia, and Egypt) and the Big Four (Britain, France, the Soviet Union, and the United States). In forty-nine meetings, the Working Group agreed on five of the eight chapters envisaged for the model. Of the remaining three chapters, financial and legal arrangements did not present serious obstacles; the major obstacle was the chapter on direction and control. The Soviets wanted all operations directly under the control of the Security Council, where they have the veto. The United States acknowledged the ultimate authority of the Council but held that day-to-day operations and implementing decisions should be delegated to the secretary general. Our negotiations in 1970, largely carried out between Ambassador Lev Mendelevich of the USSR and me, were aimed at finding an acceptable division of responsibilities between the Council and the secretary general. Personal relations between Mendelevich and me were excellent. At one point, where he conceived a possible compromise, he asked me to seek Washington approval so that it might appear as an American initiative. After receiving tentative State Department clearance to accept the compromise as a basis for discussion, Yost arranged a meeting with Ambassador Malik (USSR) at USUN, with Mendelevich and me present. Malik, with the compromise formula in front of him as an "American" suggestion, asked me to explain it. I had to do so with a straight face while Mendelevich sat there with an equally straight face. It looked as if we might reach agreement; however, Moscow's approval never came.

Yost was a great source of strength and support throughout the negotiations. He fully approved of the Soviet–U.S. effort to strengthen peacekeeping, understood the Soviet position completely, and was willing to push Washington to make reasonable concessions in an effort to reach agreement. His views were highly respected in the State Department, and his telegrams recommending various adjustments in the U.S. position were most effective. In fact, the presidential stamp of approval was given to our efforts. In his report to the Congress on February 25, 1971, Nixon stated that "a crucial development would be joint recognition by the United States and the Soviet Union of a common interest in strengthening the U.N.'s peacekeeping capacity. A major effort should be made to reach an agreement on reliable ground rules for peacekeeping operations."[13]

Unfortunately, the gap was never bridged. Yet the effort eventually paid off in a completely unforeseen way. Following a cease-fire in the 1973 Yom Kippur war, the Security Council in resolution 340 of October 25, 1973, decided "to set up immediately under its authority a United Nations Emergency Force to be composed of personnel drawn from states members of the United Nations except the Permanent Members of the Security Council." At the Council's request the secretary general prepared a report setting out the force's terms of reference, proposed plan of action, estimated costs, and method of financing.[14]

According to reliable sources in the UN Secretariat, this document was drafted in the light of proposals and statements made over many years in the Special Committee on Peacekeeping Operations and its Working Group. Remarkably, the secretary general's document avoids seriously offending any major power, incorporates all elements agreed upon, and draws up a modus operandi in which all powers can acquiesce even though they would not specifically endorse some of its features. This technique has been particularly important in the establishment, command, and control of the operations. Consequently, the future of peacekeeping might be better served by using UNEF II as a model or precedent, as in common law, rather than to attempt to codify guidelines.

Specific clauses in the secretary general's document demonstrate its achievements and advantages as a precedent. First, it states "that the force will be under the command of the United Nations, vested in the Secretary-General, under the authority of the Security Council. The command in the field will be exercised by a Force Commander appointed by the Secretary-General with the consent of the Security Council. The Commander will be responsible to the Secretary-General." This brief paragraph skillfully overcomes some of the main problems encountered in the Working Group of the Committee on Peacekeeping by clearly giving the secretary general a mandate to run UNEF operations on a day-to-day basis and to appoint a force commander, both of which duties were resisted by the USSR in negotiations on general guidelines.

Second, paragraph 3 (c) of the secretary general's document states that "the Force will be composed of a number of contingents to be provided by selected countries, *upon the request of the Secretary-General* [italics mine]." The Soviets had argued that the Security Council should make the request. The paragraph continues: "The contingents will be selected in consultation with the Security Council and with the parties concerned, bearing in mind the accepted principle of equitable geographic representation." To "bear in mind" equitable geographic representation is less rigid than the preferred Soviet version stating that "it is important to *base it* on the accepted principle of equitable geographic distribution [italics mine]."

Third, this document also indicates in its proposed plan of action that the secretary general is to appoint the commander of the emergency force as soon as possible, with the consent of the Security Council. The secretary general had already appointed the chief of staff of UNTSO, Major General Siilasvuo, as interim commander of the force. I can recall months of unsuccessful negotiations with the USSR, during our efforts to develop general guidelines, over this question of what should be done in an emergency before the secretary general could consult the Security Council about the commander. Here the problem is resolved in one brief paragraph.

Finally, the closing paragraph of the secretary general's document stipulates that "the costs of the Force shall be considered as expenses of the Organization to be borne by the Members in accordance with Article 17, paragraph 2, of the Charter." The USSR was long reluctant to agree that the General Assembly could make assessments for peacekeeping under the provisions of this article.

In these important respects the secretary general's document represents a practical answer to the real problems of running a peacekeeping force. It is apparently easier for the USSR to acquiesce in these provisions in a particular case than to endorse them as general principles or guidelines. That is why a "common-law" precedent approach may be better than an attempt at codification. The establishment of UNDOF, a UN Force on the Golan Heights, in 1974, and of the UN Interim Force in Lebanon (UNIFIL) in 1978, on the same general criteria as UNEF II, reinforces the precedent. Yet it is doubtful that the secretary general's recommendations would have been accepted with so little difficulty had it not been for the long negotiations on guidelines that clarified the limits of tolerance of the USSR and the United States and induced both of them to consider carefully during 1969–71 the problems that would be faced in finding a mutually acceptable formula.[15]

THE TWENTY-FIFTH ANNIVERSARY

Preparations for the observance of the UN's twenty-fifth anniversary began shortly after Yost became the permanent representative in early 1969. The occasion itself proved to be of little importance; however, the way the United States went about its preparations is worth recounting because of the light it sheds on the Nixon-Rogers-Yost relationship. Yost urged that substantive initiatives be taken on this occasion to strengthen the United Nations; none emerged. Yost and his staff proposed that a presidential commission be appointed and submitted the name of twenty-five citizens knowledgeable about the UN. The White House accepted the idea of a commission but sent back a completely different list distinguished by their political value to Nixon and their lack of knowledge of the UN. After some negotiations a commission of fifty was appointed, including substantial numbers from each list, as well as Senators Cooper, Fulbright, Sparkman, and Taft and Congressmen Gallagher and Morgan.

As it turned out, the commission worked well. Its chairman was Henry Cabot Lodge; Francis Wilcox served as chairman of the Working Group; and the staff was headed by two well-known scholars in the field of international affairs, Gerard Mangone and Anne Simons.

The commission's report included ninety-six recommendations for action in the UN and its specialized agencies in three broad categories: (1) Peace, Security, and Strengthening International Law; (2) Economic, Social, and Environmental Issues; (3) Organizational and Structural Reforms. In general, the recommendations were laudable, but few had any impact on policy. The notable exception was a recommendation that the United States "affirm its intention to maintain and increase its total contributions to the U.N., but that, as part of a redistribution of responsibilities, it will seek over a period of years to reduce its current contribution of 31.52 per cent to the assessed regular budget of the Organization so that eventually its share will not exceed 25 percent."[16]

The reduction of the U.S. budget assessment to 25 percent was vigorously pursued. Spurred by congressional threats to reduce the U.S. contribution to that figure unilaterally, the U.S. delegation in 1972, then headed by George Bush, succeeded in getting General Assembly approval of the reduction. But the promised counterpart, an increase in contributions for voluntary programs, was not forthcoming, nor was the reduction to 25 percent effected in the gradual way foreseen by the commission.

Also as an economy measure, not foreseen by the commission, the commemorative session was bracketed into the regular twenty-fifth session of the General Assembly. This was a move on which the Big Four stood firmly together; all four governments were then concerned with holding down the UN budget. The commemorative session, October 14–24, 1970, was addressed by the representatives of eighty-six governments, including forty-two heads of state or government, but little was stated that would not have been said in an ordinary general debate of the Assembly. President Nixon, speaking on October 23, mentioned the common objectives of furthering economic development and strengthening the UN capacity to make and keep the peace and stressed the issues of direct concern to the United States—environment, development of the resources of the sea, population control, curbing international trade in narcotics, ending hijacking, and insuring that human rights of prisoners are not violated.

The commemorative session culminated on October 24, the anniversary of the Charter's entry into force, with the adoption by acclamation of three documents:

(1) "Declaration on Principles of International Law concerning Friendly Relations among States in accordance with the Charter of the United Nations." This is an important statement of international law, worked out in seven years of negotiations, that clarifies seven basic principles of international law contained in the UN Charter: refraining from the use or threat of force against the territorial integrity or political independence of any state, settlement of disputes by peaceful means, nonintervention in the affairs of other states, cooperation among states, equal rights and self-determination of peoples, sovereign equality of states, and fulfillment of Charter obligations.

(2) "International Development Strategy for the Second U.N. Development Decade."

(3) "Declaration on the Occasion of the 25th Anniversary of the United Nations." This omnibus declaration, worked out on the basis of consensus in the twenty-five-member Preparatory Committee, is largely a collection of benign generalities, with some bite on the issue of colonialism.

It would be fair to say that nothing of consequence happened at the commemorative session that would not have happened anyway.

Another offshoot of the anniversary was the World Youth Assembly, held at UN headquarters, July 9–17, 1970. It included nearly 650 participants from 118 countries, 12 non-self-governing territories, and 28 nongovernmental organizations.

When the Youth Assembly was first proposed in the Preparatory Committee, Lord Caradon, the British permanent representative, expressed enthusiastic support, seeing it as a means of drawing the world's youth toward the United Nations. Support from the Soviet and Bulgarian representatives as well as others around the room produced a snowball effect. Representing the United States in the committee and without instructions, I avoided comment but suggested to Yost privately that the propaganda cost to the United States of trying to block the proposed Youth Assembly would greatly outweigh any dangers from it. Yost agreed fully and requested instructions accordingly. Washington then authorized the delegation to agree to the proposal on the understanding that the United States government would not pay any costs.

My Soviet colleague, on returning from Moscow, was distressed to learn that the committee was moving toward approval of the assembly. Evidently Moscow was just as much concerned as Washington about what uninhibited young people might say or do and was equally determined not to provide funds. He said he was very unhappy that his deputy, in his absence, had supported the conference and proposed a joint effort to block it. I told him it was then too late, as I sincerely believed.

Washington was worried about what the Youth Assembly might say about Vietnam, Moscow, about Czechoslovakia. Actually, three of the Youth Assembly's four commissions came out with thoughtful recommendations on development, education, and the environment. The fourth, the Commission on World Peace, was subjected to manipulation by the Eastern Europeans, representatives of the undemocratic Left, and certain international youth organizations. These maneuvers, along with the prominence of professional delegates and professional "youths" (some in their forties), were denounced in a petition signed by twenty-seven delegations. None of the four reports were adopted. Finally, the Youth Assembly adopted a consensus message to the General Assembly expressing in detail the participants' opposition to colonialism, imperialism, militarism, aggression, and racism, wherever found. It specifically called for the withdrawal of Soviet troops from Czechoslovakia, American troops from Indochina, and Israeli troops from occupied Arab territories. The Youth Assembly's consensus had no discernible impact on the work of the UN.

Yost firmly resisted any effort by Washington to instruct the American youth delegates or intervene in their selection. Most of them were politically naive compared with their counterparts from Eastern Europe, but they learned quickly. In retrospect, I still believe the risk was well worth taking.

THE SECOND UN DEVELOPMENT DECADE

As recounted in Chapter V, the first UN Development Decade was a U.S. initiative in 1961. It set general objectives and targets but was not a detailed plan. The initiative for the second Development Decade came from the developing countries, which in 1968 prevailed upon the General Assembly to decide that the strategy for the 1970s would enunciate not only goals and objectives but also concerted policy measures at the national, regional, and international levels for realizing these objectives. Accordingly, the International Development Strategy was worked out over a period of two years in the UN's Committee for Development Planning, UNCTAD's Trade and Development Board, the Preparatory Committee for the second Development Decade, the Economic and Social Council, and the General Assembly's Second Committee. The resulting eighty-four-paragraph statement represented an amalgam of international thinking on economic and social development issues and a prescription for dealing with those issues.

On October 16 the Second Committee approved the Strategy without a vote but formally recorded in its report to the Assembly some forty-five statements of interpretation, observation, and reservation. Senator Jacob Javits, speaking for the United States, spelled out reservations or interpretations on eleven of the eighty-four paragraphs, while expressing overall support for the Strategy. He stressed that the United States did not accept language in the document that it regarded as implying a legal commitment where one did not exist. He emphasized, in particular, that the United States would make "our best efforts to increase both official and private flows" of capital but could not say when it might meet the 1 percent of Gross National Product target stipulated in the Strategy or even guarantee that it would eventually meet it. The Assembly adopted the Strategy on October 24, without a vote.[17]

Opposition in Washington, principally from the Treasury Department, had to be overcome in order for the United States to join in the consensus on the Strategy. Yost and Javits together managed to overcome the opposition, in part by agreeing that Javits would make the explicit reservations described above. In fact, the percentage of GNP that the United States provides in official aid has declined from 0.49 percent in 1965 to 0.24 percent in 1977. Obviously, other factors have been more decisive than UN resolutions.

THE U.S. BUDGET AND HEADQUARTERS EXPANSION

Outsiders have no way of knowing how much private negotiation and cooperation often goes on between the Soviet and U.S. delegations even when they are attacking each other in public debate. One example was Big Four cooperation in restraining the UN budget in 1969 and 1970. This was a period when there was great concern in the Congress and the White House about holding down UN expenditures. The Soviets have always been tight-fisted on the UN budget, so on this issue they were a natural ally.

The Big Four together paid 65 percent of the UN budget. At our private sessions, where I represented the United States, we endeavored to agree on a ceiling figure to be conveyed in separate calls on the secretary general by each of our permanent representatives. The Soviets came in with the lowest figure, France the next lowest, and the United Kingdom and the United States at about the same higher figure. Finally we agreed on $168 million for 1970 and $183 million for 1971,[18] and our permanent representatives made calls on the secretary general, as foreseen.

It is, of course, the General Assembly that decides on the budget, in accordance with Article 17 of the UN Charter. Yet the budget submitted by the secretary general is an important factor in the final outcome. While he does not have to take advice from individual government representatives, he could hardly miss the point when each of the Big Four representatives— representing collectively 65 percent of assessed contributions—offered the same advice on a budget ceiling. In any case, he did come in with a restrained budget of $170 million for 1970, not too far from the Big Four suggestions. In the Assembly itself the knowledge that the Big Four stood together on the budget also served as a restraining influence. As a result, the final 1970 budget was $168 million. For 1971, however, the budget approved by the Assembly increased to $192 million, and the United States abstained in the vote—the first time it had not voted in favor of a UN budget. The United States protested against excessive costs for documentation and salaries, which exceeded U.S. Civil Service salaries by 10 to 26 percent.

In any case, the impact of the Big Four effort at budget restraint was only temporary. For the 1978–79 biennium the budget was $985 million, an increase of more than 150 percent in eight years, reflecting both inflation and growth of activities. The U.S. federal budget, it should be noted, was more than 1,000 times as much.

As activities and membership burgeoned, so did the staff and the need for space. A key question was whether this need would be filled by expanding the UN headquarters or by moving various units to Geneva, Vienna, or elsewhere. At USUN we felt strongly that it would be in the best interests of the United States and the United Nations to have as much of the expansion occur in New York as possible, for the same reason that the headquarters had been placed in New York initially—to maintain American interest and support. We noted that the percentage of Americans working in the Secretariat in New York—about 19 percent—was more than 50 percent higher than at UN agencies in Paris and Geneva and double the percentage for FAO in Rome. Incidentally, the number of Americans employed in New York was just about right in terms of the desirable range established by the General Assembly.[19] Since Congress evidently placed emphasis on these figures, we reasoned that anything which kept activities in New York would help in sustaining support for the UN.

The General Assembly at its 1968 session authorized an architectural and engineering study of plans for new construction and major alterations.[20] The plans submitted at the twenty-fourth session of the General Assembly would have provided enough additional space to meet the needs of the United Nations, the UN Development Program (UNDP), and the UN Children's Fund (UNICEF) through 1979; about $1.7 million annually was being spent in rent for these purposes in 1970, for rented offices housing about 1,250 employees. Of a total estimated cost of $80 million, the Assembly decided to authorize appropriations from the regular budget up to a limit of $25 million to be spread over ten years beginning in 1971— subject to the necessary funds being pledged and committed from other sources; that is, New York City, the U.S. government, UNDP, and UNICEF. The UN, UNDP, and UNICEF shares, totalling $40 million, could be amortized by using money anticipated for rent payments. Mayor John Lindsay, conscious of the substantial economic benefits to New York City of having a large UN Secretariat in New York—spending by the Secretariat and diplomats total about $450 million per year—pledged $20 million in city funds.[21] The whole project collapsed when Congress refused to appropriate the U.S. share of $20 million. Those congressmen who opposed the expansion because they were unenthusiastic about the UN and New York were joined in opposition by some New York City congressmen who wanted the U.S. government to pick up the city's share as well. George Bush, who had succeeded Yost as permanent representative in early 1971 when the issue came to a head, had little interest in the expansion project and did not use his considerable powers of persuasion with his former congressional colleagues. As a result UNDP, UNICEF, and a number of Secretariat units occupy rented space, and several Secretariat units have moved to Geneva or Vienna. (Vienna and the government of Austria have spent $500 million for buildings that are provided virtually rent free to UN agencies.)

VIETNAM, PRISONERS OF WAR, AND DECOLONIZATION

In his address to the commemorative session on October 23, 1970, President Nixon stressed the importance of insuring that the human rights of prisoners of war were not violated, reflecting the concern in the United States about American POWs in Vietnam. Accordingly, the U.S. delegation initiated a resolution in the Assembly's Third Committee, which deals with human rights issues. As the delegation's troubleshooter, I was assigned to the item along with Senator Claiborne Pell, who made our official statement introducing the resolution.

Knowing the resolution would have tough sledding because of its unstated but implied relationship to Vietnam, we organized a cosponsor group with wide geographic distribution: Belgium, Dahomey, Dominican Republic, Greece, Haiti, Italy, Malagasy Republic, New Zealand, Philippines, Thailand, and Togo. Brazil's delegation had tentatively agreed to cosponsor but did not receive the necessary instructions from its government. At a delegation meeting, Senator Pell expressed concern about having as cosponsors dictatorships like Brazil and Greece. I pointed out that democracies were in the minority in the UN membership, that wide sponsorship would be crucial to success, that Brazil had standing among the Latin Americans, and that cosponsorship on one issue did not imply approval of everything a government did. Senator Javits supported this position. He told Pell that when he was working for progress on civil rights in the U.S. Senate he would welcome support on such an issue from the most reactionary southern senator. That swung the delegation. (In discussing Ambassador Moynihan's tactics, pages 235–46, we shall return to this issue.)

As expected, the resolution was strongly opposed by the Soviet Union and its supporters, which characterized the U.S. initiative as a political move designed to gain support for one side in the Vietnam War. The USSR also tried to depict the resolution as a tactic against national liberation movements such as those in Africa. Nevertheless, despite repeated assaults, the resolution was adopted in the Third Committee on December 1. The General Assembly approved it on December 9 by a vote of 67 to 30, with 20 abstentions.[22] The wide cosponsorship was undoubtedly a key factor. Adoption of the resolution had no demonstrable effect on Hanoi's treatment of American prisoners of war, but once the president had raised this issue, failure in the General Assembly would have had repercussions in the Congress and on the American public.

No such success met U.S. efforts on colonial issues. From the birth of the UN the United States had generally had greater sympathy for self-determination in Asia and Africa than its Western European allies who were colonial powers there. As these issues were brought to the United Nations, USUN had a consistently greater sympathy than Washington. USUN's voting constituency at the UN had an increasingly large majority of anticolonial states; naturally, USUN did not wish to antagonize this majority on those questions, since it needed their votes on other issues. Washington, on the other hand, thought in national security terms; it attached greater importance to relations with its NATO partners, such as

Britain, France, Belgium, and Portugal. Such tension was normally worked out through consultation and compromise. On some issues—that of Indonesia in 1947–49, Suez in 1956, and the Congo in 1960—the final U.S. position came down against NATO partners for reasons of overall national interest. More often the alliance interest prevailed. In 1960, for example, the United States was ready to vote for the Declaration on the Granting of Independence for Colonial Countries and Peoples when a phone call from British Prime Minister Macmillan to President Eisenhower resulted in a last-minute switch to abstention.[23]

To implement the declaration the General Assembly established a Special Committee, which has come to be known as the Committee of Twenty-Four. Although the end of colonialism for a billion people was brought about largely through nonviolent means and, in most cases, with the acquiescence—ready or reluctant—of the administering powers, and although more than 90 percent of these people achieved self-determination *before* the establishment of the committee, in general, the attitude taken toward Western members in the committee has been one of antagonism and suspicion.

Resolutions have normally been worked out by a group of communist members and anti-Western African and Arab states. The latter, being militant and persistent, dominate the twelve-member Afro-Asian caucus of the committee. With the twelve Afro-Asian and four communist members committed, there is little disposition to compromise or negotiate within the committee. "Decisions" are presented on a take-it-or-leave-it basis to the three Latin American members and to the "other" (Western) members. (When the Special Committee of Twenty-Four was at full strength there were five "others.") The Latin American members, in conceptual support of "decolonization," generally chose to back the decisions of the Afro-Asian-communist majority even when their explanations of vote would be more consistent with a negative than an affirmative vote. Sometimes, on flagrantly obnoxious proposals, they abstained. This had led to the lopsided votes and the lack of serious consultation or negotiation that characterizes the passage of most of the committee's resolutions.

Recommendations of the Special Committee of Twenty-Four have usually gone on to become resolutions of the Fourth (Trusteeship and Non-Self-Governing Territories) Committee and the General Assembly. If such resolutions are changed from one year to the next, the change has usually been in the form of adding or inflating adjectives or inserting still more unattainable provisions.

For these reasons the United States concluded as early as January 1968 that it would be advisable to leave the Special Committee of Twenty-Four. However, after informal consultation with the members it decided to remain on the committee, at least for a time, but to frankly express its views as to the committee's shortcomings and its earnest hope that there might be some improvement. The clear implication was that otherwise the United States would find little reason to justify continued participation in the committee's work. Accordingly, in February 1968 as the U.S. representative I outlined its misgivings about the Special Committee of Twenty-Four. Specifically, I pointed out that solutions to the problems of dependent territories could be found only on the condition that the decision-making process be approached with no a priori assumptions about its outcome, that factual information be required, and that generalizations be avoided.[24] None of these conditions existed in the committee at that time.

Unfortunately, three more years then went by without any notable improvement. Praiseworthy efforts were made by two successive committee chairmen, Mahmoud Mestiri of Tunisia and Davidson Nicol of Sierra Leone, but the extremist coalition in the committee maintained its uncompromising domination.

The final straw for the United States was the failure of its efforts in 1970 to achieve meaningful consultation and negotiation on the program of action to be worked out by the committee in connection with the tenth anniversary of the Declaration of the Granting of Independence to Colonial Countries and Peoples.[25] The program was to set the guidelines for the committee's future work.

There was no real negotiation or consultation with either the United Kingdom or the United States. Instead, the program of action was drawn up in a working group whose proceedings were dominated by the representatives of the United Republic of Tanzania and the People's Republic of Bulgaria. Not only did this program carry forward all of the unworkable recommendations of previous sessions, but it added an endorsement of armed struggle and declared that "Member States shall render all necessary moral and material assistance to the peoples of colonial Territories in their struggle to attain freedom and independence."[26]

It was not the U.S. view that peoples should be denied the right to resort to any means at their disposal, including violence, if armed suppression by a colonial power required it. Indeed, the United States itself was obliged to resort to violence in order to gain independence. The difficulty lay in giving a general endorsement by the United Nations—an organization dedicated to peace—to such violence and in employing language that suggests that member states have an obligation to provide material assistance to violent action against other member states. Such action could hardly be reconciled with the requirements of the Charter of the United Nations.[27]

The United States tried, first—and in vain—by attempting to encourage meaningful consultation and then by putting forward seventeen amendments, to achieve a text that would be practical, consistent with the

Charter, and hopefully effective. Although these amendments were explained in the most conciliatory terms, all seventeen were summarily rejected. As a result, when put to the vote in the General Assembly the program of action was supported by only eighty-six members—about two thirds of the membership but still an unusually low number for a resolution on colonial matters. Even such staunch anticolonialists as the Scandinavian countries and Austria were unable to vote in favor of this program of action, which thus lost much of its meaning.

This intransigent position appears even more ill advised in the light of the constructive program of action the Western members of the committee—Italy, Norway, the United Kingdom, and the United States—were prepared to support. Such a program would have emerged either through acceptance of the U.S. amendments or of the text presented by Italy to the committee [28] just before the program of action was rammed through by the majority on October 2, 1970.

The Italian proposal would have taken the Western countries much further than they had ever gone before in condemning the suppression of the legitimate aspirations of the colonial peoples and in setting forth a program of action designed to further the exercise of their right to self-determination, freedom, and independence. Although the proposal was presented by Italy in its own name, it had in fact been worked out by an informal caucus of representatives from Western countries, including Australia, France, New Zealand, Norway, the United Kingdom, and the United States. Had such a program been adopted, it could have served as a basis for genuine cooperation. Its rejection meant that the future activities of the committee would be in the same fruitless rut as in the past. It was therefore hard to escape the conclusion that the committee could not reform itself or be reformed. In these circumstances and after many years of effort the United States believed that it had no alternative but to withdraw, as it did on January 11, 1971.

In some ways extremist positions on anticolonial issues make life easier for the U.S. delegation. Not serving on the Committee of Twenty-Four saves vast amounts of time and frustration. In the Fourth Committee of the General Assembly extremist resolutions pose no problem for the delegation; it can either abstain or vote against the resolution with a brief explanation, since positions on the perennial issues are well known. If, on the other hand, reasonable proposals are advanced the delegation has to ask new instructions, and this often means a battle with certain entrenched positions in the State Department. But, comfortable or not, it is precisely in this difficult process of negotiating changes in policy and position that the best hope lies of achieving nonviolent solutions.

The African countries are aware of this fact and, as a consequence, have increasingly brought the remaining problems in Africa, Zimbabwe

(Rhodesia), Namibia (South-West Africa), and apartheid in South Africa before the Security Council, where the major Western powers cannot escape their responsibility. Since the fifteen-member Security Council includes five Western members, three of which have the veto, and nine votes are required for a majority, there is more real negotiation in the Council. Britain, France or the United States can veto any decision of the Council; however, if this veto is used with insensitivity and without any real effort to deal with the problem, one should not be surprised to see the African states press extremist language in the General Assembly and encourage wars of national liberation.

Extreme pressure on the Rhodesia problem in March 1970 brought the first U.S. veto in the Security Council's history. A draft resolution sponsored by Burundi, Nepal, Sierra Leone, Syria, and Zambia would have made it mandatory for states to sever all ties with the Smith regime, including transportation, postal service, and all forms of communications. It would also have extended the existing mandatory sanctions against Rhodesia, as well as those in the draft, to South Africa and Portugal. Further, it condemned the United Kingdom for not using force against Smith.

The United States joined in condemning the Smith regime and had been a strong supporter of economic sanctions against it. Yost, speaking for the United States on March 14, 1970, took particular exception to the proposed ban on communications; the United States would view most seriously the prospect of leaving its citizens anywhere in the world without the means to travel and communicate. He also questioned whether the application of the sanctions to Rhodesia's neighbors would receive sufficient international support to make them effective, "or whether in seeking such action against economically powerful states in existing circumstances they would merely demonstrate the limitations of the United Nations and further entrench the Smith regime and its supporters in Southern Africa."

When the Council next met on March 17, the British representative moved for a postponement so that the members might negotiate a compromise. This motion was defeated, as was a U.S. request for a thirty-minute suspension to seek instructions. When the five-power resolution was put to a vote, the United States joined Britain in voting against it—the first American veto in the UN's twenty-five-year history. The vote had been carefully considered up to the highest levels in Washington, both for substance and precedent, and Yost did not fight it. The fact that the British veto would have been sufficient took some of the sting out of the unprecedented step, which paved the way for subsequent American vetoes on other issues, including the Middle East.

The sting was further ameliorated by the adoption of a Finnish draft resolution that included most features of the five-power draft but omitted those elements to which Yost had raised the strongest objection. The vote was 14 to 0, with 1 abstention (Spain).[29]

Another issue, since resolved, was particularly troubling to USUN in the 1964–74 decade—the Portuguese territories in Africa. The United States considered these an anachronism and an economic drain on Portugal, which was spending far more money in suppressing liberation movements in Angola, Guinea (Bissau), and Mozambique than it was deriving in trade and investments. Other Western European countries and Japan, having shed their colonies, had reached new heights of prosperity and enjoyed good economic relations with their former colonies. Unfortunately for both Portugal and the United States, Washington did not press Portugal on its African colonies as it had done with the Dutch on Indonesia and the Belgians on the Congo. The fact that Portugal, as a NATO member, received American military aid was attacked constantly by the Africans, even though the United States repeatedly declared that such arms were not for use in Africa. The Defense Department stressed the importance of the Azores base to American security, and this was useful in resupplying Israel during the Yom Kippur war in October 1973; however, it is doubtful that the base was worth its costs to the United States in its relations with African countries.

U.S. policy on Namibia (South-West Africa) did not suffer from similar restraints. When Goldberg was the permanent representative, the United States separated from Britain and France in supporting resolution 2145 (XXX) of October 28, 1966, in which the General Assembly declared that South Africa had forfeited its mandate over Namibia, for which the UN assumed direct responsibility. This pattern continued in 1970 in the Security Council where the United States voted for three resolutions concerning Namibia.

The first, resolution 276, adopted on January 30 by a vote of 13 to 0 with 2 abstentions (France, Britain), condemned South Africa's continued presence in Namibia; called upon all states to refrain from any dealings with the government of South Africa that might be inconsistent with the finding that its presence in Namibia was illegal; and established a subcommittee of the whole to study ways and means to carry out the provisions of this and previous resolutions on Namibia.[30]

The second resolution (1) called on states that maintain diplomatic relations with South Africa to issue a formal declaration that they consider South Africa's presence in the territory illegal; and (2) called on all states to refrain from relations with South Africa implying recognition of its authority in Namibia and to discourage trade, investment, tourism, and emigration there. It, too, was adopted by a vote of 13 to 0, with Britain and France abstaining.[31] On the same day, June 29, the Council decided to refer the following question to the International Court of Justice for an advisory opinion: "What are the legal consequences for states of the continued presence of South Africa in Namibia, notwithstanding Security Council Resolution 276 (1970)?" The vote was 12 to 0, with Britain, Poland, and the USSR abstaining.

Ambassador William Buffum, speaking after the votes, expressed U.S. support for both resolutions. He noted that the United States had taken policy decisions May 20 regarding trade and investment in Namibia that were reflected in the Council's resolution and particularly welcomed its request to the ICJ, the first time in its history that the Council had requested an advisory opinion.[32]

Yost fully supported U.S. policy on Namibia. He had excellent relations with the Finnish representative on the Security Council, Max Jakobson, who consulted with him closely on all moves in the Council and was particularly effective among the nonpermanent members who constituted a majority in the Council. In fact, Jakobson was one of the most effective diplomats who ever served on the Council.

GLOBAL ISSUES

Although Nixon had little regard for the UN in the areas of peace and security, he did profess to see a meaningful role for it in meeting what he called "global challenges." Among these challenges he stressed the population explosion, the uses of the oceans and the seabeds, the environment, the control of drug abuse, airplane hijacking, and cooperation in the use of outer space. These were problems that could not be solved solely through great power negotiations or in military alliances. Also, they were matters of direct and important concern to the United States and its citizens, most of whom had little interest in decolonization or the problems of economic development of the low-income countries that preoccupied the great majority of member states. Nixon observed: "These global problems are not, of course, the exclusive property of the U.N., but it is uniquely qualified to focus the energies and attention of the world on them."[33]

U.S. delegations were active in all of these issues, but the most significant breakthrough during Yost's incumbency was the conclusion of a treaty banning the emplacement on the deep seabeds of nuclear weapons or any other weapons of mass destruction. The draft treaty, worked out in bilateral negotiations between the Soviet Union and the United States, was submitted by them jointly to the Conference of the Committee on Disarmament (CCD) in 1969. Two revisions were made in response to suggestions and amendments put forward by other members of the CCD before the draft was forwarded to the General Assembly. On December 7, 1970, the Assembly adopted, 104 to 2, with 2 abstentions, a resolution commending the draft treaty, requesting that it be opened for signature, and expressing hope for the widest possible adherence to it. Yost gave full support, but U.S. involvement was largely in the hands of James Leonard, then deputy director of the Arms Control and Disarmament Agency, who had dealt with the issue in Washington and at the CCD.

Also in 1970 the General Assembly decided to convene in 1973 a new Conference on the Law of the Sea. (The proceedings and results of this highly complex and important conference are discussed in Chapter IX.)

On the environment, preparations were going forward for a conference in Stockholm in 1972. UN work on population was given a lift by the establishment in 1969 of a UN Fund for Population Activities, with $15 million pledged voluntarily by governments in its first year, of which the United States provided half.[34] The United States also moved successfully in 1970 for the establishment of a voluntary fund for drug abuse control.[35] On airplane hijacking no significant action was taken by the UN itself; however, a Convention for the Suppression of Unlawful Seizure of Aircraft was negotiated in the International Civil Aviation Organization (ICAO, a specialized agency of the UN) and signed at the Hague on December 16, 1970.[36]

At subsequent conferences on population, the environment, and the law of the sea, it became evident that the Third World countries would not give their full cooperation on the global issues emphasized by Nixon if the United States showed a lack of interest in their problems of development and other matters of general UN concern.

STAFFING AND MANAGEMENT OF USUN

Compared with Lodge and Goldberg, Yost kept a relatively loose rein on his staff, preferring to concentrate on major issues of international peace and security. Also, he had no concern with headlines or self-advertisement; on many occasions when he could have grabbed the spotlight, he let others speak for the United States. He rarely gave his top staff detailed instructions on tactics but was available with sound advice when he was sought out.

The president did not give Yost a completely free hand with his top staff. Nixon wanted a political appointee to be the principal deputy. Yost managed to keep William Buffum, an experienced career diplomat appointed by Goldberg several years earlier, but it took a struggle. To compensate, Nixon appointed two men who had been active in Republican politics to other slots: Christopher H. Phillips as deputy in the Security Council and Glenn Olds as representative to the Economic and Social Council. Phillips had served in responsible positions at the State Department and USUN during the Eisenhower administration and was, therefore, much more experienced than the usual political appointees. Olds, however, had made his career as an educator and was not accustomed to the discipline of speaking as an instructed representative; this was sometimes embarrassing. I remained as senior adviser, with the rank of ambassador, serving as the U.S. representative on various UN bodies dealing with decolonization, peacekeeping, the UN budget, and economic sanctions against Rhodesia. I also served as coordinator and troubleshooter for the General Assembly delegation.

By the fall of 1970 Yost had decided that he would retire again the following spring. Realizing that he had little influence on major policy issues, Yost was not happy about his relationship with Nixon and Kissinger. Also, he enjoyed research and writing, which he had done for two years before Nixon appointed him, and wanted to return to it. Nevertheless, he was surprised and embarrassed when the news media revealed in November 1970 that the White House had sounded out Daniel Patrick Moynihan on taking over from Yost. Moynihan's patronizing statement that he did not want to be a party to humiliating Charles Yost did not help much. The problem was solved in November 1970 indirectly, when Lloyd Bentsen defeated Congressman George Bush for a Texas seat in the U.S. Senate, thus making Bush available to succeed Yost as permanent representative.

The cruel and clumsy leak about Moynihan did get Yost more media attention than he had had before. As I told him, only half facetiously, it made him "box office." It probably improved the market for a syndicated column he undertook in early 1971. At the time of the leak, however, his private comment was that it convinced him he had been right in supporting the Democratic ticket.

Despite their differences, Yost, Nixon, and Kissinger did see eye to eye on at least one major political/security issue—the urgent necessity of reestablishing and multiplying contact and communication with Peking. The breakthrough on this issue, however, came during the term of Yost's successor, George Bush.

GEORGE BUSH

George H. W. Bush, who succeeded Yost in March 1971, was certainly one of the best-liked U.S. permanent representatives to serve at the UN. This was attributed to his engaging personality and assiduous cultivation of personal relationships, since the Nixon administration continued to show little real interest in the UN and, on African issues, moved away from the majority view.

Son of the late Prescott Bush, former U.S. senator from Connecticut,

George Bush grew up in affluent surroundings and went to Yale, where he was Phi Beta Kappa. He then moved to Texas, went into the business of oil exploration, and became independently wealthy. In 1968 he won a seat in the U.S. Congress, as a Republican. Two years later he was defeated in a race for the Senate and thus became available for the UN post.

Bush knew little about the UN when he arrived but was eager to learn and he worked hard at it. Although highly intelligent, he was not an intellectual in the sense that Yost was. Bush, like many politicians, preferred to get information and ideas through personal contacts rather than through extensive reading. This was sometimes a handicap when it came to understanding deep and complex problems but not in representing the United States on policies decided in Washington—as the pattern was during his tenure.

In personality and physical attributes, Bush reminded one of Lodge. He was tall, lean, handsome, and youthful-looking. He genuinely liked mixing with people and had a great knack for befriending them, as well as an apparently instinctive ability to avoid giving offense. He could argue persuasively and yet be a good listener. He made it a point not to act like a "big shot" (his words); he called on the ambassadors of smaller nations rather than make them come to him. He was, of course, equally courteous with the larger missions. He was punctilious about attending the many receptions and dinners hosted by other ambassadors, even though this involved a back-breaking social schedule. Both as host and guest, he had great charm. He used the family farm in Connecticut as well as the official Waldorf Tower apartment to entertain widely and well. He was also very effective in giving public speeches around the country on behalf of the UN. In 1979 he became a presidential candidate.

Bush relied heavily on career officers at both USUN and the State Department and worked very well with them. He did not replace any of the experienced officers at USUN with his people. Instead, when vacancies occurred he appointed as his deputy, W. Tapley Bennett, Jr., a career Foreign Service officer who had been ambassador to the Dominican Republic and, as representative to the Economic and Social Council, Bernard Zagorin, a veteran Treasury Department official. Both had been recommended to Bush by the State Department. Bush did bring in Thomas Lias, his former congressional aide, to help him. Lias was not a barrier between the staff and Bush; rather, he helped Bush to organize his own paperwork and was a trusted adviser. (My personal relations with Bush were excellent, but, as I told him when he took over, I had already decided to leave in September 1971 to teach at the City University of New York.)

For all these qualities, Bush had little influence on American policy in the UN, which was generally defensive rather than innovative or supportive during his term. He was a very effective instrument of policy rather than an architect or influential partner in its formulation. His position was a result of the overall Nixon-Kissinger emphasis on great power politics rather than the UN, the weak standing of Secretary Rogers, and the increasing tendency among the Third World majority to take positions that put the United States in an uncomfortable minority. Another factor was Bush's own personality; he was more adept at getting along with people of varying points of view and carrying out policy then at fighting a determined battle on the making of policy.

As for his relations with Nixon, Bush had this to say: "The appearance of closeness to the President, to the Secretary in those days, to the head of the NSC (Kissinger) was important in my ability to get things done. Frankly, there was more appearance than reality as far as the President went, although I did know him well and did have access to him when required."[37] There is no evidence that Bush was able to initiate or change any significant policy by intervention with the president, but, for that matter, neither was Yost, Scali, or Moynihan.

As for Secretary Rogers, an experienced observer who worked in a high-level position close to the secretary reports that Rogers considered Bush a "lightweight." Since Rogers himself was cool toward the UN and did not carry a lot of weight with Nixon on policymaking for the UN, he was hardly a strong support. As for Kissinger, we have already discussed his negative, almost disdainful attitude toward the UN during this period.

In a note written in January 1978 Bush indicated that, during his term, most policies and speeches were initiated in the State Department; this was in contrast with the practice under Lodge and Goldberg but tended to be the norm in cases where the permanent representative did not have considerable influence with the president. Bush was able to make some changes in the speeches, after clearing with State, but evidently none of substance. It is amazing that he was personally so popular among other delegates at a time when U.S. policy was so defensive and generally unsupportive; this is a tribute to his personal amiability and hard work in cultivating good relations. Given the Nixon-Kissinger mind set, it was probably the best that could be done.

Bush was also a loyal team player. He believed the permanent representative should not appear to be another secretary of state and that the policymaking machinery in Washington must not be bypassed. In January 1978 he wrote:

> The U.N. represents but a part of our overall foreign policy initiatives and there only a small part of our foreign policy goals are enacted. Thus the Ambassador, even though in a very visible post, must coordinate with the Secretary of State and with IO and not try to run a separate ship. He has many contacts with Ambassadors and thus gets

many insights into foreign policy; they should be cranked into the machinery. It confuses the hell out of our allies to have statements coming out of the UN or some other Embassy which may not agree with something the Secretary of State has said. The Ambassador should believe in the UN, want to strengthen it where possible. He owes the President, through the Secretary of State, his advice, his criticism, his best judgment; but when the decision is made he owes the President his support. No UN Ambassador can appear to run a foreign policy organization separate and apart from the State Department, certainly separate and apart from the policies determined by the President.[38]

Seen in that light, he did his job very well.

CHINESE REPRESENTATION

Bush showed his loyalty very clearly at the twenty-sixth session of the General Assembly, his first as permanent representative. It had become increasingly clear that the People's Republic of China could not be kept out of the UN much longer. The Lodge Commission, in its report of April 26, 1971, had recommended a two-China policy. It stated that "all firmly established governments should be included in the U.N. system" but that the United States should "under no circumstances agree to the expulsion from the U.N. of the Republic of China on Taiwan"—in effect, a two-China policy.[39]

Support for China-Taiwan had been eroding in the General Assembly. In 1970 a resolution to replace it with the People's Republic of China had majority support, 59 to 49, for the first time. It was not adopted because of a prior Assembly decision that such a move was an "important question" requiring a two-thirds majority, but even the number of countries supporting the "important question" resolution was declining. It was obvious in January 1971 that some changes in policy and tactics would be required to prevent China-Taiwan's expulsion. Also, the decision on change should have been made early so that friendly countries could be consulted, determine their own positions, perhaps make suggestions for change, and coordinate tactics for the General Assembly. Yet it was August before Washington gave the instructions to pursue a two-China policy at the forthcoming Assembly. The precious months lost would prove to be a serious handicap.

In fairness to Washington, there were serious problems in moving to a new policy. Both Peking and Taiwan rejected a two-China approach; each claimed to be the government of all of China. Chiang Kai-shek was adamant and he had some influential American supporters, mainly right-wing Republicans whom Nixon did not like to antagonize. It was probably for that reason that Nixon did not want to move before publication of the Lodge Commission Report, which recommended a two-China approach, in April 1971. The commission comprised people from a wide political spectrum, including stalwart, conservative Republicans, thus giving a degree of protective cover.

The commission, probably deliberately, left unanswered the question of representation on the Security Council. It was obviously unrealistic to expect Peking, which was in effective control of any area where 98 percent of China's people lived, to accept a situation where Taiwan continued to occupy China's seat on the Security Council, including veto privileges. Yet Washington was reluctant to bite the bullet.

Nixon had long since determined to improve communications and relations with the People's Republic of China. His historic visit to Peking a few months later (February 1972) had been preceded by three years of meticulous preparation beginning in his first few weeks of taking office. From mid-1969 onward the United States took steps to relax trade and travel restrictions, as a signal. Then, in official speeches and statements, such as Nixon's annual foreign policy reports, he signaled to the Chinese with increasing clarity the U.S. desire to reestablish and multiply contact and communication with Peking. In the spring of 1971 Peking began to show greater responsiveness; its invitation to an American table tennis team to visit China in April was one among many public signals. Then, on July 9, Kissinger secretly left Pakistan for a three-day visit to Peking, during which agreement was reached for the Nixon visit in order "to seek the normalization of relations between the two countries and to exchange views on questions of concern to the two sides."[40]

Finally, in August, the U.S. government came to an official decision that it would accept the seating of Peking in the Security Council as part of a two-China package. With the General Assembly opening only a few weeks later, there was little time to build support for the American position. Even NATO allies like Canada, Denmark, Iceland, Norway, and the United Kingdom, which recognized Peking but had supported the U.S. position on the "important question" resolution in earlier years, voted against the motion this time, while Belgium, Italy, and the Netherlands switched to abstentions. As a result, on October 25 the "important question" resolution was rejected for the first time; the vote was 55 to 59, with 15 abstentions. The change in voting occurred despite the fact that this time the resolution reflected the new U.S. position. Instead of referring to any effort to change the representation of China as an "important question," the draft resolution would have required a two-thirds majority to expel a present member. Secretary Rogers on October 4, and Ambassador Bush on October 18, had noted that the Republic of China governs a population on Taiwan larger than the population of two thirds of the UN member states and argued that it would be just as unrealistic to deny them representation as to deny the People's Republic, "which exercises control over the largest number of people of all the world's governments" a seat on the Security Council. The Assembly went on to adopt the "Albanian" resolution recognizing the People's Republic as the sole representative of China, 76 to 35, with 17 abstentions.[41] Its adoption touched off an enthusiastic and noisy demonstration, including dancing in the aisles by longtime, staunch supporters of Peking; this, in turn, led to bitter comments in Washington, strongly anti–United Nations majority in tone.

Was Nixon's anger about this result genuine and deep? It is hard to tell. In one way it was perfect for his domestic political position as well as his foreign policy aims. He had determined to improve relations with Peking, and his efforts were certainly helped by the fact that it was now in the United Nations. Peking's position on Taiwan made it doubtful that it would have accepted a two-China solution. Certainly Nixon's scheduled visit the following February would have met with a less cordial reception if the American position at the UN had prevailed. At the same time, by waging a losing battle against the expulsion of China-Taiwan and castigating the behavior of those who joyfully and publicly celebrated the event at the UN, Nixon deflected American right-wing denunciation from himself to them. His position was also helped in the United States by the Lodge Commission recommendation of April 1971.

Yet U.S. tactics had contributed substantially to the result. At USUN we felt in January 1971, as friendly countries pressed us, that an early U.S. decision on tactics at the Assembly was essential for building support and that a delay beyond June would probably make our position hopeless. The decision came in August. Kissinger's visit to Peking in July was a brilliant diplomatic stroke, but it did not help the U.S. position at the UN, especially at a time when Washington had made no decision yet on what to do at the General Assembly. Then Kissinger's visit to Peking in October, a week before the vote, while fully justified in terms of needed preparations for Nixon's historic trip, was bound to hurt U.S. chances of winning a majority for the "important question" resolution. At the time I suspected that a clever, devious Nixon had deliberately given priority to relations with Peking and, while ostensibly fighting to prevent Taiwan's expulsion, had actually contributed to that result. But in checking with Samuel De Palma, who was then assistant secretary of state for international organization affairs, I was informed that during the final days before the vote Nixon did authorize messages to heads of state and government urging support for the U.S. position. These were not first-person notes, the strongest kind, but they did swing at least one vote.[42]

With better tactics and more timely decisions it is probable that the

United States could have kept China-Taiwan in the UN at the 1971 Assembly, considering the small margin on the "important question" resolution. Even so, the erosion would have continued, and in all likelihood the seating of Peking and ouster of Taiwan would have occurred soon thereafter, perhaps in 1972. In retrospect, it was probably better for the United States to lose. It is too bad, however, that President Nixon chose to make a scapegoat of the UN majority, thus fueling anti-UN sentiments in the Congress and among the American people.

Bush carried on with complete loyalty, dedication, and skill, doing his best to win in a hopeless situation. He made no public complaint about the delayed decisions or the timing of the Kissinger visits to Peking, either before or after the U.S. defeat. Even more remarkably, he cultivated relations with Peking's representatives at the UN with great success, so much so that he was later sent to Peking as chief of the U.S. liaison office there—the equivalent of ambassador, had relations been fully normalized.

Bush faced additional frustrations in 1971. First, there was the crisis in Bangladesh, brought on initially by Pakistan's violent repression of the Bengalis in East Pakistan. A flood of millions of refugees into India and sympathy for the Bengalis led to Indian intervention. The secretary general's offer of good offices was not accepted by India. Following the outbreak of hostilities, a Soviet veto thwarted Security Council efforts in December 1971 to prevent the use of military force by one state to change the internal structure of another. Although the General Assembly voted overwhelmingly for a cease-fire and withdrawal, resolutions by that body are not mandatory and are therefore effective only to the extent that they constitute an impressive expression of world public opinion. Even then, they have effect only if the conflicting parties are sensitive to such an expression. India, in fact, ignored the General Assembly resolution.[43]

Also in December came the election of a new secretary general. U Thant was completing his second five-year term and had declared he would not serve again. The problem, as usual, was to find a candidate acceptable to the five permanent members of the Security Council. The Soviets have consistently held that the secretary general should not assume executive functions or act on his own initiative. Consequently, they had liked U Thant much better than his bold predecessor, Dag Hammarskjöld. Since Hammerskjöld, a mild-looking former Swedish finance minister, had surprised them, they preferred not to take risks on a successor. A Soviet colleague told me that Moscow refused to accept the Soviet mission's conclusion that Thant really meant what he said in declining another term until Gromyko came to New York in September 1971 and conferred with Thant himself. Then the Soviets decided to support Gunnar Jarring, the Swedish ambassador to Moscow and for some years the secretary general's representative charged with assisting the parties to the Arab-Israeli war of

1967 to negotiate a settlement. Evidently they believed Jarring, a career diplomat who was already sixty, would not be a bold or active secretary general. It soon became evident, however, that China would steadfastly veto Jarring just because he was an ambassador in Moscow and the Soviets wanted him.

The preferred candidate of the United States was Ambassador Max Jakobson, Finnish permanent representative to the UN. Jakobson had demonstrated, particularly during the two years he had served on the Security Council, that he was thoughtful, intelligent, decisive, and active. The Soviets spread the word around that the Arabs were bitterly opposed to him because of his Jewish ancestry. Actually, this was probably a smokescreen; they must have feared the very qualities of decisiveness and energy that supporters of an activist secretary general prized.

On the first ballot only Kurt Waldheim of Austria of the twelve candidates received the necessary 9 votes; the vote for him was 10 to 3, with 2 abstentions. Since all 3 negative votes were cast by permanent members, additional balloting was required. On the second and third ballots, not only Waldheim but also Jakobson and Ortiz de Rozas of Argentina received at least 9 votes; but in the latter two cases a permanent member—the USSR—had exercised the veto. (Ortiz de Rozas, in fact, had the highest number of affirmative votes—12.) Consequently Waldheim was recommended by the Security Council and elected by the General Assembly.

The result left a residue of temporary bad feeling between the Finnish and U.S. missions. At one point when the ballot was pending, Jakobson made some tactical suggestions to Bush, who rejected them and said he would not "take orders" from Jakobson.[44] After the balloting a member of the Finnish mission claimed, in private, that the United States had failed to live up to commitments made by Secretary Rogers that the United States would veto any other candidate "till the cows come home." Evidently the cows came home sooner than the Finns expected. A close associate of the secretary felt that "he didn't hang tough enough." A similar U.S. pledge to Trygve Lie in 1950 was honored during a three-year stalemate, ending in the agreed selecion of Dag Hammarskjöld. In that case, however, Lie was reappointed by the General Assembly ad interim. In 1971, on the other hand, a stalemate would have resulted in pressure on U Thant to remain ad interim. Since the Soviets wanted him to remain anyhow, it is doubtful that they would have accepted Jakobson or Ortiz de Rozas no matter how long the stalemate lasted.

Bush had better luck on the next major issue—the reduction of the U.S. assessment of the regular UN budget from 31.52 percent to 25 percent at the twenty-seventh session of the General Assembly in 1972. In principle, assessments are based on the relative capacity to pay. A complex formula is used, geared to comparative national income but making allowances for low per capita income and setting a floor and a ceiling. In the immediate postwar period an income-based scale would have had the United States paying almost half of the total budget, a situation recognized as disproportionate. Thus, in the first scale of assessments the rate of assessment of the highest contributor, the United States, was established in 1946 at 39.89 percent, although this percentage was below the estimated relative capacity of the United States to pay. The United States, which argued that the maximum contributor should be assessed no more than 25 percent, indicated its dissatisfaction with the 39.89 percent assessment but accepted it as a temporary measure because of the economic dislocations resulting from World War II.

Subsequently, as the temporary economic dislocations resulting from the war disappeared and a far more broadly based organization evolved, further adjustments were made in the scale of assessments so that eventually the U.S. assessment percentage was reduced to its 1972 level of 31.52 percent, or 1.52 percentage points above the ceiling established by the General Assembly in 1957 as a target.

In view of the fact that an additional fifty nations had become members of the United Nations since 1957 and significant additions to the membership were anticipated, the United States argued that the time had come to reduce its ceiling to 25 percent, even though its relative capacity to pay was somewhat higher. This position was in line with the Lodge Commission's recommendation and the strong views of Congress; some congressmen favored making a cut to 25 percent unilaterally. The knowledge of the latter factor must have made an impression on many delegates.

Bush and his staff did an all-out lobbying job that was highly effective. Their argument that the U.S. share could be reduced without raising the assessments of other states was buttressed by the knowledge that the expected entry of the two Germanies and upward adjustment of Japan's assessment to reflect its rapid economic growth would compensate for the reduction. Of course it was also true that other members, particularly the other developed countries, would be forgoing assessment reductions they might otherwise get; consequently, the U.S. delegation had an uphill fight. The 25 percent ceiling was won in the adoption by the General Assembly of its resolution 2961B (XXVII) on December 13, 1972, by an overwhelming majority.

Delegation lobbying had stressed the other part of the Lodge Commission recommendation—that the United States would increase its voluntary contributions to programs like the UNDP and UNICEF as its assessed contribution came down. Congress decided otherwise. In fact, U.S. contributions to the UNDP, which amounted to $90 million in 1972, were only $70 million in 1976.

The reduction to 25 percent was clearly an instance where Bush had been an effective instrument rather than an innovator of policy. When asked about instances where he had had an impact on *making* policy, Bush could recall only one, involving Israel, Syria, and Lebanon. Following the murder on September 5, 1972, of eleven members of the Israeli Olympic Team in Munich, on September 8 Israel carried out extensive air attacks against PLO bases in Lebanon and Syria, which also caused many innocent civilian casualties. Syria and Lebanon complained to the Security Council, which met on September 10. Somalia, Guinea, and Yugoslavia put forward a resolution calling on "the parties concerned to cease immediately all military operations and to exercise the greatest restraint in the interest of international peace and security." The four Western European members of the Council put forward amendments designed to change the resolution so as to apply to terrorists as well as to regular military operations, but these fell short of the necessary 9 votes. The vote on the unamended resolution was 13 to 1, with 1 abstention, the single negative vote being a U.S. veto. Explaining the vote, Bush said that the United States would have supported the resolution if the amendments had been approved; however, the unamended resolution "spoke to one form of violence and not to another, looked to effect but not to cause." Bush objected to the double standard under which "states must control their own forces but not control irregular forces. We invite more terrorism by our silence on the disaster in Munich."[45] Bush's stand was popular among Americans, shocked by the Munich murders, and his recommendation to cast a veto was accepted without difficulty in Washington.

On the larger issues of a Middle East settlement there was little activity involving Bush. The four-power talks continued throughout 1971 but produced no agreement on balanced guidelines that might assist Jarring's efforts pursuant to resolution 242. In the face of this disagreement, there were no four-power talks in 1972. Middle East policies were developed in Washington by the secretary of state and Joseph Sisco, assistant secretary of state for Middle East and South Asian affairs. In fact, after Bush made a comment about Middle East policy at his first press conference, Sisco reportedly called Bush and told him "politely but firmly that he would give out the news about this area, including the leaks."[46]

African policy was also being made in Washington, with no significant impact from Bush. This was a period when the United States emphasized "communication" with Portugal and South Africa—Option Two of the infamous NSSM-39.[47] This meant that we would try friendly persuasion rather than pressure to induce Portugal to grant self-determination to Angola, Mozambique, and Guinea (Bissau), and to induce South Africa to give up Namibia and soften the worst features of apartheid. It struck me when I first saw NSSM-39 that we were asking the wrong question: What would best serve the U.S. national interest in the next five years? In those terms, American commercial interests in South Africa and the strategic value of the Azores made the answer obvious. If the question had been put in terms of twenty years, it would have been just as evident that being friendly with Portugal and South Africa was the wrong answer. Representing the United States on colonial issues at the UN, I tried to make that point but had no impact. After all, presidents run for office every four years, not every twenty years.

As George M. Houser has pointed out, Nixon's new policies toward Africa were different in degree rather than in kind. Although the United States had consistently condemned apartheid in South Africa and supported self-determination in Africa, it had taken little action in support of those positions during the Eisenhower, Kennedy, and Johnson administrations. It had, however, supported General Assembly resolution 2145 declaring that South Africa had forfeited its mandate over South-West Africa (Namibia) and had vigorously supported economic sanctions against Rhodesia. These were gestures that the Africans appreciated, even though they wanted the United States to do much more. Under Nixon's new policies toward Africa, the United States sold civilian jet aircraft to South Africa, gave Union Carbide permission to import a shipment of chrome from Rhodesia in 1970 that was said to have been purchased before sanctions came into effect (though Union Carbide's request had been denied in 1968 and 1969), and greatly increased the number of negative U.S. votes on UN resolutions dealing with apartheid and colonialism in South Africa. Moreover, although the State Department representative testified before Congress that U.S. stockpiles of chrome amounted to seven years' supply, the White House made no real effort to defeat the 1971 Byrd amendment, under which the United States imported Rhodesian chrome in contravention of Security Council sanctions for which the United States itself has voted.[48] These policy changes were carefully noted by the Africans; consequently, it is not surprising that they took increasingly hostile positions on matters of interest to the United States, with the ready encouragement of the Soviet Union and hostile Arab states.

Nixon's lack of interest in African concerns is illustrated by the fact that, in the more than 600 pages of his memoirs covering his presidency, he does not once mention Africa.

There is no indication that Bush disagreed with Nixon's policies on Africa nor that he did anything significant to change them. Yet he remained personally popular with other UN delegates and his own staff—a tribute to his amiability and assiduous cultivation of good personal relations.

After Nixon was reelected he asked Bush to become chairman of the Republican National Committee. Bush accepted and in February 1973 was replaced as U.S. permanent ambassador to the UN by John Scali.

JOHN A. SCALI

John A. Scali was very different from George Bush in background, training, and personality. Born in 1918 in Canton, Ohio, Scali took a degree in journalism at Boston University in 1942 and worked the next three decades as a reporter. He was a war correspondent in Europe in 1944 for Associated Press and then served as its diplomatic correspondent in Washington from 1945 to 1961. He was then ABC's diplomatic correspondent in Washington for the next ten years.

Scali's most notable feat was his role as liaison between the White House and Aleksander Fomin, a counselor at the Soviet embassy in Washington during the 1962 Cuban Missile Crisis. It was Fomin who first suggested, evidently on instructions, that Khrushchev might be willing to remove the missiles from Cuba under UN inspection and promise not to reintroduce them if Kennedy would promise publicly not to invade Cuba. After a meeting of the Executive Committee, Rusk told Scali he could advise Fomin that the United States saw "real possibilities." Two hours after Scali relayed this message to Fomin came a letter from Khrushchev to Kennedy proposing a compromise similar to Fomin's suggestions. The Scali-Fomin contact became even more important when Moscow radio broadcast a second Khrushchev message, this time adding the removal of U.S. bases from Turkey as a quid pro quo. It added weight to Robert Kennedy's suggestion that the second message be ignored in the president's response to Khrushchev. To his credit, Scali not only kept strict confidentiality but did not capitalize on his role.[49]

In 1971 Nixon appointed Scali special consultant for foreign affairs, a post he held at the time of his selection for the UN post. Thus, Scali had been following foreign affairs and diplomacy for twenty-eight years when he came to USUN and was thoroughly acquainted with the issues as well as both political and career officials in the Washington foreign policy establishment. He was also bright, energetic, articulate, and forceful. In contrast to Bush, Scali was described as "abrasive" by a number of people who worked with him, knew him well, and respected his ability. His personality was, in fact, closer to the content of Nixon's policies toward the UN—skeptical, disdainful, and combative. Bush had carried out the same policies with a "nice guy" manner and a great solicitude for cultivating good relations with foreign diplomats and the American public; Scali was blunt, direct, and little concerned with public relations. He was concerned with representing U.S. policies in the Security Council and other UN bodies and won the respect of State Department professionals for his intelligence and forcefulness in doing so, as well as for his skill as a negotiator.[50]

Scali had little influence on the making of U.S. policies. Unlike Austin, Lodge, Stevenson, and Goldberg, he had no political base and was not close to the president or to the secretary of state. Instead, he tended to work through Joseph Sisco, assistant secretary for Middle East and South Asian affairs and later undersecretary for political affairs; and Samuel De Palma, assistant secretary for IO. He had known both these veteran career officers during his many years as a diplomatic correspondent in Washington. From my conversations with all three in 1978, it was clear that these were relationships based on professionalism and mutual respect and were not personal friendships. Still, the working relationship in carrying out policies and making necessary adjustments in tactics and phrasing was evidently effective. On policymaking, Scali had little impact.

When asked about issues on which he had had policy impact, Scali mentioned two: the Yom Kippur war in October 1973 and his statement to the General Assembly in December 1974 deploring the "tyranny of the majority."

Actually, the major decisions on U.S. policy during and after the Yom Kippur war were made by Nixon and Kissinger. The war started October 6 with attacks on Israel by Egypt and Syria, which won initial successes and inflicted heavy casualties on Israel. After a week of U.S. foot-dragging, attributed by various writers to Kissinger or Defense Secretary Schlesinger, Nixon decided on massive airlift to Israel of planes, ammunition, and other equipment. U.S. hesitation was occasioned by the hope that Israel could meet the invasions successfully without resupply and by the fear that U.S. resupply might trigger an Arab oil boycott, but evidence that the Soviets were airlifting massive supplies to Egypt and serious Israeli losses finally induced the United States to act. (In fact, the feared oil boycott actually came shortly after the resupply.) By October 19 the military balance had swung to Israel's favor. Thereupon Brezhnev invited Kissinger to Moscow where, on October 22, the two superpowers called for an immediate cease-fire.[51]

That same day the Soviet and U.S. delegations urgently requested the UN Security Council to adopt a resolution calling for an immediate cease-fire, which the Council promptly did in its resolution 338, October 22, 1973. Scali and his Soviet counterpart, Malik, worked effectively in securing prompt action, though there was some grumbling about superpowers arranging matters between themselves and then asking for an immediate Council endorsement.

Fighting continued despite the cease-fire order, and the Egyptian Third Army Corps was virtually encircled by Israeli forces west of the Suez Canal. On October 24 the Soviets invited the United States to intervene jointly to stop the fighting and prevent destruction of the Third Army Corps. Meanwhile, Moscow was apparently readying its forces, with the implication that Soviet troops would go in alone if the United States did not join them. President Nixon took the threat seriously enough to order an alert of U.S. Armed Forces. A serious confrontation loomed.[52]

Here began Scali's job, the most important during his tenure. Some outside force was required to separate the adversaries and assure observance of a cease-fire, and the insertion of either Soviet or Soviet plus American forces had obvious dangers. On instructions and after consultation with the Soviet delegation, Scali talked with nonpermanent members of the Security Council about the need for a UN force. It was they, the nonpermanent members, who on October 25 introduced the draft that became resolution 340 in which the Council decided "to set up immediately under its authority a United Nations Emergency Force to be composed of personnel drawn from states members of the United Nations except the Permanent Members of the Security Council." Scali took particular pride in having worked successfully for the exclusion of Soviet and U.S. forces, despite a clear Soviet desire to be part of the force. As a compromise, each sent thirty observers to serve with UN forces in the Sinai.

The Council established UNEF II on October 27, approving a report prepared by the secretary general at its request. As analyzed earlier in this chapter (in the section on Yost), in our discussion of the efforts of the Special Committee on Peacekeeping Operations to reach agreement on peacekeeping guidelines, the secretary general's report was skillfully drawn up to carefully skirt the limits of tolerance evidenced by the Soviets and the United States. As such, it may serve as a model for future operations.

A high-level knowledgeable State Department official of that period told me that Scali carried on these negotiations very skillfully and that the establishment of UNEF II had converted Henry Kissinger from an attitude of indifference toward the UN to the feeling that it could at times serve a useful purpose.

Kissinger was less pleased by Scali's other source of pride—his "tyranny of the majority" speech. According to Scali, Kissinger was upset because he himself had in mind making a similar statement and he felt "scooped," not because he differed with the content or style.[53]

Scali's statement came on December 6, 1974, during General Assembly discussion of an item on "Strengthening International Security," originally introduced by the Soviets in 1970. Though given routine clearance by the State Department, the statement apparently did not get the secretary's attention until after it came out, with a splash, in the media.

Provocation for Scali's statement had been building up for a long time, with some of the worst excesses in 1974. At the General Assembly's sixth special session on raw materials and development in May, the Third World majority of more than 100 countries had pushed through its proposals for a New International Economic Order, with little effort to negotiate compromises. These far-reaching proposals were aimed at giving the less developed countries a bigger share of the world's output and a larger role in making the decisions affecting the world economy. (They will be described in detail on pages 238–40, when we discuss the seventh special session in September 1975.)

At the twenty-ninth session of the General Assembly, an overwhelming majority rejected the credentials of the South African delegation, as had been done before. This time, however, the Assembly president, Foreign Minister Abdelaziz Bouteflika, ruled on November 12 that, as a consequence, the South African delegation could no longer participate in the Assembly at that session. A number of Western representatives challenged the ruling as contrary to the UN Charter, which provides that a member may be suspended or expelled by the General Assembly only upon the recommendation of the Security Council. (Efforts to obtain a Council recommendation to expel South Africa had been vetoed October 18 by Britain, France, and the United States.) The Assembly majority, ignoring Western claims of Charter violation, voted to uphold the president's ruling, 91 to 22, with 19 abstentions.[54]

Later in the session the Assembly voted 105 to 4, with 20 abstentions, to hear the representative of the Palestine Liberation Organization in Plenary. All members present knew very well that the PLO could have been heard in any of the seven standing committees of the General Assembly, as had been the procedure for nongovernment organizations during the entire history of the United Nations. Some delegates argued that the Palestine Liberation Organization could not be heard in committee, since the item had been assigned to the Plenary. This argument overlooks the evident fact that the Assembly could easily have assigned the item to the Political Committee or Special Political Committee, both of which are committees of the whole, and then taken final action in Plenary. The issue, therefore, was not whether the PLO views could be heard but whether it could be given enhanced status by being heard in the Plenary session. The U.S. representative called this "a dangerous precedent," and even representatives sympathetic to the PLO on questions of substance questioned this breaking of precedent. The Algerian president of the General Assembly added frosting to the cake by having on the platform a chair traditionally reserved for heads of state—a chair that was not used even by Nikita Khrushchev, Harold Macmillan, and Fidel Castro, or other heads of government who spoke before the General Assembly.

Another resolution adopted at the same session gave the Palestine Liberation Organization status as an observer at the United Nations General Assembly. The vote on this resolution (3237[XXIX]), was 95 to 17, with 19 abstentions.[55] In the past such observer status had always been reserved to states. One must ask whether this precedent would enable such groups as the Eritreans, the Kurds, the Nagas, and the Estonians to have observer status. Once the principle of according only states the right to have observer status at the General Assembly starts to break down, it is hard to know where the new practice will stop. In all likelihood, it will stop wherever the political majority at any given time wants it to stop.

Also at the twenty-ninth session the General Assembly adopted over Western opposition a Charter of Economic Rights and Duties of States, first proposed by President Echeverria of Mexico at the third UNCTAD Conference in 1972. Its underlying premise was that existing international law had been developed primarily by the industrialized countries and favored their interests; now, with a majority of the world's nation-states having become independent since 1945, it was time to draw up new rules. Despite two years of negotiations, serious differences remained between the Third World majority, egged on by the Soviet bloc, and the West. The main sticking points were: (1) the attempt, by using the term "Charter" and other wording devices, to give a General Assembly resolution a legal character normally accorded to conventions or treaties ratified by governments; (2) provisions that foreign-owned property might be expropriated without regard to international obligations; (3) endorsement of producer organizations such as OPEC; (4) claims for restitution for alleged losses resulting from colonialism, neocolonialism, racial discrimination, and "all forms of foreign aggression"; (5) the indexation of commodity prices to the price levels of manufactured goods.

The charter resolution was adopted, 120 to 6, with 10 abstentions; however, the 16 countries that either voted against it or abstained represent more than 80 percent of world trade and investment. Senator Charles Percy, in explaining the negative U.S. vote, criticized the charter as "unbalanced," as did most Western representatives. Under the UN Charter, resolutions of the General Assembly are recommendations that are not binding on member states, except for regular budget assessments. It is extremely doubtful that the industrialized Western countries, whose cooperation would be essential to making the Charter of Economic Rights and Duties effective, will accord it any validity; however, courts in Third World countries may be inclined to give it standing.

It was against this background that Scali, warned that governments of sovereign states cannot be browbeaten by "the tyranny of the majority" and that attempts to do so might make the UN increasingly irrelevant to international action. It was not a question, he noted, whether the United States would withdraw from the UN. If the United States decreased its interest in the UN and decided to deal with its international problems elsewhere and a number of other Western nations did the same, the UN would diminish in importance at a time when it was needed more than ever.

Scali was preceded by the French representative, who argued in much the same vein, and was followed by the British representative, who said: "Recently we have seen resolutions adopted in which the interests of a minority whose cooperation may be essential for their implementation were brushed aside. We have resolutions which, by denying from the start any particle of justice to a different point of view, can only damage the prospects for a solution to the problems which they purport to address." The Danish representative warned: "Only by close adherence to and respect for the basic principles, by compromise and avoidance of unrealistic adoptions of decisions shall we be able to safeguard the universal support from the peoples of our nations." Similar warnings were expressed by other Western representatives.[56] (The tactic had been planned in the Western caucus, with Scali playing a leading role.)

A number of Third World and Soviet bloc speakers responded by observing that the West had not been reluctant to use its voting strength when it controlled the UN majority during the UN's first decade. Some Third World spokesmen acknowledged the need for genuine negotiation on resolutions if they were to be meaningful; however, this would have to involve understanding and flexibility on the Western side. Amen! There is little doubt that Nixon's lack of concern with Third World objectives in southern Africa and with economic development led to U.S. policies in the UN that made efforts at compromise appear futile and strengthened the influence of Third World extremists.

In some ways the exchange served as a catharsis, with both sides adopting a more conciliatory attitude when the General Assembly next convened at its seventh special session in September 1975.

Meanwhile in 1974 Henry Kissinger was finding the UN very helpful in his step-by-step approach toward a Middle East peace. On January 18 Secretary General Waldheim informed the Security Council that, with Kissinger's good offices, an Egyptian-Israeli Agreement on Disengagement of Forces had been signed by Egypt, Israel, and the UN. On May 31 the Security Council, in a resolution cosponsored by the USSR and the United States, welcomed a similar Syrian-Israeli disengagement agreement and decided to establish the UN Disengagement Observer Force (UNDOF) along lines similar to those of UNEF II. These UN peacekeeping forces, by stabilizing the disengagement of forces, were a real asset to Kissinger's efforts to work toward peace in the slow, step-by-step manner that he then saw as the realistic approach.

GLOBAL ISSUES

U.S. interests were also involved in a series of conferences on global issues—environment, population, use of the seas and seabeds—which Nixon considered an appropriate area of UN concern. In his 1972 report to the Congress, Nixon said:

These problems constitute a major opportunity for the United Nations system. At a time when political realities inhibit the UN's ability to meet some of its original purposes, the new dimension of diplomacy gives to the UN an agenda of urgent tasks. Their successful accomplishment will not only be a significant contribution to the well-being of mankind, but will also serve to inoculate and nurture among nations the habit of cooperation for the general good—and for the ultimate acceptance of the rule of law to govern international relations. That, after all, is the heart of the purpose for which the UN was founded.

The UN possesses special and unique capacities for dealing with these problems. It has in being a trained Secretariat. It can attract the expert talent required. It can direct attention to the transcendent global interest in these problems, to which national interests must be accommodated. Finally, it can use its moral authority to stimulate international action.[57]

The UN Conference on the Human Environment, the first worldwide conference ever held on this subject, met at Stockholm, June 5-16, 1972. One hundred and thirteen countries sent delegations, including the People's Republic of China, attending a UN conference for the first time. It aligned itself with the less developed countries and argued that they should receive "reparations." The Soviet bloc, except Romania, did not attend because the General Assembly majority had decided on an invitation formula that excluded the German Democratic Republic (East Germany).

Discussion and debate were of a generally high quality. Although political issues intruded from time to time, such issues were muted. Delegations focused their presentations on overriding concern for problems of the human environment and the necessity for concerted international action. The problem of atmospheric nuclear weapons tests entered the discussions more than had been anticipated, however, primarily because the conference coincided with France's nuclear tests in the South Pacific.

The conference adopted unanimously a Declaration on the Human Environment containing twenty-six principles to guide nations in developing approaches to the solution of problems of the human environment. It was unable to reach agreement on a twenty-seventh principle concerning the obligation of countries adequately to inform one another of potential environmental effects of their activities and decided, therefore, to refer it to the General Assembly for further consideration.

It unanimously adopted an Action Plan containing 109 recommendations for international action and referred an equal number to countries for action at the national level.

On December 15, 1972, the General Assembly adopted, 116 to 0, with 10 abstentions, a resolution cosponsored by the United States that approved the institutional arrangements recommended by the Stockholm conference. It also adopted unanimously a resolution deciding to locate in Nairobi, Kenya, the secretariat of the new UN Environment Program. In the Second Committee the United States had voted against the designation of Nairobi because it believed that the coordinating responsibility of the new environmental secretariat could best be discharged in New York or Geneva; however, in Plenary it went along with the strongly expressed desire of the Third World that the headquarters be in a less developed country.[58] (All the specialized agencies and the UN itself are headquartered in developed countries.)

The Third World Population Conference, the first to be held at an intergovernmental level, met in Bucharest, Romania, in August 1974. The conference, after many stormy sessions during which Third World countries insisted on references to the New International Economic Order, adopted a World Population Plan of Action by the acclamation of 135 governments, with only the Holy See dissenting because of the direct fertility control measures mentioned therein. At the twenty-ninth session of the UN General Assembly, where the conference report was considered in the Second Committee, Brazil and Uruguay proposed an amendment to add a paragraph stressing that "the implementation of the World Population Plan of Action should take full account of the New International Economic Order and thus contribute to its implementation." After rejection of a U.S. proposal to delete the last six words of that paragraph, on the grounds that the language violated the consensus reached in Bucharest, the United States abstained on the resolution as a whole, because of that paragraph. The vote, on December 17, 1974, was 131 to 0, with 4 abstentions (the United States).[59]

Also in 1974 began the Third United Nations Conference on the Law of the Sea, which after five years and nine sessions had still not come to an agreement in 1979; the main stumbling block is the question of a regime for the deep seabeds.[60] Since the issues are highly complex and did not substantially involve John Scali, we have not dealt with them here. For similar reasons we have dealt only briefly and superficially with the conferences on environment and population, where neither Scali nor USUN was involved. They have been mentioned, however, because of Nixon's expressed interest in UN concern with global issues.

Scali, as a professional diplomatic correspondent, respected professional competence among career diplomats. He kept the professional staff left by George Bush, including the top deputies. The only significant change was the appointment of C. Clyde Ferguson, a very able black professor of law, as representative to the Economic and Social Council in October 1973. Ferguson, now teaching at Harvard Law School, had served as a member of the UN Subcommission on the Prevention of Discrimination, as Ambassador to Uganda (1970–72), and as assistant secretary of state for

African affairs. Scali was able to obtain something for the staff that his predecessors had tried in vain to get for almost two decades—housing allowances for those who had representational functions at USUN.

When asked why he had resigned, Scali replied that he felt the new president, Gerald Ford, should have the opportunity to name his own man. As Ford took office in August 1974, he evidently had more urgent matters on his mind. In any case, it would have been difficult to change the permanent representative just as the twenty-ninth session of the General Assembly was to begin in September. In the event, Scali's successor, Daniel Patrick Moynihan, did not take over until June 1975.

DANIEL PATRICK MOYNIHAN

John Holmes, an experienced and knowledgeable Canadian observer of the United Nations and the United States, has commented: "There was no mistaking abroad President Nixon's dislike of the U.N. It was probably necessary for Americans to go through the brief fling at Moynihanism just to show that it was counterproductive."[61]

Ironically, Moynihan was not appointed by Nixon but by his successor, President Ford, in June 1975. Yet Moynihan's tactics of confrontation against the Third World did represent the culmination of Nixon's attitude toward the UN; hence he is included in this chapter.

Another irony is that Pat Moynihan first came to prominence in the U.S. government in the Democratic, pro–United Nations administration of President Kennedy, working for a lifelong liberal Democrat, Arthur Goldberg. When Goldberg was secretary of labor during 1961–63, Moynihan served as special assistant and executive assistant to the secretary, then became assistant secretary of labor, 1963–65. When Goldberg came to the UN in July 1965, he wanted Moynihan for his deputy; he had great esteem for Moynihan's unusual capacity for hard work, for his intellectual brilliance, and for his skillful articulation. Moynihan declined the offer, preferring to accept an academic appointment in Wesleyan University, Connecticut, followed by an appointment at Harvard.

Moynihan returned to Washington when Nixon became president in 1969, serving as a presidential assistant for urban affairs and, later, as counselor to the president. Moynihan's penchant for graphic and striking phrases made him unpopular with many in the black community when, as part of a report on federal poverty programs, he recommended "benign neglect." In late 1970 news leaks disclosed that President Nixon was considering the appointment of Moynihan to replace Yost at the United Nations. Perhaps because of the embarrassing leak, this did not happen. Moynihan kept his academic appointment at Harvard but was a special consultant to the president during 1971–73. He was then named ambassador to India, where he remained until 1975.

Moynihan's first real exposure to the UN came in the fall of 1971 when he served on the U.S. delegation to the twenty-sixth session of the General Assembly. He was assigned largely to the Third Committee, which deals with social, humanitarian, and human rights questions, in view of his long concern with these issues in the United States. Unfortunately, the Third Committee has traditionally had the lowest priority of all Assembly committees in the thinking of the United States and many other delegations. In the male chauvinism that most governments have displayed at the UN as well as at home, the Third Committee had by far the largest number of women representatives of any Assembly committee and its work was considered relatively unimportant. If its procedures were often disorderly and its discussions propagandistic, no one worried much. The communist states took a more serious interest, seeing the committee as an excellent forum for propaganda with the Third World representatives. During my own years at USUN there was a very striking contrast in moving from the Second (Economic) Committee, where the United States had much more widespread contacts and substantially more influence than the Soviets, to the Third Committee, where the reverse prevailed. Yet the same governments, all the members of the UN, were in both committees.

It is not surprising that Moynihan's service in the Third Committee gave him a jaundiced view of the UN. The same thing happened to William Buckley, who served in the Third Committee at the session in 1973 and later wrote a book about his experience that was an entertaining but, because of Buckley's narrow exposure, not a very balanced picture of the UN General Assembly.[62] Based on these and other experiences, it behooves the United States to take both the Third Committee and the issues before it more seriously and to avoid assigning high-powered, highly articulate representatives exclusively to it for an entire session.

That experience, combined with the evolution of his own thinking, was reflected in Moynihan's widely noted article, "The United States in Opposition," which appeared in the March 1975 issue of *Commentary*. Moynihan's target was the Third World, more than 100 member states, mostly new countries, which has used its majority to dominate the UN agenda. Of the new nations he wrote: "To a quite astonishing degree they were ideologically uniform, having fashioned their politics in terms derived from the general corpus of British socialist opinion as it developed in the period roughly 1890–1950." In his view the new nations were carrying out the "British revolution" of Fabian socialism, the welfare state, as expounded by Harold Laski and other professors at the London School of Economics. The main elements of this socialist doctrine, as he saw it, were:

(1) emphasis on the redistribution of wealth rather than on production; (2) an anti-American, anticapitalist, antiprofit bias; (3) the belief that the new nations, former colonies, had been exploited in the same way as the industrial proletariat; (4) resentment against ethnic discrimination, corresponding to class distinctions in industrial society; (5) demand for reparations to the peoples that had been victims of exploitation and discrimination; and (6) an emphasis on legislative procedures (the General Assembly) to right the wrongs.

Moynihan alleged that this doctrine was responsible for the decline of the British economy, which in 1973 accounted for only 3.1 percent of the world's production compared with 5.8 percent in 1950. Naturally, in his view, British protéges such as Burma, India, and Sri Lanka were doing badly for the same reason.

In his article Moynihan considered the preceding session of the General Assembly, the twenty-ninth, a disaster following "a massive failure of American diplomacy." He pointed to sections of the UN's *World Social Report*, particularly its 1970 edition, that showed a pro-Soviet, anti-American bias and charged that U.S. officials had been asleep in not attacking the report at its earliest appearance. He noted with strong disapproval the emphasis at the 1972 UN Conference on the Human Environment and the 1974 Population Conference on the redistribution of the world's wealth. At the latter conference it was alleged that the cause of poverty was not excessive population growth but injustice and exploitation. In similar vein, he denounced the Charter on Economic Rights and Duties of States adopted at the Assembly's twenty-ninth session.

The remedy? It was time for the United States to go into opposition, to abandon "appeasement," to stop being apologetic, to stand up for its beliefs. "It is time . . . that the American spokesman came to be feared in international forums for the truths he might tell." Thus, according to Moynihan, U.S. representatives should strike back at Third World representatives who criticized the United States by exposing inequities and injustices in their countries. They should stress that, under the present economic order, the last three decades had seen the most rapid growth in world product in human history and that even the less developed countries have experienced faster economic growth than did the industrialized countries at a similar stage. They should emphasize the role of free enterprise in making the West so productive and the contributions of the multinational corporation, "arguably the most creative international institution of the 20th century." They should point to the economic failures of new countries operating on socialist principles and the success of private enterprise nations like Brazil, Nigeria, Singapore, South Korea, and Taiwan. They should also strike out aggressively for individual liberty and *against* examples of its suppression. Kissinger, who had become disenchanted with Scali, liked Moynihan's article and suggested that he become Scali's successor.

Although there is much truth in Moynihan's diagnosis and even his criticism of American acquiescence of the 1970 *World Social Report*— which he criticized trenchantly as U.S. representative to the Third Committee in 1971—his application of his own remedy during a brief tenure as permanent representative showed how counterproductive it could be if applied literally. George Ball observed: "Although the Moynihan article made some valid points, it generalized too much from the author's limited exposure. Two states that led the drive for an increased share of the world's income were Algeria, a former French colony, and Mexico, which had not been a colony since 1821."[63] (Ball used these examples against Moynihan's thesis that Fabian socialism, as expounded by the high priests of the London School of Economics, was the destructive philosophy transmitted through leaders of former British colonies and was the heart of the Third World campaign for redistribution of wealth and reparations.)

Ironically, Moynihan's first major appearance, before the seventh special session of the UN General Assembly on September 1, 1975, was not a statement of opposition to the New International Economic Order; on the contrary, it was unusually accommodating. The statement had been prepared for Henry Kissinger, but the secretary was at a critical point of his Middle East shuttle diplomacy, and Moynihan read it in his name. It was a carefully prepared, comprehensive statement, reflecting the views of experts throughout the government. It was clearly intended as a signal that we were ending a year and a half of confrontation between the United States and the Third World, during which the United States had stood almost alone. Its most dramatic specific proposal was Kissinger's suggestion that a $10 billion facility be established in the International Monetary Fund (IMF) for compensatory financing to help developing countries that produce raw materials to weather the vicissitudes of erratic markets. The speech represented a major change in Kissinger's thinking about the Third World and the UN.

The Third World leaders accepted the Kissinger statement as a significant effort toward accommodation, and serious negotiations ensued. The result was an agreement on the following goals of the less developed countries: (1) stabilizing their income from commodity exports; (2) obtaining preferential tariff treatment in industrialized countries for their manufactured goods; (3) improving their access to capital and technology; and (4) obtaining a greater voice in the World Bank and the IMF.[64]

There were, however, significant differences as to how these goals should be approached. The developing countries' call for the "indexation" of commodity prices to the prices of manufactured goods was rejected by most industrialized countries. The United States and other industrialized countries agreed that development assistance should be increased, and the United States expressed its intention of doing so; however, the United States representative specifically disavowed any firm commitment to a target of 0.7 percent of GNP in official development assistance set by the developing countries. While agreeing with the general objectives of placing special drawing rights (SDRs) in the center of the international monetary system, the United States expressed reservations about the setting of specific targets for the use of SDRs for development assistance until there was agreement on all of the interrelated components within a fully reformed international monetary system. Also, while agreeing that there should be an increased role for the developing countries in decision making in the international financial institutions, the United States argued that "participation in decision making must be equitable for all members and take due account of relative economic positions and contributions of members to the institution as well as the need for efficient international decision making."[65]

It is most significant that the developing countries accepted the central role of the World Bank group (along with bilateral assistance) in providing capital for development. The principal stress of the resolution is not on creating new institutions but on increasing capital flow from existing institutions and improving the terms. This is a major change from the 1950s and 1960s, when the developing countries strongly supported SUNFED and its successor idea, the United Nations Capital Development Fund (UNCDF), as the principal instruments for soft loans. (These would have placed control under the one-country, one-vote General Assembly.) The resolution adopted at the seventh special session does urge developed countries, and developing countries in a position to do so, "to make adequate contributions to the United Nations Special Fund [the name given to a token SUNFED] with the view of early implementation of a program of lending, preferably in 1976"; however, this appears to be little more than a pious hope. It seems to be generally realized that the parliamentary bodies in the major industrialized countries will not provide the massive sums required for development assistance to an international institution that does not have weighted voting. (In fiscal year 1979, the World Bank and IDA committed over $8 billion.) It is also significant that countries like Iran, Saudi Arabia, Iraq, Kuwait, and Venezuela, which were staunch advocates of SUNFED in earlier years when the United States was asked to provide the bulk of the funds, chose to place their money elsewhere when the twelve-fold increase of oil prices gave them the billions of dollars that could make the Special Fund meaningful.

Unfortunately, the sluggishness of the world economy, inflation, and the weakening of the dollar tended to slow the movement toward these goals, especially with respect to official aid. Still, the U.S. move toward accommodation appeared to presage a less confrontational, more constructive General Assembly.

Instead, the thirtieth session of the Assembly became highly controversial, due in part to Arab aggressiveness and in part to Moynihan's flamboyant, demagogic style. During discussion of racism and racial discrimination, Arab representatives introduced an amendment stating that "Zionism is a form of racism and racial discrimination." Given the Arab position as part of the Afro-Asian group (which includes a majority of the members of the UN), the 22 Arab votes and the support of the Soviet bloc, any Arab proposal has a long head start toward a majority. The Soviet Union gave its strong support both to curry favor with the Arabs and because a movement like Zionism, which encourages people to leave the Soviet paradise, is an embarrassment to Moscow. As I learned in Budapest during Stalin's anti-Zionism campaign in 1952, anti-Zionism quickly translates into anti-Semitism, still easily aroused in Eastern Europe.

On this issue the Third World did not act as a bloc. Most of the Latin American countries and some African states opposed the amendment because they considered it anti-Semitic, likely to hinder peace efforts in the Middle East, and certain to disturb the consensus reached on the Programme for the Decade for Action to Combat Racism and Racial Discrimination. A number of countries, including the United States, stated that they could not support the programme if the language defining Zionism as racism were included. Faced with this prospect, several African representatives tried to get the Zionism issue sidetracked, but they told me that Moynihan's flamboyant statements handicapped their efforts. An African ambassador who had been Moynihan's classmate at the London School of Economics said privately that he and many of his colleagues resented the way the U.S. representative talked down to them. The Libyan ambassador, who led the drive to define Zionism as racism, told Ambassador Piero Vinci of Italy that he could never have succeeded if Moynihan had not provoked so much resentment among the African delegates.

The final vote, taken on November 10, 1975, was 72 to 35, with 32 abstentions.[66] This was an unusually small number of affirmative votes for an Arab-sponsored proposal in the post–oil boycott period. Clearly, the proposal could not have been voted down, but there were indications that a combination of those countries that had voted against or abstained with some of those who had reluctantly voted for the proposal could have been mustered as a majority to defer action if Moynihan had been restrained; at least, some of the Africans thought so. Moynihan, on the other hand, believed that his vigorous efforts had increased the strength of the opposition and that nothing could have headed off the Arab proposal.

Later he also complained, to Kissinger's obvious annoyance, that his efforts were not being supported adequately by State Department officials in Washington and in foreign capitals. Moynihan's vigorous efforts on this issue as well as in Security Council debates on the Middle East made him something of a folk hero among many American Jewish and conservative groups. This support was a factor in his campaign for the U.S. senate in 1976, though he vehemently denied that he was courting such political support while he served as U.S. permanent representative, and there is no clear evidence that he did.

Also on November 10 the General Assembly requested the Security Council to adopt measures to enable the Palestinian people "to exercise their inalienable rights" in accordance with General Assembly resolution 3236(XXIX). It urged that the PLO be invited to participate in all conferences on the Middle East held under UN auspices and in the Geneva Peace Conference on the Middle East.[67] That same day the Assembly established a twenty-member Committee on the Inalienable Rights of the Palestinian People to prepare a program of implementation to enable them to exercise the right of self-determination and the right to return to their homes and property.[68] Clearly the Arabs were riding high in the General Assembly, which was sinking correspondingly low in American public opinion.[69]

The Arabs struck again in the Security Council on December 3. Lebanon had brought a complaint against Israeli air attacks in Lebanon, undertaken in reprisal to Palestinian guerrilla attacks launched from there. Five Third World countries—Cameroon, Guyana, Iraq, Mauritania, and Tanzania—proposed that the PLO be invited to participate in the Council on the same basis as a state that is not a member of the Council, despite the fact that the PLO did not even claim to be a government in exile. Contending groups with an interest in an item under discussion had been heard by the Council on various occasions—for example, the two groups contending for power in the Dominican Republic in 1964–65—but always under rule 40 of the Council's rule of procedure, which did not imply status similar to that of a state. Western members of the Council would have been willing to hear the PLO under rule 40, but not on the basis proposed. Despite their objections, the five-nation proposal on seating the PLO was adopted by a vote of 9 to 3 (Costa Rica, United Kingdom, United States), with 3 abstentions (France, Italy, Japan). Since the matter was procedural, the veto did not apply.

The Council then proceeded to discuss a draft resolution presented by the same five countries. The draft would have condemned Israel strongly for its "premeditated air attacks against Lebanon," warned that the Council would have to consider taking "appropriate steps and measures" to give effect to its decisions if Israel repeated such attacks, and called upon

Israel to desist forthwith from all military attacks against Lebanon. The Council vote was 13 to 1, with 1 abstention (Costa Rica).[70] This time, however, the negative vote of the United States counted as a veto, since substance was involved, not just procedure.

Again on January 26, 1976, the United States exercised its veto. This time, Benin, Guyana, Pakistan, Panama, Romania, and Tanzania introduced a draft resolution that would have affirmed that "the Palestinian people should be enabled to exercise its inalienable right of self-determination, including the right to establish an independent state in Palestine." After two weeks of debate, the draft resolution was put to the vote; the result was 9 to 1 (United States), with 3 abstentions (Italy, Sweden, United Kingdom), and China and Libya not participating.[71]

For balance it should be noted that, while these controversial debates and resolutions were getting public attention, the Council in October 1975 renewed the mandates of the UN peacekeeping forces in the Sinai and on the Golan Heights. These forces were most helpful in separating the Egyptian, Syrian, and Israeli forces and thus reducing violence. In real importance they far outweigh the propagandistic resolutions that engage public attention.

By January 1976 Moynihan's performance at the UN had occasioned public criticism by other representatives at the UN, including old allies like the British, and his criticism of inadequate support by the State Department—leaked to the press—did not endear him to Secretary Kissinger. The secretary was also irritated by Moynihan's "overkill" tactics.[72] At that stage I was asked by the Long Island newspaper *Newsday* to write a guest column on Moynihan. As a college professor, no longer in government, I was able to write freely. The column appeared on February 3, 1976, the day after Moynihan announced his resignation, but had been submitted two weeks before. The only change required was in the verb tense in the third sentence. It read as follows and is, I believe, still valid:

> Daniel Patrick Moynihan is undoubtedly one of the most colorful, energetic, scholarly and articulate representatives the United States has ever had at the United Nations. He has shown courage, energy and skill in defending positions that should be defended. He has now rendered a great service to the United States and the United Nations by leaving his present post.
>
> Ambassador Moynihan has worked hard for worthwhile American objectives. He has also defended Israel against blatantly one-sided resolutions and cast the American veto against harmful decisions in the Security Council. He has eloquently reminded other members of the long-range peril to the existence of the United Nations contained in

unrealistic resolutions rammed through the General Assembly by automatic majorities—resolutions that have no hope of implementation because those who are called upon to make them effective have not supported them. (Members cannot be forced to obey General Assembly resolutions.) At the seventh special session of the United Nations General Assembly last September, he worked tirelessly for the resolution on improved economic relations between the poor countries and the industrialized countries of the world. Why, then, do I believe he had become a liability?

It is not so much a matter of substance as of tactics and style. Moynihan has been unduly provocative, widening the circle of enemies and antagonizing our friends.

Item: In his speech to the AFL-CIO in San Francisco last October, he included a statement condemning Ugandan President Idi Amin as a "racist murderer." I have no quarrel with that. But Moynihan then gratuitously insulted more than 40 other African countries by stating that it was no accident that Amin was president of the Organization of African Unity. In fact, Amin's presidency was an accident—the accidental result of the fact that 1975 was the year for Uganda to host the organization, and by tradition the president of the host country becomes president of the organization.

It is perfectly true that some African countries insult the United States, and the American representative should reply. It is counterproductive, however, when the representative of a country with the political maturity of the United States insults the African countries *en masse.*

Item: In December I heard Ambassador Moynihan on a Sunday morning TV interview show predicting defeat on the anti-Zionism resolution on the ground that the overwhelming majority of member states had anti-democratic regimes. This follows his thesis that there are probably no more than two dozen liberal democracies in the world. He may have some basis for that estimate. The fact is, however, that there is no pure democracy and few absolute dictatorships. Most countries are ranged along a spectrum somewhere between ideal democracy and total dictatorship.

Tactically, it makes little sense to place in an enemy category more than 120 member states of the United Nations which do not measure up in Moynihan's concept of liberal democracy. On the more than 100 items before the United Nations General Assembly, we shall find allies and opponents among governments at all parts of the spectrum between dictatorship and democracy. What counts on any issue is how they stand on that issue.

During the 15 years I spent at the United Nations, we never rejected a vote from a government whose democratic standards were not all they should be. Doing so would have put us in a constant minority. How do you condemn 120 countries as authoritarian regimes hostile to liberal democracy and then try to win their votes?

Item: In introducing the recent draft resolution calling for a worldwide amnesty for political prisoners, Ambassador Moynihan did not consult normally friendly delegations, such as the western Europeans. Again, experience at the United Nations demonstrates that few, if any votes are won through speeches, however eloquent. The key to success in moving a resolution is thorough organization and preparation, including *prior consultations* with key delegates from various parts of the world. British annoyance at Moynihan's tactics was forcefully expressed last November by Ambassador Ivor Richard, who referred to him as a "trigger happy Wyatt Erp," and "a vengeful Savonarola."

Another important factor in taking initiatives at the General Assembly, or countering attacks on the United States, is the effective use of the mission staff. Several senior officers on that staff expressed dismay at his failure to consult them on various moves in areas for which they were responsible. Lobbying with more than 140 other delegations is a team effort.

Moynihan's cablegram to Kissinger and U.S. diplomats last week carried in it certain important misconceptions. Contrary to the impression given, he was not the first American representative to speak forcefully and forthrightly at the United Nations. Henry Cabot Lodge, Arthur Goldberg, George Ball and John Scali never shrank from a confrontation with opponents and were not reluctant to use strong language. Ambassador Scali's tough but well-reasoned statement to the 29th session of the General Assembly on the "tyranny of the majority" had a strong and helpful impact.

The point is to use strong language when it helps your cause and not when it is harmful. It is all right to trade insults with someone who has insulted you first, but you should not use a broad brush in insulting a large number of other delegates whose support you may need on various issues.

Second, Moynihan was mistaken in asserting that last year was the first time that advocates of Puerto Rico's independence tried to put the matter on the General Assembly's agenda. Such a move has been made repeatedly for at least the past 10 years and has been consistently defeated.

Third, breaking up the "nonaligned" bloc is not done successfully by grouping them into an enemy category of undemocratic, hostile and ungrateful regimes. Ambassador Moynihan was perfectly correct in pointing out that these nations are "extraordinarily disparate, with greatly disparate interests."

But in order to avoid their behaving mindlessly as a bloc, it is important to demonstrate to the more moderate members of the nonaligned group that with reasonableness and cooperation, they can achieve something. This was done at the seventh session of the General Assembly last September with great effort by Secretary Kissinger, Ambassador Moynihan and many others in the American government.

Much of the good will achieved at the special session was dissipated by Moynihan's style and tactics, particularly his blanket assaults and condemnations. Such tactics do not break up blocs; they solidify them and tend to drive the "Third World" toward the Soviets.

To be sure, successful diplomacy does not mean being a nice guy to everybody on all occasions. There are times when toughness and doing things people do not like are essential to success. We should, for example, take seriously into account whether a country has consistently opposed American interests at the United Nations when we get requests for aid. Aid cannot buy friends, but should it reward enemies? But this weapon must be used with care and precision, not with Moynihan's verbal carpet bombing.

There is also the matter of choosing targets—not replying to every insult or attack, lest one appear constantly on the defensive. Righteous indignation should be feared, but it loses its impact when it is overused.

What we need at the United Nations is an ambassador who is tough but sensitive to the views of others; who speaks eloquently but also listens attentively; who is a team player, not just an individual star; who constantly strives to narrow the circle of our enemies and widen the circle of our friends; who has pride in America but recognizes that other countries also have their pride. Moynihan did not measure up to these criteria.[73]

Moynihan returned to teaching at Harvard and went on to win election as U.S. senator from New York as a Democrat, defeating the incumbent, James Buckley. Despite serious reservations about his performance at the UN, I voted for him in the Senate race; the qualities required would be different.

NOTES

1. Richard Nixon, *RN: The Memoirs of Richard Nixon* (New York: Grosset and Dunlap, 1978), p. 338.

2. See, for example, Henry A. Kissinger, *American Foreign Policy* (New York: Norton, 1974), esp. pp. 51–98. See also John G. Stoessinger, *Henry Kissinger: The Anguish of Power* (New York: Norton, 1976).

3. Conversation with Samuel De Palma, March 8, 1978.

4. Charles W. Yost, *The Insecurity of Nations* (New York: Praeger, 1968), pp. 217–20.

5. Ibid., p. 77.

6. Ibid., p. 254.

7. Ibid., pp. 256–58.

8. Conversation with De Palma, op. cit.

9. Conversation with Charles Yost, February 21, 1978, in Washington, D.C.

10. Conversation with De Palma, op. cit.

11. Richard Nixon, *U.S. Foreign Policy for the 1970's* a report to the U.S. Congress, February 25, 1971, pp. 123–32.

12. See S. M. Finger, "Breaking the Deadlock on U.N. Peacekeeping," *Orbis* (Summer 1973); 385–98, for an account of the background and negotiations.

13. Nixon, *RN*, p. 201.

14. UN Security Council, *Report of the Secretary-General on the Implementation of Security Council Resolution 340* (S/11052/Rev. 1), October 27, 1973.

15. For a fuller discussion see S. M. Finger, "U.N. Peacekeeping and the U.S. National Interest" in S.M. Finger and J. R. Harbert, eds., *U.S. Policy in International Institutions* (Boulder, Colo.: Westview, 1978), pp. 71–77.

16. *Report of the President's Commission for the Observance of the Twenty-fifth Anniversary of the United Nations* (Washington, D.C.: GPO, April 26, 1971) [the Lodge Commission].

17. *Twenty-fifth Annual Report on U.S. Participation in the U.N.,* Report by the President to the Congress for the Year 1970, U.S. State Department publication 8600, September 1971, pp. 69–72.

18. Classified USUN telegrams.

19. See *Twenty-fifth Annual Report on U.S. Participation in the UN,* op. cit., pp. 252–53.

20. For construction details see *Twenty-fifth Annual Report on U.S. Participation in the U.N.* (Report by the President to the Congress for the year 1969, Washington, D.C., U.S. Government Printing Office, 1974, pp. 216–17.

21. A report by the New York City Commission for the United Nations estimates that expenditures by the Secretariat staff and missions to the UN in the city amount to some $450 million annually.

22. G.A. Res. 2676 (XXV), Dec. 9, 1970.

23. Conversation with De Palma, op. cit.

24. UN Doc. A/AC.109/SR. 574, pp. 5–7.

25. G.A. Res. 1514 (XV), December 14, 1960.

26. G.A. Res. 2621 (XXV), October 12, 1970, paragraph 3(2).

27. Charter considerations with respect to such actions are thoughtfully analyzed by Rupert Emerson in his article, "Self-Determination," *American Journal of International Law* 65, 3 (July 1971): 459–75.

28. UN Doc. A/8066, Annex 1.

29. *U.S. Participation in the U.N.* (1970), op. cit., pp. 194–96.

30. S.C. Res. 276, January 30, 1970.

31. S.C. Res. 277, January 30, 1970.

32. *Twenty-fifth Annual Report on*

U.S. Participation in the U.N. (1970), op. cit., pp. 188–90.

33. Nixon, *RN.*, pp. 205–6; see also pp. 207–24 for a discussion of the global issues.

34. *U.S. Participation in the U.N.* (1970), op. cit., p. 89.

35. Ibid., p. 100.

36. See S. M. Finger, "Terrorism and the United Nations," in Yonah Alexander, ed., *International Terrorism* (New York: Praeger, 1976), pp. 327–29.

37. Response to a question the author put to George Bush in January 1978.

38. Ibid.

39. Lodge Commission Report, op. cit., p. 36.

40. Nixon, *RN*, pp. 17–18.

41. This paragraph is based on information in *U.S. Participation in the U.N.* (1970), op. cit., pp. 54–56.

42. Conversation with De Palma, op. cit.

43. Nixon, *U.S. Foreign Policy for the 1970's* (IV), May 3, 1973, p. 186.

44. Conversation with De Palma, op. cit.

45. *Twenty-seventh Annual Report on U.S. Participation in the U.N.* (1972), Washington, D.C., U.S. Government Printing Office, 1973, pp. 41–42. See also my testimony on UN sanctions, "Rhodesia as a Case Study," Hearings before the Subcommittee on International Organizations and Movements of the Committee on Foreign Affairs, House of Representatives, 92d Cong., 2d sess., June 15, 1972, pp. 93–129.

46. *Washington Post*, March 18, 1971.

47. National Security Study Memorandum 39. For a discussion, see Rhodesia section in Chapter XIII. See also Anthony Lake, *The "Tar Baby" Option* (New York: Columbia University Press, 1976), pp. 124–34, 276–85.

48. George M. Houser, "U.S. Policy and Southern Africa," in F. S. Arkhurst, *U.S. Policy Toward Africa* (New York: Praeger, 1975), pp. 88–129.

49. Arthur M. Schlesinger, Jr., *A*

Thousand Days, John F. Kennedy in the White House, New York, Houghton Mifflin, pp. 825–28.

50. This paragraph is based on conversations in February 1978 with five men who had been in key State Department positions while Scali served as permanent representative.

51. Stoessinger, op. cit., pp. 179–92, describes the events and the charges against Kissinger and Schlesinger.

52. See Frederic L. Kirgis, Jr., "NATO Consultations as a Component of National Decisionmaking," *American Journal of International Law* (July 1979); 400.

53. Conversation with John Scali in Washington, D.C., February 23, 1978.

54. *Twenty-ninth Annual Report on U.S. Participation in the U.N.* (1974), Washington, D.C., U.S. Government Printing Office: 1975, pp. 112–18.

55. For text of General Assembly Res. 3237 (XXIX) inviting the PLO to participate in the work of the General Assembly and of all international conferences in the capacity of an observer, see J. Vambery, *Annual Review of United Nations Affairs 1974* (Dobbs Ferry, N.Y.: Oceana, 1976), pp. 107–08.

56. UN General Assembly, *Provisional Verbatim Records* (A/PV.2307, 2313, 2314, 2316), twenty-ninth session.

57. Richard Nixon, *U.S. Foreign Policy for the 1970's* (III), a Report to the Congress by Richard Nixon, President of the United States, Washington, D.C., US Government Printing Office, 1972.

58. *U.S. Participation in the U.N.* (1972), op. cit., pp. 104–05.

59. *U.S. Participation in the U.N.* (1974), op. cit., pp. 200–203.

60. Bernard H. Oxman, "The Third United Nations Conference on the Law of the Sea: The 1977 New York Session," *American Journal of International Law* (January 1978): 57–83. The U.S. evaluation is summarized on p. 59.

61. John W. Holmes, "A Non-American Perspective," in David A.

Kay, (ed.) *The Changing United Nations,* New York, The Academy of Political Science, 1977, p. 35.

62. William J. Buckley, *United Nations Journal: A Delegate's Odyssey* (New York: Putnam, 1974).

63. George W. Ball, *Diplomacy for a Crowded World* (Boston: Atlantic–Little, Brown, 1976).

64. UN Doc. A/Res. 3362 (S. VII), September 6, 1975.

65. Statement by Ambassador Jacob Myerson, U.S. representative in the Ad Hoc Committee of the seventh special session of the UN General Assembly, September 16, 1975.

66. G.A. Res. 3379 (XXX), November 10, 1975.

67. G.A. Res. 3375 (XXX), November 10, 1975, adopted by a vote of 101 to 8 (United States), with 25 abstentions.

68. G.A. Res. 3376 (XXX), November 10, 1975, adopted by a vote of 93 to 18 (United States), with 27 abstentions.

69. See Benjamin Rivlin and Jacques Fomerand, "Changing Third World Perspectives and Policies Towards Israel," in M. Curtis and S. A. Gitelson, *Israel in the Third World* (New Brunswick, N.J.: Transactions Books, 1976), pp. 325–60, for an analysis of the factors building up Arab political influence in Third World countries. See also S. M. Finger, "The Third World Countries and the Arab Israeli Question at the U.N.," *Middle East Review* (Spring 1975): 23–28.

70. Joseph T. Vambery, ed., *Annual Review of United Nations Affairs, 1975,* (Dobbs Ferry, N.Y.: Oceana, 1976), pp. 52–53.

71. William A. Landskron, ed., *Annual Review of United Nations Affairs, 1976,* (Dobbs Ferry, N.Y.: Oceana, 1977), p. 72.

72. Stoessinger, op. cit., p. 169.

73. See Seymour Maxwell Finger, "Moynihan at the UN: Diplomacy by Insult," in *Newsday,* February 3, 1976, op. ed. page.

CHAPTER VIII

The Turnaround in American Policy: Scranton and Young

WILLIAM W. SCRANTON

The appointment of William Scranton as permanent representative marked a turning point in U.S. policy toward the UN, with a renewed emphasis on accommodation rather than confrontation.

Scranton was a man of recognized stature, like Austin, Lodge, Stevenson, and Goldberg. As a former governor of Pennsylvania and onetime candidate for the Republican nomination for president, Scranton was recognized by other national representatives as a leading political figure. His known friendship with President Ford added to the respect in which he was held at the UN, as did his calm, dignified, self-assured, but low-key manner.

Scranton had been reluctant to leave private life to take the UN job, but Ford finally persuaded him to do so. He represented a return to the U.S. practice during the UN's first two decades of having an outstanding political figure at the head of its mission to the UN, a sign that the United States took the organization seriously. This reflected, among other things, a change in Henry Kissinger's attitude toward the UN and the Third World.

Scranton's background, temperament, and style were in sharp contrast to Moynihan's. Scranton was born to wealth; Moynihan's early life was a struggle. Moynihan was flamboyant, Scranton low-key. Moynihan believed in public confrontation, Scranton in quiet diplomacy. Moynihan irritated Kissinger; Scranton flattered and cajoled him.

After getting a law degree at Yale in 1946, Scranton entered on a successful career in law and business, interspersed with politics. He served as special assistant to the secretary of state in 1959-60, was elected to Congress as a Republican in 1960, and served as governor of Pennsylvania from 1963 to 1967. In the spring of 1964 he was regarded by liberal

Republicans as a presidential candidate, but Barry Goldwater won the party's nomination. When Ford became president in August 1974, he wanted Scranton to take a high government post, but Scranton was reluctant to leave private life. Instead, he served as an occasional consultant to the president until March 1976, when he finally agreed to take the UN job.

Scranton set out consciously to change the tone of U.S. relations with other representatives at the UN and succeeded remarkably well. Piero Vinci, who served as Italy's permanent representative to the UN from 1966 to 1979, reports that Scranton was liked and respected by all groups. The representative of Libya, a country opposed to the United States on a wide range of issues, said of Scranton: "He disarmed us completely." A day's outing for the UN diplomatic corps at his Dalton, Pennsylvania, estate was a memorable event; the Scrantons were at their charming, informal best. It should be noted that wealth and position are no handicap in dealing with the representatives of Third World countries. Even those who come from poor nations are usually the elite of their own countries and enjoy dealing with other elites. After the leaders of Laos visited Peking for the first time in 1956, they told me with obvious pleasure that Chou En-lai was a true aristocrat. There are many other examples.

Scranton was equally assiduous about cultivating good relations in Washington. He went there every two or three weeks and made it a point to attend meetings of the cabinet, of which he was a member, whenever he could possibly do so. He sought out Henry Kissinger on each visit. He would usually take Joseph Sisco or Philip Habib, Sisco's successor as undersecretary for political affairs, with him, then meet with Kissinger alone afterward. He did see the president alone frequently but always made sure it was with Kissinger's knowledge. He kept Kissinger, Habib, and Samuel Lewis, the assistant secretary for international organization affairs, informed about his talks with the president. "Henry wanted to see everything." He flattered Kissinger by calling him "Boss" or "General-issimo," and it worked. He also found it politic to feed the "big ego" of James Schlesinger, then secretary of defense.[1]

Another part of Scranton's tactical campaign in Washington was a conscious effort to build up the position of the Bureau of International Organization Affairs and its chief, Samuel Lewis. This, too, represented a return to the situation prevailing under Lodge, Stevenson, and Goldberg, after IO had declined in prestige and influence during the Nixon years, and even more during Moynihan's service at the UN.

At USUN Scranton kept the staff left by his predecessors. He evidently did not intend to stay beyond January 1977. He was, according to veteran staff members, an excellent chief of mission whose leadership encouraged staff morale, loyalty, and effectiveness. Many bilateral contacts were used by Scranton in New York and in foreign capitals, for lobbying on Korea and Puerto Rico. As a result, neither of these items was discussed at the thirty-first session of the General Assembly.

The Korean item had been a perennial, using up a lot of time for sterile results during more than twenty sessions of the Assembly. Scranton found that a number of Eastern European representatives, notably from Poland and Romania, did not like the North Koreans or the item. Moreover, developments at the thirtieth session, when two contradictory resolutions, one pro-North, had been adopted, demonstrated the futility of the discussion. Further, Henry Kissinger, addressing the General Assembly on September 30, 1976, had called for a serious dialogue between North and South Korea and indicated that the United States would be prepared to have the UN Command in Korea dissolved as long as the armistice agreement was either preserved or replaced by more desirable arrangements. In these circumstances, Scranton, working through the Romanian representative, negotiated an agreement not to discuss the Korean item at the thirty-first session.

Scranton and his staff also argued successfully against any new resolution equating Zionism with racism, as had been done the previous fall, and none was adopted.[2]

Scranton's appointment came at a time when U.S. policy toward Africa was changing. The 1974 revolution in Portugal and the decision of the new Portuguese government to accept self-determination in the former Portuguese "provinces" (colonies) in Africa freed the United States of any constraints it had felt because Portugal was a NATO member and made its Azores base available to the United States. By September 1975 Guinea-Bissau, the Republic of Cape Verde, the Democratic Republic of São Tomé and Príncipe, and the People's Republic of Mozambique had been admitted to the UN. Angola, the only remaining formerly Portuguese territory, was still the scene of fighting among three factions.

By the time Scranton assumed his UN post in March 1976 it had become clear that the forces of Agostinho Neto (People's Movement for the Liberation of Angola), aided by the Soviet equipment and Cuban troops, had gained the upper hand over the rival groups in Angola, headed by Holden Roberto (National Force for the Liberation of Angola) and Jonas Savimbi (National Union for the Total Independence of Angola). The United States had provided minor covert support to the latter groups, but Congress balked at providing more; its key members were irritated because they had been kept in the dark and feared another Vietnam. On December 19, 1975, the Senate voted to end all covert aid to Roberto and Savimbi. South African troops had fought alongside Savimbi's forces in the South, thus swinging the sympathies of the other African states over to Neto. By March 27 South Africa declared it had withdrawn its forces from Angola.

On March 31 the UN Security Council in its resolution 387 condemned South Africa's aggression by a vote of 9 to 0, with 5 abstentions (France, Italy, Japan, United Kingdom, United States). China did not participate in the vote. The abstainers and China condemned South African intervention but said they would have liked to see that condemnation extended to all foreign forces. Supporters of the resolution drew a distinction between aid requested by a "legitimate" government and an invasion opposed by it.

Fighting continued in Angola, but the Neto regime, now recognized by the Organization of African Unity (OAU) and bolstered by 3,000 Cuban troops, was dominant. In June, Neto's government applied for UN membership, which was vetoed by the United States. On November 22 the United States abstained on the Security Council resolution recommending Angola's admission. Scranton explained that the United States would not support admission because of the continued presence of Cuban troops but would not veto it because Angola's admission had been endorsed by the OAU. In December the General Assembly admitted Angola by a vote of 116 to 0, with 1 abstention (United States). China, which also opposed Soviet-Cuban intervention, did not participate in the vote.[3]

The emergence of Marxist regimes in Angola and Mozambique caused Secretary Kissinger and others in Washington to rethink U.S. policy toward Africa, especially toward Rhodesia (Zimbabwe) and Namibia. Kissinger now believed that the United States must put pressure on South Africa and the Smith regime to move toward a nonviolent achievement of majority rule and self-determination in Rhodesia and Namibia lest the black population there, seeing no alternative, turn toward Soviet and Cuban support. Scranton not only agreed with this more active support for African aspirations; he encouraged it. Because of his views on the importance of a forthcoming American policy on southern Africa, he recommended to President-elect Jimmy Carter the appointment of Andrew Young as his successor to the United Nations.[4]

Scranton also showed his interest in Africa by visiting eleven countries there in June 1976. At the UN he developed good relations with a number of Africans, notably Salim A. Salim, Tanzanian permanent representative and one of the most dynamic leaders of the African countries working for decolonization in southern Africa. To American audiences and American officials in Washington, Scranton pointed out that U.S. trade with Nigeria alone had surpassed trade with South Africa.

Meanwhile, a reformed Henry Kissinger was engaged in a serious and urgent effort to bring self-determination and majority rule to the last two former colonies in Africa still ruled by white regimes, Rhodesia (Zimbabwe) and Namibia (South-West Africa). Kissinger made his first trip to Africa in the spring of 1976, conferring with the leaders of neighboring African states and working closely with the British. In his statement to the UN General Assembly on September 30, 1976, Kissinger called for a commitment to majority rule in Rhodesia within two years. For Namibia he proposed independence within a short time limit. He advocated a constitutional conference in a neutral location under UN auspices, with the participation of all authentic national forces, including SWAPO (South-West Africa People's Organization).

In line with its new policy in Rhodesia, the United States joined in a unanimous resolution of the Security Council on April 6, 1976, extending economic sanctions against the Smith regime to include insurance, trade names, and franchises. Yet, because of a 1971 act of Congress that included the Byrd amendment, the United States continued to import chrome and nickel from Rhodesia. As a result, the United States was singled out for condemnation in General Assembly resolution 31/154B, adopted on December 20, 1976, by a vote of 124 to 0, with 7 abstentions. The United States voiced its objection to being singled out because of its "honesty"; it was evident from the reports of the Security Council's committee on sanctions against Rhodesia, established in 1968 under Council resolution 253, that many other countries were allowing the importation of Rhodesian products through lax enforcement. The offending U.S. law was finally repealed in 1977, by which time it had done serious harm to U.S.-African relations and had brought no benefit to the American economy.[5]

While the change in U.S. policy on Rhodesia and Namibia was welcomed, American policy toward South Africa did not move in the direction demanded by the African countries. Kissinger believed that there would have to be a different timetable for South Africa, where the problem was not classic colonialism but racism. He also felt that Johannes Vorster, South Africa's prime minister, could be a major factor in bringing about majority rule in Rhodesia and self-determination in Namibia. Given the need of the Smith regime for South African support, Kissinger urged Vorster to put pressure on Smith to move toward majority rule— apparently with a measure of success, however limited. In Namibia, South Africa remained in de facto control, even though officially shorn of its mandate in 1966 by General Assembly resolution 2145. Kissinger was understandably more interested in prompt action by Vorster in Namibia than in pushing for reform in South Africa itself, where change would inevitably be slower and more difficult.

Events in South Africa did not permit the United States to be comfortable in its policy. In June, Africans in Soweto, near Johannesburg, demonstrated massively against a new South African regulation that Afrikaans be used as the medium of instruction in African schools. When the demonstrators announced a strike and used force to prevent black workers who wanted to work from doing so, the government resorted to massive violence and killing. On June 19 the Security Council, in its resolution 392 (1976), condemned South Africa's action.

On July 30 the Council in its resolution 393 strongly condemned an alleged armed attack on July 11 by South Africans against Zambia. The vote was 14 to 0. The United States, abstaining, said it would have liked a full-scale investigation, since South Africa claimed it had no knowledge of such an attack and would accept an investigation.[6]

Against this background it is not surprising that many African representatives listened with some skepticism to Kissinger's statement in the UN General Assembly September 30 that in South Africa "the pace of change had accelerated."

THE MIDDLE EAST AND ENTEBBE

Scranton's debut in the Security Council, March 24, put him in a difficult position vis-à-vis Israel and the American Jewish community. A complaint had been brought by Jordan against a ruling by a lower Israeli court that would have had the effect of altering the status of the Haram esh-Sherif, a Moslem holy place in Jerusalem. (The ruling was later reversed by the Supreme Court of Israel.) Scranton reiterated the view of the U.S. government that no change could be made unilaterally in the status of Jerusalem. He declared: "The United States position could not be clearer. Since 1967 we have restated here, in other fora and to the Government of Israel that the future of Jerusalem will be determined only through the instruments and processes of negotiation, agreement and accommodation. Unilateral attempts to predetermine that future have no standing."[7]

With respect to the occupied territories in general, Scranton quoted Article 49 of the fourth Geneva Convention Relative to the Protection of Civilian Persons in Time of War, to which Israel and its Arab neighbors are signatories. It states: "The occupying power shall not deport or transfer parts of its own civilian population into the territory it occupies." From this Scranton reasoned: "Clearly then substantial resettlement of the Israeli civilian population in occupied territories, including in East Jerusalem, is illegal under the Convention and cannot be considered to have prejudged the outcome of future negotiations between the parties on the location of the borders of states of the Middle East. Indeed, the presence of these settlements is seen by my Government as an obstacle to the success of the negotiations for a just and final peace between Israel and its neighbors."[8]

Although this had been a consistent U.S. position since 1967, Scranton's reiteration of it precipitated demonstrations against him at the approaches to the UN. The issue remains a bone of contention between the present American administration and the Israeli government.

Scranton's position was soon restored, however, by his veto two days later of a draft resolution (document S/PV.1899) that would have censured Israel for "persisting in a policy aimed at changing the religious character of the city of Jerusalem." In explaining his vote he said: "We believe, *my government and I*, that this conclusion is incorrect. Quite to the contrary; we think that Israel's administration of the Holy Places in Jerusalem has literally and actively minimized tensions [italics mine]." Scranton noted that the United States was at that moment engaged in an effort to regain momentum in the process of negotiating a peaceful settlement and added: "It is our belief and our strong feeling that this draft would not help that peaceful settlement process."[9]

The United States had vetoed four earlier resolutions affecting Israel that were brought before the Security Council in 1972, 1973, 1975, and in January 1976. Many other Council resolutions on the Middle East over the years passed with American delegates backing them, or abstaining from voting.

Scranton further enhanced his standing with Israel and its sympathizers when the Entebbe rescue operation was discussed at the Council in July 1976. An Air France airbus had been hijacked en route from Athens to Paris and taken to Entebbe Airport, Uganda. The hijackers then released non-Jews and some non-Israeli Jews but continued to hold more than 100 Jewish hostages, mostly Israelis. On July 4 Israel sent a small military force to Entebbe, which after an hour and a half on the ground rescued the hostages and returned with them to Israel. Three of the hostages, one Israeli soldier, and a number of Ugandan soldiers were killed, and several Ugandan aircraft were destroyed. Of the action Scranton said:

In this episode, that responsibility lay with the Government of Israel to protect her citizens, hostages threatened with their very lives, in mortal danger in a faraway place. Those innocent people were subject to the terrorist hijacking of the airplane on which they were rightfully flying and further subjected to a six-day terrorizing experience in a foreign country, seeing other persons freed while the Jews were forced to remain. Subjected at gunpoint to seven hijacker terrorists who know no law. Aware that the only possibility of freedom came from a government whose head had previously rejoiced at the slaying of Israeli athletes at Munich, called for the extinction of Israel, and praised that madman, Hitler, who had on his evil conscience, if he had a conscience at all, the murder of six million Jews.

Under such circumstances, it seems to me, the Government of Israel invoked one of the most remarkable rescue missions in history, a combination of guts and brains that has seldom if ever been surpassed. It electrified millions everywhere, and I confess I was one of them.[10]

These comments were delivered as personal remarks at the end of

Scranton's statement on July 12, following his statement of the official U.S. position, in which he refuted allegations that Israel had breached the UN Charter's prohibition against the violation of the sovereignty or territorial integrity of another state.

> Israel's action in rescuing the hostages necessarily involved a temporary breach of the territorial integrity of Uganda. Normally such a breach would be impermissible under the Charter of the United Nations. However, there is a well-established right to use limited force for the protection of one's own nationals from an imminent threat of injury or death in a situation where the State in whose territory they are located either is unwilling or unable to protect them. The right, flowing from the right of self-defense, is limited to such use of force as is necessary and appropriate to protect threatened nationals from injury.

> The requirements of this right to protect nationals were clearly met in the Entebbe case. Israel had good reason to believe that at the time it acted Israeli nationals were in imminent danger of execution by the hijackers. Moreover, the actions necessary to release the Israeli nationals or to prevent substantial loss of Israeli lives had not been taken by the Government of Uganda, nor was there a reasonable expectation such actions would be taken. In fact, there is substantial evidence that the government of Uganda cooperated with and aided the hijackers.[11]

Scranton then urged that the Council address itself to the cause of incidents like the one at Entebbe, that is, the scourge of hijacking. Accordingly, on July 14 the United States and the United Kingdom presented a draft resolution under which the Council would have condemned hijacking and all other acts that threatened the lives of passengers and crews. On September 9, 1970, the Council itself had adopted by consensus resolution 286 appealing for the immediate release of all passengers and crews held as a result of hijackings and calling on states "to take all possible legal steps to prevent further hijacking or any other interference with international civil air travel." Again, on June 20, 1972, the Council had stated its grave concern "at the threat to the lives of passengers and crews arising from the hijacking of aircraft." Moreover, twelve of the fifteen states that sat on the Council in 1976 had ratified the Convention for the Suppression of Unlawful Seizure of Aircraft by Hijacking, signed at the Hague on December 16, 1970. In effect, then, the U.K.–U.S. draft was a reaffirmation of views already endorsed by the Council, not a breaking of new ground. Yet this time, because of political overtones, the U.K.–U.S. draft received only 6 votes, with Panama and Romania voting in the negative and the other 7 members not voting. Since 9 votes are required, it was not adopted.

On the other hand, a draft resolution introduced by Benin, Libya, and Tanzania, which would have condemned Israel's "flagrant violation" of Uganda's sovereignty, was not pressed to a vote. Evidently the sponsors knew that they could not get the required 9 votes. In light of the anti-Israel bias of a majority of the Council's members, the standoff could be considered an Israeli success.

I was around the UN during the Council's discussion of Entebbe and was struck by the esteem in which Scranton was held. In separate conversations top-ranking members of the Israeli and Arab delegations expressed high regard for his fairness and ability. Scranton's standing with Ford and Kissinger remained high, and he continued to have impact on policy. The one notable exception was his effort to persuade Kissinger against a veto of Vietnam's admission to the UN. Scranton felt that pettiness on this issue would damage relations with the Third World. Kissinger was adamant, however, and on November 15 Scranton, on firm instructions, vetoed a 14 to 1 resolution of the Security Council, citing Vietnam's failure to give an adequate account of Americans missing in action. In 1977 Vietnam was admitted, with U.S. acquiescence.

ECONOMIC DEVELOPMENT

By September 1976 the euphoria of agreement on a broad-scale resolution on economic development at the seventh special session of the UN General Assembly a year earlier had dissipated. The Third world countries were disappointed over the lack of results at the Paris Conference on International Economic Cooperation. There was mutual disenchantment at the fourth session of the UN Conference on Trade and Development (UNCTAD) in Nairobi, May 5–31, 1976. The conference did agree on integrated commodity programs to help stabilize and increase the earnings of the less developed countries, with details to be worked out later, and on certain measures to encourage their exports of industrial goods. There was disagreement, however, between the industrialized and the less developed countries on debt and balance-of-payment problems, monetary reform, and the flow and terms of aid. Draft resolutions on these matters were referred to a subsequent meeting of the Conference on Trade and Development: a Belgian draft resolution by which the conference would have decided that "early consideration" should be given to a U.S. proposal for the establishment of an international resources bank was rejected by a vote of 31 to 33, with 44 abstentions.[12]

This action annoyed Kissinger, who had put forward the idea to the conference. In his general debate statement at the thirty-first session of the General Assembly, he deplored the practice of nations making decisions before even listening to the debate on an issue, based on bloc or regional positions or on decisions by prior conferences containing more than a majority of the membership. Thus, he felt, they came prepared for battle rather than for negotiations. The less developed countries, he argued, had often made demands for change that were as confrontational as they were unrealistic. "Such tactics lost more than they gained; they undermined political support in the industrial democracies, which was important to provide resources and market access—available nowhere else—to sustain development."[13]

Some of Kissinger's feelings were reflected in the voting on two General Assembly resolutions at the thirty-first session. Resolution 174, which reiterated the Assembly's appeal to industrialized nations to meet the target of 0.7 percent of Gross National Product for official development assistance, was adopted by 117 to 1, with 18 abstentions. Resolution 178, on the implementation of economic resolutions adopted by the Assembly, was approved 128 to 1, with 8 abstentions. In both cases the United States cast the sole negative vote. But most resolutions on economic development issues were adopted without dissent, and the overall tone was one of watchful waiting rather than of bitter confrontation. The less developed countries wanted to see what the new administration of President-elect Carter would do and what would happen at the Paris Conference on International Economic Cooperation. Accordingly, the Assembly did not adjourn its thirty-first session on December 22. Rather, it decided to reconvene in a resumed session to discuss the only outstanding agenda item: "Development and international cooperation: implementation of the decisions adopted by the General Assembly at its seventh special session." The reconvened session was held in September 1977, just before the opening of the thirty-second session, when Andrew Young was the permanent representative.

Scranton did not become much involved in economic matters, preferring to concentrate on political and security issues, particularly those concerning southern Africa and human rights.

On November 24, 1976, Scranton spoke on "Human Rights: Let's Mean What We Say" in the Third Committee, a body in which the U.S. permanent representative had rarely appeared during its thirty-two-year history. The statement came shortly after Carter's election to the presidency and, interestingly, foreshadowed the approach Carter was to take as president on the international aspects of human rights.

Scranton contrasted the active role of the United Nations in adopting declarations, resolutions, and conventions setting human rights standards with the paucity of action to make them effective. He observed:

Today the only universality one can honestly associate with the Universal Declaration of Human Rights [adopted in 1948] is universality of lip service. Why is the United Nations so long on declarations and so short on implementations? Why does it spend so much energy recognizing rights and so little providing remedies for the wronged? Why did the year 1968—the twentieth anniversary of the adoption of the Declaration, designated as the International Year for Human Rights—follow the 19th Century pattern of treating human rights as little more than a political issue? Why did the Tehran Conference all but restrict its focus to anti-Israeli grievances and the black-white problems of southern Africa, and consciously ignore other obvious and egregious instances of oppression on every continent? The reason is simply this: human rights are still treated almost exclusively in a political context, even though positions are cloaked in high moral principles. As a result compliance with human rights standards is measured not by the standards themselves, but by vote-gathering ability.

Those imprisoned for political dissent, those tortured because they refuse to abandon what they know to be true, cannot await the day their case might happen to come under the international political spotlight. For the literally hundreds of thousands suffering and denied their dignity as humans, the damage is irreparable. In short, in the field of human rights, justice delayed, as it is by slow and easily obstructed United Nations procedures, becomes mass murder condoned.

Addressing the situation in the Soviet Union, he said:

In the Soviet system any genuine respect for human rights encounters the harsh opposition of basic Marxist dogma: that individual rights stand in the way of a planned and directed society. Then there is their cynical approach to human rights discussion itself. For example, by putting forward in the Human Rights Commission what they call "the right to life" they attempt to justify, in the name of national security the limitation of every other human right—the right to speak freely, to write, to worship, to be free of arbitrary action by the state.

The Soviet Union's efforts to manipulate the developing world are very destructive. Using the guise of neocolonialism to discredit the ideas and forms of freedom, they hope to strengthen the ideas and forms of totalitarianism.[14]

Scranton pointed to President-elect Carter's statements on human rights and legislation by Congress enacted in 1976 as evidence of the U.S. commitment to encourage the worldwide observance of human rights. He noted that consistent patterns of gross violations of human rights already affected decisions on U.S. security assistance abroad and votes in multilateral lending agencies. "Future legislation may well extend the range of our concern." He then urged that the UN take action to make its declarations, resolutions, and conventions effective by improving its performance on the review of petitions that reveal "a consistent pattern of gross and reliably attested violations," as provided in resolution 1503 of the Economic and Social Council (1970); by concerning itself with massive violations of human rights around the world and not just a few countries that were unpopular with the UN majority; and by giving serious attention to proposals for a UN commissioner for human rights, an International Human Rights Court, or a permanent body to meet and review complaints regularly throughout the year.

None of the remedies Scranton called for has been applied to date. This is not surprising, considering the attitudes of most member states and the dismal record since the early 1950s. Yet Scranton's statement did serve a purpose; the United States came forth as a champion of human rights rather than being on the defensive as it had too often been in recent years. Andrew Young was to carry this new U.S. approach further. Clearly, the approach embodies many of Moynihan's ideas on human rights, but without his abrasiveness.

ANDREW YOUNG

Andrew Young's appointment shattered a number of traditions. He was the first ordained minister, the first black, and the youngest man (forty-four) ever named to the job.

This was not the only time Young broke a precedent. In 1972 he became the first black congressman elected from Georgia since Reconstruction a century earlier; a majority of his constituents were white.

Yet in another sense Young's appointment represented a return to a U.S. tradition—naming a prominent political figure who has influence with the president. Such was the case, in varying degrees, with Austin, Lodge, Stevenson, Goldberg, and Scranton, who collectively accounted for about 80 percent of the time the United States had been in the UN. Young had played a vital role in helping Carter win 83 percent of the black vote in the 1976 election. He had also helped Carter by serving as a bridge to northern white liberals. Carter called him his "best friend in public life."

Young grew up in a New Orleans neighborhood that was predominantly lower-middle-class white. His father was a dentist and his father's father, whom Young describes as a "bayou entrepreneur," had also been prosperous. Among his ancestors was a mulatto woman who became the mistress of a New Orleans shipping magnate, a Pole named Czarnowski.[15]

Young makes no bones about his sheltered youth in a black bourgeois environment. He attended Howard University, the college of America's black elite, graduating at the age of nineteen. It was in his last year at Howard, where he had gone to prepare for either medical or dental school, that Young developed a serious social consciousness. He was impressed by the dedication of a young minister who had come to live in his parents' home. The minister was getting up to study and work at 5:00 A.M. when Young was just coming home from a night of fun. That presented a challenge to Young's life-style and values. Then, while driving home to New Orleans after his graduation, Young spent the night at a church conference in Kings Mountain, North Carolina, and had a white roommate who was on his way to Rhodesia as a missionary. The thought that a white man was sacrificing material comforts to go to help Africans evidently stirred Young's social consciousness; he decided on the ministry.[16]

Young studied at Hartford Theological Seminary in Connecticut, was ordained as a Congregational minister in 1955, and served as pastor in several southern towns. In 1957 he and his wife, Jean, whom he had married in 1954, moved to New York City. He worked for the National Council of Churches and lived comfortably in Queens. But the news photos of blacks sitting in at lunch counters in the South moved him deeply, and he decided to go where the action was. The Youngs moved to Atlanta in 1961, where Andy soon became the top lieutenant to Dr. Martin Luther King, Jr., leader of the Southern Christian Leadership Conference—spearhead of the nonviolent civil rights movement.

After King was murdered in 1968, Young decided that politics was the key to black progress in America. He lost a race for Congress in 1970 but was elected in 1972 and reelected in 1974. His backing for Carter in the Florida primary in 1976 may have been crucial in Carter's victory over George Wallace.

Although many black leaders advised Young against taking the UN job, believing it would be better to have him in Washington working on behalf of American blacks, Young himself had had the UN in the back of his mind for a long time. This was mainly because of Ralph Bunche's outstanding role as an undersecretary general of the UN; he was the first black man with whom Young had identified as a child. Thus, Young was ready when Carter, soon after the election, said, "I've been feeling for a long time that the U.N. is going to be important again. We're going to make it important in foreign policy and, though I respect your wish to stay in Congress, I'd really like for you to take the position." Young was delighted but did ask for time to consult his wife before accepting the president's offer.[17]

Young talked of redeeming the United States at the UN and the UN in the United States, of putting the United States on "the right side of the moral issues of the world." This put him at the opposite pole from Moynihan, whose rhetoric, Young believes, had "fairly disastrous results."

Young readily acknowledged that the trend he favored had already been instituted and helped along by his predecessor, Scranton.[18] It is also a trend favored by the president and the secretary of state.

Although he had no diplomatic experience before he came to the UN, Young was not without international experience. He had traveled to thirty nations in most parts of the world and had many friends both in and out of their governments, particularly in Africa and the Caribbean. In the House of Representatives he had been active on a number of foreign policy issues. More important, even though he flouted certain aspects of protocol, he had some important qualities of a diplomat. He was intelligent and personable, spoke well, and had influence with the president. These are the things that really count at the UN, not where the ambassador rides in his car. Moreover, UN diplomacy has always been more informal and less protocolar than traditional diplomacy, despite the many stilted public speeches. Also, foreign diplomats are used to dealing with noncareer American permanent representatives, who held the post for thirty-two of the first thirty-four years since the UN was founded. Some, however, were upset by Young's indiscretions in dealing with the media and by his frequent absences.

Young considered himself a politician rather than a diplomat. Asked about the difference, he replied: "A diplomat, in the traditional sense, is instructed by his government to maintain the status quo. A politician is generating activity, hoping to produce change, trying to make things happen in a positive way for his country. I find that the State Department trains people not to take chances, to do the safe thing for their careers."[19] In truth, a good politician will use diplomacy to achieve his goals, as Young has. And there have been many career Foreign Service officers, of whom George Kennan is the best known, who have worked to change policy. But no career officer could have the influence with the president and the "star" quality with the public that Young had, and these are important assets in the job at the UN. Nor would he have had the unauthorized meeting with the PLO representative at the UN that ultimately led to Young's resignation.

Asked what any one individual could do as "the servant of policy," Young replied: "But you're not. . . . When you make up your mind to do something, by the sheer power of the human spirit you can do it. If you believe and nobody else believes and you're willing to work your behind off to make it happen, it will happen."[20]

Most important is the fact that Young represented and was part of an administration that has consciously chosen a more forthcoming approach to the UN and Africa. Speaking in New York December 3, 1977, Assistant Secretary of State Maynes declared:

The Carter Administration's approach to the United Nations has been characterized by changes in three major areas.

The *style* has been changed primarily through the presence of Andy Young and his energetic efforts to cultivate leaders in the Third World and to broaden our comprehension of shared interests. But there are other steps, including the President's decisions to give two major addresses here at the United Nations, to invite Secretary General Waldheim to Washington at a very early stage in his Administration, and to spend 2 full days here at the United Nations in October.

The *substance* of our relations with the United Nations has changed through our recognition that the United Nations is a vital ingredient in the conduct of the world's business and by our determination to make greater use of all of its machinery.

The *funding* aspect of our policy has shifted as we have tried to reverse 10 years of decline in American contributions to components of the U.N. system to the point where many of our voluntary contributions, percentagewise, are now below our assessed contributions.[21]

As noted earlier, U.S. neglect of Africa had finally ended in 1975, in Kissinger's alarm over the installation of Marxist regimes in Angola and Mozambique. Ford, Kissinger, and Scranton had begun a new policy of supporting the early attainment of self-determination and majority rule in Namibia and Rhodesia. Young threw himself wholeheartedly into this new American policy and was a major factor in moving it along in Washington, in Africa, and at the United Nations. When Carter was welcomed in Nigeria in March 1978, the first visit by an American president to Africa, it was clearly Young who had paved the way. At a UN Conference on Apartheid at Lagos in August 1977, Foreign Minister Joseph Garba of Nigeria said that the Carter administration had done more than any other to combat South African racial practices and hailed Young as the "symbol of a new and constructive United States policy toward Africa." Such praise is striking coming from a Nigerian leadership that long barred a visit by Secretary Kissinger. Young described the African community's reception of him as "outstanding" and "exceptionally warm."[22]

Young applied to African problems many of the principles learned in the civil rights campaign—in particular, nonviolent struggle; patient negotiation; and the belief that large corporations, if convinced that it is in their interest, can be a potent ally. He won few converts among either the militant black Africans or the diehard white South Africans. Both sides tended to feel that his analogies with the U.S. civil rights movement were too simplistic. But he has neither lost faith nor relented in his efforts, even after resigning from his post at the UN.

Young has friends among radical, socialist, and Marxist leaders in Africa, as well as the moderate ones, but is himself a firm believer in free enterprise. Speaking to a group of South African businessmen in Johannesburg, he said: "I hear a lot of talk about revolution around the world. There are many, many ideologues that promise a transfer of power from one group to another, and yet as I have traveled around this world the places where I see the hungry being fed, the places where I see the naked being clothed, the places where I see the sick being healed are places where there happens to be a free market system. Where there's no ideology at all of change. And yet, in fact, in those free market countries more social change, more revolution is in fact taking place."[23]

Young went on to point out how banks and corporations in Atlanta, Georgia and Birmingham, Alabama, had finally become convinced that the civil rights movement was in their own interest, that it would avert violence, and that they had become more prosperous after the blacks, with increased opportunity, enlarged their markets. While persuasion had been used in both places, it took a massive nonviolent protest and a six-month economic boycott in Birmingham to make the business community aware of its responsibility. Young acknowledged that South Africa was a vastly different problem but still urged that South Africa avoid the human and economic repressions that would surely lead to widespread violence. Instead, it should seek racial justice and peace and thus open up to itself the vast economic potential of the African continent, just as Atlanta had become a city "too busy to hate," busy making money, "enjoying the prosperity of the market system."[24]

Young's statement might be considered as tailored to his business audience, except that he consistently used similar arguments with black African leaders, Marxist as well as non-Marxist, both in Africa and at the UN. For example, in his statement at the UN Conference for Namibia and Zimbabwe, held on May 19, 1977, at Maputo in Marxist Mozambique, Young argued for nonviolent struggle and negotiation and for a constructive role that multinational corporations might play. Referring to the nonviolent civil rights struggle in the United States, Young said: "And so it was in fact [from] many of the multinational corporations that we maligned, that we somehow gained our first impetus for freedom and support, long before our Congress and even before our Supreme Court and certainly before we had a President that cared anything about black Americans."[25]

Young also reminded his Maputo audience that the majority of the nations of Africa achieved independence through negotiated settlement and that those countries that had obtained independence by negotiation "moved much more rapidly in their development." He conceded that "it may be difficult, if not impossible, to reconcile the differences which exist in Zimbabwe or . . . Namibia," but he argued that every possible effort must be made to do so, for the benefit of both blacks and whites. He noted that, in the struggle for change, "one finds that quite often blanket sanctions do not produce the desired results. But somehow a combination of pressures and incentives for change can prove more effective even as tactics of wise restraint in the armed struggle have produced significant advantages. And so I would say that those of us committed to negotiated settlement should be respected for the tactics that we attempt to utilize and that even when there are differences it is very hard to adapt tactics of armed struggle to the problems of negotiated settlements. People who are engaged in negotiated settlements hardly have the moral right to tell the people who are engaged in armed struggle how to run their paths and determine their freedom."[25] As he had done in Johannesburg, Young again held forth the hope of mutual benefit for blacks and whites in Africa through cooperation in economic development, as had happened in Atlanta.

The Maputo exercise provided a most interesting insight into the way Young functioned. When he first discussed Maputo with his Western colleagues on the Security Council, they were against participation. They argued that it would be used as a forum for attacking Western collaboration with the white regimes in southern Africa; hence, it would be better not to enliven the proceedings and draw greater media attention through Western participation. Young heard them out, then stated he was going anyway. After that, the other Western countries decided that they, too, would attend. As predicted, the West was denounced and the final document of the conference was anti-Western. These developments, which he anticipated, did not bother Young; for him the important thing was to convey a sense of feeling, not to battle over the wording of a document. USUN officers who accompanied Young to Maputo believe that his participation there did much to strengthen his credibility with the Africans, who were impressed by his sincerity, dedication, and conviction, even on points where they disagreed. By recognizing that those who seek change by fighting should be respected by those whose tactics were to work for peaceful change, and vice versa, Young paved the way for cooperation by the "front line" African states in working toward negotiated settlements in Rhodesia and Namibia.

Young's work with the African countries in seeking peaceful solutions was widely appreciated, even by Western ambassadors who sometimes found his unorthodox style irritating. One of them said: "You owe Ambassador Young a considerable debt. More than most Americans understand, he has developed a link with the Third World countries. Young has assured them of America's intentions as perhaps no one out of the conventional white establishment could have done. That is a distinct gain and one that, all things considered, is likely to stand you in good stead in the future."[26] But some French-speaking African representatives, particularly those from smaller countries, felt that Young had neglected them.

On numerous occasions Young cautioned against full economic sanctions against South Africa. For example, he is quoted in the *Chicago Tribune* of February 6, 1978, as saying that "if we cut off investments we would lose jobs and we wouldn't necessarily help blacks in South Africa."[27] This attitude is consistent with his overall belief that enlightened corporate policy could help to bring social justice in South Africa as it did in the American South.

Young also believes that American business should be much more active in black Africa, in both trade and investment. He has noted that Peugeot and Mercedes have developed substantial markets in black Africa, whereas American manufacturers of cars and trucks have not exploited the market.

YOUNG AND WASHINGTON

An important factor in Young's influence, besides his special relationship with the president, was his rapport with Secretary of State Vance, lasting almost to the end of Young's tenure. Vance is a competent, solid, modest, indefatigable, and unpretentious man with a great deal of experience and no yearning to compete for the spotlight. A liberal Democrat, Vance shares Young's general view on U.S. policy goals in Africa and toward the Third World.[28] Also, more than any other secretary of state in history, Vance has a deep interest in the UN. During a decade of law practice in New York before he became secretary, Vance headed the policy studies program of the UN Association of the U.S.A. and took a very active interest in the UN. When Young had policy differences with William Schaufele, assistant secretary of state for African affairs, Schaufele was replaced by Richard Moose, then deputy undersecretary for management. Moose had traveled to Africa with Young in May 1977 and demonstrated that he could get along with Young, a key factor.[29] (Schaufele became Ambassador to Poland, indicating that his differences with Young did not damage his standing among the career professionals.)

Vance and Young also took pains to see that their own man, Charles W. ("Bill") Maynes was installed as assistant secretary of state for international organization affairs. Maynes had been in the State Department but was secretary of the Carnegie Endowment for International Peace during the Nixon-Ford years. He is highly intelligent, able, and energetic and was a firm supporter of Young's. His predecessor at IO, Samuel W. Lewis, had done an excellent job, recognized as such by Scranton and the State Department's professionals. Lewis was named ambassador to Israel.

A further indication of the mutual trust between Young and Vance was the way Young's principal deputies were selected. Young did not really know either James Leonard or Donald McHenry when he appointed them. Vance did, and Young took his recommendation. According to McHenry, it was also Vance who suggested Melissa Wells for the post of U.S. representative to the Economic and Social Council. The result was unusually close working relationships between Young's top staff at USUN and the key people in IO and the Bureau of African Affairs. Maynes, Moose, and McHenry have known each other for many years, worked together in the Carnegie Endowment, and share similar outlooks toward the UN and southern Africa. Consequently, Young did not need to use his influence with the president to advance policies against a reluctant State Department bureaucracy, as had sometimes happened in the past. Agreement was reached at the working level. Also noteworthy is the fact that Vance was in direct telephone contact with the secretary general very frequently, yet this raised no problem with Young. The secretary used occasional private weekends in New York to chat with Young about the UN and southern Africa.[30]

Vance fully supported Young's work at the United Nations, particularly with Africa and other parts of the Third World, but certain key problems were reserved for the secretary, for example, the Middle East and relations with Europe, Japan, and the Soviet Union. Also, at crucial points, Vance was the principal U.S. negotiator on African problems, notably in dealing with the British foreign secretary on Rhodesia. This division of labor was generally satisfactory to both, until Young became involved in a meeting with the PLO representative in July 1979, leading to his resignation shortly thereafter.

Like Goldberg, Young had a fully staffed office on the executive floor of the State Department. It was run by his own appointee, Anne Forrester Holloway. Young attended cabinet meetings regularly.

Young pushed for looking at Africa in African terms, not in terms of Soviet-American rivalry, and this was much appreciated by Third World countries at the UN. Also appreciated was the fact that in April 1977 the United States for the first time accepted a UN visiting mission to one of its territories, the Virgin Islands.

Young's concern with combating the cold war optic in viewing African problems may have led him into his off-the-cuff comment early in 1977 that the Cubans were a "stabilizing" factor in Angola. This was the first instance in which Vance publicly disagreed with him. Evidently embarrassed as Cuban military intervention continued in Angola and then spread to Ethiopia, Young later tried to clarify, explain, and modify his position. In a statement to the First Committee of the UN General Assembly on December 6, 1977, he said that "the presence of nearly a quarter of Cuba's armed forces and the interjection of Cuban military advisers in troubled areas throughout the continent can only lead to more deaths and suffering, both Cuban and African" and "step up tension, spread conflict and lead to unnecessary loss of life." In a television interview in March 1978 he explained more fully.

> When I spoke about Cubans being a stabilizing force in Angola, there was no fighting going on in Angola; they were basically doing technical assistance. They were in fact protecting Gulf Oil's installation in Cabinda, and essentially that role I thought was not against the United States interests, because they were contributing to the development of the economy and the viability of a society in Angola.

> When they began the search and destroy missions in southern Angola and when they used military means to try to resolve a conflict of Angolans themselves, I had no hesitation to condemn that military role.[31]

With respect to the nature of the Soviet threat in Africa, Young had some sharp differences of opinion with Zbigniew Brzezinski, special assistant to the president for national security affairs—the post Henry Kissinger held from 1969 to 1973, before becoming secretary of state. Brzezinski expressed deep concern about Soviet and Cuban involvement in Angola and Ethiopia. In May 1978 he charged in a television interview that the rebels who killed large numbers of white and black civilians in the Shaba Province of Zaire had been trained by Cubans in Angola—a view later supported by Carter and Young. He also reemphasized concern about Soviet-Cuban involvement in Ethiopia and other parts of Africa, which he called a threat to détente.[32] Young feared that the United States might overreact to the Soviet-Cuban presence by becoming actively involved itself, thus bringing on a Soviet-American confrontation in Africa and heating up the cold war.

Despite setbacks in Angola, Ethiopia, Iran, and Afghanistan, Young believed it was the United States, not the Soviet Union, that was winning the competition in the Third World. He noted the Soviet failures in Guinea, Egypt, and Somalia. He was convinced that Third world governments, even those with Marxist leaders, would find that it is the West that can offer the trade, technology, and capital they need, not the Soviet Union. In particular, he was convinced, on the basis of his contacts with Angolan representatives at the UN, that the current Marxist government of Angola would welcome improved relations with the United States, particularly economic. (Gulf Oil has had no problem in continuing operations there.) He also believed that U.S. recognition of Angola's government would speed the departure of the Cubans.[33]

"OPEN DIPLOMACY"

Young's outspoken style, which he called "open diplomacy," caused problems. In talking with reporters at various times, he called the British, Russians, and Swedes racist, along with former Presidents Nixon and Ford, bringing howls of protest. Young's definition of racism included not only conscious acts but also subconscious attitudes of superiority, condescension, and discrimination that result from insensitivity. He also attributed much of the criticism of the UN, with its majority of nonwhite states, to racist attitudes.

Young provoked another storm of criticism in the United States early in 1977 when he called the Cubans a "stabilizing" influence in Angola (a problem discussed earlier).

Two months after his appointment there were rumors that Young's penchant for off-the-cuff remarks were embarrassing Washington and that he would not remain long. Those who spread or believed the rumors did not know much about Jimmy Carter and Young's relationship with him. Young's influence with the president stemmed primarily from his role in the 1976 elections and his standing in the black community, but there was also a degree of personal affinity. Both are religious men as well as practical politicians. Both grew up in a racist, segregated South that was substantially desegregated in their lifetimes. Young was a major leader, as aide to Martin Luther King, Jr., in the civil rights struggle. Carter was not actively involved in the struggle but owed his presidency to its successful outcome, with the huge increase in black voters in the South.

By August 1977 Young's outspokenness had been reassessed. An editorial in the *New York Times* in 1977, entitled "Rediscovering Andrew Young," reflects the reassessment.

> There was a time not so many weeks ago when it was fashionable to pick on Andrew Young, the former preacher, civil rights worker and Georgia Congressman who now represents the United States at the United Nations. His off-the-cuff remarks—about racism in Sweden and in Queens, about racist former Presidents here, about Cuban troops in Africa being a stabilizing force—constantly seemed to get him into trouble. He was, so said many a commentator, a free-floating, free-speaking zealot whose foot was constantly in his mouth and who had only the most remote connection with the foreign policy of the country.
>
> One hears fewer complaints about the Ambassador's comments these days. One hears, instead, remarks of a very different sort. Indeed, some of his colleagues from other governments now say he has become the most influential person at the United Nations, and that his

presence at the head of the American delegation has swung more than a few votes, or has prevented issues from coming to a vote when the outcome would have been against the United States. And some say, with little irony or exaggeration, that Andy Young is currently the most influential person in Africa as well.[34]

Eleven months later, in July 1978, Young was again in trouble because of indiscretion in talking to a reporter about "political prisoners" in the United States. His lack of discretion with reporters undermined his standing not only among some segments of the American public but also with some foreign representatives at the UN.

Consistent with his belief in talking foreign policy with the American people, Young made an unprecedented number of public speaking appearances. He also made an unusual number of trips abroad, on policy missions to Africa and the Caribbean and to attend UN conferences in Lagos (on apartheid), Guatemala City (Economic Commission for Latin America), and Geneva (Economic and Social Council), all in his first year. Moreover, he was in Washington frequently for policy discussions and attended the cabinet meetings there with conscientious regularity. As a result, Young was at USUN only about half the time. When he was there he concentrated on the substance of major issues, particularly in regard to southern Africa. He paid little attention to the specific wording of resolutions; for him, it was the "sense of feeling" that counted. Nor did he have much time for, or interest in, overseeing the operation of the mission; that was left to subordinates. In that sense, according to an experienced senior staff officer at USUN, there were two missions in New York— Andrew Young and the rest of USUN. Experienced Western ambassadors at the UN expressed a similar view in my conversations with them. One of them referred to Young as an "absentee landlord" who was rarely around for Western caucuses during the General Assembly.

In the effort to do his job conscientiously and still be the open, accessible man he has always been, Young tended to drive himself into periodic states of exhaustion. He would talk with visitors into the small hours of the morning, then be up at six o'clock to start a busy day. At the end of six weeks or so of this superhuman schedule, Young would become so exhausted that he sometimes disappeared for a few days to rest, incommunicado.

In an ideally constructed mission, Young's freewheeling would have been complemented by a highly organized, experienced staff. Such was not Young's objective. He was determined to make a clean break with the past, to give USUN a new image, and to underscore that a new approach and a new policy were the order of the day. He replaced all four deputies at the ambassadorial level. Moreover, he brought in members of his congressional staff, filling slots that would otherwise have been available to career officers. Most of the new appointees were able; however, USUN was not the well-organized, highly professional mission it had been for most of its history. The drastic shakeup and new operating style upset some veteran Western ambassadors but did not hinder Young's popularity with Third World representatives; in fact, it was probably enhanced.

Young's principal deputy was James Leonard, an unusually able former Foreign Service officer with long experience in disarmament and arms control. Leonard has an inquisitive and inventive mind in dealing with substantive issues; he is less interested in the details of management. In 1979 Leonard was appointed deputy to Robert Strauss, ambassador at large for Middle East peace negotiations.

Young's deputy for the Security Council, Donald McHenry, had also had many years of government experience. I remember McHenry, a black, as one of the most intelligent and effective State Department officials I had contact with in dealing with colonial issues at the UN. Conversations with experienced USUN officers and foreign diplomats at the UN indicate that he is highly respected for his integrity, thoroughness, and rigorous analysis of issues. McHenry is blunt and direct in stating his views, to Europeans, to black Africans, to white South Africans, and was so even to his chief, Young. Concentrating principally on the tough problem of Namibia, McHenry carried the ball on most of the important, detailed negotiations on that territory.

In addition to Leonard and McHenry, Young appointed two more new aides at the ambassadorial level: Melissa Wells, former ambassador to Guinea-Bissau as representative to the Economic and Social Council, and Allard Lowenstein, a former colleague in the civil rights struggle and ex-congressman, as deputy for special political affairs. (Lowenstein, a politician and an idealist, had difficulty adjusting to USUN operations and left in June 1978.) Young also brought in from his congressional staff Stoney Cooks as a personal aide and Tom Offenburger as press secretary; both had been with Young for twelve years, including eight at the Southern Christian Leadership Conference. Other Young appointees included press assistant Karen Jones; and Kay Jackson, one of his two secretaries.

Shortly after his arrival Young made it clear that, in addition to these former associates, he intended to fill positions with people too long ignored by the system—women and members of the minority groups—the latter so that the mission would have "ethnic diversity"; naturally his position was not appreciated by the existing staff.

Fortunately, Young made some exceptions. Among the senior staff holdovers from Scranton's period, the highest ranking and most influential was Ambassador Richard Petree, the senior adviser. An able Foreign Service officer with more than thirty years' experience, Petree was respected by Young as well as by the staff and foreign ambassadors. He had the principal responsibility for management of the political affairs staff. He also gave substantive backstopping to Young. The economic and social staff was run by Amassador Wells; the legal staff consisted of two veterans, Herbert Reis and Robert Rosenstock, who had worked together for many years. Apparently no one was pulling it all together, as was done under most of Young's predecessors.

Young himself preferred to concentrate on policymaking and communicating with the American people as well as foreign delegations rather than on the management of USUN.

Another new departure at USUN was the appointment of a full-time representative to the UN Commission on Human Rights, Edward Mezvinsky. This reflected the Carter administration's new emphasis on human rights, as also manifested by the designation for the first time of an assistant secretary of state for human rights and humanitarian affairs, Patricia Derian. As a further sign of changed U.S. policy, in the spring of 1978 Carter signed two ten-year-old UN covenants, one on civil and political rights and other on economic and social rights.

The turnaround in U.S. policy on human rights has not changed the UN's preoccupation with human rights in three areas—South Africa, Chile, and the territories occupied by Israel; however, at its thirty-fourth session in 1978 the Human Rights Commission did decide to study the situations in Uganda, Uruguay, Equatorial Guinea, Paraguay, Bolivia, Indonesia, South Korea, Ethiopia, and Malawi, against which complaints had been received. It also asked the government of Kampuchea (Cambodia) to respond to information on human rights violations. It adopted a Nigerian resolution calling for the establishment of regional human rights commissions where none existed (e.g., Africa) and an Indian-sponsored resolution on the creation of national human rights institutions by all UN members. Still, the commission made no major headway on a Swedish effort to get it to draft a convention against torture; there was little progress on the proposal to establish a UN high commissioner for human rights; and the condemnatory resolutions adopted again reflected the Third World majority's "selective morality," zeroing in on South Africa, Israel, and Chile, while ignoring massive violations elsewhere.

We have already described Young's views on southern Africa and apartheid and his advocacy of negotiated, peaceful settlements. Now it might be well to look specifically at two areas where he was involved in negotiations looking toward independence under majority rule; Rhodesia (Zimbabwe) and Namibia.

RHODESIA (ZIMBABWE)

For five years after Ian Smith announced on November 11, 1965, that Rhodesia would henceforth be independent, the United States had a relatively comfortable position. It was based on emphasizing British responsibility for dealing with the white settler regime and supporting Britain at the United Nations. On October 29, two weeks before Smith's declaration, President Johnson had sent him a personal message stating that a Unilateral Declaration of Independence (UDI) would be a tragic mistake and making it clear that the United States would support the British in opposing such an act. After Smith nonetheless declared independence unilaterally, the United States backed the British policy of No Independence Before Majority Rule (NIBMAR). When Britain urged selective UN Security Council sanctions against Smith in December 1966, the United States gave its full support. In May 1968 the United States again backed a British proposal, this time for comprehensive sanctions and the establishment of a committee to monitor compliance.[35] As noted in Chapter VI, Ambassador Goldberg was a key factor in bringing about agreement in both instances. At the same time, the United States supported the British in their refusal to use military force against Smith. It was Britain, rather than the United States, that took most of the heat at the United Nations. The Africans were occasionally irritated with the United States but never so seriously as to lead them to jeopardize African-American relations.[36] I served as U.S. representative on the Rhodesian Sanctions Committee from 1968 through the summer of 1971 and was generally in the position of urging, on instructions, that sanctions enforcement be tightened. This position was popular with the Africans and the British but not with some of our Western European allies, whose enforcement of the sanctions was halfhearted. Even when the U.S. government in November 1970 permitted Union Carbide to import 150,000 tons of Rhodesian chromite, which it had allegedly paid for before mandatory sanctions became effective—a dubious case—the African reaction was relatively subdued. Evidently the earlier active American advocacy of strict enforcement of sanctions had left a temporary residue of goodwill.

This residue was destroyed a year later when Congress adopted the Byrd amendment. Attached to a military procurement bill as section 503, the amendment read: "Notwithstanding any other provision of law, on and after January 1, 1972, the President may not prohibit or regulate the importation into the United States of any material determined to be strategic and critical pursuant to the provisions of this Act, if such material is the product of a country or area not listed as a Communist-dominated country or area in general headnote 3(d) of the Tariff Schedules of the United States (19 U.S.C. 1202) for as long as the importation into the United States of material of that kind which is the product of such Communist-dominated countries or areas is not prohibited by any provision of law."

Although sponsors of the amendment stressed the alleged danger of becoming increasingly dependent on Soviet chrome, the language covered seventy-one other materials as well. Ironically, because of market factors, the percentage of U.S. chrome imports of Soviet origin *increased* from 45 percent in 1971, the year before the amendment became effective, to 60 percent in 1972 and 54 percent in 1973. In 1973 only 2 percent of U.S. chrome imports came from Rhodesia, but imports of Rhodesian ferrochrome put two of the four American producers of ferrochrome out of business.[37]

If the economic effects of the Byrd amendment were dubious, its political impact was disastrous. It put the United States in the company of South Africa, colonial Portugal, and nonmember Switzerland as the only acknowledged violators of the UN sanctions. It undercut the authority of the UN and gave heart to the Smith regime. Some African delegates told observers they had voted against the United States on a terrorism resolution in 1972 because of their dislike for the Byrd amendment. David Newsom observed: "In my four years as Assistant Secretary [for African Affairs] the exemption on Rhodesia sanctions has been the most serious blow to the credibility of our African policy."[38]

Unfortunately, the Nixon administration showed little interest in either Africa or the United Nations. Ambassador George Bush made several calls to the White House, with no discernible effect. Although the administration's official position was against the Byrd amendment, neither Nixon nor Secretary Rogers was active in trying to persuade congressmen to oppose it. The White House was unwilling even to go on record against the amendment in the fall of 1971. In May 1972, when Senator Gale McGee of Wyoming tried to get the Byrd amendment repealed, he thought he had a White House commitment to help. But the White House was unwilling to show its hand on the issue either in statements or through the activity of its staff and their political allies. (The White House did allow John Irwin, the undersecretary of state, and David Abshire, assistant secretary of congressional relations, to write letters to the Congress supporting repeal of the amendment.) When the showdown vote approached, McGee vainly appealed for five or six telephone calls to "marginal" senators. He later stated on the Senate floor that only three White House calls—which never came—would have made the difference. Apparently, Nixon was more concerned about not antagonizing conservative senators a year before the 1972 presidential elections than he was about U.S. relations with Africa or the U.N.[39]

As noted earlier in this chapter, Scranton and a reformed Kissinger worked hard at rebuilding American relations with the Africans in 1976. President Ford, who had voted for the Byrd amendment as a congressman, did support its repeal, but successful action did not come until after Carter became president in 1977.

Young, Vance, and Carter gave the matter high priority. Testifying before a congressional committee hearing on February 24, 1977, Young stated: "I think we realize that had we repealed the Byrd Amendment on our first, or even second try, we probably could have avoided significant bloodshed and potential disruption to that entire area." He also told the committee that, on his just concluded trip to Africa, almost every one of the seventeen heads of state he met asked: "What are you going to do about the Byrd Amendment?" Young noted that this was considered by both the black Africans and Ian Smith as a test of American sincerity and commitment to majority rule in southern Africa. He also observed that he would be president of the Security Council in March and would feel personally bolstered if Congress could act by then. In fact, it did. Thus, Young's credibility with African leaders was given a significant lift at a critical early period of his service at the United Nations.

Despite the American lapse of four years and even more substantial covert evasion of the sanctions by many other countries over the past decade, sanctions did hurt the Rhodesian economy. Rhodesia was paying an estimated 10 percent of its gross domestic product in transport subsidies and agricultural and export incentives in order to stimulate exports and bypass sanctions. It had to sell cheap and buy dear. While able to overcome these handicaps from 1968 through 1975, by 1976 Rhodesia's economy was spiraling downward. The global slump in the steel industry and U.S. repeal of the Byrd amendment had caused mineral exports to slacken. South Africa imposed a surcharge on imports from Rhodesia that cost the Rhodesian economy $20 million in 1977. Meanwhile, the cost of fighting the revolutionaries had escalated to over $250 million in 1976, 25 percent higher than in 1975. By April 1978 it was running at an annual rate of $475 million, more than half the national budget. Capital investment dropped by 19 percent in 1976. In agriculture there was disinvestment as farmers abandoned their estates because of guerrilla activity. Moreoever, there was an increasing emigration of whites, including doctors, teachers, and engineers. (The 1978 population included less than 270,000 whites and over 6.5 million blacks.)[40]

The economic pressure was increased on May 27, 1977, when the Security Council adopted a resolution expanding the scope of sanctions against the Smith regime. The United States, having repealed the Byrd amendment, rejoined the group of countries zealously working for strict enforcement of the sanctions and was a cosponsor of the May 27 resolution.

The Carter administration joined with the British government early in 1977 in working toward a plan for peaceful transition to majority rule. Key participants in the endeavor were Foreign Secretary David Owen and Ambassador Ivor Richard on the British side and Vance and Young on the American. The credibility Young had established with the African states was a significant asset in getting their cooperation, usually tacit, but sometimes openly expressed. On September 1, 1977, the British permanent representative sent to the president of the UN Security Council "proposals for the restoration of legality in Rhodesia and the settlement of the Rhodesia problem." (UN Security Council Document S/12393). The proposals had been drawn up by the British government, "with the full agreement of the Government of the United States of America and after consulting all the parties concerned." The Anglo-American consultations had been held with leaders of all the nationalist factions, the neighboring ("Front Line") states and the Smith regime, both bilaterally and in groups. The main features of the proposals were as follows:

1. The surrender of power by the illegal regime and a return to legality.
2. An orderly and peaceful transition to independence in the course of 1978.
3. Free and impartial elections on the basis of universal adult suffrage.
4. The establishment by the British government of a transitional administration, with the task of conducting the elections for an independent government.
5. A United Nations presence, including a United Nations Force, during the transition period.
6. An Independence Constitution providing for a democratically elected government, the abolition of discrimination, the protection of individual human rights and the independence of the judiciary.
7. A Development Fund to revive the economy of the country which the United Kingdom and the United States view as predicated upon the implementation of the settlement as a whole.[41]

The deteriorating situation in Rhodesia and the presentation of the Anglo-American proposals put additional pressure on Ian Smith. On March 3, 1978, he announced an agreement with three African leaders in Rhodesia to bring about "majority rule on the basis of universal adult suffrage."[42] The preamble to the agreement acknowledged the impact of sanctions and armed conflict and presented it as a means of leading to their termination. It represented certain significant concessions by Ian Smith, such as agreement to the principle of universal suffrage and to independence as of December 31, 1978; a sharing of power among the participating groups; and a commitment that he would eventually step down. But, as Young declared in his statement to the Security Council on March 14, 1978, the Salisbury agreement was not adequate to bring out a peaceful solution. It fell short of the Anglo-American proposals in the following ways:

1. It did not involve all the nationalist leaders, omitting those who were doing the fighting against the Smith regime. "Thus it threatens to further divide rather than unify the people of Zimbabwe and threatens to prolong violence rather than end it."
2. The Executive Council, which determined policy during the transition period, had to make all decisions by consensus. (Its four members were Smith, and the leaders of the nationalist groups within Rhodesia— Sithole, Muzorewa, and Chirau.) Thus, Smith had a veto over any changes.
3. There was no provision for the fair and impartial conduct of elections. In the Anglo-American proposal, a British resident commissioner would help insure that result, as would the presence of impartial observers.
4. The authority to maintain law and order would continue to reside in the white-dominated army, police, and courts. The Anglo-American proposal suggested that a UN peacekeeping force assist the resident commissioner and the police force in maintaining tranquility and in insuring the impartiality of the political process.
5. It lacked the entrenched Bill of Rights, which was in the Anglo-American proposal.[43]

Despite Anglo-American and UN objections, Smith and his three black collaborators went ahead with the Salisbury agreement. Elections in March 1979 resulted in victory for Muzorewa, who became prime minister, with Smith in the cabinet as minister without portfolio. But white power remained entrenched and the fighting between the Muzorewa-Smith forces and the Mugabe and Nkomo troops continued, even intensified. No other government recognized the new regime of Zimbabwe Rhodesia, and UN sanctions continued.

On August 6 the Commonwealth heads of government, meeting in Lusaka, Zambia, came to an accord aimed at "finding satisfactory solutions to the remaining problems of this region." The accord "recognized . . . that the internal settlement constitution is defective in certain important respects"; accepted Britain's constitutional responsibility to grant legal independence to Zimbabwe on the basis of majority rule; called for the adoption of "a democratic constitution including appropriate safeguards for minorities" and for "free and fair elections properly supervised under British Government authority, and with Commonwealth observers"; and set as a major objective the "cessation of hostilities and an end to sanctions as part of the process of implementation of a lasting settlement."

Earlier there had been hints that the new Conservative government, which came into office in the spring of 1979, might recognize the Muzorewa regime and move to end British sanctions. But concerned with possibly vehement reactions at the Commonwealth Conference, which might even have led to its breakup, Prime Minister Thatcher moved cautiously. On the eve of the conference, Nigeria nationalized British shares in Nigerian oil production and marketing. Although Nigeria said the action was in protest of British oil sales to South Africa, it was also a clear warning to the Thatcher government not to lift sanctions against Zimbabwe Rhodesia.

The U.S. position was also of key importance to Mrs. Thatcher. Here Young's strong position on this issue was undoubtedly a factor in the action by Carter and Vance to resist congressional pressure to lift sanctions.

In September 1979 the British government invited the parties, Abel Muzorewa, Robert Mugabe and Joshua Nkomo to a London meeting aimed at implementing the Lusaka accord. The negotiations were extremely difficult as the parties disagreed on fundamental issues; e.g., whether there would be a new constitution or amendments of the existing one, who would supervise new elections, and what the composition of the armed forces would be. Finally, in December 1979, an agreement was reached, based on the following elements: (1) The United Kingdom would resume its sovereign control over Zimbabwe, ending the illegal declaration of independence of 1965, pending the establishment of a new government based on majority rule elections to be held in February 1980; (2) Hostilities would cease and the armed forces would regroup at designated points; (3) A 1300-man force of Commonwealth troops would supervise the cease-fire; (4) Economic sanctions against Zimbabwe Rhodesia would be ended. The agreement was made possible in part by British skill and toughness; in part, by the strong desire of Muzorewa and the Rhodesian whites to see an end to the sanctions and fighting (Young had contributed to this pressure by his energetic efforts to repeal the Byrd amendment in 1977 and his intercessions with Carter in the summer of 1979 urging the President not to yield to Congressional pressure to remove the sanctions); and in part by the pressure on Nkomo and Mugabe by the neighboring African states, notably Zambia, Mozambique, Tanzania, and Botswana, whose economies were being severely damaged by the long civil war in Zimbabwe. Young's cultivation of good relations with the leaders of these African states during the preceding two and a half years had also helped significantly.

NAMIBIA

When the UN General Assembly declared in 1966 that South Africa's mandate over South West Africa (Namibia) had terminated, Arthur Goldberg played a leading role in negotiating the resolution (2145 [XXI]). (See Chapter VI.) In May 1967, however, the Assembly adopted resolution 2248 (S-IV), calling for measures to force South Africa out, and the United

States became one of 30 abstainers. Goldberg argued that efforts must be made toward a peaceful solution through dialogue. Because of this and other differences of viewpoint, the United States stayed off the Council for Namibia, as did France and Britain.

For almost a decade there was a standoff. South Africa refused to recognize the Council for Namibia and ignored the resolution of the General Assembly. The 1974 revolution in Portugal, as a result of which an independent Angola emerged, brought a new situation to the northern border of Namibia. South Africa intervened unsuccessfully in Angola on the side of Jonas Savimbi against the Soviet and Cuban supported forces of Agastinho Neto, which emerged triumphant. The South-West African People's Organization (SWAPO), which had been waging a political and guerrilla campaign for control of Namibia, now had a friendly neighbor country as a base as well as the support of the OAU, the Council for Namibia, and the General Assembly.

Faced with this new situation, South Africa finally began to take steps looking toward ending its mandate. The leaders of South-West Africa's National party, on instructions from the South African prime minister (who had been prodded by several U.S. demarches), began in September 1975 talks with black leaders inside Namibia (but not with SWAPO) leading to a Constitutional Conference. On August 18, 1976, the Constitutional Conference issued a statement fixing December 31, 1978, as the date for Namibia's independence. Two days later the UN Council for Namibia rejected the proposals in the statement as ambiguous, equivocal, and totally lacking in legitimacy. SWAPO's leader, Sam Nujoma, denounced the constitutional talks in Namibia, which he charged were being carried out with "puppet chiefs," and declared that SWAPO would go on with its struggle for liberation.[44]

Earlier that year the Security Council, in its resolution 385 adopted unanimously on January 30, 1976, had declared that there must be "free elections under the supervision and control of the United Nations to be held in the whole of Namibia as one political entity" and that "there should be adequate time to enable the UN to establish the necessary machinery in Namibia to supervise and control such elections." This resolution was ignored by South Africa in working out its proposals for independence; however, it became the basis for Western efforts to work out a compromise solution.

In December 1976 the General Assembly adopted resolutions denouncing South Africa for its continued occupation of Namibia and for organizing the constitutional talks in Namibia. It accorded SWAPO observer status in the Assembly and at all conferences convened under UN auspices. It also adopted without objection a concept of a "Nationhood Programme" of assistance by the UN system, covering both the period of struggle for independence and the initial years of independence.[45] A year later in its resolutions 3219A and 3219B, adopted without objection, the Assembly allocated $500,000 to the UN Fund for Namibia and appealed to states, the specialized agencies, and other international institutions to provide assistance. (On six other resolutions concerning Namibia, resolutions 32/9 C, D, E, F, G, and H, the United States abstained, following patterns established in earlier years.)

Young made little effort to change U.S. positions on General Assembly resolutions on Namibia at the thirty-second session, his first, nor did he try to negotiate compromise language. Instead, he concentrated throughout 1977 on private discussions of the core issues involved in arriving at a peaceful transition to independence. Characteristically, he was more concerned with a sense of feeling than with words. He started, soon after his arrival at the UN, by inviting some key African and other nonaligned representatives to a series of early morning breakfasts. His first objective was to establish credibility. Then he asked them to think, not in terms of resolutions, but about a serious undertaking to bring genuine and early independence to Namibia.

The African representatives said in private what they could not state publicly—that it was necessary to enter into some kind of discussions with the South African government. But they said: "You have to do it because you are the only ones who maintain communications with both groups." They added: "you have to do it without coming to us for a mandate, we will give you one which so ties your hands that you will never get anywhere. You go ahead and undertake this.[46]

After talking with Vance and Carter, Young asked the other four Western members of the Council in 1977—Britain, Canada, France, and the Federal Republic of Germany—to form a contact group, which came to be known informally around the UN as the "Gang of Five." Basing themselves on Security Council resolution 385, the Five undertook a year of long, patient, and frank discussions with South Africa, SWAPO, and the key African states. Both at the UN and in capitals, they searched for an acceptable compromise formula. Initially their efforts met with suspicion and mistrust on all sides and in particular from the principal interested parties, South Africa and SWAPO. During the period April 1977–January 1978, the Five took no position whatever on the elements that might lead to a practical implementation of resolution 385. Instead, they explored thoroughly the concerns of the parties.

In January 1978 the first draft of a proposal was prepared, mainly by Donald McHenry of USUN and Gerald Helman of the Bureau of International Organization Affairs. In February the five foreign ministers held proximity talks in New York with Foreign Minister Botha of South Africa and Sam Nujoma, president of SWAPO, as well as with the secretary general of the United Nations and senior representatives of Zambia, Tanzania, Nigeria, Botswana, Angola, Mozambique, Mauritius, and Gabon. These February talks convinced the five governments that their proposal embodied a reasonable means of implementing resolution 385, but that certain provisions required clarification or improvement in drafting. The proposals were finalized and presented to the interested parties at the end of March, then circulated on April 10, 1978, as Security Council document S/1263.[47]

The key elements in the proposal were the provisions for free elections for the whole of Namibia, as one political entity, with appropriate UN supervision and control. Elections were to be held for a Constituent Assembly which would adopt a Constitution for an independent Namibia. Balloting was to be secret and all adults would be eligible to vote, with provision for those who could not read or write. Before the elections a UN special representative was to assure that all discriminatory laws and regulations were eliminated and political prisoners freed and that all refugees who wished to return would have an opportunity to do so. There was also to be a cease-fire and a phased withdrawal from Namibia of all but 1,500 South African troops within twelve weeks and prior to the elections, as well as the demobilization of all "citizen forces, commandos and ethnic forces." The remaining South African forces would be restricted to one or two bases and would be withdrawn entirely after certification of the election. The UN special representative was to be assisted by a Transition Assistance Group (UNTAG), consisting of a civilian team and a peace-keeping force.

This proposal was tentatively accepted by the government of South Africa on April 25, 1978. Speaking to the General Assembly three days later, SWAPO President Sam Nujoma expressed a conditional acceptance, depending on certain clarifications and additional conditions. UNTAG "should consist of a civilian team of no fewer than 1000 people as well as a United Nations peacekeeping force of no fewer than 5000 men . . . under authority and direction of the United Nations Special Representative." Nujoma also stipulated that the remaining 1,500 South African troops should be confined to a base in the *southern* part of Namibia. The main problem, however, was his insistence that the Walvis Bay enclave, which had never been part of the mandate, was part of Namibia and essential to its territorial integrity. It is the only deep-water port accessible to Namibia.

The five Western governments had omitted any mention of Walvis Bay because they saw no way of settling that difficult question in the context of the current negotiations. They stated: "We feel strongly, however, that the issue should not delay the long-sought-after independence of Namibia. We consider that all aspects of the question of Walvis Bay must be subject to discussion between the South African

Government and the elected government of Namibia. We have, furthermore, obtained assurances that the strength of the South African force in Walvis Bay will not be increased during the transitional period and that Namibians in Walvis Bay will be able to participate in the political life of the Territory during the transitional period, including by voting on the elections."[48]

After further meetings of the Five with Nujoma, SWAPO also accepted their proposals; these formed the basis of Security Council resolution 431, adopted on July 27, 1978. At the same meeting the Council adopted resolution 432 in which it declared that "the territorial integrity and unity of Namibia must be assured through the reintegration of Walvis Bay within its territory" and that the Council "will remain seized of the matter until Walvis Bay is fully integrated into Namibia." The five Western members of the Council voted for both resolutions.

Secretary Vance, speaking for the United States, said that the West supported the second resolution, recognizing that there were geographic, political, social, and administrative arguments favoring unification with Namibia. But he balanced this with an interpretation intended to mollify South Africa, saying that there was no prejudgment of legal issues, no intention to "coerce," and that in calling for steps toward "reintegration," direct negotiations between the parties were being suggested.

South Africa protested strongly against the second resolution, pointing out that Walvis Bay had never been part of the Namibia mandate. Obviously, the South Africans wanted to hold on to the port so that they could use it as a bargaining chip in negotiating a number of crucial issues with the new country. They would like assurances that use of the port not be given to a hostile power, that South African commerical holdings would not be seized, and that they could have access to airfields, since they are denied such facilities elsewhere in Africa and the enclave is closer to Europe than their own airports are. Despite these misgivings about the second resolution, the South Africans indicated in 1979 that they would go along with UN procedures under resolution 431—essentially the Western plan they had accepted in April 1978. At the UN the agreement was considered to have justified the Africa policy of Vance, Young, and McHenry and a notable achievement made possible by skillful diplomacy rather than bluster.[49] Unfortunately South Africa has continued to quibble and place new obstacles in the way, preventing implementation of the plan.

A critical factor in gaining SWAPO's acquiescence to the Western proposals was the attitude of Angola. Here Young and McHenry did a commendable job of building channels of communication to a government with which the United States has no official diplomatic relations. One result was quiet Angolan work with SWAPO, persuading its leaders to go along with the Western plan. Another was an assurance to McHenry that the Angolan government would try to prevent any recurrence of attacks on Zaire's Shaba Province by rebels living in Angola, such as occurred in May 1978 and a year earlier.[50] In fact, Young and his staff had had a working relationship with the Angolan mission to the UN for some time. Young discussed "a whole range of things" with President Neto when both attended an African festival in Nigeria in February 1977. Subsequently, there were repeated contacts with Angolans at the UN, including a meeting between Vance, Young, and the Angolan foreign minister when Vance attended the UN disarmament session in June 1978.

OPEN MOUTH DIPLOMACY AGAIN

Just as Young's work on African issues was bearing such important fruit, he caused a furor by another inept and inopportune statement, this time to a reporter for *Le Matin* on July 12, 1978. The reporter brought up the trials of the Soviet dissidents. With feelings running very high in the United States, Young told the reporter that "there are hundreds, perhaps thousands of political prisoners in the United States," apparently alluding to poor blacks. He noted that there were "likely to be tens of thousands" of political prisoners in the USSR and that there is nobody in prison in the United States for criticizing the government or "for writing a style of literature or for having a monitoring system of our human rights." Despite these nuances, the statement was a major blunder and an embarrassment to the president. Carter let it be known publicly that he had phoned Young and told him he was "very unhappy about his choice of words and several of the statements" made that week—the first public rebuke. Secretary Vance had already expressed his displeasure to Young.[52] Young himself, a day after his gaffe, issued the following press statement:

> Let me assure you that I am fully in accord with the strong statements condemning the persecution of Soviet dissidents issued by President Carter and Secretary Vance and have actively supported the movement for universal human rights and freedoms and especially the cause of Soviet Jewry from my earliest days in the U.S. Congress.
>
> Nor have I ever equated the status of political freedom in the United States with that in the Soviet Union. I know of no instance in the United States where persons have received penalties for monitoring our Government's position on civil or human rights.[53]

Young's blunder also brought forth denunciations by congressmen, especially conservative whites, some of whom called for his impeachment.

But this call was not taken seriously, and President Carter, even in rebuking Young, had made his continued confidence in him clear. When asked whether Young had offered to resign, White House Press Secretary Jody Powell said: "I can say with assurance that if there had been an offer, the President wouldn't have accepted it." Even so, Young appeared chastened for some time thereafter.

When I interviewed Young in July 1979 he defended his "political prisoners" remarks on the grounds that they were designed to help Shcharansky and other Soviet dissidents. He said he had been working through private channels to prevent or mitigate Shcharansky's sentencing. He believed that the Soviets were likely to ignore public criticism by the United States but might be influenced by leftist European criticism of the trial. By acknowledging that the United States, too, had sometimes transgressed, he had hoped to win support for Shcharansky and other dissidents from European leftists who were also critical of the United States.

Seven months later Young slipped again. Interviewed on January 7, 1979, he said that the PLO's relationship to the UN "has made it possible for there to be some moderating influences present in the whole Palestinian equation. The people who are representing the PLO at the U.N. are very skilled politicians and very intelligent, decent human beings." In the 1960s I could have said the same about many South African delegates I met at the UN but would have considered it insensitive toward the American black community to make such observations public.

Young's comments alarmed Jewish organizations. The day after his interview appeared, the Conference of Presidents of Major Jewish Organizations charged that his remarks appeared to condone the philosophy and tactics of the PLO, which it characterized as a terrorist organization. His remarks were especially unfortunate and ill timed, coming at a moment when delicate peace negotiations were under way between Egypt and Israel—negotiations in which Young was not involved.

The dam finally broke in August 1979 when it was revealed that Young had on July 26 held an unauthorized, private meeting with the PLO representative at the UN. He did not report the meeting to Carter or Vance (or through official channels), and the revelation caused them serious embarrassment. Moreover, he first described the meeting as accidental but later conceded that it had been prearranged. His purpose, to arrange postponement of Security Council consideration of a resolution that the United States would have vetoed, can hardly be faulted, but the meeting was in contradiction of U.S. promises to Israel, and public revelation of it caused serious problems for U.S. efforts to further Middle East peace negotiations. Carter, having changed two able cabinet officers a month earlier because he wanted "team players," would have found it difficult to explain retaining

Young. The Senate majority leader, many other prominent politicians, and many public groups demanded his resignation. And Young himself, who believes in communication as a way of tackling problems—he met with Ku Klux Klan leaders in the South during the civil rights struggle—was unwilling to go along with the policy of no PLO contacts to which his government was publicly committed. Thus, his resignation was inevitable.

Young's resignation aroused a furor among American black organizations. His importance as a symbol to the black community had been emphasized by Benjamin Hooks, executive director of the NAACP, who in 1978 observed: "No black person has ever had such a forum (especially with the backing of a sympathetic and supportive President) for advocating policies on Africa that challenge white minority rule and oppressive domination."[54] After Young's resignation, the leader of the Southern Christian Leadership Conference had lunch with the PLO representative at the UN, then issued a press statement endorsing human rights for the Palestinians, including the right of self-determination. Although neither Israel nor the leadership of American Jewish organizations pressed for Young's resignation—many, in fact, were his old comrades from the civil rights struggles of the 1960s—the incident sparked latent hostilities between black and Jewish Americans.

In conclusion Young's performance merits a mixed review. His habit of talking to reporters off the top of his head often embarrassed the administration and irritated friendly governments. His frequent public appearances all around the country helped to promote understanding of the UN, but they involved such prolonged absences that other Western ambassadors at the UN felt that he was too often not available for consultation and caucuses. Also, USUN was not as well organized as it had been under chiefs like Lodge, Goldberg, and Scranton. He is a man of ideas rather than of organization, who appeared to be bored with the day-to-day slogging that characterizes so much of the UN's work.

Yet, all things considered, he served U.S. interests well. His personal charm, quickness of mind, stamina, and ability to communicate were important assets, as was his warm relationship with Carter and Vance, who shared and supported his views on African policy. He had outstandingly good relations with the Africans and other Third World representatives. While Scranton started the improvement of the U.S. relations with the Third World after years of serious deterioration, Young succeeded in this regard as no representative had since Adlai Stevenson.

Young must also be given credit for his dedication to working for peaceful transition of power in Zimbabwe Rhodesia and Namibia. It is still not certain that negotiations will succeed in Namibia. What is certain is that Young's efforts improved such prospects from what might otherwise have been hopeless.

Given the new importance of the Third World to the United States politically, economically, and strategically, these were no small achievements.

McHENRY AS PERMANENT REPRESENTATIVE

Donald McHenry, Young's deputy for Security Council Affairs, succeeded him as permanent representative and served for the balance of the Carter presidency. In one sense, McHenry was a career official, having served with the State Department for a decade. He resigned from the department during the Nixon administration because of policy differences and was with the Carnegie Endowment when Vance and Young selected him in 1977. The circumstances of his appointment, following Andrew Young's resignation, gave McHenry a political constituency. The black community took pride in Young, was disturbed by his resignation, and would undoubtedly have been upset if McHenry, also black, felt obliged to resign.

Consequently, McHenry had appreciable clout in Washington. He saw the president to discuss policy much more frequently than Young did. He was also much respected by the secretary of state. Indeed, it was Vance who recommended McHenry, whom he had known for many years, to serve as Young's deputy. Moreover, McHenry's years of service as a highly respected career official gave him both a wide circle of useful contacts and an intimate knowledge of how the bureaucratic machine works. Those were significant assets in bringing his influence to bear on policy. He used his knowledge and contacts to strengthen USUN's staff, which resulted in a better organized and more effective mission.

The early months of 1980 showed some fruits of the Carter-Vance-Young-McHenry efforts to reach out toward understanding with the Third World at the UN. In January the General Assembly voted overwhelmingly (104–18, with 18 abstentions) to condemn the Soviet invasion of Afghanistan. This vote exploded the neoconservative myth that there is a solid Soviet–Third World bloc in the UN. At the same time Cuba was obliged to abandon its campaign for election to the UN Security Council. (Note also that in November 1979 the Assembly had adopted a resolution, against Soviet opposition, calling for the "withdrawal of foreign forces" [the Vietnamese] from Cambodia and refused to recognize the government installed in Pnom Penh by the Vietnamese.) In February elections held in Zimbabwe under British supervision led to a landslide victory for Robert Mugabe. His government, though Marxist, sought constructive relations with the United States and saw to it that an American Embassy was established in the capital of Zimbabwe well before the Soviets.

McHenry's performance as permanent representative was marred by a serious mistake in the policy-making process on one issue in the Security Council. On March 1, 1980, the Council unanimously called upon Israel "to dismantle the existing settlements and in particular to cease, on an urgent basis, the establishment, construction and planning of settlements in the Arab territories occupied since 1967, including Jerusalem." The affirmative vote by the United States sent shock waves through Israel and the American Jewish community.

Two days later, President Carter disavowed the U.S. vote, terming it a mistake based on a communications failure. He said it violated two basic U.S. principles: first, in accordance with the Camp David accords, there should be an undivided Jerusalem; and, second, "during the time of the negotiations we would not call for the dismantling of existing settlements." However, much skepticism was expressed about the disavowal. I believe the affirmative vote was a serious mistake, for the reasons Carter himself gave.

The resolution is, in any case, a nonbinding recommendation. More important is whether the U.S. vote signaled a changed American policy toward Israel. Evidently it did not, as Vance made clear in his statements to the Senate Foreign Relations Committee on March 20, 1980, when he reiterated the U.S. commitment to Israel's security and the other basic elements of American policy.

The resolution, however, involved an issue that has long been a bone of contention between the United States and Israel. U.S. opposition to Israeli settlements beyond the June 4, 1967, boundaries has been consistent and publicly expressed for more than a decade—under Presidents Johnson, Nixon, Ford, Carter, and Reagan. Israel, on its side, has just as consistently upheld the rights of Jews to settle in Judea and Samaria.

Discussion of the resolution that the Security Council adopted on March 1 showed clearly that, notwithstanding the difference on settlement policy, no other country supported Israel to the extent that the United States did. (Indeed, many countries criticized the U.S. sharply for that support, and no other country spoke in favor of the Israeli position.)

Why, then, did the policymakers in the State Department press for an affirmative vote at that particular time on such a sensitive issue? From reading relevant documents, articles, and statements and interviews with directly involved American officials in Washington and New York, I conclude that an important reason was an increasing sense of frustration with Begin's restricted vision of autonomy and his continued policy of establishing new Jewish settlements at a time when negotiations on Palestinian autonomy appeared, in American eyes, to be approaching a crucial stage.

In the fall of 1978, at Camp David, Carter, Begin, and Sadat had succeeded in negotiating an agreement that enabled Egypt and Israel to sign a peace treaty the following March. Thus Egypt recovered the Sinai and Israel had its first peace treaty with an Arab state, and the most powerful one to boot. But Camp David had also included an Israeli commitment to recognize "the legitimate rights of the Palestinians" and envisaged negotiations leading toward the exercise of those rights through some form of autonomy. Carter believed that Begin had also agreed to suspend settlements on the West Bank pending the completion of negotiations. Begin, however, did not and, consequently, was perceived in Washington as being uncooperative on the settlements issue and too narrow in his definition of autonomy.

Protests to Begin fell on deaf ears. Washington sought some way to show its deep concern. The idea of reducing or delaying aid, as Henry Kissinger had done, was rejected as too harsh. Then came the resolution in the Security Council and a possible opportunity to send the message.

McHenry was instructed to negotiate modifications in the draft, to eliminate references to Jerusalem and to dismantling of settlements, and to make the resolution hortatory rather than mandatory. His success was only partial (the resolution is hortatory), but—intent on sending the message—the State Department recommended to the president that he authorize a "yes" vote, with a statement that the United States regarded the dismantling of settlements as not "practical."

Carter, preoccupied at the time with Iran, Afghanistan, hostages in Colombia, and the election campaign, failed to give the proposed resolution the attention he should have—hence the grave error and the disavowal. (I am informed by a reliable State Department authority that McHenry was not in direct contact with the president on this issue, though he definitely favored an affirmative vote.)

The administration's ineptitude on this issue was costly to Carter. His disavowal of the affirmative vote two days later aroused Arab antagonism, even among those relatively friendly to the United States. And the vote itself shocked the American Jewish community shortly before the Democratic presidential primary in New York, which Carter lost.

McHenry, on the other hand, retained the respect of other UN representatives for the remaining nine months of the Carter administration, despite the disavowal. He was not blamed for the administration's ineptitude on this issue; he and his top staff were recognized as experienced, competent professionals, and they continued to function effectively.

NOTES

1. Conversation with William Scranton, January 12, 1978.
2. Ibid. See also USUN press release 191 (76), Revision 1, *United States Positions on United Nations Issues in 1976*, p. 109.
3. USUN press release 191, op. cit., pp. 99–102.
4. Conversation with Scranton, op. cit.
5. *UN Monthly Chronicle* (February 1978): 20, lists thirteen countries that did not respond to Sanctions Committee inquiries about suspected violations. For an account of the disastrous impact of the Byrd amendment on U.S.-African relations see Anthony Lake, *The "Tar Baby" Option* (New York: Columbia University Press, 1976).
6. USUN press release 191, op. cit., pp. 31–32.
7. UN Security Council Official Records, March 24, 1976.
8. Ibid.
9. UN Security Council Official Records, March 26, 1976.
10. UN Security Council Official Records, July 4, 1976.
11. Ibid.
12. *Annual Review of United Nations Affairs, 1976* (Dobbs Ferry, N.Y.: Oceana, 1977), p. 152.
13. UN General Assembly, *Official Records*, A/31/PV. 11. September 30, 1976.
14. U.S. Mission to the United Nations Press Release, November 24, 1976.
15. "Outspoken Andy," *Newsweek*, March 28, 1977, pp. 1–5.
16. Ibid., p. 5.
17. Peter Ross Range, "Andrew Young," an interview in *Playboy*, July 1977, p. 61. See also Joseph Lelyveld, "Our New Voice at the U.N.," *New York Times Magazine*, February 6, 1977, p. 17.
18. Young's opening statement, press conference at the UN, December 21, 1977.
19. *Time*, July 18, 1977, p. 8.
20. *Newsweek*, March 28, 1977, p. 3.
21. Address by Charles William Maynes, assistant secretary of state for international organization affairs, to the Association of American University Women, New York, December 3, 1977.
22. Interview in *Africa* (March 1977), p. 18.
23. Statement by Andrew Young to South African businessmen, Johannesberg, South Africa, May 21, 1977.
24. ibid.
25. Statement by Andrew Young at the UN Conference on Namibia and Zimbabwe, Maputo, Mozambique, May 19, 1977.
26. Marquis Child's "Are We Understanding Andrew Young?," *Washington Post*, May 30, 1978. This perception was also brought out in numerous conversations I had with senior USUN officials and Western ambassadors at the UN, March–May 1978.
27. *Chicago Tribune*, Feb. 6, 1978.
28. For background on Vance and his organization of the State Department, see *New York Times*, September 18, 1967, pp. 1, 16.
29. Robert Shrum, "Andy Young Takes on the World", New York Times, July 8, 1977, p. 23.
30. Conversation with Donald McHenry, May 3, 1978.
31. Remarks on "Meet the Press," telecast March 12, 1978, Kelly Press, Washington, D.C.
32. Remarks on "Meet the Press," telecast May 28, 1978.
33. My interview with Andrew Young on July 23, 1979.
34. *The New York Times*, August 18, 1977, Editorial page, col. 1.
35. S.C. Res. 253 (1968).
36. Lake, op. cit., pp. 120–22.
37. Ibid., pp. 148–57.
38. Ibid., pp. 245–47.
39. Ibid., pp. 216–26. See also *Sanctions as an Instrumentality of the United*

Nations—as a Case Study, Hearings before the Subcommittee on International Organizations and Movements of the Committee on Foreign Affairs, House of Representatives, June 13, 15, and 19, 1972.

40. Michael T. Kaufmann, "Rhodesia's Economy Badly Needs Peace," *New York Times*, January 15, 1978, Sec. E, p. 4. See also John T. Burns, "For White Rhodesia, 'Pretty Bad and Getting Worse,'" *New York Times*, April 26, 1978, p. A1.

41. For the text of the Anglo-American proposals see *UN Monthly Chronicle* (April 1978): 79–80. Positive African responses to them are cited in the same issue, pp. 25, 32.

42. The text of the agreement, as published in the *New York Times*, March 5, 1978, is used as the basis of analysis.

43. Young's statement is in USUN press release 10 (78), March 14, 1978.

44. *Annual Review of United Nations Affairs, 1976*, op. cit., p. 87.

45. Ibid., pp. 88–91.

46. Statement by Ambassador Donald F. McHenry to the Cape Town Press Club, Cape Town, South Africa, April 7, 1978.

47. Statement at the General Assembly by Canadian Foreign Secretary Jamieson (Doc. A/S-9/PV. 3), April 25, 1978, pp. 38–53; and conversation with Donald McHenry, May 3, 1978.

48. Jamieson, op. cit., p. 51.

49. "UN adopts Namibia and Walvis Bay Resolutions," *New York Times*, July 28, 1978, p. A1. This article also gives the test of the two resolutions. See also Anthony Lewis, "Diplomacy Not Bluster," *New York Times*, July 17, 1978, Op-Ed Page, for an appraisal of the contributions made by Young and McHenry in gaining the quiet cooperation of African states, including Angola.

50. "Angola Vows to Thwart Rebel Attacks," *Newsday*, June 28, 1978.

51. "US-Angola Ties Kept Alive at UN," *Interdependent* (July–August 1978), p. 5.

52. "Carter Tells Young of Unhappiness at Comment on Political Prisoners," *New York Times*, July 16, 1978, p. 1.

53. Ibid.

54. Foreword to NAACP *Task Force on Africa Report and Recommendations* (New York: NAACP, 1978), p. 14.

CHAPTER IX

Jeane J. Kirkpatrick: Return to Confrontation

Jeane J. Kirkpatrick represented a dramatic change in approach from her immediate predecessors and, in her confrontational predilections, from all previous American ambassadors to the United Nations except for Daniel Patrick Moynihan. Her political philosophy, her attitude toward the UN, and her relations with African delegates were diametrically opposed to those of Andrew Young and Donald McHenry. They were liberals, while she is a staunch neoconservative on foreign policy issues. They saw the UN as a helpful forum for arriving at peaceful solutions; she considers it a "dangerous place" where conflicts tend to be exacerbated. They cultivated the African representatives at the UN and frequently represented black African viewpoints in Washington; she reflected the Reagan line, which was perceptibly friendlier to South Africa. These differences are not merely personal; they reflect differences in policy between the Carter and Reagan administrations.

To understand Jeane Kirkpatrick, one must first understand her political philosophy. In foreign policy she is a conservative. She has acted and spoken out of ideological conviction, as the representative of an administration that is, by American standards, unusually ideological. She is critical of those who believe that Americans "should concern ourselves with universal values, with abstract supranational goals, with what they are predisposed to call democracy and freedom, and not with such mundane matters as American power."[1] Her criticism does not mean that she is skeptical about the virtues of democracy and freedom; as her essays and speeches show, she is firmly convinced that the American concepts of democracy and freedom are superior to Marxism or any other collectivist society. Rather, her criticism is directed against those who would subordinate U.S. national interests to abstract moral concerns that may handicap the United States in its struggle against communism, which she sees as the predominant moral and political issue.

Her ideological affinity with the president is made clear in the speeches collected in her 1983 book, *The Reagan Phenomenon*.[2] The foreword, by Robert Nisbet, emphasizes her involvement in the formulation of foreign policy, not only as the permanent representative to the UN but also as a member of the Cabinet and the National Security Council. According to Nisbet, "her admiration for the President is very admirably deep," and evidence "suggests accord between the two on matters dealt with in this book." Those matters include policy toward Central America, Israel, Afghanistan, southern Africa, human rights, the Soviet Union, and the United Nations. Like Reagan, she tends to view foreign policy issues in terms of Soviet-U.S. confrontation and considers détente to have been a mistake.

In the first address of the book, "The Reagan Phenomenon and the Liberal Tradition," originally delivered on May 28, 1981, Kirkpatrick declares that "the liberal democratic and the Marxist-Leninist traditions are antithetical in their conceptions of human life and politics as well as in their practices." She sees American power as "necessary for the survival of liberal democracy"; notes Soviet gains in Ethiopia, Angola, Nicaragua, Southern Yemen, and Afghanistan in the 1970s; sees Reagan's election as the end of the Vietnam era and a return of the nation's self-confidence; and calls for greater clarity and firmness toward the Soviet Union.

That speech, clear in its application to relations between the industrialized Western countries and the Soviet bloc, does not resolve the issue of how to deal with more than a hundred countries that fit in neither category. What about countries that profess a brand of Marxism but reject domination by either superpower? What about dictatorships like Zaire, South Korea, and many others that are anti-Communist but are clearly not liberal democracies? Kirkpatrick addresses that question in her best-known essay, "Dictatorships and Double Standards," which appeared in *Commentary* in November 1979 and brought her to Reagan's attention.[3]

Her essay begins with an attack on the Carter administration, "whose crowning achievement has been to lay the groundwork for a transfer of the Panama Canal from the United States to a swaggering Latin dictator of Castroite bent." She then charges that in Iran and Nicaragua, "it actively collaborated in the replacement of moderate autocrats friendly to American interests with less friendly autocrats of extremist persuasion." She argues that the United States was wrong in trying "to impose liberalization and democratization on a government confronted with violent internal opposition—not only in Nicaragua and Iran but also in Angola, Vietnam, Cuba before the triumph of Castro and China before the fall of Chiang Kai-shek." This is indeed a formidable and striking catalogue, indicating clearly that (at least in hindsight) she would have favored unquestioning U.S. support of Portuguese colonialism, Ngo Dinh Diem, and Fulgencio Batista, as well as Chiang. All of these cases were far more complex than her analysis suggests, and it is difficult to find a "moderate" autocrat among them. In the case of Chiang's China and Diem's South Vietnam, the regimes were so weak and unpopular that the real question is whether the United States acted wisely in giving them as much support as it did.

Yet Kirkpatrick has a point. The overwhelming majority of nations in the world are not liberal democracies; hence, we rarely have the choice between dealing with "good" democracies and "bad" dictatorships. Nor, as she points out, does the United States have the capacity to democratize and modernize these countries. Still, if we are to deal with a nation at all, we must deal with its government, however imperfect. (The Carter administration, despite its emphasis on human rights, maintained relationships with right-wing dictators in Latin America, Asia, and Africa, as well as with left-wing ones, such as in Yugoslavia.)

There are, of course, gray areas, such as the 1979 "internal settlement" government of Zimbabwe/Rhodesia where the United States followed the British lead in withholding recognition, a policy sharply criticized by Kirkpatrick in her article. Had the United States recognized the Muzorewa government, it could not have had a useful relationship with the present government of Zimbabwe. While professing Marxism, Robert Mugabe has been notably less friendly toward the Soviet Union than toward the United States.

Kirkpatrick makes a distinction between "traditional" dictators like the Shah and General Somoza, who allegedly offer a hope of gradual democratization, and totalitarian (communist) dictators, who offer no such hope. As Theodore Draper points out, however, there are Marxist regimes that have introduced degrees of liberalization (e.g., Yugoslavia, Hungary) and right-wing dictators who have not liberalized at all. He also notes that it was not traditional in Nicaragua for the dictator to own 50 percent of all property and that the Shah's downfall was precipitated in part by his efforts to modernize a traditional society too fast.[4]

However much scholars may dispute the pros and cons of Kirkpatrick's thesis, Ronald Reagan welcomed it; it fitted in perfectly with his policy of confronting communism. Indeed, he has made the doctrine his own, particularly in Central America, with military aid to the government of El Salvador fighting rebels there and to rebels fighting the Marxist government of Nicaragua. And Kirkpatrick was in the inner circle of policymaking for Latin America. She served as the president's representative to the Kissinger commission on Central America and had a major responsibility for the harder line toward Nicaragua evident since mid-1983.

Clearly Kirkpatrick's political philosophy had a decisive impact on her attitude and actions at the UN. She returned to the Moynihan tactics of confrontation with the "nonaligned" majority. Like Moynihan, she is convinced that the United States must state its views clearly and consistently at the UN, and she and her team did so. She did not hesitate to stand alone on issues and did so with great regularity. No one can doubt the consistency, coherence, and firmness of U.S. behavior at the UN during her tenure, and that gained a measure of respect even from opponents.[5]

But speeches and resolutions are not all that happen at the UN, even though they consume the bulk of its time and are most visible to the public. Most speeches and General Assembly resolutions are soon forgotten. Important actions can be taken only by governments, and influence on them can usually be effected by informal conversations and a persuasive ear rather than public rhetoric and votes. Indeed, in my own fifteen years at the UN, I found these informal conversations more important and productive then public rhetoric. One of Kirkpatrick's principal deputies referred to the UN as a "soapbox" rather than a place for negotiations, and that appears to have characterized the approach of her U.S. mission.

Underlying this approach is Kirkpatrick's belief that the UN as it now functions has strayed from the goals of the Charter and that it is now an arena where conflicts are exacerbated rather than resolved. She concedes that the UN of the 1960s played a useful role in ameliorating dangerous situations in the Congo (now Zaire), Cyprus, and the Indo-Pakistan war of 1965. But, she argues, current debates at the UN tend to exacerbate conflicts for three main reasons:

1. The number of parties to the conflict is extended, as countries feel constrained to participate in debates and vote on issues in which they have no direct interest.
2. The pressure to vote and choose sides breeds polarization.
3. The blocs at the UN are mechanisms for conflict exacerbation and extension; for example, the use by the Arab group of its position within the Afro-Asian bloc to generate speeches and resolutions against Israel and the United States.[6]

In an interview with the author on April 7, 1983, Ambassador Kirkpatrick was asked whether, on balance, she considered the United Nations' influence as positive or negative. In reply, she said there were two UNs. The UN of the High Commissioner for Refugees, the Children's Fund (UNICEF), World Health Organization (WHO), and Food and Agriculture Organization (FAO) was a constructive force. On political and security issues, however, she considered the UN a negative influence, for the reasons cited above.

Kirkpatrick is on solid ground when she notes that most debates in the General Assembly are ideological. Also, discussion and voting in the General Assembly naturally widen the circle of participation. And sometimes bringing an issue to the UN is a hostile act, as when the Arab countries bombard the General Assembly with a plethora of resolutions against Israel.

But the United Nations' record on conflict resolution, while far below the expectations of 1945, has much more to its credit than the three examples cited by Ambassador Kirkpatrick. One could add a host of examples, such as the peaceful settlement of the dispute between Indonesia and the Netherlands on West Irian, Iranian agreement to allow a UN referendum that resulted in the independence of Bahrain, and the presence of a UN peacekeeping force to stop the conflict between Saudi Arabia and Egypt in Yemen. In fact, of more than 150 disputes submitted to the Security Council and the General Assembly, only a dozen long-range problems have thus far defied solution.[7] The others have been resolved through the UN or between the parties themselves.

Ambassador Kirkpatrick could point out, with justification, that these successes are in the past; the UN has had little impact on current disputes like the Iran-Iraq war, Arab-Israel disputes, the Soviet invasion of Afghanistan, the Vietnamese invasion of Kampuchea, and the conflicts in El Salvador and Nicaragua. But there have been "slumps" before, notably from 1952 to 1956; consequently, it may be premature to give up on the UN as an instrument of peace.

Her negative view of the UN is reflected in "Standing Alone," an address Kirkpatrick made in October 1981.[8] She refers to the United States as "impotent" at the UN, noting that the United States and Israel are the only two countries that are not members of geographic blocs; for example, Afro-Asian, Latin American, Eastern European, and Western Europe and Other (WEO). There are also subgroups, such as the EEC (Common Market), the African, Asian and Arab blocs, and ASEAN (Southeast Asia). These groups play a key role in deciding on candidacies, proposing agenda items and resolutions, and mobilizing votes. The Soviets dominate a bloc of about a dozen countries that, except for Romania on occasion, can be expected to do their bidding. By contrast the United States is not a member of any bloc, and this is a handicap.

Yet the handicap need not be crippling. The United States has frequent informal meetings with the WEO group and has friends in all the other groups except the Soviet bloc. And foreign representatives to the UN are not fools, even though many occasionally make foolish speeches. They recognize that the UN cannot do anything important without U.S. cooperation. It should be noted that the membership went through an entire session of the General Assembly in 1964–65 without voting rather than risk the withdrawal of either superpower.

What the nonaligned countries, constituting almost two-thirds of the membership, do control are the agenda and the flow of resolutions in the General Assembly, as Kirkpatrick notes in "Standing Alone." They have used that majority to focus on Israel-Arab issues, Namibia, South Africa, and the New International Economic Order (NIEO)—all issues on which the United States is in the minority opposition. The Soviets take an opportunistic position on these issues, supporting the nonaligned majority on self-determination as long as it is against Western interests. On Afghanistan, the majority has voted for several resolutions calling for the withdrawal of Soviet troops; there Soviet belief in self-determination is less evident.

Whether the nonaligned countries have been using their majority wisely is questionable. The fact that they have focused so much on anti-Western issues, with inflamed and repetitive rhetoric and resolutions, has seriously undermined confidence in the UN among Western peoples, governments, and media. Without such support useful results cannot be achieved. And the disenchantment in the United States has produced the Moynihan and Kirkpatrick reaction of embattled confrontation in the UN. Still, the United States has some responsibility to lead in more constructive directions and not just exchange brickbats. If there is no hope of constructive dialogue the nonaligned majority will have no incentive to desist from rhetoric invective and sterile resolutions. (The 1984 revolt of the "moderates" among the nonaligned, to be discussed later, may offer a window of opportunity for mutual accommodation.)

Kirkpatrick's response, like Moynihan's, emphasized that the United States should take very seriously what representatives say and do at the UN. In criticism of previous representatives, she says: "We operate as though there were no difference between our relations between supporters and opponents, with no penalties for opposing our view and no rewards for cooperating" and "as though we had no coherent national purposes that link issue to issue."[9] At her initiative American officials in foreign capitals were instructed more frequently to object to antagonistic votes or speeches made in the UN by representatives of the host country. Such tactics, if not used to excess, can be very helpful and should be employed on important matters. But there is a limit to the number of issues that can be usefully discussed in capitals. Often an embassy representative who has only a superficial understanding of an issue must talk with a foreign ministry official who understands even less. Moreover, such a step should normally be taken *after* consultation with the other country's representative at the UN; otherwise, one may needlessly antagonize the representative and multiply the number of contacts in the capital beyond the point of diminishing returns.

The difference between Jeane Kirkpatrick and her predecessors is most notable in relations with African delegations. They frequently differed with Andrew Young on particular resolutions and issues, but they liked him and were convinced of his sincerity and understanding. They would even, where possible, try to avoid embarrassing him with the U.S. government. With Kirkpatrick, on the other hand, they felt little sympathy.

Kirkpatrick has shown that the United States can strike back, both in words and action. A notable example was her reaction to the Communiqué of the Ministers of Foreign Affairs and Heads of Delegations of the Non-Aligned Countries, issued on September 28, 1981, in New York. On October 6 she sent a letter to virtually all UN ambassadors who represent nonaligned countries, expressing surprise that the ambassadors of their countries "would or could associate yourselves with a document composed of such base lies and malicious attacks upon the good name of the United States." The letter also noted that the USSR, which was conducting or supporting occupations of Afghanistan, Kampuchea, and Chad, was not mentioned in the communiqué, while the United States, which was then occupying no country, was criticized nine times. While Kirkpatrick's points were noted, her manner of presenting them provoked widespread resentment among the nonaligned ambassadors, including those friendly to the United States.[10]

Subsequently, she managed to develop reasonable working relationships with several friendly nonaligned ambassadors, but the sense of confrontation persisted. U.S. handling of the Law of the Sea Conference (to which we shall return) left particular scars: T. T. B. Koh, the astute and veteran ambassador from Singapore, observed: "The tough tactics of the U.S. [at the Law of the Sea Conference] didn't go down well with their friends in the [nonaligned] movement." Since Koh is widely respected and has been one of the staunchest U.S. friends over many years, his observation must be taken seriously. And, referring to the nonaligned summit meeting of March 1983, Nigeria's deputy permanent representative to the UN said his country and other moderates backed off from an effort to delete specific references to U.S. intervention in Latin America because "we couldn't afford to be seen publicly as giving in to Washington."[11]

As part of the "get tough" campaign, Washington has been computerizing individual Third World country votes in order to take them into account when considering aid requests. But adjusting the aid spigot to accord with UN votes may be difficult, given all the other factors that must be considered. The Soviet Union votes with the United States nearly as often as Jordan does; Zimbabwe, for several years the recipient of the largest U.S. aid program in Sub-Saharan Africa, votes with the United States less often than does Libya.[12]

Even after Prime Minister Mugabe visited President Reagan in Washington in September 1983, Zimbabwe abstained on the Security Council resolution condemning the Soviets' shooting down a Korean civil airliner. According to the *New York Times,* Kirkpatrick proposed that aid to Zimbabwe be cut substantially but was opposed by Chester Crocker, assistant secretary of state for African affairs, and the Congressional Black Caucus.[13] Subsequently, aid was cut.

THE PERSONAL SIDE: KIRKPATRICK, HER RELATIONS WITH WASHINGTON, AND HER STAFF

Jeane Jordan Kirkpatrick had had many careers—as scholar, teacher, author, lecturer, and mother—before she came to the UN in 1981. Born in Duncan, Oklahoma, in 1927, she attended Stephens College (Missouri) and received her B.A. from Barnard in 1948, her M.A. from Columbia in 1950, and her Ph.D. from Columbia in 1968. Her doctoral dissertation, on Peronist Argentina, was an important factor in her becoming a specialist on Latin America. She is married (since 1955) to Dr. Evron M. (Kirk) Kirkpatrick, long-time executive director of the American Political Science Association and now resident scholar at the American Enterprise Institute. They have three sons. They have also shared a long-time interest in political science and U.S. politics.

An adult lifetime of managing a family and a career has made Jeane Kirkpatrick a disciplined person who makes optimal use of time. She told a reporter, "Next to having children, work gives meaning to your life." Before her appointment to the UN, she wrote three books

(*Leader and Vanguard in Mass Society,* 1971; *Political Women,* 1974; and *The New Presidential Elite,* 1976) and numerous articles in scholarly and influential journals. During this time, while rearing a family she carried on a career of teaching and research, principally at Georgetown and the American Enterprise Institute.[14]

Her husband, a friend of the late Hubert Humphrey, led Jeane Kirkpatrick from a scholarly interest in politics to active participation in the Democratic party. Disappointed by the nomination of George McGovern, they helped in 1972 to found the Coalition for a Democratic Majority. These are Democrats who espouse traditional liberalism on domestic issues but are hard line conservatives on foreign policy and are popularly known as "neoconservatives." She became vice-chairman of the coalition, which included Norman Podhoretz, editor of *Commentary* magazine, Eugene Rostow, and the late Senator Henry Jackson.

As noted earlier, her *Commentary* article, "Dictatorships and Double Standards," fitted in admirably with Ronald Reagan's own hard-line conservatism and brought her to his attention. She served in his foreign policy advisory group in the 1980 campaign. Her appointment as representative to the UN was a natural, from his standpoint. She was a Democrat and the only woman in his initial cabinet—an important consideration for a president whose position on women's rights has been strongly criticized by feminists. Above all, she shared his conservative, anti-Soviet views on foreign policy and could be counted on to be a tough, articulate advocate at the UN. At a Cabinet meeting he referred to her as "our heroine."[15]

Her personal relationship with the president and their shared ideology on foreign policy gave Kirkpatrick a strong position in the administration. She sat not only in the Cabinet but also in the National Security Council and took both of these positions seriously; consequently, she was in Washington much of the time. With no strong deputy in overall charge at USUN, she tended to run the mission by telephone during her frequent absences.[16]

The chain of command for the U.S. ambassador at the UN has often been a source of confusion and occasionally friction; after all, since Lodge the ambassador has had Cabinet status. Yet instructions to New York come at least formally from the State Department, with rare exceptions, and in many past periods the department's Bureau of International Organization Affairs (IO) has been a major participant in framing and executing policy decisions. In Ambassador Kirkpatrick's case, the assistant secretary for IO was initially Elliott Abrams. The son-in-law of Norman Podhoretz, Abrams clearly shared the Podhoretz-Kirkpatrick line of thinking. When he became assistant secretary of state for human rights affairs, he was replaced by Gregory Newell, a Mormon in his thirties who had little background in international politics. Neither could compete with Kirkpatrick in terms of influence; she continued to run things her way, reporting more directly than almost any predecessor to the secretary of state and on frequent occasions to the president.

There were some well-reported differences between Kirkpatrick and Alexander Haig when he was secretary of state. The best known was a controversy over her negotiations during Security Council consideration in July 1981 of the Israeli bombing of an Iraqi nuclear reactor under construction. Under instructions from the State Department to veto any resolution involving sanctions or other punitive measures, she negotiated a condemnatory resolution with Iraq that was mild enough to be acceptable to the United States. Some days later, aides to Haig let out word that she had been prepared to support a resolution that would have imposed sanctions on Israel but that Haig had stepped in to stop it. Haig himself announced the day after the story was made public that there was no truth to it. Still, there was much speculation that the "leak" by the aides reflected a feeling that Haig was not getting due credit.[17]

Although there was serious concern in Israel that the U.S. vote for condemnation might signal a change in U.S. policy and Kirkpatrick's stance,[18] her subsequent actions and statements dispelled such fears. A knowledgeable Israeli observer at the UN described her as "the best representative Israel ever had."

By the summer of 1982, Haig's differences with Reagan's inner circle of conservatives and his constant pressure to be publicly acknowledged as the president's "vicar for foreign policy" led to the acceptance of his resignation. Kirkpatrick was on a trip to Africa at the time, leading to a quip by Oleg Troyanovsky, the Soviet permanent representative to the UN, that she was the only hunter who had bagged her prey in Washington while on safari in Africa.[19]

In any case Haig's replacement by George Shultz ended conflict between Kirkpatrick and the secretary of state, at least on matters directly related to her UN job. Shultz appears to be much more secure in his position and much less concerned with getting credit and jockeying to be closer to the president.

Kirkpatrick filled the controlling upper echelon of USUN—including all key jobs—with people who shared her views.[20] Her first alter ego in the Security Council was Ambassador Charles Lichenstein, an old family friend. Lichenstein was a campaign aide to Richard Nixon in the 1960s and served in the Nixon White House from 1969 to 1974, as an assistant for public information and policy development and as a congressional and political liaison; in the Ford administration, he was deputy to Counsel Dean Birch.

Kirkpatrick's first representative to the Economic and Social Council was José Sorzano, an anti-Castro refugee from Cuba who came to the United States two decades ago, received his Ph.D. in political science from Georgetown, and served as a research assistant for Kirkpatrick's book on Perón. Sorzano's deputy, Mark Plattner, who came from a position with the Twentieth Century Fund, is also an antileftist neoconservative. Her chief counselor was Carl Gershman, for years head of the militantly anti-Communist Social Democrats-USA and a writer known for his opposition to special allowances and moral dispensations for the Third World. Gershman has done public relations work for Jonas Savimbi, leader of the anti-Communist insurgents in Angola. It was a team long on loyalty to Kirkpatrick and on ideological consistency but short on experience in international diplomacy.

Initially the deputy permanent representative was Marshall Brement, a career Foreign Service officer who came to the post from an assignment on the National Security Council and considered himself compatible with the new team. Nevertheless, he was generally shut out of Kirkpatrick's inner circle and left by mutual accord after seven months to become ambassador to Iceland. He was replaced by Kenneth L. Adelman, who had served on Reagan's transition team and shared Kirkpatrick's views fully. In fact, Adelman's tough anti-Soviet speeches earned him the sobriquet of USUN's "hit man" among UN diplomats.[21] A man of considerable charm and intellect and an accomplished writer, he was, however, handicapped by a lack of diplomatic experience. Adelman was nominated in January 1983 to be director of the Arms Control and Disarmament Agency, and after several months of controversy over his lack of experience in arms control, he was confirmed by the Senate. José Sorzano, Kirkpatrick's Georgetown protégé, replaced Adelman, thus assuring control by her inner circle.

The only top-level holdover was Ambassador Richard Petree, deputy representative to the Security Council, an able, experienced career Foreign Service officer who had served at USUN under three other permanent representatives, including William Scranton, a Republican. He was fully prepared to serve loyally under Kirkpatrick but, like Brement, found himself an outsider. After six months Petree decided to retire and accept a position as president of the U.S.-Japan Foundation. He was replaced by William C. Sherman, another veteran Foreign Service officer. Despite his title, Sherman rarely spoke in the Security Council; Lichenstein and subsequently Sorzano served as Kirkpatrick's alter ego there. Instead, Sherman's principal job was running the Mission's staff. But because he was not one of Kirkpatrick's insiders, Sherman was left out of key policy discussions, as were a number of veteran staff members.

While U.S. permanent representatives have usually brought some congenial individuals with them, often as deputy, secretary, or press spokesman, they have generally kept experienced staff and assigned key roles to capable Foreign Service personnel to a much greater degree than did Kirkpatrick. Even Andrew Young, though he was determined to have a strong personal influence on policy, had a number of experienced professionals in key spots, and they had influence on him. His principal deputy was James Leonard, a veteran Foreign Service officer. His deputy for the Security Council, Donald McHenry, had long years of experience in the State Department dealing with UN affairs. McHenry was used fully in the Security Council and in working, with substantial authority, toward a settlement in Namibia. Finally, there was Petree, who had ambassadorial status and succeeded McHenry as deputy for the Security Council in 1979. Thus, prior to Kirkpatrick three of the four deputies with ambassadorial rank were professionals; they knew the UN, had wide contacts, and were respected by other delegations and key Secretariat officials.

Interestingly, Kirkpatrick herself has decried the amateurism and ineptitude of U.S. representation at the UN; she has complained that our permanent representatives and assistant secretaries for International Organization changed so rapidly that it took much of their tenure to gain the necessary experience.[22] Given the turnover in American presidents, a comparable turnover in U.S. Permanent Representatives appears inevitable. Yet Austin served for six years, Lodge for seven and a half, Stevenson for four and a half, and Goldberg and Young for almost three years. More important, even short-term permanent representatives can serve successfully if they come with political skills and use an experienced staff. Scranton, Ball, and McHenry were highly effective in mobilizing support for U.S. positions and cultivating good relations with other delegations even though their tenure as permanent representative was relatively short.

Based on her experience, Kirkpatrick has proposed that Foreign Service officers serve longer at USUN than the usual two or three years, a sound idea in light of the complexity of multilateral diplomacy at the UN and the importance of knowing people as well as issues. Yet these changes will mean little unless the career professionals feel that they have meaningful input into the formulation and implementation of policy and are not shut out by the inner circle of ideologues. Throughout the 1940s, 1950s, and 1960s, USUN was the most professional and experienced of all missions and was respected as such. Then the experienced professionals were in the inner circle, had an impact on policy, and many rose to ambassadorial rank at USUN. With the loyal support they provided, even a new permanent representative could function effectively. During the 1970's rapid turnover of staff officers at USUN, combined with a frequent change in permanent representatives, led to a deterioration in the US Mission's professionalism. Under Kirkpatrick the lack of experienced professionals in key roles was a particular handicap in dealing with other UN missions, including those of friendly Western European allies. Another problem was Kirkpatrick's limited availability. She spent much of her time in Washington, abroad, or making speeches and was rarely in the UN building except for specific purposes, such as making a statement or seeing the secretary-general. Neither she nor her principal deputies spent much time in the Delegates Lounge, the time-honored center for informal contacts, picking up information, consulting, and getting acquainted.[23] This is where early warning signals can be picked up on the projected moves of other delegations and where preliminary soundings can be made quickly on UN initiatives. It is especially important for the United States, which is not a member of any geographical group.

However, when Kirkpatrick did appear, she had clout. Though characterized as a "hard-line conservative" and tough in the sense of standing firm on her convictions, Kirkpatrick was not bombastic and did not shout. Her political philosophy and attitude toward the United Nations was very much like Moynihan's, but where he was flamboyant she was low-key. Yet she commanded attention, not only as the representative of a superpower who was clearly supported by the president, but also as a person who crafts her statements with care. Delegates listened carefully, knowing that she meant what she said. But many were turned off by her professiorial style of lecturing and the fact that she did not spend much time listening to other people. A senior diplomat representing one of America's closest allies observed that the Reagan-Kirkpatrick ideology put the United States in a difficult position at the United Nations, and that her confrontational style made it worse.[24]

Kirkpatrick was also criticized for her tendency to lecture Third World representatives as if they were undergraduates, for not learning the intricacies of UN politics, and for preferring to express her ideology rather than focus on concrete political goals. These views were expressed to me in interviews with representatives of friendly NATO allies as well as by Third World representatives and coincide with those gleaned by reporters for major newspapers and a national magazine (which stated, "Friends and foes alike consider Kirkpatrick's staff inexperienced and inept.")[25] A Canadian professor who polled about eighty UN diplomats in connection with a book he is writing told me that they expressed the same types of criticisms I had heard and read.

While she may differ from her critics as to the reasons, Kirkpatrick herself testified to the fact that the United States has been isolated at the UN.[26] In "Problems of the Alliance," she noted:

> At the United Nations, the alliance is not very strong. At the United Nations, the United States frequently stands alone on controversial issues, some of which are very important to us, some of which are important to others. At the United Nations, our European allies often prefer a posture of nonalignment between us and the Group of 77 on the so-called North-South issues, which consume much of the time of that organization. On some other issues, they vote with our adversaries.[27]

On the positive side, Kirkpatrick was credited with giving strong, effective responses to Soviet attacks. She is fluent in French and Spanish, two major languages at the UN. Also, even those who criticize her ideological fervor and style acknowledge that she is not personally vindictive or petty. And her performance improved perceptibly as she gained experience at the UN, particularly in her fourth year, as will be discussed later.

Another plus was her good working relationship with Javier Perez de Cuellar, who became secretary-general of the UN in January 1982. An experienced Peruvian diplomat who has served as his country's ambassador to Moscow, Perez de Cuellar is liked and respected by UN diplomats and the Secretariat's top staff, with whom he worked for almost a decade. He served as Peru's permanent representative to the UN, 1971–75, and was the secretary-general's special representative to Cyprus, 1975–77, and UN undersecretary-general for special political affairs, 1979–81. It is also well known that he did not campaign for the job; consequently, he has no need to bend to political pressures from any member or group of members. Kirkpatrick called him "a man of great intelligence, high integrity; he is an unusually fair, reasonable, decent man."[28] She told me she briefed him regularly on the Middle East, Central America, Namibia, and other areas where the UN and the United States share concerns and that he was most appreciative.[29]

She also expressed full support for the secretary-general's efforts aimed at strengthening the capacity of the United Nations to maintain peace. In a most candid and perceptive introduction to his annual report to the UN General Assembly in September 1982, Perez de Cuellar noted that the Security Council, which the UN Charter charges with primary responsibility for the maintenance of international peace and security, too often finds itself unable to take decisive action to resolve international conflicts. Its resolutions are increasingly defied or ignored. Too often the Council seems powerless to generate the support and influence necessary to insure that its decisions are respected.[30]

Kirkpatrick expressed full support for the secretary-general's efforts to strengthen the UN's role in the maintenance of international peace and security. Despite some skepticism as to prospects for success, she participated actively in informal meetings of the Security Council to consider the secretary-general's suggestions.

ISRAEL

No U.S. representative to the UN has been a firmer friend of Israel than Jeane Kirkpatrick. She did not hesitate to urge using the American veto in the Security Council or voting alone with Israel when she believed that Israel was being treated unfairly. Given the Arab influence with the "nonaligned" movement, which constitutes a majority of UN membership, along with Soviet opportunism, and West European ambivalence, that is often. In the Security Council she also used the potential U.S. veto to secure changes in draft resolutions. The resolution concerning Israel's attack on the Iraqi nuclear reactor was a notable example.

Support for Israel fit her neoconservative philosophy on foreign policy. Her personal sympathy was made clear when she attended the Third World Conference on Soviet Jewry in Jerusalem, March 15–17, 1983. Israel is a democracy, strong, and a firm friend of the United States. And the blatant one-sidedness of the UN majority on Arab-Israeli issues outrages her sense of fair play, as she makes clear in *The Reagan Phenomenon*. In "Israel as Scapegoat," she contrasts UN procedures with the Camp David process, which was oriented toward practical results and limited to the parties directly concerned and the United States as mediator. By contrast, she finds that at the UN the objective has not been to find common ground but to isolate and denigrate Israel and "ultimately to undermine its political legitimacy." A decisive role in this endeavor to undermine Israel's legitimacy has been played by the Palestinian Liberation Organization.[31]

The Security Council was at its biased worst in considering an incident in April 1982 when a foreign-born Jew went berserk and committed violence in one of Islam's most sacred mosques, the Dome of the Rock. A draft resolution implied that responsibility for the act lay not with the individual but with the Israeli authorities, who had unequivocally denounced the act. When the draft resolution came to a vote April 11, the United States vetoed it. Meanwhile the Council was ignoring the bloody Iran-Iraq war, the Vietnamese invasion of Kampuchea, and the Soviet invasion of Afghanistan.

On one important issue of substance—Israeli settlements in the West Bank—Ambassador Kirkpatrick consistently took a position significantly different from that of the Carter administration. She consistently vetoed resolutions condemning these settlements, while recording the Reagan position that, though not illegal, they are "obstacles to peace."

Ambassador Kirkpatrick was like her predecessors in taking a totally firm and strong stand against the repeated and blatantly unfair efforts of certain Arab states to deprive Israel of the right to participate in the UN General Assembly. The procedure specified in the UN Charter for suspending or expelling a member requires a recommendation from the Security Council. Such a recommendation would certainly be vetoed by the United States and probably by Britain and France as well.

A more likely threat is action in the General Assembly to deny Israel participation in its work by rejecting the credentials of its delegation. Such action was taken in 1974 against South Africa, which has not participated in the UN since then. Similar action against Israel, whose delegation is chosen by a representative, democratic government, would not only be contrary to the UN Charter but also grossly unfair. Though the General Assembly condemned the Soviet invasion of Afghanistan, there has been no suggestion that the Soviets be barred from participation. And in 1981, while Iraq was invading Iran, an Iraqi was elected president of the Assembly. Israel, surrounded by enemies, has resorted to arms against threats to its survival, certainly under more serious threat than the Soviet Union and Iraq when they undertook their invasions.

On October 16, 1982, Secretary of State Shultz made the U.S. position clear. He stated that such action would be a clear-cut violation of the UN Charter, would create further conflict and division and "would do grave damage to the entire United Nations system". He warned that, if the action were taken, the U.S. would withdraw from participation in the General Assembly and withhold its assessed contributions.[32]

The attempt to exclude Israel came during the 37th Session of the General Assembly in the fall of 1982. Shultz's warning, made more credible by the withdrawal of the U.S. delegation to the Conference of the International Atomic Energy Agency following the rejection of Israeli credentials there, had a strong impact on UN delegations, including the Arabs. Moreover, Kirkpatrick and her delegation worked hard at persuasion and the Secretary General forcefully lobbied against the attempt to expel Israel, arguing that it would spell disaster for the organization.

The majority of Arabs then backed away from such action, whereupon a non-Arab country, Iran, attempted to bring the issue to a vote. That attempt was easily blocked through a procedural move by Finland which won overwhelming support. The Finnish representative said privately that, having tested the waters, he knew it would be "a piece of cake".[33]

LATIN AMERICA AND PUERTO RICO

Latin America has been an area of great interest to Jeane Kirkpatrick since she began work on her dissertation on Perónist Argentina almost two decades ago. It is not surprising that she has focused major attention on Latin American issues at the UN and had great influence on policymaking in Washington. Her positions have been consistent with the hard-line conservatism expounded in "Dictatorship and Double Standards," particularly with regard to El Salvador and Nicaragua. It seems clear that she and William Clark, then head of the National Security Council, were principally responsible for the replacement of Assistant Secretary of State Thomas Enders and Ambassador to El Salvador Dean Hinton. Enders and Hinton, neither of whom has a notably dovish record in the career Foreign Service, were identified with a two-track approach, that is, negotiations with the rebels in El Salvador and with Nicaragua while continuing military aid to El Salvador. This approach was apparently not hard-line enough for Clark and Kirkpatrick.

In line with its traditional position that Central American and Caribbean issues should be dealt with in the Organization of American States (OAS), a regional organization of the type envisaged in Chapter VIII of the UN Charter, the United States has not brought such issues to the UN. But other countries have, and the United States has had to face the issues there.

At the thirty-sixth session of the General Assembly (1981), a draft resolution was introduced reaffirming the Franco-Mexican communiqué, which supported a negotiated settlement between the government of El Salvador and the rebels. Despite U.S. opposition the resolution was cosponsored by five of its NATO partners. Nine of the ten EEC countries supported it; only the United Kingdom abstained. The resolution was adopted, over the negative votes of some twenty Latin nations. Kirkpatrick deplored this as "an ominous pattern," showing her own conviction that the United States was right and its European allies wrong and that they should have displayed greater solidarity.[34]

At the thirty-seventh session (1982) Nicaragua was elected to one of the two Latin American seats on the UN Security Council. It garnered the necessary two-thirds majority, despite strenuous U.S. efforts to forestall its election. This was in marked contrast with the failure of Cuba in 1979, when it had the chairmanship of the nonaligned group, to win a seat on the Security Council.

On March 23, 1983, Nicaragua brought to the UN Security Council a charge that the United States was aiding rebel groups in their efforts to overthrow the government in Managua. Nicaragua said it did not seek a resolution but rather a public forum to express its concern.

In response, Kirkpatrick described the Nicaraguan complaint as the claim of a new right—"the right of repression of its own people with impunity and with immunity from the consequences thereof." She pointed out that the Nicaraguan ruling group had reneged on its promises to the OAS, in a letter dated July 17, 1979, of "a broadly representative democratic government," with "full observance of human rights" and free elections. She observed that the independent political parties representing the private sector withdrew from the Council of State in protest against the violence and jailing of their leaders and the suppression of free speech; that labor unions "were harnessed and harassed when they tried to resist being incorporated into the state"; that the churches had been progressively repressed; and that no free elections had been held or even scheduled.[35]

Speaking again on March 25, Kirkpatrick found it necessary to take issue with certain friendly or neutral governments (i.e., Mexico, Pakistan, Panama, Zimbabwe, Tanzania, and China), whose statements she said, indicated that "the confusion and intimidation had already had insidious effects."[36]

It is hard to believe that these governments, regardless of the wisdom of their positions, expressed views different from the American assessment as a result of confusion and intimidation. Indeed, Kirkpatrick's statement appears to stand in contrast with her evaluation in her *New York Times* essay of March 31, entitled "U.N. Mugging Fails." There she argued that "the Nicaraguans did not secure broad support for their preferred bilateral approach. Instead support developed for a regional approach to what were clearly regional problems." She cites Venezuela's backing for a conference of the Central American countries "plus five neighboring democracies," Colombia, Mexico, Venezuela, the Dominican Republic, and Panama.

She concluded:

The losers in this unconventional United Nations drama were those who seek to use United Nations arenas and procedures to polarize nations, spread hostility and exacerbate conflict for short-range political advantage. The winners are all those who hope it is not too late to restore the Security Council as an arena for the rational discussion and management of international disputes.[37]

But the support the United States received was in favor of a negotiated settlement, not of the "Contras" trying to destabilize the Nicaraguan government.

It is doubtful that the Sandinistas considered themselves losers. They came to the Security Council in order to have a forum to express their views and get media attention—which they did. U.S. backing of the "Contras" received little support and U.S. enthusiasm for a regional settlement has been notably lacking. Indeed, after Nicaragua accepted the Contadora draft proposal in September 1984, the United States rejected it and exerted pressure on Honduras and El Salvador to demand changes in the proposal. Administration policy to date has emphasized aid to the "Contras" and a negotiated settlement between them and the Sandinistas leading toward a democratic, pluralistic government.

In the Falklands (Malvinas) crisis, Kirkpatrick found herself torn between our British and Latin American allies. Initially she tried to dissuade the U.K. representative, Sir Anthony Parsons from bringing the issue to the Security Council. She felt that airing it there would make the Argentines less willing to compromise. Nevertheless, the British went ahead and the Council began discussion of the issue on April 1, 1982. The next day Argentine troops invaded the Falklands, President Galtieri having ignored Reagan's telephone advice not to resort to force.[38]

Because of the diplomatic skills of Parsons and his team, British démarches in certain key capitals, and the character of the Argentine invasion, Britain won support for a resolution demanding an immediate cessation of hostilities and withdrawal of all Argentine forces from the Falklands (Resolution 502, April 3, 1982). The vote was ten in favor, one against (Panama), and four abstentions (USSR, Poland, China, and Spain). The United States voted with its British ally, and Kirkpatrick, despite her initial misgivings about their bringing the issue to the Council, subsequently expressed admiration for the great skill of Parsons and his team at the UN.[39] Guyana and all five African and Asian members voted with the British, despite the fact that Argentina is sometimes considered a Third World nation and was arguing the question as a colonial issue.

In the ensuing weeks, while Britain prepared its military counterattack, Secretary Haig undertook an exhausting mission of mediation, shuttling between London, Buenos Aires, and Washington. Then on May 2 Secretary-General Perez de Cuellar, who had discreetly stood aside during Haig's attempt, began mediation efforts with the Argentine and British representatives at the UN. (On that same day Haig announced the failure of his mission and the *General Belgrano* was sunk, followed two days later by the sinking of H.M.S. *Sheffield*.) By May 14 Perez was cautiously optimistic that he had an agreement on a "set of ideas for a negotiated settlement"; that is, mutual withdrawal, diplomatic negotiations for a definitive settlement of the dispute, the lifting of sanctions and exclusion zones, and the establishment of transitional arrangements in the Falklands under UN auspices pending the outcome of diplomatic negotiations.

The British, in an earnest effort toward a peaceful solution, accepted the proposal, suggesting only minor alterations designed to clarify provisions concerning troop withdrawal and the participation of the Falkland Islanders in the transitional administration. Kirkpatrick was convinced that it was a good arrangement and spent the whole of one evening trying to persuade Argentina's representative to the UN, Enrique Ros, that Buenos Aires should go along. Unfortunately for all the interested parties, and especially Argentina, the Argentines on May 18 rejected it. That was the end of the secretary-general's mediation effort.[40] On that same day H.M.S. *Fearless* sailed into the waters of the total exclusion zone of the Falklands, and the war began in earnest.

Following the failure of Haig's efforts at peaceful mediation, the United States, to the dismay of the Argentines, gave some logistic and full political support to Britain. Kirkpatrick, concerned about the damage this was doing to U.S. relations with Latin American states, held several meetings with Argentina's foreign minister and its representative to the UN. Even though she cleared these meetings in advance with the president and the State Department, Haig was furious and accused her of being "mentally and emotionally incapable of thinking clearly on this issue" because of her close links with the Latins. She, in turn, criticized him as being incapable of understanding Latin American sensibilities. Her efforts, in fact, were aimed at bringing an end to the fighting.[41]

Meanwhile, at the UN Security Council, Spain and Portugal proposed on June 4 a draft resolution calling for an immediate cease-fire. Britain, whose forces had gained the upper hand, was determined to veto it. Kirkpatrick, with an eye toward the Latins, requested State Department authorization to abstain rather than vote against the resolution, which would in any case be nullified by a British veto. Haig, in Versailles, was finally persuaded to authorize an abstention five minutes after Kirkpatrick had cast the negative vote his earlier instructions required.[42]

Certainly Kirkpatrick cannot be faulted for her determined efforts at the UN to maintain good relations with the Latins, while not abandoning Britain and principle. Yet one has to wonder whether her pursuit of the ideas advanced in "Dictatorship and Double Standards" might not bear some responsibility for Argentina's invasion. During Carter's administration, the Argentine military dictators would have had no doubts about the United States siding with Britain in the event of an Argentine invasion. In contrast, Reagan and Kirkpatrick had been going all out in showing good will toward the Argentines, who in turn were providing military help to the U.S.-supported government in El Salvador. Would President Galtieri have launched the invasion if he had known in advance that, in a showdown, the United States would side with Britain? One cannot be certain, since Galtieri was having domestic problems and the invasion was to some extent an attempted diversion from those problems.

Kirkpatrick was more successful on Puerto Rico. In 1953 the UN General Assembly, in Resolution 748, formally recognized that the people of Puerto Rico had exercised their right to self-determination and removed Puerto Rico from the list of non-self-governing territories. In elections held since then, parties espousing either statehood in the United States or a continuation of the present commonwealth status have averaged about 95 percent of the vote. In a second referendum on status, 60 percent of those voting opted for commonwealth, 39 percent for statehood, and only 1 percent for independence. Nevertheless, in 1982 Cuba, which argues that independence is the only true expression of self-determination for Puerto Rico, requested the inscription on the General Assembly agenda of an item concerning the status of Puerto Rico. It had done the same in 1971. Again, as in 1971, the Cuban move was rejected by a majority. True, the same result had been achieved before, and Cuba has been unsuccessful for more than a decade. Nevertheless, such victories never come easy; the Kirkpatrick team worked hard to achieve it. USUN officers lobbied energetically in New York and, at Kirkpatrick's initiative, Washington instructed a number of American ambassadors to intervene with their respective foreign offices.

OTHER ISSUES

With continued strong support from and lobbying by the ASEAN countries, the Kirkpatrick team also managed to maintain majority support for resolutions calling for withdrawal of foreign (Soviet) forces from Afghanistan and Vietnamese forces from Kampuchea. In the Afghan case, the McHenry team in 1980 achieved a vote of 104 in favor, 18 against, and 18 abstentions, a very solid vote attesting to the aversion of most nonaligned states to superpower aggression and, incidentally, flying in the face of the Moynihan-Kirkpatrick thesis that there is a nonaligned coalition with the Soviet bloc. That strong majority had held up in subsequent sessions. In November 1982 the vote was 114 in favor, 21 against, and 13 abstentions, and similar resolutions were adopted overwhelmingly in 1983 and 1984.

On Namibia little progress has been made. The five-nation contact group, formed in 1977 on the initiative of Andrew Young, has continued its efforts to reach settlement, but the central U.S. role previously played by Donald McHenry has now been transferred almost wholly to Assistant Secretary Chester Crocker and his colleagues in the State Department's Bureau of African Affairs.

The process has on several occasions appeared to be close to fruition, but South Africa has always found some reason to stall or hold out. The Reagan administration's approach to South Africa of "constructive engagement" has produced no visible South African concessions.[43] The current stumbling block, initially introduced by the United States and eagerly embraced by South Africa, is a condition that Cuban troops be withdrawn from neighboring Angola simultaneously with the withdrawal of South African forces from Namibia.

The most dramatic and potentially far-reaching change of position adopted by the Reagan administration was on the Law of the Sea Convention. The convention, comprising more than 300 articles, deals with territorial waters, transit rights through international straits, 200-mile Exclusive Economic Zones, the continental shelf, protecting the marine environment, and facilitating scientific research. Negotiations on the convention went on intensively for ten years, spanning the Nixon, Ford, Carter, and Reagan administrations. By early 1981 agreement seemed near.

The Reagan administration, with its ideological emphasis on unfettered private enterprise, took a very skeptical view of certain provisions of the convention, especially those concerning seabed mining and the establishment of an International Seabed Authority. More than 150 other nations waited for a year while the United States reviewed the provisions of the draft. Then in March 1982 the United States spelled out in dogmatic terms its objections to the provisions that require any mining company to assist the International Seabed Authority (ISA) in exploiting sites equal in size of value to the site it was mining and to transfer technology to the ISA for that purpose. The United States also objected to production ceilings on the mining of the mineral nodules designed to protect land-based producers from oversupply and consequent price declines. Moreover, it opposed the provision under which treaty articles can be amended by agreement among three-quarters of the parties; theoretically at least, the United States could be bound by a treaty provision without ratification by the United States on the advice and consent of the Senate.[44]

Efforts to reach a compromise on the U.S. objections failed. When the convention was voted upon on April 30, 1982, 130 nations were in favor, 4 against (Israel, Turkey, the United States, Venezuela), and 17 abstained (9 Soviet bloc and Belgium, Italy, Luxembourg, the Netherlands, Spain, Thailand, Britain, West Germany).

Ambassador T. T. B. Koh (Singapore), president of the conference that negotiated the convention, and now ambassador to the United States, was deeply disappointed in the U.S. position. After all, the idea of sharing seabed sites resulted from a compromise suggested in 1976 by then Secretary of State Henry Kissinger in a speech at the Pierre Hotel in New York, evidently with clearance from President Ford. As for the required transfer of technology, Koh pointed out that technology was more than just plant and equipment; consequently, mining companies would be far from powerless in dealing with the ISA.[45]

The formulation and presentation of positions on this issue seem to have been directed from Washington rather than by Kirkpatrick.[46] When I asked her in April 1983 about the U.S. position, she replied, "No comment."

The United States has been even more isolated on disarmament issues at the UN. At the thirty-seventh session of the General Assembly, for example, it cast the lone negative votes on Resolution 73, which addressed the urgent need for a Comprehensive Test Ban Treaty, 111–1–35 (abstentions); Resolution 78A, Report on Bilateral Discussions, 114–1–32; Resolution 83, Prevention of an Arms Race in Outer Space, 138–1–7; and Resolution 98A, calling on the Soviets and the United States to resume bilateral negotiations on the proliferation of chemical weapons, 95–1–46.[47] Other NATO powers and the Soviet Union and its allies abstained on these resolutions, except for Resolution 83, which they supported. These lone negative votes were further evidence of the Reagan administration's inclination to confront the nonaligned countries that supported these resolutions.

On budget issues, however, the United States has found allies among the other principal contributors, particularly the Soviet Union. It voted with the Soviet bloc, on the losing side, on budgetary resolutions concerning the International Civil Service Commission, the UN Institute for Training and Research, and the UN Disaster Relief Organization. In November 1982 the United States, Soviet, and British ambassadors made a joint approach to the secretary-general demanding that he put a lid on the total UN budget, which was about $800 million for 1983 (roughly one-thousandth the size of the U.S. budget). The United States assessment is 25 percent of the assessed UN budget, the Soviet (including the Ukranian and Byelorussian SSR) about half of that.

But the American delegations went one step beyond the other principal contributors by unilaterally submitting an amendment to each Assembly resolution that called for additional spending. The amendment said that "in no case will financial obligations incurred exceed the level of resources approved" for the original 1983 budget. Michael J. Berlin suggests that "underlying the policy is the feeling by Kirkpatrick and others in the Reagan Administration that the U.N. Secretariat is becoming the enemy." In a 1982 speech in Washington, Kirkpatrick charged that diplomats at the United Nations and UN bureaucrats themselves are engaged in a Marxist "class war" against the United States and its corporations and are seeking to use the UN in an effort to redistribute the world's wealth to achieve "global socialism."[48]

The Soviets and the Americans have long been strange bedfellows in opposing the rapid growth of the UN budget, which has increased by 73 percent over the last five years. I recall organizing similar joint démarches with the Soviets, British, and French in the late 1960s, when the UN budget was about a fourth of its present level, and the coordinated actions did serve to restrain budget increases for a number of years.

CONCLUDING OBSERVATIONS

In the winter 1983–84 issue of *Foreign Affairs,* I evaluated Kirkpatrick's first three years at the UN.[49] The article maintained that she had, indeed, lived up to her own criteria as she expressed them in January 1982:

"We take the United Nations very seriously . . . we make certain that when we speak we are serious and credible . . . and pursue a consistent policy over time, letting our actions demonstrate that we are, indeed, serious people who notice and who care and who can distinguish between actions and between countries who behave like friends and supporters of democratic institutions—and those who do not."

She also emphasized that these are the policies of President Reagan.[50] Certainly she has shown that the United States can be tough and consistent, but is that the same as being influential? While influence is always hard to measure, the record of her tenure, along with that of the only other U.S. permanent representative who followed a confrontational policy, Moynihan, suggests the contrary. In her first three years, Kirkpatrick cast fourteen vetoes (a high proportion of the thirty-six vetoes the United States had cast); Young, in a comparable period, cast only three. For 38 years the United States had never had to stand alone in voting against a Security Council resolution critical of American action, but it was forced to do so on October 28, 1983; no other member voted against the draft resolution deploring the US invasion of Grenada and calling for the withdrawal of forces.

The failure of the United States to block the election to the Security Council of either Guyana or Nicaragua by the General Assembly in 1981 and 1982, respectively, is in marked contrast to the defeat of Cuba's election effort in 1979. Also noteworthy is the great difficulty the United States experienced in mustering nine votes on the Security Council on September 12, 1983, for a resolution deploring the Soviets' shooting down of a civilian Korean airliner with 269 innocent victims aboard. The unfortunate remark by Ambassador Charles Lichenstein on September 19, 1983, suggesting that, if UN delegates did not like New York, the U.S. delegations would cheerfully bid them a fond farewell as they "sailed off into the sunset," may have been good domestic politics but did not play well among UN delegates. Kirkpatrick's own statement, in an NBC television interview October 30, that "the U.N. is against us" does not suggest a state of mind that would view the organization as a place where the United States can win friends and influence people.

Her consistency, seriousness, and toughness were respected by other delegations. So was the fact that she clearly had the ear of the president. And, unlike Andrew Young, she has not embarrassed the president by public actions or statements contrary to established policy. Yet, overall, most UN representatives, including those of European allies and other friendly governments, are critical of her performance for three main reasons:

1. Her ideological approach involved repeated, often unnecessary, confrontations with Third World representatives and made cooperation difficult even for friendly delegations. Diplomacy normally strives to expand one's circle of friends and narrow the circle of enemies. Her approach tended to do the opposite, though it may have provided comfort to beleaguered friends. Her approach also tended to diminish public support for the UN because she spoke more often in public as a critic than a supporter.

2. Her professorial speaking style, her lack of diplomatic experience, and her relative inaccessibility have also hampered her effectiveness. Delegates complained that she had little time to listen to them in New York.
3. Her top staff, especially her close ideological friends in the USUN, also lacked diplomatic and UN experience. They had to learn on the job the skills of listening, lobbying, and negotiating, and did not progress rapidly. In the 1960s USUN had the experienced staff and network of friends at the UN, while the Soviet staff was relatively inexperienced. Now the roles are reversed.

The *Foreign Affairs* article concluded:

> Yet the fundamental issue is not technique or speaking style; it is the approach the United States and other members take toward the United Nations. Should the UN be primarily an arena for confrontation or a forum for accommodation? And in which direction should the United States, as a major power, lead? The experience of the Moynihan and Kirkpatrick incumbencies appears to suggest that the strategy of confrontation serves the interest neither of the United States nor the United Nations.

In 1984, Kirkpatrick's last full year at the UN, these observations still seemed fair and well-grounded. Yet the United States was clearly more successful at the thirty-ninth General Assembly in the fall of 1984 than at the previous three. There was much less harsh rhetoric directed at the United States; references singling out the United States and Israel in a resolution on military relations with South Africa were deleted in a separate vote; Thailand won a Security Council seat against the Soviet candidate, Mongolia; and the budget increase was held to a bare minimum. The United States continued to vote in a small minority or alone on many resolutions dealing with South Africa, the Palestinians, disarmament, human rights in El Salvador, Guatemala, Chile, and the Law of the Sea, but the mood of accommodation on many significant issues was notable.

What factors were responsible for the improvement in 1984? First, there was a "revolt of the moderates" (Kirkpatrick's term) in the Third World. Some observers attribute the revolt to the tough Reagan-Kirkpatrick tactics—keeping records of votes and speeches at the UN, cutting aid to Zimbabwe, and speaking out sharply in response to attacks on the United States.[51] These tactics may have influenced some Third World delegations, but it should be noted that they were counterproductive when used by Moynihan in 1975–76 and by Kirkpatrick in her first three years.

My own investigation and conversations with well-informed UN representatives and Secretariat officials indicate that more important factors were involved. The most significant was a change in the situation and attitudes of the Third World countries. During the year preceding the thirty-ninth General Assembly, a majority of them had realized that their politics of confrontation and demands for global negotiations had become counterproductive. This realization was manifested at the sixth session of the UN Conference on Trade and Development in Manila and at the Nonaligned Conference in New Delhi. The passage of the chairmanship of the conference from Castro to Indira Gandhi helped to shift the leadership from extremists to moderates. Notable at New Delhi was the emphasis on urgent, specific problems—debts, commodity prices, protectionism, actions by the World Bank and the IMF—rather than global negotiations on an entire new economic order. The desperate situation of many developing countries virtually thrust this wisdom upon them. And, as they looked at these urgent problems, it was clear that, however much they might be disappointed with Western responses, there was no other place they could turn to for the capital, the technology, and the markets they need. Experience over many years has taught them that they can expect very little from the Soviet bloc.

It also became clear that resolutions or actions that outrage public opinion in the Western democracies could harm prospects for cooperation by Western governments. This realization strengthened the hands of moderate leaders in the Third World.

One of these, Ambassador P. J. F. Lusaka of Zambia, said in his initial address as president of the General Assembly:

> What is required at this critical juncture is a time to pause, to reflect deeply and to reevaluate the direction in which we must move if our Organization is to regain its credibility and full acceptance. This is not the time for factious rhetoric. . . . What is required is a return to that period of our history and development when the formulation of decisions was an effort requiring close consultations with all those concerned.[52]

His efforts struck a responsive chord among other moderate leaders, notably delegates from the ASEAN countries, moderate Africans, the Caribbean states, the West Europeans, and some key Latin Americans.

On the specific issue of the Israeli credentials, Lusaka urged that "we should avoid any step that would vitiate the principle of universality of membership." He had, in fact, been working privately for months with Third World delegations against any move to bar the Israeli delegation. Another major factor was the firm U.S. statement that any action to deny Israeli participation in the Assembly would bring about American withdrawal. The move to reject Israeli's credentials was rejected by an even larger margin than in previous years.

Three other political factors deserve mention. The continuing Soviet devastation of Afghanistan and the Vietnamese invasion of Kampuchea have had a significant impact on the thinking of Third World countries. The long war between Iran and Iraq has weakened Arab and Moslem cooperation. And the split in the PLO has reduced its leverage. PLO representatives indicated that Yasir Arafat was planning to address the Assembly; however, when they were informed that he would not receive protocol treatment equivalent to a head of state, as he did in 1975, the planned visit was shelved.

The disastrous famine in Africa and the sympathetic Western response to it had an important impact on the Africans. The West Europeans worked closely with the Africans to develop a UN program for aid to Africa and then all agreed to wait until the American delegation could get authorization to go along on a consensus resolution.

Further, there has been disenchantment with the Arabs among many African states. The flow of aid from OPEC's bonanza in the 1970s was disappointing, and the weakening oil market has lowered expectations even more. Moreover, many Africans realized that the 1975 insertion of a phrase equating Zionism with racism, at Arab and Soviet instigation, substantially weakened Western support for the first UN Decade Against Racial Discrimination and damaged the United Nations' standing in Western eyes. The Assembly's resolution on the second Decade made no such reference, and was adopted by consensus.

These favorable developments were significantly influenced by changes in the American stance. Reagan's address at the opening of the General Assembly, coming at a time when the president had moved from a confrontational posture toward one of negotiation with the Soviets, set the tone for the entire discussion on disarmament. Moreover, Reagan's toning down of his own rhetoric provided a good example to other member states. The new American pragmatism was further demonstrated by close cooperation with the Soviets in staving off challenges to the Antarctica treaty and in holding down the UN budget.

One final factor should be mentioned. There has been a tendency for the General Assembly during American presidential election campaigns either to postpone its meeting until after the elections or to act moderately during the campaign. The thirty-ninth session tended to fit the latter pattern.

Jeane Kirkpatrick, recognized as a loyal, dedicated, and authoritative representative of the president, clearly benefited from his effective presentation and change in stances. Her credibility and seriousness were never in doubt, and the experience she had gained during her four-year tenure resulted in a more effective performance. Ironically, the session demonstrated that the United States has major power and influence at the UN, in contrast to Kirkpatrick's earlier assertions that it had neither and was, in fact, "impotent."

Indeed, the United States has always had the power to make the UN ineffectual. No military action can be taken against the U.S. or Soviet veto. No international economic program of any consequence can succeed without American participation. The real question is whether this power will be used to reinforce the United Nations' effectiveness (if others are willing to cooperate) or simply to limit damage, restrain the budget, and castigate and punish opponents. If the United States chooses the latter option, moderates in the Third World will be disillusioned and discredited; the glimmer of hope evidenced in 1984, that there can be a return to negotiation and accommodation rather than rhetoric and confrontation, will soon vanish.

Jeane Kirkpatrick resigned early in 1985, to be succeeded by General Vernon Walters. Having served four years—the longest of any U.S. permanent representatives since Adlai Stevenson—she decided to return to Georgetown University, to teach, write, and speak.

NOTES

1. Jeane J. Kirkpatrick, address to the National Committee on American Foreign Policy, New York, June 2, 1982, reproduced in the *American Foreign Policy Newsletter,* August 1982. See also J. J. Kirkpatrick, "U.S. Security in Latin America" and "Reflections on Totalitarianism" in *Dictatorships and Double Standards* (New York: Simon and Schuster, 1982), pp. 53–91 and 96–138.

2. Jeane J. Kirkpatrick, *The Reagan Phenomenon—and Other Speeches on Foreign Policy* (Washington, D.C.: American Enterprise Institute, 1983), pp. 3–16.

3. Jeane J. Kirkpatrick, "Dictatorship and Double Standards," *Commentary,* November 1979, pp. 34–45. This essay is reprinted in her 1982 book of collected essays and speeches, *Dictatorships and Double Standards,* (Washington, D.C.: American Enterprise Institute).

4. Theodore Draper, review of *Dictatorships and Double Standards,* in *New York Times Book Review,* July 25, 1982, pp. 12–13. See also Alan Tonelson, "Human Rights: The Bias We Need," *Foreign Policy,* Winter 1982–83, pp. 55–61.

5. Interviews with UN ambas-

sadors, a veteran journalist, and an experienced scholar on the United Nations.

6. "The Problem with the United Nations," in *The Reagan Phenomenon,* op. cit., pp. 92–98. See also A. Yeselson and A. Gaglione, *A Dangerous Place* (New York: Viking, 1974), which is a source that Kirkpatrick quotes in expounding her philosophy.

7. A. Leroy Bennett, *International Organizations,* 3rd ed. (Englewood Cliffs, N.J.: Prentice Hall, 1984), pp. 130–31. See also S. M. Finger, *Your Man at the U.N.: People, Politics and Bureaucracy in Making Foreign Policy,* (New York: New York University Press, 1980), for additional examples of how decisions at the United Nations have contributed to the settlement of both political and economic disputes, especially pp. 4–9, 53–54, 57–64, 116–24, 172, 179–89.

8. Reproduced in *The Reagan Phenomenon,* op. cit., pp. 79–91.

9. Ibid., p. 104.

10. *Time,* on October 26, 1981, referred to the letter as an undiplomatic "letter bomb."

11. David J. Shapiro, "Third World Moderates Rebound," *The Interdependent,* March/April 1983.

12. Ibid.

13. *New York Times,* October 21, 1983.

14. See Marian Christy, "The Frenetic World of Jeane Kirkpatrick," *Boston Globe,* July 19, 1981.

15. *The Reagan Phenomenon,* op. cit., inside dust jacket.

16. Interview with senior official at USUN, April 13, 1983.

17. Dorothy Rabinowitz, "Reagan's 'Heroine' at the U.N.," *New York,* July 20, 1981, p. 36.

18. Leon Hadar, "Jeane Kirkpatrick: Joining the Jackals," *Jerusalem Post,* June 26, 1981.

19. Interviews with a senior West European diplomat, February 22,

1983, and a former senior USUN official, April 14, 1983. See also *Washington Post,* November 25, 1982, p. A-33.

20. See Rabinowitz, op. cit., pp. 40–41. Also, press releases from USUN and Bernard Nossiter, "New Team at U.N.: Common Roots and Philosophies," *New York Times,* March 3, 1983.

21. Interviews with a senior West European diplomat, November 19, 1982. Also, interview with a professor who had surveyed more than 80 UN missions, May 6, 1983. See also James Fallows, "The Ordeal of Kenneth Adelman," *The Atlantic,* June 1983.

22. *The Reagan Phenomenon,* op. cit., pp. 103–5.

23. A series of more than twenty personal interviews conducted from November 1982 to May 1983.

24. Personal interviews, January–May 1983.

25. *Time,* October 26, 1981.

26. "Standing Alone," reproduced in *The Reagan Phenomenon,* op. cit., pp. 79–91.

27. "Problems of the Alliance," reproduced in *The Reagan Phenomenon,* op. cit., pp. 174–75.

28. Ibid., p. 215.

29. Interview with Jeane Kirkpatrick, April 7, 1983.

30. Introduction to the Annual Report of the Secretary-General on the Work of the Organization, *UN Chronicle,* October 1982, p. 2. See also Ernst B. Haas, "Regime decay: Conflict management and international organization, 1945–81," *International Organization,* Spring 1983, p. 189.

31. Reproduced in *The Reagan Phenomenon,* op. cit., pp. 109–18.

32. *New York Times,* October 17, 1982, p. 20. See also S. M. Finger, "How U.S. Can Protect Israel in the U.N.," *Newsday,* July 15, 1982.

33. *The Interdependent,* March/April 1983, p. 5.

34. *The Reagan Phenomenon,* op.

cit., pp. 174–75.

35. USUN Press Release 21 (83), March 24, 1983. For further insight into Kirkpatrick's thinking see "U.S. Security and Latin America," in *Dictatorships and Double Standards*, op. cit., pp. 53–95.

36. USUN Press Release 23 (83), March 25, 1983.

37. *New York Times,* March 31, 1983, p. A23. The reference to the "swaggering dictator" and the Panama Canal is from her article, "Dictatorships and Double Standards," discussed earlier.

38. *Sunday Times of London* Insight Team, *War in the Falklands,* (New York: Harper and Row, 1982), pp. 111–30.

39. *The Reagan Phenomenon,* op. cit., p. 103.

40. *War in the Falklands,* op. cit., pp. 176–84.

41. Ibid., pp. 256–57.

42. Ibid., pp. 257–58. See also Anthony Parsons, "The Falklands crisis in the United Nations, 31 March–14 June 1982," *International Affairs* Spring 1983, pp. 169–78, for a superb account by an insider.

43. See Robert Rotberg, "On Southern Africa," *New York Times,* December 10, 1982, op-ed page. See also S. M. Finger, "Viewpoints," *Newsday,* April 12, 1981.

44. *UN Chronicle,* June 1982, pp. 3–22. See also Elizabeth Mann Borgese, "Law of the Sea: The Next Phase," *World Politics* 83/84 (Guilford, Conn.: Dushkin, 1983).

45. Interview with Ambassador T. T. B. Koh, New York, January 4, 1983.

46. See Leigh S. Ratiner, "The Law of the Sea: A Crossroads for American Foreign Policy," *Foreign Affairs,* Summer 1982, pp. 1006–21. This article by one of the U.S. negotiators goes into great detail on the positions of individuals and departments in Washington and also describes the events of spring 1982. It contains no mention of Ambassador Kirkpatrick or of the U.S. delegation to the United Nations.

47. *UN Chronicle,* January 1983, pp. 135–39.

48. Michael J. Berlin, "U.N. Budget Growth: Major Donors Shout They Won't Take It Anymore," *The Interdependent,* January 1983, p. 5.

49. S. M. Finger, "The Reagan-Kirkpatrick Policies and the United Nations," *Foreign Affairs,* Winter 1983–84, pp. 436–57.

50. *The Reagan Phenomenon,* op. cit., pp. 117–18.

51. See Walter Goodman, "Kirkpatrick's View of U.N. Job: Leader of a Revolt," *New York Times,* December 22, 1984, p. 2; Michael J. Berlin, "U.N. Session Marked by U.S. Resurgence," *Washington Post,* December 24, 1984, p. 8; and William Korey, "A Turning Point on the East River," *Wall Street Journal,* January 14, 1985, editorial page.

52. General Assembly Official Record, September 18, 1984, Statement by Amb. Paul J. F. Lusaka, President of the thirty-ninth session of the U.N. General Assembly.

CHAPTER X

A General at the UN: Vernon A. Walters

Vernon A. (Dick) Walters succeeded Jeane Kirkpatrick in May 1985. He represents a formidable array of talents and experience: a career army officer who rose to the rank of Lieutenant General; deputy director of the Central Intelligence Agency; and ambassador-at-large, who went to 108 countries on special missions for President Reagan between 1981 and 1985. He speaks seven foreign languages, five of them fluently.[1]

Like his predecessor, Jeane Kirkpatrick, Walters is a conservative and staunch anti-Communist in international politics. He describes himself as "slightly right of center, not a superpatriot, a believer in the values of the country" and as "a pragmatist tinged with idealism." He is clearly an enthusiastic supporter of President Reagan whom he calls "a man who has given the country back a pride in being American."[2] He has also had a record of firm support for right-wing dictatorships, notably in Chile and Argentina.

Their shared conservatism in foreign policy notwithstanding, there are significant differences between the way Walters and Kirkpatrick have functioned at the UN. His approach is much less confrontational. He does not hesitate to make pungent statements when the situation requires, nor to veto a resolution unfair to the United States or Israel. But he has made a noteworthy effort to cultivate other representatives, uses his language skills effectively, is an entertaining raconteur and is more accessible. He is not an eloquent speaker, but he does not give the feeling that he is talking down to other representatives.[3]

Walters has been handicapped somewhat by his frequent absences on special missions abroad at President Reagan's behest. He appears to welcome such assignments, even though they take him away from New

York and contact with other delegates. These assignments, made in recognition of the experience and success Walters has had as special emissary over the years, also provide him with the stimulation of dealing with top governmental leaders; they probably make some of his UN colleagues appear less important or interesting. One longtime observer of the UN reports that, while Walters tries to be chummy with foreign representatives, he is more adept at expressing his own viewpoint and telling anecdotes than at listening. Still, his more positive approach toward the UN and his genuine efforts to be friendly have made him more popular than his predecessor.

There is also a distinct difference in the way they have chosen their key associates. Kirkpatrick picked dedicated, intelligent ideologues with little diplomatic experience. Walters made it a point to replace all her top deputies and has brought in people with diplomatic experience. His clean sweep, however, included Ambassador Harvey Feldman, who was a career diplomat. His top political deputies, Ambassadors Herbert Okun and Patricia Byrne, have each had more than thirty years experience in the career foreign service. Ambassador Joseph Reed, representative to the UN Economic and Social Council, had five years of experience with the World Bank and was Ambassador to Morocco, 1981–85. Ambassador Hugh Montgomery, Alternate Representative for Special Political Affairs, is a Ph.D. from Harvard, served for 28 years on a variety of CIA assignments in Europe and was director of the Bureau of Intelligence and Research in the State Department when he was selected by Walters. Montgomery, a personal friend and former colleague of Walters in the CIA, has spent very little time at the United Nations, remaining in Washington most of the time. As Counselor for Press and Public Affairs Walters picked Richard C. Hottelet, a veteran correspondent who had covered the UN for CBS News for more than three decades. Though all are experienced professionals, only Hottelet was steeped in UN affairs when he was appointed. Walters, a lifelong bachelor, takes his responsibility seriously. He is liked by his staff and knows and cares about what they are doing.

While Walters's appointment was under consideration Secretary Shultz reportedly suggested that he not have cabinet rank and not sit in on National Security Council meetings. But Walters did not accept the post until he was assured of status equal to that of his predecessor.[4] Since he spent four years as ambassador-at-large carrying out more than a hundred missions for the President, he obviously has a good rapport with Reagan. Yet it remains to be seen whether Walters has the clout on foreign policy issues that Kirkpatrick had. Her reputation was made as a thinker and articulator of policy, his as an implementer.

Now over two years into his assignment, Walters and his team have a creditable record of achievement under very difficult circumstances.

At its fortieth session the General Assembly, for the first time ever, unanimously and openly condemned international terrorism.[5] It also criticized, for the first time, human rights violations in Soviet-occupied Afghanistan and in Iran. By larger majorities than before, it demanded the withdrawal of Soviet troops from Afghanistan and Vietnamese forces from Cambodia. At the initiative of the Secretary General, strongly supported by the United States, the Assembly decided to convene a World Conference on Drug Abuse Control in 1987. It also adopted a resolution calling for renewed efforts in the Geneva Conference on Disarmament to negotiate a convention to prohibit the development, production and stockpiling of chemical weapons.[6]

The fortieth session was notable for "greater sobriety in debate and in voting," which made it "more productive and promising." A USUN assessment observed further:

> The United States has reason to be satisfied with what appears to be a change in the confrontational tactics and hostile voting patterns noted in recent years. It still took exception on occasion, to the tone of debate and the language of draft resolutions containing attacks on itself as well as on friends and allies. But when the United States, for instance, challenged seven invidious references in draft resolutions on Namibia, it obtained the necessary broad support to have the offending phrases and paragraphs deleted. More important than the immediate issue was the willingness of Third World countries to vote with the United States for civility and objectivity in highly political matters.[7]

But the big crisis for Walters was yet to come. In 1986 the UN was threatened with financial strangulation. The withholding of assessed payments by many members had left the UN with a serious shortage of funds, which assumed crisis proportions when the United States in 1985–86 unilaterally made drastic cuts in its assessed contributions.

The seeds of this crisis were planted in 1964–65, when the General Assembly failed to enforce Article 19 against member states more than two years behind in their assessments, notably the Soviet Union and France. As described in Chapter VI, Arthur Goldberg then pointed out that "if any member can insist on making an exception to the principle of collective financial responsibility with respect to certain activities of the Organization, the United States reserves the same option to make exceptions if, in our view, strong and compelling reasons exist for doing so. There can be no double standard among members of the Organization."[8]

Some may question how "strong and compelling" American reasons were, but there is no question that the cuts were draconian. The Kassebaum amendment called for a unilaterally declared reduction from 25 percent to 20 percent unless voting on the budget was weighted in proportion to assessment, resulting in a cut of $42 million. An additional cut of over $10 million resulted from an action sponsored by Congressman Don Sundquist (R. Tenn.) allegedly to counteract those portions of the Secretariat salaries remitted by Soviet nationals to their government; it is difficult to know how this sum was calculated. A unilateral decision by Washington to change the budgetary formula for handling U.S. taxes resulted in an additional cut of $15 million. A further $7 million reduction represented the U.S. share of the difference between the budget initially proposed in September 1985 and the final budget adopted by the General Assembly that year, which reflects factors of inflation, exchange rate fluctuations, and additional program costs. These cuts, plus $35 million not paid in 1985, added up to about $100 million, an insignificant part of the U.S. budget but a crippling blow to the UN. They would be far more than required to satisfy the average cuts mandated by Gramm-Rudman-Hollings, yet the Administration interpreted the law to be a double whammy, putting the Gramm-Rudman cuts on top of the others.

This shortfall, combined with the delinquencies of other governments, put the UN in desperate straits. As a result the secretary general instituted severe austerity measures: a freeze in recruitment; non-extension of staff beyond the age of 60; a delay in promotions and cost-of-living adjustments, a reduction in travel, consultants and overtime and other economies which should effect savings of about $30 million. He subsequently recommended, and the Assembly agreed to, savings of an additional $30 million through the deferment of major capital expenditures; a reduction in meetings, documentation, and publications; and the reduction of certain low priority programs.[9] Some of these economies were healthy, but others represented a threat to the muscle and bone of the organization. Our NATO allies were troubled by the U.S. position, which would either threaten the viability of the UN or shift the burden of the U.S. shortfall to them. Even the Soviets, notorious for their stinginess towards the UN and for withholding huge sums of assessments, made a contribution of $10 million in 1986 to ease the crisis.

In this emergency Walters and his staff worked energetically and effectively toward a compromise which offered the hope of averting disaster—the overriding issue of the forty-first General Assembly.

Groundwork for the compromise was laid by the report of a broadly representative eighteen-nation "Group of High-Level Intergovernmental Experts to Review the Efficiency of the Administrative and Financial Functioning of the United Nations" (G-18), established by the Fortieth General Assembly on Japan's initiative.[10] The objective was to deal with the complaints of the United States and other major contributors who provide over 80 percent of the financing, against waste, inefficiency and the majority-vote adoption of budgets which they opposed. Another goal was to satisfy the aims of the Kassebaum amendment without necessarily introducing weighted voting in a formal way.

The Group of Experts met in four working sessions between February 25th and August 15th to review a state of affairs in which the General Assembly established "new organs, committees, commissions, and expert groups leading to overlapping agendas and duplication of work." The Group's report to the General Assembly spoke of significant growth in the number of conferences and meetings and a volume of documentation that has "surpassed the limit of what can be studied and constructively used." It found parallel growth in the personnel of the UN Secretariat from 1,546 in 1946 to 11,423 in 1986, the structure "complex, fragmented and top-heavy" with inadequately qualified staff, particularly in the higher categories. The experts recommended severe cuts in staff among some seventy steps to reduce administrative fat, procedural lethargy, and wasteful expense. While recognizing the need for change, the Group was not able to agree upon a new process for drawing up the budget that would check these ills at the source. The United States, the Soviet Union, Japan, Canada, the members of the European Community, Singapore, and India, among others, urged the requirement of decision by consensus in the budgeting procedure. In an enhanced Committee on Program and Coordination, whose twenty-one members included the large contributors, representatives of the entire UN membership could reconcile their views on a budget ceiling, its broad priorities, and a contingency fund to cover unforeseen supplemental expenditures. Those who opposed such a course professed to see it as giving the large contributors an effective veto on the Assembly's budgetary prerogative and contravening the one-nation-one-vote provision of the Charter.

On September 22nd, 1986, President Reagan addressed the Assembly—for the fifth time, more than any U.S. President before him—with words of admonition and reassurance. "The United States," he said, "remains committed to the United Nations. For over forty years, this organization has provided an international forum for harmonizing conflicting national interests and has made a significant contribution in such fields as peacekeeping, humanitarian assistance and eradicating disease." He noted:

This organization itself faces a critical hour . . . that is usually stated as a fiscal crisis. But we can turn this 'crisis' into an opportunity. The important reforms proposed by the Group of Experts can be the first step toward restoring the organization's status and effectiveness. . . . And you have my word for it: My country, which has always given the U.N. generous support, will continue to play a leading role in the effort to achieve its noble purposes.[11]

Speaking to the Assembly on October 15, Ambassador Walters warned:

The United Nations is at a critical juncture. It is facing a crisis of reform, the root causes of which are political and bureaucratic. . . . If the agreed recommendations of the G-18 report are enacted, hand in hand with the establishment of a program and decision-making mechanism operating on the basis of consensus, the Organization's ability to live up to the goals of the Charter . . . to fulfill the hopes of the peoples of the United Nations, particularly the poorest and most defenseless, will be measurably increased.

It took two months of arduous negotiation to bring that wish to fruition. At one point, as negotiations in New York seemed to be deadlocked, President Reagan intervened with personal letters to a number of key African leaders. Stressing the importance of the issue, he reaffirmed his Administration's desire to preserve the UN's credibility and its adherence to the original goals. Mr. Reagan appealed for each leader's assistance in correcting the current disagreement, noting that this would help him to gain the approval of Congress.[12]

On December 19 the Assembly adopted a resolution approving the essential recommendations of the Group of Experts, spelling out the budget-making procedure, which was to take effect fully with the beginning of the next biennial budget cycle in 1988.[13] Whether it would actually provide a solution would depend on the actions of the governments involved. On the one hand, a resort to voting by the majority to override objections by the major contributors would cause a breakdown of the arrangement. Conversely, failure of the major contributors to pay their assessed contributions or an abuse of the consensus procedure to enforce their will on individual items would also cause a collapse. Thus the solvency of the United Nations would depend on the willingness of member governments to live up to the principles of the compromise resolution.

Another important element is the implementation of recommendations by the Group of Eighteen to reduce the number of organs, committees, and commissions, the excessive documentation, and Secretariat staff. While there was general agreement on the need for such reductions, there was bound to be resistance from governments as their own nationals and favorite programs were targeted. Only a realization of the grave consequences of not carrying out these resolutions can overcome such parochialism, and the Secretary General does have a strong mandate in the Assembly's resolution.

On the U.S. side, President Reagan called the resolution "historic." Ambassador Walters called it "a great day for the United States . . . great for the United Nations, a great day for mankind" and said he would recommend "that the United States meet its assessed contribution."[14] In February 1987 the administration indicated that it would ask Congress for authorization of the full assessments for the United Nations and its specialized agencies for fiscal years 1988 and 1989.[15] In March the Department of State submitted suggested language to the relevant congressional committees that would modify the Kassebaum amendment. The proposed language recognized that "with the adoption of General Assembly Resolution 41/213, the United Nations has taken a first concrete step toward fundamental reform on its decision-making procedures on program budget matters." It would leave it to the President to determine whether the decision-making procedure established by that resolution "is being implemented and its results respected by the General Assembly" and, on that basis, authorize payments of assessments in excess of 20 percent.[16]

The underlying problem was, of course, political. While Congress was concerned about holding down expenditures in light of huge deficits in the national budget, the sums involved can have little impact on those deficits. The problem was the perception among many, if not most, Congressmen that the United Nations majority had turned the UN into a wasteful organization that is hostile to the United States—a perception fed by Jeane Kirkpatrick and the Heritage Foundation. The compromise resolution emerging from the financial crisis could succeed only if the majority of UN members took American concerns into account in their actions and if the Congress were to change its perception of the United Nations and the organizational changes.

In other respects the forty-first session was routine. The great international political issues—Cyprus, Namibia, South Africa, the Iran-Iraq War, Arab-Israel peace, Afghanistan, Cambodia and Nicaragua—were discussed but not moved perceptibly toward solution. Once again resolutions were adopted by large majorities calling for the withdrawal of foreign troops from Afghanistan and Cambodia, though the Soviets and Vietnamese were not cited by name. On the other hand, the United

States was condemned by name for its air raid on Libya in April 1986. The vote on that resolution was 79 in favor, 28 opposed, 33 abstentions. For comparison, the vote on the Afghanistan resolution was 122–20–11 and on Vietnam 115–21–16; only the Soviet-bloc and client states voted against these two resolutions.

There was the usual plethora of anti-Israel resolutions, spurred by the Arab and Soviet groups. Yet a substantial majority, with a strong position taken by the United States, again rejected a proposal to deny the validity of the Israeli delegation's credentials, which would have prevented Israel's participation in the Assembly. The proposal was rejected by a vote of 77–40, with 16 abstentions.

More noteworthy was the thirteenth Special Session of the General Assembly (May 1986), convened to deal for the first time with the problems of a single region, the critical economic situation in Africa. The Special Session's theme was partnership. On the African side, responsible spokesmen led by President Abdou Diouf of Senegal, chairman of the Organization of African Unity, overrode the radicals. They discarded the old confrontational clichés which portrayed Africa's troubles as the legacy of colonial rule and their solutions in terms of transfers of wealth from the industrial north to the developing nations of the south. They dealt, instead, with Africa's responsibility to cope with its needs as best it can if it is to call for help from outside—in short, policy reform and self-help. A Program of Action for African Recovery and Development 1986–1990 underscored the "primary responsibility" of the governments of Africa for the economic and social development of their countries. It eschewed grandiose proposals in favor of such realistic steps as: moving toward self-sufficiency in food by placing "primary focus" on women farmers who dominate food production in most countries; eliminating pricing policies that discourage production and strengthening incentive schemes; radical change in the educational systems to generate skills, knowledge, and attitudes relevant to Africa's needs; encouraging "the positive role of the private sector;" and South-South cooperation.[17]

At the forty-first session of the General Assembly, however, there was an increased incidence of solo votes by the United States, often withdrawing from a consensus in situations where our close allies and friends were willing to go along. It is difficult to assess the degree to which this practice resulted from the permanent representative's own convictions or from instructions from the State Department, influenced by the hard-line attitude of Alan Keyes, the assistant secretary of state for international organization affairs.

The United States also had a setback at the February-March 1987 meeting of the Human Rights Commission in Geneva. On February 24 it submitted a draft resolution that expressed deep concern over reported "serious human rights violations in Cuba, in particular of the rights to freedom of expression and association, freedom from arbitrary arrest and detention and freedom of thought, conscience and religion." It also appealed to the Government of Cuba "to release all those detained for their political views and activities and to allow any Cuban who might wish to leave or return to Cuba to do so without hindrance" and it called for an investigation of the situation (E.CN 4/1987.L29/Rev.1).

The United States made a major effort to build support for its resolution. President Reagan stressed its urgency in personal notes to other heads of state. Ambassadors in forty-two capitals called on Foreign Ministry officials, and other Administration officials sent out more than four hundred cables urging support. Walters himself went to Geneva to present the resolution to the Human Rights Commission, made impassioned speeches on its behalf and made personal contact with five Latin American heads of state.[18]

Cuba countered with a draft resolution calling attention to alleged human rights violations in the United States, particularly with respect to Indians, blacks and other minorities. Then India launched procedural motions not to consider either resolution. The purported reason was a desire not to "politicize" the Human Rights Commission, though India had shown no such solicitude when human rights complaints singled out Chile, Israel and South Africa. The Commission voted, 19–18, with six abstentions, not to consider the United States resolution and 17–15, with eleven abstentions, not to consider the Cuban proposal. The United States voted against both motions; it was prepared to have decisions on the Cuban proposal as well as its own. The Soviet Union, and its satellites, voted for both Indian motions, as did Peru, Argentina and Mexico, while Colombia and Venezuela abstained. It was a distressing setback for the United States, which had mounted a major campaign against human rights violations in Cuba. Particularly distressing was the lack of support from the Latin American members, except for Costa Rica.

CONCLUDING REMARKS

At this writing (March 1987) Walters has been at his post two years, which may be only the midpoint of his service; consequently, evaluations made now may be subject to change. Nevertheless, certain tentative conclusions can be drawn.

1. He has demonstrated a commitment to the survival of the

United Nations, with active U.S. participation, based on joint efforts by
the members to act responsibly on UN budgets and drastically reduce
waste, duplication and bloated bureaucracies.

2. He has restored professionalism in the upper ranks of the Mission, naming experienced diplomats as his principal deputies.

3. He has made a conscious effort to cultivate other delegates,
using his extraordinary language talents and fund of anecdotes. Though
he is frequently absent on special assignments for President Reagan and
may talk better than he listens, Walters has nevertheless been effective
in his interpersonal contacts.

4. His outstanding achievement may be the compromise resolution of December 19, 1986, aimed at resolving the financial/political
crisis of the United Nations and improving the administrative functioning of the organization. As indicated earlier, the success or failure of
that compromise depends on actions he cannot control—the degree of
cooperation of other countries, the acts of Congress, and the vigor of
the president's support with Congress. But at least he tried.

NOTES

1. *New York Times,* May 31, 1985,
p. 2.

2. Ibid.

3. David Remnick, "Vernon Walters, Back in His World," *The Washington Post,* December 16, 1985, C-1.

4. Ibid. Also, interview with Walters by the author, April 7, 1986.

5. GA Res. 40/61, December 9, 1985.

6. GA Res. 40/92, December 12, 1985.

7. US UN Press Release 204(85), December 18, 1985, p. 6.

8. US UN Press Release 4615, August 16, 1965, p. 4.

9. UN Press Release SG/SM/3860, GA 27279, April 28, 1986.

10. Report of the Group of High-Level Intergovernmental Experts to Review the Efficiency of the Administrative and Financial Functioning of the United Nations. GAOR, Supplement No. 49.A/41/49.

11. US UN Press Release 187-86, December 31, 1986. p. 3.

12. Ibid., p. 4.

13. GA Res. 41/213, December 19, 1986.

14. US UN Press Release 18-7-86, p. 4.

15. *Washington Weekly Report* XIII-5, UN Association of the U.S.A., February 6, 1987.

16. *Washington Weekly Report* XIII-11, March 20, 1987.

17. GA 13th Special Session Res. 13/2.

18. "Reagan's Mighty Effort to Condemn Cuba," *The New York Times,* March 24, 1987, p. 10.

CHAPTER XI

Summing Up: Who Should Represent Us at the United Nations?

We have looked at the record of forty years, 1945–85, and sixteen permanent representatives. Now it is time to consider this record, to put it into perspective in order to think clearly about the future and, in particular, about the kind of representation the United States should have at the United Nations.

We shall be examining the following issues, in the light of this record:

1. What kind of role should the United States play in the current UN? What are its policy options?
2. What type of permanent representative can best serve such policies? Should he be a career diplomat or a political appointee? What kind of relationship should he have with the president, the secretary of state, the Congress, the media and the American people?
3. What sort of staff should the permanent representative choose? Should all of his top deputies be career people or political appointees, or should there be a mixture of the two? Should the rest of the staff be career? How long should they serve?
4. What kind of delegates should be chosen to represent the United States at the UN General Assembly? What mixture of professional diplomats, members of Congress, and political appointees is desirable? How can the participation of nonprofessionals be made more effective?
5. What is the role of the permanent representative and his staff in developing, nurturing, and executing U.S. policy at the UN?

First, let us look at the present and future policy options of the United States in the United Nations. One possible option is the extreme one of withdrawal. This would, of course spell the end of the United Nations as an effective international institution. Such a step is as unlikely as it would be unwise. Despite U.S. irritation with some of the distasteful resolutions passed by the General Assembly, a *New York Times*/CBS News poll taken in September 1983 indicated that 89 percent of Americans believed that the U.S. should stay in the UN and 65 percent that the UN should remain in the U.S. The same general attitude has been indicated in polls taken over the past three decades, although the percentage of those expressing satisfaction with UN performance has oscillated. Furthermore, the percentage of support for U.S. participation in the UN is highest among the young, the college educated, and the elites from which American political leaders emerge.[1]

Realistically, then, the question is not whether the United States should participate in the UN, but how. Should the model be the "benign neglect" of the Nixon administration, the confrontational attitude of Moynihan and Kirkpatrick, or the active, supportive stances of Austin, Lodge, Stevenson, Goldberg, Young, and McHenry?

Public opinion does not appear to support the confrontational approach. In a June 1983 Roper Poll commissioned by the United Nations Association of the U.S.A., only 19 percent of the respondents believed that the U.S. should answer more directly to attacks made in the UN. An equal number, 19 percent, favored working behind the scenes with friendly countries "to have our point of view prevail," while 48 percent favored working for "agreement on major global issues that are acceptable to the broadest number of countries possible." Faced with these three alternatives, 14 percent answered "don't know."

My own views coincide with those of the Atlantic Council Working Group on the United Nations. In its report, *The Future of the UN*, the group declares: "The United Nations, with all its weaknesses, is presently irreplaceable. U.S. national interests require that we continue to play a full and constructive part." The group recommends a pragmatic, pluralistic strategy, using the UN when it is best suited to deal with certain aspects of problems but using other institutions when they are better placed for our purposes.

"Where the primary aim is to air grievances and exchange views, or to design and launch needful initiatives and programs at the global level, the General Assembly is the appropriate forum. . . . But where concrete action on economic, financial or technical policy is required, smaller bodies can often be more effective. Such smaller bodies can exist inside or outside the United Nations. In many cases, peripheral organizations with partial membership based on regional location or on functional necessity should take on more substantial portions of the international agenda."[2]

On economic and technical issues, for reasons outlined in Chapter I, I believe that the U.S. interest is better served through negotiation in the appropriate specialized agency than in the UN. Agencies like the World Bank, the International Monetary Fund, and GATT, in their respective functional areas of development financing, monetary issues, and trade, have a creditable operating record. Moreover, because of weighted voting, professional emphasis and decision-making procedures, they offer the United States a degree of influence comparable to its economic importance— not 1 vote among 159, as in the UN General Assembly. Functional necessity has fostered the development of the OECD, INTELSAT, the IMF's Interim Committee, and various informal meetings of a core group of the major industrial powers to discuss inflation, growth rates, and international monetary issues. Such groups are clearly less cumbersome than universal bodies like the UN. In addition to the inherent advantages of such functional approaches, they also make it clear that no "tyranny of the majority" in the UN can do appreciable damage to U.S. interests.

On the other hand, full and constructive participation in the UN can provide substantial opportunities for the United States. It is the arena where the deep concerns of the Third World are brought forcefully to our attention. The language is often strident; the demands are exaggerated; the criticism of the United States is often unfair; and the politics of the UN frequently produces biased resolutions on human rights and the Arab-Israeli problem. But, because of the veto in the Charter, the United States can block any action, as opposed to rhetoric, damaging to us or our allies. Yet it would be at our own peril to ignore the voices of the Third World at the UN. Our preoccupation over the past three decades has understandably been with the USSR, China, Japan, and the major Western powers. In the face of this preoccupation, U.S. representatives at the UN have often been important allies of those elements in Washington who were concerned about the insensitivity of much of the American bureaucracy to the issues of colonialism and economic justice, issues that preoccupy the UN majority.

A former secretary of state once discovered that, if he turned the earpiece upside down in the General Assembly hall, he would hear nothing and could think about other problems while appearing to listen to the speeches. This was symbolic. His four years as secretary came during a period when the United States, under Nixon, turned a deaf ear to African views on Rhodesia, Namibia, and South Africa; U.S. concern with the problems of the less developed countries languished; and anti-American feelings in the UN grew. Although we should not be commanded by the Third World countries, neither can we afford to ignore them if we want to deal effectively with issues of international peace and security and global survival.

How, then, can the U.S. participation in the UN serve American and world order interests? The UN today is a reflection of a turbulent, pluralistic diverse world. We may not like it, but prudence requires that we face it and formulate policies in that context.

Our first priorities in the UN should remain those of peacekeeping and peacemaking. The UN which has no armed forces, cannot deal effectively with any direct conflict between the USSR and the United States, both because of the veto in the Charter and the power realities. Yet it did serve a useful ancillary role in the resolution of the Berlin Blockade in 1949 and the Cuban Missile Crisis in 1962. Where the UN is of critical importance is in the control of violent conflicts in the Third World. Left unabated, some of these might bring about Soviet-American confrontation as the superpowers are drawn in on opposite sides. Prime examples of helpful UN intervention are the peacekeeping forces in Zaire (Congo) and the Middle East, especially in 1973.

Proposals for a peaceful transition in Namibia also depend on a UN presence to bring about cease-fires and supervise free elections to the satisfaction of the contending parties. Given the known costs and risks of unilateral intervention (Vietnam), it is clearly in the U.S. interest to support a UN role in troubled areas of the Third World wherever feasible. As the Atlantic Council Working Group has put it, "there should be a new presumption in U.S. policy that the outcomes of most local conflicts will in the long run be more consistent with basic U.S. interests if recourse is made to the Security Council rather than if attempts are made to act unilaterally."[3] Conflicts in the Third World have averaged, according to one study, one and a third per year, and the probability is that this rate will continue in the foreseeable future.[4] Clearly, it is in the U.S. interest to support the UN's capacity to contain such conflicts through peacekeeping and peaceful settlement. Changes there will be. How peacefully or violently they are wrought may depend to a significant degree on the behavior of states, especially the powerful ones, acting through or outside the UN. Although the UN has been unable to deal with certain problems—Hungary, Vietnam, Czechoslovakia—it has helped to deter or stop fighting in many other dangerous situations. Its potential must not be ignored.

This is not an either/or proposition. A former secretary general has stressed the need for complementary bilateral action and multilateral diplomacy. He has cited as helpful examples the U.S. actions in negotiating disengagement agreements between Israeli, Egyptian, and Syrian forces buttressed by UN peacekeeping forces; the U.K.–U.S. efforts to bring about a peaceful transition to majority rule in Rhodesia; and the work of the five Western members of the Security Council to bring independence to Namibia on the basis of Security Council resolution 385. UN concern with an issue is not a substitute for national policy but can provide useful support for it if used wisely.[5] As corollary, bilateral efforts in capitals and meetings with caucus groups should be used to support our objectives in the UN and other multilateral institutions.

The Security Council members should endeavor to return to its practices of the 1960s and 1970s, when the emphasis was on good offices and private negotiations as a means of settling disputes. At the initiative of Secretary General Perez de Cuellar, Council members are holding regular informal private meetings to discuss how the Council can be made more effective in its primary functions—facilitating the settlement of disputes and the maintenance of international peace and security. Success will depend, of course, on the attitudes of member governments and whether they want to emphasize polemics or quiet diplomacy.

In the UN's first decade, the United States could usually muster a majority on political and security issues. The Uniting for Peace resolution and other U.S. initiatives were introduced in order to strengthen the authority of the General Assembly in case a veto blocked action in the Security Council. In the 1970s, by contrast, the United States was often in the minority and denounced the "tyranny of the majority" in the Assembly. Consequently, it tended to emphasize the role of the Council, where it has the veto, rather than the Assembly. The shift in majority sentiment, as membership grew, is illustrated by the use of the veto. In the first twenty-five years of the UN, the Soviet veto was cast to defeat 105 resolutions in the Security Council; the United States cast 1 veto (1970). From 1971 to 1984, by contrast, the United States vetoed 49 resolutions, the Soviet Union 5. The United States vetoed resolutions on the Middle East and southern Africa that were considered too one-sided or extreme and on membership for Angola and Vietnam. (Later, the United States refrained from the veto on resolutions admitting both countries.) It is worth noting that in January 1980 the Soviet Union used its veto twice, against resolutions mandating economic sanctions on Iran and condemning the Soviet invasion of Afghanistan.[6]

Yet the General Assembly, despite its domination by Third World countries, is still important to the United States. As noted above, it is one of the few places where American representatives are exposed and sensitized to the demands of the Third World. Moreover, the Assembly has demonstrated its value as an outlet for ventilating complaints, as a legitimizer of international agreements, as a place for assimilating newer countries into the changing international system, and as a forum for new approaches to global problems. It cannot compel the United States or any other country to do its bidding, but it has been and can continue to be an important instrument for building international cooperation when its member states can agree on a course of action; for example, the UN Development Program, the World Food Program, the International Atomic Energy Program, UNICEF, the outer space treaties, the UN

Environment Program, and the UN Fund for Population Activities. It is this aspect that President Carter had in mind when he said in his report to Congress of March 2, 1978, on UN reform: "If we are to develop adequate machinery for management of the world's common problems, a central concern of our foreign policy in the remaining years of this century must be the building of a more effective UN system."

With these objectives in mind, we can now turn to the question of U.S. representation at the UN. Let us begin by making explicit some of the analytical themes that have been implicit throughout this book, primarily by considering three central factors as they affected the record of the U.S. permanent representatives to the United Nations. These factors are: (1) the context of international politics, UN politics, and American electoral and bureaucratic politics within which the permanent representatives had to act; (2) the background and style of the representatives themselves; and (3) developments at the UN and relations between the UN and the United States during the representatives' tenures. We can then proceed to an analytical comparison of these records and base upon them suggestions for the selection and the policy of representatives in the future.

First, a further explication of these three factors is in order. By context, I refer to the international setting, including the nature of superpower relations, North-South relations, and the major international crises of the period; the internal politics of the UN, including the balances in the Assembly, the Security Council, and other organs; the major issues with which these organs concerned themselves and the international crises the UN ignored; and American politics, including the concerns and ideology of the presidents and their administrations, relations between the executive branch and Congress, the public, the press, foreign policy priorities and goals, and the nature of the relations between the president, the State Department, and the representative and his staff.

Turning to the representatives themselves, we shall consider the past record and public stature of the representative; his political independence and style; his personal strengths and weaknesses; and his own role and how closely that perception and his view of the UN desire accorded with reality during his tenure.

We shall then discuss performance, by which we mean the accomplishments at the UN and its public image in the United States during the representative's tenure; the American record in the UN, both in terms of positions taken and battles won or lost; and of course the direct impact of the representative on these matters and on the course of U.S.–UN relations generally.

The international context within which the sixteen permanent representatives had to operate changed substantially during the forty-nine years with which we are concerned, and four phases can be identified, keeping in mind that the transition from one phase to the next was not usually clean and clear-cut. The first phase was the cold war period, lasting approximately from 1946 to 1962. During this period the dominant issue of international politics was the superpower confrontation, which manifested itself in a seemingly unending series of crises, from Iran (1946) to Greece, Berlin, and Palestine (1948), to China (1949), to Korea (1950), to Indochina (1954), to Suez and Hungary (1956), to Lebanon (1958), to Laos (1959), to the Congo (1960), to the Bay of Pigs (1961), and to the Cuban Missile Crisis (1962). Through most of this period, the United States could usually muster a solid majority in the General Assembly. It frequently used that majority for cold war purposes and, on occasion, to bypass the Soviet veto in the Security Council. However, throughout the 1950s the pro–U.S. majority shrank as the UN admitted one newly independent nation-state after another to membership. Decolonization, then, was changing the nature of the UN politics beneath the surface of U.S.–USSR confrontation, as the nations of what would come to be called the Third World began pressing their own concerns on the organization, among which the Soviet-American rivalry was relatively minor.

Owing to its control of the Assembly on major issues and its use of the UN for propaganda victories, the United States considered the UN an important factor in foreign policy during this period, and except for the extreme Right-Wing, most Americans strongly supported this view. Presidents Truman and Eisenhower repeatedly stressed their strong belief in the UN and appointed men of stature—Senators Warren A. Austin and Henry Cabot Lodge—to be U.S. permanent representatives, men who often enjoyed close and direct access to the presidents. The foreign policy of the United States was concerned almost exclusively with containment of expansive communism, and the UN fit into this policy so long as it followed the American lead.

During this period USUN worked actively in Washington to develop policies responsive to Third World pressures for economic development and decolonization. In large part, this activity was stimulated by a desire to get Third World backing on cold war issues. Thus, the United States developed initiatives for the Universal Declaration of Human Rights (1948), the UN Expanded Program of Technical Assistance (1950), the UN Special Fund (1957), and International Development Association (1959), and the UN Development Decade (1961). USUN also tried repeatedly to influence U.S. policies in the direction of supporting self-determination, with varying degrees of success (e.g., Indonesia, Suez, Tunisia). With the entry of sixteen new countries in 1960, most of them African, the end of Western domination of the General Assembly was foreshadowed.

In the second phase, 1963–68, the U.S. presidents became increasingly preoccupied with Vietnam, and the growing numerical strength of the

Third World began to have its impact at the UN. The fact that the UN, because of the positions of the major powers and Hanoi, could do little about Vietnam made the UN less important to the key policymakers in Washington. Moreover, the Third World majority increasingly pressed issues of decolonization and economic development that put the United States and other Western nations on the defensive. Thus, the UN was no longer an instrument of American policy; rather, it came to be regarded as a source of problems.

Inevitably, this independent and critical new United Nations lost support in the United States. This was reflected by the decreasing emphasis on, and support for, the UN in the thinking of the American presidents. Kennedy and especially Johnson were less interested in the UN than their predecessors. Nevertheless, they both appointed men of stature—Stevenson, Goldberg, Ball—to the position of permanent representative, though they did not give the representative a strong role on the dominant foreign policy issue, Vietnam. Moreover, Stevenson and Goldberg had impact on U.S. policies in the UN concerning Africa and the Middle East; both continued to work for active and constructive U.S. involvement in the UN; and both lent importance to the organization by their stature and their firm belief in its purposes and principles.

The third phase, 1969–75, was the détente period. Nixon and Kissinger concentrated on major power politics—the USSR, China, NATO, and Japan—while winding down the U.S. involvement in Vietnam. The superpower conflict was eased somewhat, though indirect conflict with the Soviets continued in such crises as the Indochina war (1969–75), the Bangladesh war (1971), the Arab-Israeli war (1973), the Angola civil war, and in growing tensions throughout southern Africa. These latter crises were evidence of the growing Third World influence on international politics, since they were issues of decolonization and self-determination. Increasingly strident demands by the Third World countries for a new international economic order, coupled with the concern of the industrial countries for resources, especially after the OPEC revolution of 1973, brought North-South relations to the fore. These changes brought the UN back to prominence in international politics as the instrument (at least in the General Assembly) of Third World countries, while at the same time the superpowers discovered new uses for the Security Council as an instrument of détente (as in the Middle East). For the most part, however, the superpowers avoided the UN and its Third World members, making the latter ever more truculent, especially toward the United States.

Anti–UN sentiment in the United States increased during this period as well, reflected by the attitude of Nixon and Kissinger that it was irrelevant to their global concerns. Nixon's appointees to the post of U.S. representative were generally ignored by him, and his contempt for the UN was evident. He and Kissinger concentrated on great power relationships, giving little thought to the Third World except for crises with implications for the superpowers. By September 1975, with Nixon gone, Kissinger could see that unless the United States became constructively involved with the Third World on economic issues of concern to them and on self-determination in southern Africa, its own economic and strategic interests would suffer.

The latest phase can be called the pluralistic period and has lasted from 1975 and is likely to continue for some time. No longer can it be said that there is a single dominant issue in international politics. Rather, Soviet–U.S. relations have taken their place alongside economic, social, political, and security problems of differentiated natures, such as those of southern Africa, the Middle East, international economic relations, oil, resource arrangements, and so on. The UN has continued to be an arena of conflict, but the conflict has been primarily between the Third World and the West, especially the United States. Presidents Carter and Reagan, while taking very different attitudes toward the UN, have both appointed representatives in whom they have confidence and who have special access to the president.

In the light of these contextual factors, we can now turn to a consideration of the representatives themselves. There were five men appointed to be U.S. permanent representatives to the UN during the cold war period, 1946–62: Stettinius, Austin, Lodge, Wadsworth, and Stevenson. Stettinius and Wadsworth served only briefly and had little impact. Austin and Lodge, however, served six and seven years, respectively. (Stevenson was appointed in 1961 but served until 1965; consequently, we shall consider him in the next group of representatives.)

Austin was a man of public prominence who, as senator from Vermont from 1931 to 1946, had his own political base. Though a Republican, he was close to Truman and shared his internationalist outlook. Austin's standing in the Senate and his Republicanism were substantial assets to Truman in gaining bipartisan support; and the president valued him highly. Nevertheless, Austin received his instructions and his speeches from Washington. He was a low-key personality who enjoyed good relations with other delegations and with the secretary general, and his skills as a negotiator, developed during his congressional career, served him in good stead. But his efforts were hampered by a conservative, noncombative nature and his poor health. Austin perceived the UN as a bridge between East and West, a view that contained more aspiration than reality as cold war tensions steadily increased during his tenure. By 1952 he had been converted reluctantly into a cold warrior.

Lodge, even more than Austin, was a major public figure, as a U.S. senator from 1936 to 1944 and 1946 to 1952, and as son of a distinguished political family. He was close to Eisenhower, who appointed him to cabinet status and looked to Lodge as a general political adviser on major issues. He was secure enough to challenge State Department instructions, especially those at lower levels. His strengths were primarily managerial and oratorical; he was a decisive man, not afraid of responsibility, who appointed a staff he expected to be competent, creative, and loyal. He was a confirmed cold warrior who saw the UN primarily as an arena for U.S. propaganda against the USSR.

During the Vietnam period, there were also four permanent representatives—Stevenson, Goldberg, Ball, and Wiggins. The latter two served briefly, with little real impact; Stevenson served four years and Goldberg three.

Stevenson continued the trend begun with Austin and Lodge of representatives with high public standing. He was given the post, not as a position of influence, but rather to give some satisfaction to the Eleanor Roosevelt wing of the Democratic party. Stevenson and Kennedy had been rivals for the Democratic nomination in 1960 and were by no means as close as were Lodge and Eisenhower; moreover, few of Kennedy's staff had much respect for Stevenson. As a result, Stevenson had very little influence, and his challenges to Rusk and the State Department heightened tensions and diminished his effectiveness in that he had no effective channels of his own to the president. Nevertheless, his personal stature and his skills as an orator made him an influential figure at least in public opinion, both at the UN and in the country. But his outside commitments, self-doubts, and inbred distaste for conflict reduced his effectiveness at the UN and in Washington. Stevenson was torn between his idealistic belief in the UN as the last hope of mankind and his felt need to be an effective cold warrior in the service of Kennedy and Johnson.

Goldberg was also a major public figure, a former labor lawyer and secretary of labor who stepped down from the U.S. Supreme Court to take the UN post. He was initially very close to Johnson, who persuaded him personally to give up his Court seat for the UN position, promising Goldberg major foreign policy input, including on Vietnam. Goldberg, with his direct links to the president, had more clout than Stevenson had. His speeches and many policy ideas were initiated at USUN, but in the end he too was deeply disappointed at his lack of influence on Vietnam policy. Although an indifferent speaker, Goldberg was a master negotiator and a good administrator, and he considered the UN to be an important instrument in the search for global peace. Although frustrated in his efforts to bring peace to Vietnam through the UN, Goldberg had substantial impact on U.S. policy in the UN, especially on Africa and the Middle East.

During the Nixon period there were three permanent representatives—

Yost, Bush, and Scali. Each served about two years. None had any significant impact on policy.

Yost was a career diplomat, the first to be appointed to the UN post. He was selected by Nixon primarily because he was a Democrat who, though a distinguished professional, would not make waves. He had no meaningful relations with Nixon or Kissinger, who were directing the action in U.S. foreign policy from the White House throughout Yost's tenure. He received his orders from Secretary of State Rogers, himself overshadowed by Kissinger. Yost was an extremely able diplomat with strong convictions, but his lack of political clout meant that he had virtually no impact on policy, and Nixon clearly wanted it that way. Yost believed in the UN, but he had no illusions about it or about his own ability to influence events there or in Washington.

Bush was an oil millionaire and former congressman whose loyal service as a Republican was rewarded by his appointment to be U.S. representative. Policies during his tenure also were decided in Washington and passed along to USUN through channels. Bush had no more influence with Nixon and Kissinger than Yost. Yet, while carrying out Nixon's generally negative policies toward the UN without serious protest, Bush was personally popular with other UN delegates and his own staff. He was a good and courteous listener, worked hard at personal relationships, and did not needlessly antagonize people.

Scali had been a journalist and later foreign affairs adviser to Nixon before his appointment to USUN. He had no political base or public stature of his own, nor was he close enough to Nixon or Kissinger to enjoy any real influence. He was, however, knowledgeable about international affairs and Washington because of his long career as a journalist, and he developed good working relationships with career professionals in the State Department. He was also a good negotiator. If his attitude toward the UN was often skeptical, combative, and disdainful, this attitude mirrored that of the president.

The Pluralistic period at the UN, from 1975 to the present, has seen the appointment of a variety of representatives under presidents of distinctly different world views: Moynihan and Scranton, appointed by Ford, Young and McHenry by Carter; Kirkpatrick and Walters by Reagan.

Moynihan, though a public figure of some stature, had served in government at the pleasure of presidents and had no independent political base. An ambitious neoconservative ideologue, he was appointed after publication of his article in *Commentary* calling for U.S. combativeness at the UN, a stance that Scali had already begun to adopt without Moynihan's penchant for the limelight. Moynihan was not close to Ford, and Kissinger was a rival. He complained publicly about State Department undercutting of his position. He was a flamboyant orator who enjoyed growing public support by exploiting hostility toward the UN. In that sense he was demagogic and used the UN post as a stepping-stone to the U.S. Senate. His view of the UN was an arena of conflict in which the United States confronted a hostile world, and, perhaps inevitably, so it became when he was there.

Scranton, a former governor of Pennsylvania who had run for president in 1964, began a sharp turnaround in U.S. attitudes at the UN. A patrician like Lodge and Stevenson, he had a political base of his own and agreed to serve at the UN only after repeated, persistent pleas from Ford. He had close personal ties to Ford and learned how to appease Kissinger with flattery, enabling him to enjoy the best relations with Washington of any permanent representative since Lodge. Scranton was low-key and diplomatic in his dealings with other delegations and was widely respected both at the UN and in Washington. While standing firm on U.S. vital interests, he looked upon the UN essentially as an arena for cooperation rather than for conflict.

Young was a major public figure, a leader of the civil rights movement, a former U.S. congressman with his own political base, and an important factor in President Carter's election. Consequently, he had considerable influence with the president. He also had good working relations with Secretary Vance, but there were tensions between him and other State Department officials whom he was not averse to challenging. Young's open criticisms of racism in the United States and elsewhere, as well as his being the first black in the UN post, helped him to establish good relations with the Third World delegations, but his indiscreet outspokenness often embroiled him in domestic controversy. He was a mediocre administrator and his many outside commitments drew him away from USUN, which was not as well managed as it should be. Nevertheless, because of his relationship with Carter, his views on the UN as an important arena of international politics and on policy in general carried weight, particularly on southern Africa issues.

McHenry, appointed to succeed Young for the last sixteen months of the Carter administration, was a skilled professional with long experience on UN issues. He had served in the State Department in the 1960s and then as Young's deputy for more than two and a half years. He generally shared Young's views on the UN, Africa, and the Third World, though he did not hesitate to argue with his chief where they differed.

Jeane Kirkpatrick, appointed by Reagan, represented a return to the confrontational approach of Moynihan, though without his flamboyance. She is strongly anti-Communist and ideological in her approach. She defended U.S. positions in clear, blunt, and carefully crafted language. She did not hesitate to speak out or vote in isolation in defense of her beliefs. For that reason and because she represented a superpower, her statements had impact and she was respected. But she was handicapped in her first three years by her lack of experience in UN and international politics and by a professorial style of speaking that struck many Third World representatives as condescending. With experience, her performance improved in her fourth and last year.

Kirkpatrick's successor, Vernon Walters, had a long career in the army and the CIA, as well as Ambassador-at-Large. While sharing Kirkpatrick's strong anti-Communism, he has been less confrontationist in his approach.

It is clear that the sixteen U.S. permanent representatives to the United Nations have been persons of wide diversity in background, ideology, and style. How, then, did each perform in the position? And what was the record of the United States and the UN during each tenure?

Stettinius, appointed to clear the State Department position for Byrnes, had successfully led the San Francisco delegation, but his illness and the brevity of his tenure prevented him from having any real impact at USUN. Austin, however, as the first major permanent representative, created precedent with every action. Owing to his personal prestige and known integrity, he was able to secure USUN's position as an important entity in American foreign policy and to maintain good relations with all parties. Because of the majority the United States enjoyed in the UN Austin was influential there, too, and won almost all the contests in which the United States was engaged. Austin was hampered by ill health in the latter part of his tenure, but strong deputies and an excellent staff helped to fill the gap. Concomitantly, the UN enjoyed high prestige in the United States, and most international issues were brought before it. The UN was directly involved in many of them, such as the Palestine conflict, the Indonesian crisis, and the Korean War; and indirectly involved with crises in Iran and Greece and the Berlin Blockade. Austin, who came to the UN in 1946 with strong hopes of using it as a bridge to build friendly relations with the Soviet Union, was gradually converted into a cold warrior, especially after the outbreak of the Korean War.

Lodge not only continued the practice of using the UN for cold war objectives; he brought a new energy, verve, and flair to it. Moreover, the UN became increasingly important in world affairs and in U.S. policy, playing major roles in the crises in Suez, Lebanon, and the Congo. Owing to Lodge's prestige, USUN gained in stature as the "Other State Department," and Lodge achieved cabinet status for the permanent representative. He was also instrumental in initiating a number of programs with which the United States gained favor in the eyes of the nascent Third World, including the International Atomic Energy Agency, the UN Development Program, and the World Food Program. Lodge increased the stature of the United States in the UN, and of the UN in the United States, and he won a series of propaganda battles with the USSR that were impressive. His temperament and skills were ideally suited to the cold war UN.

When Stevenson arrived at USUN, it was generally assumed that the mission would have even greater prestige and influence. On the contrary, USUN lost influence in Washington because of the preoccupation of both Kennedy and Johnson with power politics and the belief, especially in Lyndon Johnson's mind, that Stevenson was swayed too much by idealism. Stevenson, on his side, became increasingly disturbed by U.S. interventions in Vietnam and the Dominican Republic and disheartened by his lack of influence on presidential policymaking, which further reduced his effectiveness. Still, Stevenson represented the United States well, particularly during the Cuban Missile Crisis, and his very presence and stature lent importance to the UN.

Arthur Goldberg, arriving at USUN with a strong mandate from Lyndon Johnson, did much to restore the mission's effectiveness and its influence in Washington. He won significant successes on some issues, especially on South-West Africa, Rhodesia, the India-Pakistan war, the Nonproliferation Treaty, the *Pueblo* incident, and the Middle East, due as much to his own skills as to U.S. prestige and influence. Overall, Goldberg was highly successful at the UN, in contrast with his subsequent dismal performance as a political campaigner. But he was bitterly frustrated on his primary goal—to influence U.S. policy toward peace in Vietnam—and his relationship with Johnson turned sour in his last year. Johnson's distaste for the UN and distrust of Secretary General U Thant increased during Goldberg's tenure; consequently, Thant's efforts to promote Vietnam negotiations were rebuffed. Even so, Goldberg did play a role in getting Johnson to turn down the military's request in the spring of 1968 for a further increase in U.S. troops in Vietnam—a crucial decision. Ball, who succeeded him, won a propaganda victory during the Soviet invasion of Czechoslovakia in 1968, but the days when such a success might materially affect U.S. foreign policy were over. Wiggins, who followed, was an interim appointee serving out the end of the Johnson administration.

The three representatives appointed by Nixon had no significant political influence with the president; that was the way he wanted it. Yost was a superb professional diplomat; Bush, a politician with an unusual flair for getting along with people; Scali, a seasoned, shrewd journalistic observer of international affairs. But none had any impact on policy, which was controlled by Nixon and Kissinger. The American record at the UN was poor during this period, as the Third World majority indulged its resentments, and the stature of the UN in the United States declined steadily toward its nadir under Moynihan. The UN was disdained as a Soviet-Third World arena for propaganda, and USUN declined in stature as well, losing much of its input and prestige.

Moynihan set out to challenge the Third World and his own vision of its alliance with the Soviet. Third World anti-Americanism rose correspondingly. U.S.–UN relations plunged to an all-time low as Moynihan's own political star soared. While some U.S. defeats in the General Assembly were inevitable, adoption of the anti-Zionist resolution may be fairly attributed to Moynihan's style and rhetoric and to the insults he often delivered to Third World delegates and countries and even to America's friends. Moynihan generally ignored USUN's staff, and his relations with the State Department were poor.

Scranton, by contrast, was relatively successful. It was during his tenure that the U.S.–UN relationship began to make a recovery. As a result of the peacekeeping role in the 1973 Middle East conflict, Kissinger had evinced new respect for the UN, and its image in the United States improved somewhat. Scranton's low-key, dignified, accommodating approach; his excellent relations with Ford and Kissinger; and his skilled use of USUN staff were particularly effective after Moynihan's truculence. He managed to avert a number of anti-American (and anti-Israel) resolutions and began the rehabilitation of USUN, as well as the UN's image generally in American public opinion.

This trend continued under Young. Although an indifferent administrator, he restored the post of U.S. representative to something approaching its earlier stature. Young, with the Carter administration behind him, made the UN an arena for compromise on certain issues, especially those concerning southern Africa. His unique standing and skills led to a marked improvement in relations between the United States and the Third World as well as between the United States and the UN as a whole. Unfortunately, he often undercut his own standing by indiscreet media statements that embarrassed Carter. Finally, he held an unauthorized meeting with the PLO representative to the UN at a time when U.S. relations with Israel were particularly sensitive; did not report the meeting to Carter, Vance, or any other Washington official; and refused to promise that he would not have such communications in the future. His resignation became inevitable. Still, on balance, he served U.S. interests well at the UN.

McHenry, though not a political figure, acquired a degree of political clout because of the circumstances of his appointment and the fact that he is black. He enjoyed good relations with Secretaries of State Vance and Muskie and the career professionals in the State Department. He was also widely respected around the UN for his professionalism and integrity, and he performed very competently.

Jeane Kirkpatrick's directness and integrity were also respected around the UN, but her ideological stance, her evident lack of enthusiasm for the UN as an institution and her rather limited availability did not make her popular with other representatives, including those of America's friends and allies. Moreover, her inner circle was made up of ideologues like herself, without experience in U.N. or international politics, rather than seasoned diplomats with extensive contacts around the UN.

Walters, a skilled linguist and raconteur, has had a better reception among foreign delegates. He has also brought in experienced diplomats as his deputies. Unfortunately, he has often been away on special missions for the President, limiting his availability. He has been skilled in the implementation of policy, but it remains to be seen whether he has a significant impact on policy-making.

In viewing the performance of these sixteen permanent representatives, I have evaluated only their performance *in that job*, not their life's work. For example, Goldberg was a more effective Representative at the UN than Stevenson, but the latter had immeasurably greater impact in his lifetime as a political leader.

With this review in mind, we can now turn to the question of what kind of permanent representative the United States should send to the United Nations. I think the record, as well as my own experience, is convincing in one respect: the United States representative should be an influential political figure rather than a career diplomat. This opinion is shared by the many knowledgeable, experienced people I talked with in preparing this book, including former career diplomats who served at the UN.

By contrast, I believe that almost all ambassadors to foreign countries, including the most important ones, should be career diplomats rather than political appointees. I agree with Charles Yost's critical observation concerning the tendency of presidents to make political appointments to the most important diplomatic posts:

> A curious American habit, practiced very rarely in other countries, is that of appointing a substantial proportion of its ambassadors not from the career service but from a variety of other unrelated walks of life. No one would dream of so acting in the choice of generals or admirals, of corporation executives, of university professors or of senior partners of law firms, but it seems to be supposed in our country that any reasonably bright individual can take on so simple a task as conducting our relations with a foreign nation.[7]

However, the job of permanent representative to the UN is unique, as Yost, the only career diplomat ever to hold it, would agree. Other countries gauge the importance the president attaches to the UN by the political and international stature of the person he chooses to have represent him there. Men like Austin, Lodge, Stevenson, Goldberg, Scranton, and Young have been able to wield far more influence at the UN and in policymaking than other representatives, however able. They have given the United States stature in the UN and the UN importance in the United States, both essential functions. They are also able to exploit the great opportunities afforded by the media focused on the UN much better than career diplomats, whose training and discipline lead in a different direction. An indication of how the most prominent of U.S. representatives brought prestige to the job, rather than vice versa, is the way they chose to be addressed. Austin was called "Senator," Stevenson and Scranton "Governor," Goldberg, "Mr. Justice," and Lodge "Mr. Lodge." None preferred the title "Mr. Ambassador."

In many cases permanent representatives with great personal prestige have been frustrated by their inability to effect policy changes. Stevenson was kept in the dark about the Bay of Pigs operation, which he totally disapproved; he was thwarted in his efforts to get U.S. policy on Chinese representation changed; he was upset by the intervention in the Dominican Republic; he was unable to get a U.S. contribution to help resolve the UN's financial crisis in 1965; and he was very uncomfortable defending U.S. actions in Vietnam, particularly the massive bombing. Yet Clayton Fritchey, who was at all times close to Stevenson, feels that he had a benign influence on U.S. foreign policy in the UN, as did Arthur Goldberg, his successor. Thus Fritchey, referring to "Our Heroes at the UN," concludes that the job has been frustrating for its incumbents but beneficial to their country.[8] I worked with both Stevenson and Goldberg throughout their service at the UN and agree with Fritchey.

Nor does the prominence of the position assure a bright political future. Most of its illustrious incumbents went nowhere politically afterward. Lodge, Bush, Moynihan, and Kirkpatrick were the exceptions. Lodge gained spectacular public prominence during his last year at the UN; he was seen frequently on television scoring points against the Soviets in the Security Council, particularly on the RB-47 issue. As noted in Chapter IV, this prominence was an important factor in his nomination as Republican candidate for vice-president in 1960. Moynihan gained prominence by being spectacularly combative at the UN at a time when it was particularly unpopular in New York; this undoubtedly helped him win nomination and election as a U.S. Senator. Bush, who became a candidate for the presidency in 1979 and was elected vice-president in 1980, pointed to his service at the UN as part of his qualifying experience. Kirkpatrick, who was not a major political figure when appointed, gained considerable prominence while serving as the permanent representative.

The prominence of permanent representatives has been attacked from another angle, that is, that it distorts media perceptions of the relative importance of the UN. Senator Henry Jackson, who said in 1962 that "the conduct of UN affairs absorbs a disproportionate amount of energy of our highest officials," also stated:

> I have been struck, for example, by the serious disproportion in the press, radio and television coverage of our UN delegation and the coverage of the Department of State. The space and time devoted to

the former does not correctly reflect the relative importance of what is said in New York against what is said in Washington. . . .

Should our delegation in the United Nations play a larger role in the policy-making process than our representatives to NATO or to major world capitals? I think the answer is no and the burden of proof should lie upon those who advocate a unique role for our Embassy in New York.[9]

There is now much less media coverage of the UN than there was in 1962. Nevertheless, Jackson's statement goes to the heart of the issue: How important is the UN to the United States? When one looks at the sources of frustration for Stevenson and Goldberg in the 1960s (Vietnam), it is hard to escape the conclusion that the United States would have been better off if they had had *more* influence on American public opinion and policy. Also, the world has changed since 1962, becoming less bipolar, and those with whom the United States must maintain working relationships, especially Third World countries, regard the UN as a very important forum. Downgrading our representation would only antagonize them.

Moreover, the United States continues to hold a special position in the UN. It had the major role in establishing and drafting its Charter; it is the host country; it has worldwide interests and involvements; and it has a major stake in the development of a peaceful and orderly world. No other country can do as much to make or break the UN, and this makes the role of the U.S. representative crucial in the building of public and congressional support for the role of the UN in American concerns. The appointment of persons of prestige, political influence, and independence may at times upset the tidy discipline that is dear to the hearts of traditional bureaucrats, but the initiative, dynamism, and political astuteness they bring has more than compensated for the disruption of organizational charts.

There is a second and equally important aspect to this question, and that is the nature of the relationship between the appointee to the UN post and the president who gives him the job. As the contrast between the Nixon appointees and those of Eisenhower or Carter shows, only a president who understands the importance to U.S. foreign policy of the UN can be expected to allow the permanent representative to be as influential and important as were Austin, Lodge, and Young. The most successful U.S. representatives were those who enjoyed close personal relations with the president and a significant amount of political and bureaucratic autonomy.

As part of this, the permanent representative should continue to be a member of the cabinet. There is a degree of administrative anomaly involved in having a cabinet officer report through an assistant secretary; however, it is vital to demonstrate to the world at large and to the American people that the president considers the UN important and is in constant and routinized contact with the U.S. representative. The Washington bureaucracy, furthermore, has been slow to adapt to the increasing importance of multilateral diplomacy, despite a number of studies of how the government should be restructured to deal with the new dimensions of foreign policy.[10] There is still no high official and no mechanism in Washington to assure that top policymakers give adequate attention to UN issues, and it appears unlikely that such changes can or will be made in the near future. Consequently, only the cabinet status of the permanent representative can assure that adequate attention is paid to the multilateral option in considering foreign policy questions.

Richard Petree, a former career diplomat who served at USUN under Scranton, Young, McHenry, and Kirkpatrick, takes a different view. He believes the permanent representative should be an outstanding career diplomat and should have a rank equivalent to undersecretary of state. In his view the rank would assure an adequate hearing in Washington and the choice of a career professional would provide greater assurance of discipline and consistency. It would also place USUN clearly under the secretary of state, thus simplifying the chain of command. Petree makes a good case, but I still believe the national interest would be better served by continuing the practice of appointing an influential political figure who has direct access to the President. In my view this is the only way to assure that U.N. issues will get adequate attention in Washington. Given the U.S. practice over the past 39 years, a change along the lines Petree suggests would be interpreted by most other countries as an American downgrading of the U.N.

Beyond these considerations, there are a number of important personal attributes that successful Representatives have displayed:[11]

1. Diplomatic skills, primarily the techniques of negotiation. This involves being thoroughly knowledgeable, not only about his own case, but also about that of other participants so that he may find and stress points of mutual interest. He should arrive quickly at the core of an issue and not be distracted by peripheral matters. He should establish trust and credibility and must never promise more than he can deliver. He must have the stamina and patience to remain cool and clearheaded under great stress and, ideally, should also be creative and imaginative in finding ways around roadblocks. He should be tough in defending U.S. interests but never unnecessarily provocative or insulting and always willing to consider practical accommodation. Both Goldberg and Young were known for their negotiating talents well before they came to USUN, having acquired them in such domestic political areas as the labor and civil rights movements.

2. He should be a good listener and have sensitive antennas, what Dean Rusk used to call "the persuasive ear." Representatives of smaller countries become incensed if they feel they are not getting due attention,

and they often say things it is important for the United States to hear. The U.S. representative cannot promote American initiatives or cope successfully with the initiative of others unless he is aware of the winds of opinion. Here, as in military defense, "early warning" is important. Above all, he should be careful not to appear to be throwing his "superpower" weight around, nor be arrogant or haughty. Lodge, for instance, made it a point to call personally on each of the delegation heads soon after his arrival; Scranton, Bush, and Young, facing a much larger UN membership, managed to convey a sense of respect and friendship by other means.

3. He should be a good public speaker, capable of clarifying and dramatizing issues for other delegates, as well as for Congress and the American public. Of course, this skill can be used for ill (e.g., Moynihan) as well as for good (e.g., Lodge, Stevenson, Young); and it has not hampered the performance of some who lacked it (e.g., Goldberg).

4. He should be experienced, or at least familiar, with foreign affairs. Such experience need not come from traditional diplomacy. Many congressmen and cabinet officers other than the secretary of state have had experience with foreigners and have been involved in foreign policy concerns on the now very broad agenda of international relations with which the U.S. representative must be familiar. Men of stature acquire foreign acquaintances and international outlooks even when not directly concerned with foreign policymaking, as did Austin, Lodge, Stevenson, Goldberg, Scali, Scranton, and Young.

5. He should be able to accommodate himself when necessary to the foreign policy bureaucracy in Washington; direct appeal to the president must be infrequent if it is to be maximally effective. On most issues the permanent representative and his deputies should endeavor to work out policies with their counterparts in the State Department, particularly the secretary of state, the assistant secretary for international organization affairs, and their key staff. Since the UN post takes its occupant away from Washington most of the time, he needs reliable and effective friends there, both in the executive branch and in Congress.

6. He should be sensitive to the main currents of opinion in Congress and the American public. In order to lead or change such opinion, he must first know where it is and how strong it is on a given issue. Of course, most men in politics have well-developed abilities to keep in touch with diverse sources of opinion, whether mass or elite.

7. He should be a good manager, able to pick and retain qualified staff and make clear-cut delegations of authority to avoid becoming bogged down in detail, while providing leadership and letting the staff know that he is aware of achievements and failures.

Of all these considerations, the most important is that the president pick a figure of public stature to whom he is close and with whom he is comfortable both personally and politically, and who is skilled at negotiation and conciliation. For the representative to be fully effective, he must retain the full support of the president; have access to the White House; maintain good relations with other delegations, his own staff, and key Washington officials; and be sensitive to the main currents of congressional and public opinion.

Theoretically, the position of permanent representative, with cabinet status, is a challenge to the authority of the secretary of state and the national security adviser. We have seen that serious differences on policy do arise, such as during the Vietnam War where both Stevenson and Goldberg were more dovish than Rusk, or on Cuban involvement in Africa, where Young's views clashed with those of Brzezinski. The record shows that the secretary of state and the national security adviser have usually prevailed in such instances, since both are better positioned, based in Washington, and with better resources (the State Department and the National Security Council). The evidence indicates that the UN representative has been much more successful working with the Washington policymakers rather than against them. Once again it is up to a president to choose a harmonious team and to serve as the final arbiter.

Young's resignation, following his unauthorized meeting with the PLO representative at the UN, resulted from his unwillingness to guarantee that he would give up freewheeling and follow established policy—as the permanent representative must do if American foreign policy is to be coherent.

USUN STAFF

Although I have endorsed the notion that a political figure is preferable to a career diplomat in the UN post, I think it wise that the USUN staff be comprised of competent, experienced, professional career diplomats. The UN is enormously complex; four or five important meetings may be going on simultaneously; and sensitivity and skill in dealing with foreign representatives and with fast-changing political situations are a critical attribute that career officers are more likely to have than outsiders. Also, career officers are skilled at reporting, negotiating, and drafting speeches, skills that can be of great help to the representative.

Arthur Goldberg in early 1967 made a radical change in his top deputies, choosing career professionals to succeed political appointees. The result was a better-coordinated, fully professional mission that ran more effectively than had been the case with too many political stars at the top. Andrew Young, while making a strong pitch for the representation of minorities and women, nevertheless appointed experienced professional diplomats as his top deputies. His staff was not as tightly managed as Goldberg's, perhaps a reflection of their respective interests and personalities. Stevenson, while selecting mostly political appointees, did choose well, and he strengthened the political staff greatly by choosing Charles Yost, a distinguished professional, as his deputy for the Security Council.

The arguments for professionals as top deputies apply, a fortiori, to the rest of the mission staff. Yet there is room for a few outsiders, particularly as personal aides and press secretaries. And a person of exceptional competence is always desirable, whether career or not.

Because the UN is so complex, and there are over 150 delegations to deal with, continuity is more important there than at other U.S. missions. Hence the tour of duty for Foreign Service officers, about three years at most posts, should normally be four to five years at USUN. Also, the Foreign Service should give its career officers more training in multilateral diplomacy and provide more incentives for specialists in that area.

THE GENERAL ASSEMBLY DELEGATION

Concern with fielding the best possible team should also extend to the General Assembly delegation. Although there is merit in having citizens from various parts of the country, different ethnic backgrounds, and both sexes, such representation can be achieved without compromising on fitness, if enough care goes into the selection and if the representation pattern is sought over a number of years rather than in a single delegation.

Having been involved in General Assemblies for fifteen years, both as staff and representative, I believe the delegation works best when the top deputies serve as representatives (or alternate representatives). In this way the year-round ambassadors who serve in the Security Council and the Economic and Social Council as well as their subsidiary bodies can bring experience and continuity to bear in the Assembly. Also, their standing with other delegations is apt to suffer if they must take a back seat in the Assembly. Since there are five representatives and five alternates, who for all practical purposes have the same status in the Assembly, this still leaves at least five places for political appointees. If a sixth place is desired for an outside appointment, one of the year-round deputies can serve as secretary general, coordinator, and troubleshooter of the delegations.

We noted in Chapter II that many outside appointees have made outstanding contributions to a delegation's effectiveness. Congressional delegates in particular have usually caught on quickly and served well. They are selected from the Senate Foreign Relations Committee or the House International Affairs Committee; consequently, they are familiar with the major issues. Also, their parliamentary experience makes it easier for them to adapt to the Assembly. Especially noteworthy have been Senators Vandenberg, Austin, Connally, Humphrey, Mansfield, Church, and Javits and Congressmen Judd, Fascell, and Frelinghuysen. It is doubtful whether the 1957 U.S. initiative for a UN Special Fund would have succeeded without the strong involvement of Walter Judd who, arriving at USUN with a negative view of UN technical cooperation, became a fervid convert. The presence of two congressmen on the delegation each year also provides a valuable link with Congress and, in particular, a means of deepening congressional understanding of the UN.[12]

The appointment of prominent personalities from the spheres of business, labor, science, and the academic community can also provide substantial benefits as well as certain hazards. Many have brought inventive minds and fresh viewpoints or have been valuable in contacts with other delegations because of their personal prominence—Eleanor Roosevelt, Dr. Charles Mayo, George Meany, I. W. Abel, and Henry Ford II. Skillful regular staff can provide the necessary technical and tactical expertise, and as noted in Chapter II, the blend has often been most productive.

Particular caution should be exercised in considering the appointment of celebrities from the entertainment world. It is, of course, possible to be a star and be well informed about world affairs, but the two do not usually go together. A three-month assignment to a General Assembly delegation seems like an easy political payoff for campaign support, but a president who regards the UN seriously should beware.

One must also be careful with regard to committee assignments. The fact that William J. Buckley and Daniel Patrick Moynihan (before his appointment as permanent representative) were assigned to the Assembly's Third Committee, the most propagandistic and least professional of the sessional committees, undoubtedly fueled their antagonism toward the UN.

Timing is most important. In my own experience at fifteen Assembly sessions, the delegation was usually announced just before the session began. (The two congressional delegates, however, were informed of their assignments months earlier.) There was rarely enough time to brief the new delegates adequately; most learned their jobs about midway through the session. Yet it was rare that a good delegate was ever brought back for another session.

Delegations should also include ambassadors from other important posts, as area and special advisers, even if some of them cannot stay for the entire three months. Their area experience, expertise, and stature can add to the delegation's effectiveness. Equally important, since most of their own work now deals with multilateral issues, such ambassadors will be enriched by the experience. Yet ultimately the delegation must be backstopped by an effective and competent staff at USUN and led by an influential and dedicated permanent representative. In this way, the entire delegation can become an important part of the foreign policymaking process.

THE PERMANENT REPRESENTATIVE, USUN,
AND POLICYMAKING

We have been concerned throughout our narrative with the role of the permanent representative in the making and execution of policy. We have noted, in particular, the cases where strong permanent representatives, enjoying the confidence of, and access to, the president, have been able to persuade him to initiate or change policies. Notable examples were the establishment of the IAEA, the UN Special Fund, and the World Food Program during Lodge's stewardship; the U.S. stand in favor of majority rule for Rhodesia (Zimbabwe) and South-West Africa (Namibia) pressed by Goldberg; and the vigorous resumption of that policy stimulated by Scranton and Young. Such initiatives frequently overcame bureaucratic inertia or infighting standoffs in Washington, for reasons discussed in Chapter II.

Moreover, almost all permanent representatives have pressed Washington to take a more forthcoming attitude toward self-determination for colonial peoples. They have been exposed repeatedly to the forceful pressures of the growing Third World majority and were frequently concerned with garnering votes from those countries on issues of concern to the United States. For similar reasons they have often drawn the president's attention to the economic concerns of the less developed countries; as a result, the United States has initiated or encouraged economic programs in the UN itself (the UN Development Program, the World Food Program, and the UN Development Decade) and also at the World Bank (the IDA) and the International Monetary Fund (compensatory financing). Whether U.S. responses on anticolonialism and economic development have been adequate is open to question. What is certain, however, is that the United States would have been less responsive to Third World concerns if the permanent representatives had not stressed them repeatedly and strengthened those elements in the Washington bureaucracy that wanted to be responsive.

We have observed that the influence of the permanent representative on policy has varied, depending primarily on his relationship with the president and the secretary of state; his own stature and leadership qualities; and the strength, inventiveness, and organization of his staff, as well as the political and economic environment in the United States and the world. We have also observed that USUN is an action-forming, action-inducing agency. Faced with an agenda at the UN, it must propose courses of action to Washington and seek guidance to meet deadlines. With Washington so close, a symbiotic relationship has developed with concerned departments in Washington, so that courses of action are often worked out through joint consultation. In fact, many exchanges of telegrams issuing or modifying instructions are actually confirmations of informal understandings reached by phone or through personal contacts.

Because of the fast-changing situations that characterize a General Assembly, particularly in its final weeks, USUN must have considerable latitude in the execution of policy instructions, though not so much as do delegations whose capitals are farther away. Draft resolutions and amendments thereto come in thick and fast, and responses must be made quickly if the delegation is to play an active and constructive role in the Assembly's work. Of course there will be times when the United States will want to disassociate itself from a resolution, but this, too, requires rapid consultation with friendly delegations and with Washington.

Francis O. Wilcox has studied the USUN-Washington interactions on the making and implementation of policy for some three decades, as chief of staff of the Senate Foreign Relations Committee, as assistant secretary of state for international organization affairs, as dean of the School of Advanced International Studies at Johns Hopkins University, and as director general of the Atlantic Council of the United States. Following our interview in February 1978, he wrote the following comments on the making and execution of policy, in reply to questions I had raised:

Foreign policy has to be determined here in Washington because of the importance of Congress, the White House, and the various departments of the government in the policy process. We cannot expect the Ambassador in New York to formulate policy because he does not have access to all the sources of information which the Department of State has access to. In addition to his role of carrying out policy, he should also be the President's adviser on important questions concerning the UN. He knows the delegations in New York, he knows the atmosphere there, and he and his staff should know what the traffic will bear. While the President may turn to the Secretary of State to advise him on UN matters, he would certainly want to confer also on other important issues with our Ambassador there.

The Ambassador's recommendations on UN matters should of course, like recommendations from other sources, go through the regular policy making machinery. Otherwise, the Secretary of Defense, the missions abroad, the intelligence community, the Congress, the American public and various departments of the government would not have an opportunity to make their contributions to the policy process. This does not mean the Ambassador should not have direct access to the President to discuss UN matters with him. In any event, the Ambassador should not be in a position to make policy without taking into consideration the views of other parts of our government. Policy cannot be made in New York except within the framework of policy guidelines that have been set up by the US government.

Like all top officers in the government, our Ambassador to the UN has much to do with the formulating of alternative courses of action. In the Suez, Hungarian, Lebanese and Congo crises, for example, the Mission often formulated alternative courses of action for the Department to consider. We, in the Department, would consult closely with the Mission before sending formal instructions to New York. In other words, the best judgment of both the Department (that is, the government) and the Mission would be taken into account in the formulation of instructions that are sent to New York. Good instructions will have some flexibility so the officers in the field will be able to exercise their judgment in the execution of policy.

There is always the possibility also of the Ambassador and his staff using their judgment in applying policy decisions that are sent to them by the Department. If he thinks the atmosphere is not conducive to getting our policy accepted, he will, of course, report this to the Department and possibly ask for a change in policy. Or, in some cases, the policy might be applied in a somewhat less vigorous fashion—if the Ambassador is not entirely sympathetic.

USUN is in a good position to initiate policy because lots of policy actions are started there either by the UN Secretariat, by other delegations, or by committees of the UN. In reporting these actions to the Department, the Ambassador will normally ask for instructions but he usually also makes suggestions about the courses of action that should be pursued by our government. In other words, lots of ideas emerge in New York; as a result the Ambassador has a good opportunity to identify them and to make recommendations about them while policy discussions are still underway.[13]

In talks and correspondence with virtually all living former permanent representatives and several former assistant secretaries of international organization affairs, I have found nothing that would conflict with Wilcox's views. Having had fifteen years of experience at USUN, I, too, agree with him, except that I would place more emphasis on direct access to the president on important ideas that might otherwise be mired in bureaucracy. The processing through other relevant departments, bureaus, and agencies can then take place in the manner described by Wilcox. Perhaps our difference in viewpoint on this issue arises from the fact that his career has been in Washington, whereas my experience was at USUN and abroad.

Our NATO allies and Japan find it exasperating to wait for months while policy battles are waged within the executive branch, with decisions often coming just before joint actions of governments must be taken, so that there is little time or opportunity for intergovernmental consultation.

Since Vietnam and Watergate the process has become even more cumbersome. The foreign policy consensus that prevailed for more than two decades has been shattered, and no new consensus has taken its place. Presidential leadership has been weakened; Congress has become more assertive in its foreign policy role. For the U.S. permanent representative this means that he must work with key congressmen on issues that concern him and enlist the help of the president and the secretary of state. Since he can spend relatively little time in Washington, teamwork with the secretary of state has become more important than ever.

In sum, our representative at the UN must have political stature, the full confidence of the President, a creative and analytical mind, negotiating skills, experience in foreign affairs and sensitivity to the Congress, to foreign representatives and to trends in American public opinion. He or she must also be a leader, a good team player and an effective organizer and manager. This is no small order, but neither is the job that must be done. It is a job that can have a significant impact on world peace. We need the best.

NOTES

1. Alfred O. Hero, Jr., "The United States Public and the United Nations," in David A. Kay (Ed.), *The Changing United Nations*, New York, The Academy of Political Science, 1977, pp. 12–29.

2. The Atlantic Council Working Group on the United Nations, *The Future of the UN* (Boulder, Colo.: Westview, 1977), pp. xx–xxii. A similar approach is suggested in S. M. Finger, "United States Policy Toward International Institutions," *International Organization*, 30, 2 (Spring 1976); Richard M. Gardner, *Blueprint for Peace* (New York: McGraw-Hill, 1966), p. 9; Harlan Cleveland, *The Third Try at World Order* (New York: Aspen Institute, 1976); and Stanley Hoffman, "The Uses of American Power," *Foreign Affairs* (October 1977): 27–40.

3. Atlantic Council Working Group, op. cit., pp. 18–24.

4. L. P. Bloomfield and Amelia C. Leiss, *Controlling Small Wars* (New York: Knopf, 1969).

5. See, for example, Kurt Waldheim's statement of May 12, 1977, in Winnipeg, Canada, in *Canada and the United Nations in a Changing World* (Ottawa: UN Association in Canada, 1977), pp. 19–20.

6. U.S. Mission to the UN, Research and Reference Section, *List of Vetoes Cast in Public Meetings of the Security Council,* May 18, 1983.

7. Charles W. Yost, "Diplomacy and Politics," *Foreign Service Journal* (July 1977): 2.

8. Clayton Fritchey, "Our Heroes at the UN," *Harper's*, February 1967, pp. 30–36. See also Peter Grose, "Post at UN Brings Prestige to Holder But Little Power," *New York Times*, December 17, 1976.

9. Senator Henry Jackson, *Congressional Record*, March 21, 1962.

10. See, for example, *Foreign Policy Decision Making: The New Dimensions,* (New York: UN Association of the USA, 1973), the *Report of the Commission on the Organization of the Government for the Conduct of Foreign Policy* (Washington, D.C.: GPO, 1975); and G. Allison and P. Szanton, *Remaking Foreign Policy* (New York: Basic Books, 1976).

11. This section on desirable qualities of the permanent representative is distilled from analysis presented in the previous chapters; my own experience of fifteen years at USUN; and conversations with, and letters from, former permanent representatives and assistant secretaries of state, notably Francis O. Wilcox, Harland Cleveland, and Joseph J. Sisco. It also reflects conversations with knowledgeable permanent representatives of other countries at the UN.

12. See Robert E. Riggs, "One Small Step for Functionalism: UN Participation and Congressional Attitude Change," *International Organization*, 31 (Summer 1977): 515–39.

13. Letter to the author, dated April 6, 1978, from Francis O. Wilcox, Director General of the Atlantic Council of the United States.

Index